Bloom's Modern Critical Interpretations

Alice's Adventures in
  Wonderland
The Adventures of
  Huckleberry Finn
All Quiet on the
  Western Front
Animal Farm
As You Like It
The Ballad of the Sad
  Café
Beloved
Beowulf
Billy Budd, Benito
  Cereno, Bartleby the
  Scrivener, and Other
  Tales
Black Boy
The Bluest Eye
Brave New World
Cat on a Hot Tin
  Roof
The Catcher in the
  Rye
Catch-22
Cat's Cradle
The Color Purple
Crime and
  Punishment
The Crucible
Darkness at Noon
David Copperfield
Death of a Salesman
The Death of Artemio
  Cruz
The Divine Comedy
Don Quixote
Dracula
Dubliners
Emerson's Essays
Emma
Fahrenheit 451

A Farewell to Arms
Frankenstein
The General Prologue
  to the Canterbury
  Tales
The Grapes of
  Wrath
Great Expectations
The Great Gatsby
Gulliver's Travels
Hamlet
The Handmaid's Tale
Heart of Darkness
I Know Why the
  Caged Bird Sings
The Iliad
The Interpretation of
  Dreams
Invisible Man
Jane Eyre
The Joy Luck Club
Julius Caesar
The Jungle
King Lear
Long Day's Journey
  Into Night
Lord of the Flies
The Lord of the Rings
Love in the Time of
  Cholera
Macbeth
The Man Without
  Qualities
The Merchant of
  Venice
The Metamorphosis
A Midsummer Night's
  Dream
Miss Lonelyhearts
Moby-Dick
My Ántonia

Native Son
Night
1984
The Odyssey
Oedipus Rex
The Old Man and the
  Sea
On the Road
One Flew Over the
  Cuckoo's Nest
One Hundred Years of
  Solitude
Othello
Paradise Lost
The Pardoner's Tale
A Passage to India
Persuasion
Portnoy's Complaint
A Portrait of the Artist
  as a Young Man
Pride and Prejudice
Ragtime
The Red Badge of
  Courage
The Rime of the
  Ancient Mariner
Romeo & Juliet
The Rubáiyát of Omar
  Khayyám
The Scarlet Letter
A Scholarly Look at
  The Diary of Anne
  Frank
A Separate Peace
Silas Marner
Slaughterhouse-Five
Song of Myself
Song of Solomon
The Sonnets of
  William Shakespeare
Sophie's Choice

Bloom's Modern Critical Interpretations

Bloom's Modern Critical Interpretations

Beowulf
Updated Edition

Edited and with an introduction by
Harold Bloom
Sterling Professor of the Humanities
Yale University

CHELSEA HOUSE
PUBLISHERS
An imprint of Infobase Publishing

Chelsea House
An imprint of Infobase Publishing
132 West 31st Street
New York NY 10001

Library of Congress Cataloging-in-Publication Data
Beowulf / Harold Bloom, editor. — Updated ed.
   p. cm. — (Bloom's modern critical interpretations)
 Includes bibliographical references and index.
 ISBN 0-7910-9301-8 (hardcover)
 1. Beowulf—Examinations—Study guides. 2. Epic poetry, English (Old—Examinations—Study guides. 3. Civilization, Anglo-Saxon, in literature. 4. Civilization, Medieval, in literature. 5. Beowulf. I. Bloom, Harold. II. Title. III. Series.

 PR1585.B58 2007
 821'.1—dc22   2006031072

Chelsea House books are available at special discounts when purchased in bulk quantities for businesses, associations, institutions, or sales promotions. Please call our Special Sales Department in New York at (212) 967-8800 or (800) 322-8755.

You can find Chelsea House on the World Wide Web at http://www.chelseahouse.com

Contributing Editor: Janyce Marson
Cover designed by Ben Peterson

Printed in the United States of America
Bang EJB 10 9 8 7 6 5 4 3 2 1

This book is printed on acid-free paper.

All links and web addresses were checked and verified to be correct at the time of publication. Because of the dynamic nature of the web, some addresses and links may have changed since publication and may no longer be valid.

Contents

Editor's Note

My Introduction agrees with my late friend, E. Talbot Donaldson, that *Beowulf* is a pagan poem composed by an only ostensibly Christian writer. I contrast Donaldson to another scholarly friend, Fred Robinson, who argues for a double perspective, pagan and Christian. With great respect for Robinson, nevertheless I agree with Donaldson that this is a poem about heroism and the glory of Beowulf in particular.

In this volume's first essay, Arthur Gilchrist Brodeur finds the unity of a doomed king who dies for a doomed people.

In Richard J. Schrader's judgment, Beowulf's rise to the throne brings the Danes to a new glory, after which John D. Niles attempts to delineate the precise place of the poem *Beowulf* in literary history.

Grendel's ghastly glove is shown by Seth Lerer to provide *Beowulf* with a further command of literary tradition, while Andy Orchard analyzes the psychology of both of the poem's monsters.

Edward B. Irving Jr. illuminates the pagan versus Christian argument as to *Beowulf* by telling us it cannot be resolved, ever, after which John D. Niles returns to indicate that the poem's exact relation between myth and history cannot be determined.

Irony, another insoluble question as to *Beowulf*, is investigated by Scott DeGregorio, while Phyllis R. Brown believes a Christian optimism transforms this epic.

Beowulf's own funeral is described by Gale R. Owen-Crocker as being both Christian and pagan, after which Judy King concludes this volume by contrasting Beowulf with Scyld, the monarch described in the poem's prelude.

HAROLD BLOOM

Introduction

Whether any particular poem can be termed "Christian" or even "religious" is a much more problematical question than we tend to recognize. *Beowulf* is generally judged to be a Christian poem on a Germanic hero. I myself would deny that even *Paradise Lost* is a Christian poem, because John Milton was a Protestant sect of one, and his epic reflects his highly individual spiritual stance. More crucially, the distinction between a sacred and a secular poem never seems to me a *poetic* distinction. You can regard all strong poetry as being religious, or all strong poetry as being secular, but to judge one authentic poem as being more religious or more secular than another seems to me a societal or political matter rather than an aesthetic finding.

Why then care whether or not *Beowulf* is a Christian, as well as being a heroic, poem? The answer is partly historical, partly imaginative or poetic. During the first half of the fifth century the Angles, Saxons, and Jutes overran Roman Britain. By the end of the seventh century these Germans, and the Celts they ruled, mostly had been converted to Christianity. *Beowulf* is assigned by some scholars to the first half of the eighth century, and its nameless author undoubtedly was a Christian, at least nominally. But if *Beowulf* is to be considered a Christian poem, we must ask, Can there be Christianity without the figure of Jesus Christ, and without the presence of the New Testament? Every biblical allusion in *Beowulf*, all scholars agree, is to what Christians call the Old Testament. E. Talbot Donaldson, distinguished scholar-critic of medieval English literature, expresses this oddity with his usual laconic good sense:

> Yet there is no reference to the New Testament—to Christ and His Sacrifice which are the real bases of Christianity in any intelligible sense of the term. Furthermore, readers may well feel that the poem achieves rather little of its emotional power through invocation of Christian values or of values that are consonant with Christian doctrine as we know it....
>
> ... One must, indeed, draw the conclusion from the poem itself that while Christian is a correct term for the religion of the poet and of his audience, it was a Christianity that had not yet by any means succeeded in obliterating an older pagan tradition, which still called forth powerful responses from men's hearts, despite the fact that many aspects of this tradition must be abhorrent to a sophisticated Christian.

I first read *Beowulf* as a graduate student, and have just reread it, cheerfully using Donaldson's splendid prose translation to eke out my faded command of the text. Certainly Donaldson describes what I have read: a heroic poem celebrating the same values that Tacitus discerned in the Germans of his day. Courage is the prime virtue exalted in *Beowulf*. No one reading the poem would find Beowulf to be a particularly Christian hero. His glory has little to do with worship, unless it be justified self-worship, and he fights primarily for glory, to increase his fame, to show that he occupies the foremost place among all Germanic heroes. It is true that Grendel and his even more monstrous mother are portrayed for us as descendants of Cain, but neither they nor the fatal dragon at the poem's end can be said to fight against Christ, or the things that are Christ's. When Beowulf goes forth to battle, he is in quest of reputation and treasure, but not of Christ or God or the truth.

The subtlest defense of a Christian reading of *Beowulf* is by Fred C. Robinson, who finds in the poem an appositive style that balances Dark Age heroism and Christian regret, and that enables the poet to "communicate his Christian vision of pagan heroic life." The dominant tone of *Beowulf*, according to Robinson, is one of "combined admiration and regret" for heroic paganism, as it were. The Christian present confronts the Germanic past, admires its heroism, and supposedly regrets its paganism. In much the most sophisticated critical reading yet afforded the poem, Robinson sets out to correct the view of Tolkien, who somehow could give us Hrothgar as Christian surrounded by pagan companions:

> Because Hrothgar advises Beowulf against overweening pride, avarice, and irascible violence, some scholars have wanted to see this as a Christian homily on the Seven Deadly Sins, and many parallels in Scripture and commentary have been adduced. But there is nothing in the speech that is not equally accordant with Germanic pre-Christian piety.

For Robinson, the entire poem manifests a double perspective of a remarkable kind:

> Reading *Beowulf* is, in a way, like reading the centos of Proba, Luxorius and Pomponius, who composed entire poems on Christian subjects by rearranging the verses of Virgil, Horace, and Ovid in order to make them convey Christian meanings. Students of these curious works hold two contexts in mind at the same time, for their pleasure is in following the Christian level of the narrative while remaining aware of the source of the poetic language. Just as in reading the centos we think simultaneously of Aeneas and Christ, so in reading *Beowulf* we should hear distant echoes of Thunor and Woden when the men of old appeal to their "mihtig dryhten" and "fæder alwalda." We know to whom these words refer in the Christian present, but we also know that they once referred to other, darker beings.

A polysemous theological diction thus dominates *Beowulf*, just as it does *Paradise Lost*, if Robinson is wholly correct. Holding Christian and pagan terms in patterns of apposition, the *Beowulf* poet is able to imply Christian values without repudiating ancestral virtues, and yet, in Robinson's judgment, the poem ends upon a kind of modified repudiation, with the statement that Beowulf was *lofgeornost*, translated by Donaldson as "most eager for fame." To say with your last word that the hero, above all men, desired to be praised, wanted a glory bestowed by his fellows, is to insinuate that the hero is wanting, by Christian standards. To maintain his case, Robinson is compelled to this reading, which seems to me to possess a fine desperation:

> The people of Christian England can never reenter the severe, benighted world of the men of old, nor would they. All the poetry

of *Beowulf* can do is bring the two together in a brief, loving, and faintly disquieting apposition.

But here is the conclusion of *Beowulf*, in Donaldson's translation:

> Then the people of the Weather-Geats built a mound on the promontory, one that was high and broad, wide-seen by seafarers, and in ten days completed a monument for the bold in battle, surrounded the remains of the fire with a wall, the most splendid that men most skilled might devise. In the barrow they placed rings and jewels, all such ornaments as troubled men had earlier taken from the hoard. They let the earth hold the wealth of earls, gold in the ground, where now it still dwells, as useless to men as it was before. Then the brave in battle rode round the mound, children of nobles, twelve in all, would bewail their sorrow and mourn their king, recite dirges and speak of the man. They praised his great deeds and his acts of courage, judged well of his prowess. So it is fitting that man honor his liege lord with words, love him in heart when he must be led forth from the body. Thus the people of the Geats, his hearth-companions, lamented the death of their lord. They said that he was of world-kings the mildest of men and the gentlest, kindest to his people, and most eager for fame.

Does this indeed end with a disquieting apposition? Do we feel that the mildness, gentleness, and kindness of Beowulf (to *his* people, not to monsters, enemies, traitors, or whatever) is in apposition to his lust for renown? Heroic poetry can do little with the virtues of the New Testament Christ, though considerably more with certain epic qualities of the Old Testament. The *Beowulf* poet may have felt no personal nostalgia for the beliefs of his Germanic ancestors, but after all he had chosen to write a heroic poem rather than a work on the finding of the True Cross. Is a poem Christian only because it undoubtedly was written by a Christian? There is nothing about God's grace in *Beowulf*, though something about God's glory as a creator. And there is much tribute to Fate, hardly a Christian category, and rarely is Fate set in apposition with the will of God, as Robinson's pattern might lead us to expect.

Rereading *Beowulf* gives one a fierce and somber sense of heroic loss, in a grim world, not wholly unlike the cosmos of Virgil's *Aeneid*. In spirit, the poem does seem to me more Virgilian than Christian. Though addressed to a Christian audience, it seems not to be addressed to them as Christians but as descendants of heroic warriors. Beowulf does not die so as to advance the truth but so as to maintain his own glory, the fame of a man who could slay a monster with only his own bare hands to do the heroic work. The bareness of those unfaltering hands counts for much more than does the monster's descent from the wicked line of the accursed Cain.

ARTHUR GILCHRIST BRODEUR

The Structure and the Unity of Beowulf

The poem of *Beowulf*, Klaeber tells us, "consists of two distinct parts joined in a very loose manner and held together only by the person of the hero." Like W. P. Ker, Klaeber finds some reason to regard the second part as a late-conceived sequel to the first, rather than as integral with it in the poet's original plan.[1]

J. R. R. Tolkien, on the other hand, maintains that the structure of the poem, "simple and static, solid and strong," is "not really difficult to perceive, if we look to the main points, the strategy, and neglect the many points of minor tactics. We must dismiss, of course, from mind the notion that *Beowulf* is a 'narrative poem,' that it tells a tale or intends to tell a tale sequentially ... the poem was not meant to advance, steadily or unsteadily. It is essentially a balance, an opposition of ends and beginnings. In its simplest terms it is a contrasted description of two moments in a great life, rising and setting; an elaboration of the ancient and intensely moving contrast between youth and age, first achievement and final death." Tolkien has won the assent of R. W. Chambers; and his view of the structure of the poem has received the weighty approval of Kemp Malone: "More striking is the originality of *Beowulf* in structure.... The two main parts balance each other admirably, exemplifying and contrasting as they do the heroic life in youth and age."[2]

From *The Art of* Beowulf, pp. 71–87. © 1959 by the University of California Press.

Tolkien's symbolical interpretation, moreover—lately challenged by T. M. Gang and ably defended by Adrien Bonjour,—supplies us with a new and pleasing theory of the unity of the poem. Chambers' tribute is well deserved: "Towards the study of *Beowulf* as a work of art, Professor Tolkien has made a contribution of the utmost importance."[3] Whether or not we accept Tolkien's symbolism, he is certainly right with respect to the structure; and matters which he may have regarded as "points of minor tactics" clearly indicate that the poet was aware of the problems of unity posed by his balanced structure, and elaborated a carefully considered and effective design for the whole.

The poem seems to break in two only if we think of it exclusively in terms of its main action. At the end of Part I we leave the hero in his uncle Hygelac's court, a young champion who has done glorious deeds in Denmark, and whose loyal love for Hygelac is warmly returned; at the beginning of Part II we find him an old man, about to crown his own fifty-year reign with a final heroic sacrifice. The breach of continuity is not adequately bridged— indeed, it is made all the more apparent—by the brevity and swiftness of the transitional passage (lines 2200–10a) at the beginning of Part II. Obviously, if he had wished, the poet might have gone far to bridge this gap: whether or not he had traditional basis for any exploits of his hero during the fifty-year reign, he surely knew—for in lines 2354–96 he tells us—of Beowulf's gallant stand in Frisia, his slaying of Dæghrefn and his escape, his refusal of the crown, his protection of the boy-king Heardred, and his expedition against Onela. This is God's plenty; and it is exactly the kind of stuff of which heroic lays were made. The poet could have made much of all this if he had wished; and he might easily have accounted for the long reign without revealed incident as the direct result of the power won by Beowulf in his alliance with Eadgils and through the defeat of Onela. Indeed, he seems to have conceived it so: for Beowulf, as he lies dying, asserts that 'there has not been a king of any neighboring people who has dared approach me with weapons' (lines 2733b–35).

If we compare the treatment, in *Grettissaga*, of the Icelandic outlaw's fight against the trolls of the waterfall with Beowulf's triumphs over Grendel and his dam, we see at once how capable our poet was of transforming into noble epic narrative the thinner stuff of folk-tale. How much more, then, might he have made of the hero's deeds in those middle years, from his valiant fight in Frisia through his magnanimous service to Heardred, and his retaliation for Heardred's death! He preferred to present them in a summary of intervening action; and this must have been his deliberate choice.

What determined that choice was evidently his judgment as an artist—a sound judgment; for to have treated these intervening events at length would have been to destroy his calculated balance, the exemplification of the heroic ideal in its two contrasted and most meaningful stages—first and last—of his hero's life. We are forever indebted to Tolkien for his perception of this. The poet wisely elected to subordinate, but *not* to sacrifice, such record as tradition gave him of his hero's exploits in the wars of peoples, and to use as his major theme the victories over monsters too formidable for any other champion to encounter. Through these he has revealed to us the matchless young hero, wise and loyal, brave and strong, beyond the measure of other men; and on the other hand, the old man still mightiest, facing certain death with unshrinking fortitude to save his people from the fury of the dragon. The sacrificial and triumphant death of Beowulf derives its meaning from this contrast. Had the poet stuffed his story with Beowulf's conquests of mortal foes, the incomparable "opposition of ends and beginnings" would have been lost: we should have gained a kind of English *chanson de geste*, and lost the world's noblest *Heldenleben*.

The poet carefully reinforces and points his "opposition of ends and beginnings": at the end of each part he has summed up the character and the *ethos* of his hero as revealed in the preceding narrative. Beowulf's loyalty to his lord, readiness to help the distressed, and magnanimity are emphasized in the fifty-five lines with which Part I concludes; his matchless courage despite the weight of years, his generosity and kindness to his followers, his devotion to his people, and his desire to deserve the esteem of men are expressed in the comment of Wiglaf and the Messenger in Part II, and in the eulogy uttered by his bereaved retainers as they perform his funeral rites. Most appropriately, the author places in Beowulf's own mouth the just and modest appraisal of his life: 'I have ruled this people fifty winters; there has been no king among the neighboring nations who has dared approach me with weapons, to threaten me with terror. I have awaited my appointed destiny in my own homeland, have held my own well; I have not sought strife, nor sworn oaths unrighteously. For all this, though sick with mortal wounds, I can rejoice; for the Ruler of Men will have no cause to reproach me with murder of kin when my life departs from the body.' (lines 2732–43a).

Herein lies the only *advance*: in the first part of the poem Beowulf has been presented as the ideal retainer and champion; in the second, he is the ideal king. In his passage from the lesser role to the greater, his heroic virtues inevitably find larger, though similar, modes of expression. We do not see his temper change, or his character develop: we see them reveal themselves appropriately and consistently in every action and situation.

In a heroic poem so conceived and constructed as "an opposition of ends and beginnings," the person of the hero must provide the essential bond between the balanced parts. It is so in the *Iliad*, the structure of which is very different from that of *Beowulf*: it is the person of Achilles through which the inner unity is maintained. But the hero functions within a very complex action, which must not be allowed to escape his domination. Therefore Homer confines all the action within the period of the wrath and reconciliation of Achilles: the fortunes of all the Greeks and Trojans depend upon *his* action or inaction, so that we feel the portent of his spirit behind all that is said or done; all that occurs falls within the few days of the wrath and in the period immediately following its resolution. The fate of Troy lies in the heart of Achilles, and is decided with the death of Patroclus.

There is no such unity of time or place in the *Odyssey*; though here also the resourceful, indomitable hero makes himself continuously felt. The structure of the poem arises out of the person of the hero: all the sorrows and wanderings of Odysseus result from a single act of his—the blinding of Polyphemus; and the story is brought together as Odysseus himself tells his toils and buffetings to Alcinous and the Phaeacian court. The resolution comes as the direct consequence of this narration by the hero; and in that moment the poet makes his hero appear to Homer's audience at his greatest and most sympathetic, through the eyes of the Phaeacian audience of Odysseus himself.

The nature of the main action of *Beowulf*, split as it is by a time-gap of more than fifty years, confronted its poet with a problem more difficult than Homer had to face. Beowulf's return home after his victories in Denmark, and the beautiful scene at the Geatish court, successfully avert a breach of the unity of place; but the very need to maintain a calculated balance compelled discontinuity of action. But it is only the main plot which suffers discontinuity; the action of the subplot is continuous, and is made, in all its parts, to pivot upon a single historical event. This event has the most decisive effect upon the hero's career, and upon the fates both of his people and of the Danes. It is through the poet's management of the death of Hygelac, and of Beowulf's relations to Hygelac, that the effect of discontinuity in the main action is overcome, and unity achieved.

I think that Klaeber—who has seen quite clearly the pertinence and the effectiveness of the legendary "episodes" in the first part of *Beowulf*—has failed to perceive the significance of the historical traditions which occupy so much of the second part. He thinks of these as "a little too much in evidence"; he feels that they "retard the narrative ... rather seriously" (pp. liii–liv).

Now these historical stories are not episodes, at least not in the same sense as the tale of Finn and Hengest, of Sigemund, or of Offa and Thryð. They have a function much deeper and more vital than the mere supplying of background and setting. Unlike most of the episodes of Part I, they are conceived as falling, not in a heroic age anterior to the events of the poem, but within the hero's lifetime and personal observation or experience. Though they are more "in evidence" in Part II, they are present, and important, in Part I as well. Although Beowulf is not thought of as participating in all the events concerned in them, they all have intense and immediate meaning for him; they affect his life and the destiny of his people. They are, moreover, carefully distributed: in Part I we find historical stories dealing with the fates of the Danes; in Part II, historical stories of the wars between Geats and Svear.

They are, indeed, an essential part of the drama of the hero's life; they deal with situations and relationships which the poet had scarcely less at heart than he had the monster-quellings of the main action. It has been observed repeatedly, and by no one more acutely than by Klaeber,[4] that Beowulf is a hero of finer mold and nobler spirit than other champions of Germanic story; that he lives and dies as the selfless protector of those who suffer beyond their power to resist or to bear. In all this he has God's help; in the triumphant monster-slayings of Part I—as the poet tells us plainly—God, and the hero's courage, averted fate.

But at the very beginning of Part II, in the first twelve lines, we are made aware that doom impends over the hero and his people: the season of youth and conquest is long past. A theme which had been sounded in Part I now becomes dominant, and brings to our full understanding the nature of the poet's conception of his hero. It is more than the death of Beowulf which constitutes the tragedy of Part II, and so of the whole work: in death he is victorious; and he is old enough, and sufficiently full of honors, to die happily. His tragedy is that he dies in vain—indeed, that his death brings in its train the overthrow of his people.

For the poet clearly conceives Beowulf, the noble champion and happy warrior unconquerable in personal encounter, as born to fight a losing battle against destiny. He has saved the Danes from the kin of Grendel, and he saves his own people from the dragon; but in each exploit all he has accomplished is the postponement of their destruction. Part I divulges, by skillful implication, the failure of the alliance between Danes and Geats which Beowulf and Hrothgar had hoped to promote: because of its failure, civil war will bring about the murder of Hrethric (and presumably that of Hrothgar as well), and in due course the fall of Hrothulf and the extinction of the Danish kingdom.[5]

Part II reveals the stages by which the power of the Geats declines through a succession of conflicts and the fall of kings, until only Beowulf remains to save them from conquest. When he dies, their last hope perishes with him. And so, justly, in Part II the allusions to fate (*Wyrd*) are to a power which God is no longer concerned to forestall, and which sweeps away both the hero and his nation.

The historical traditions which so deeply interested the poet do not impede the action; they are part of it. The downfall of the Danish and Geatish kingdoms, and Beowulf's involvement in the tragedies of nations, constitute the matter of the subplot. No one has failed to see how steadily and specifically Beowulf's last fight and death are related to the ruin of the Geats; but it has not been fully perceived how significantly this relation parallels Beowulf's frustrated hope of saving Hrethric and the integrity of Shielding rule. The ultimate and impelling cause of both national catastrophes, in the poet's eyes, was a historical event: the defeat and death of Hygelac in Frisia.

Beowulf's qualities of mind and heart, no less than those of body, are established before he is first required to act before our eyes. They are fixed and constant; they govern, and are exhibited with complete consistence in, all that he says and does. This consonance between the man and all his actions, in youth and age, in life or death, establishes the inner unity of his *Heldenleben*; and it is through the steady exhibition of those qualities in him which impel his actions and speak in his words that the heroic ideal is so admirably illustrated throughout the poem. It is delightful to observe how pellucidly Beowulf's character discloses itself on first meeting: not only to the audience, but to the personages of the poem—to the Captain of the Shore, to Wulfgar, Hrothgar, and Wealhtheow. It is this recognition of the character of the man that makes it possible for the Danes so easily to accept this foreigner as their champion. The surest evidence of his transparent nobility is Wealhtheow's appeal to him to protect her sons.

His selfless loyalty is exhibited in Part I in the scene at Hygelac's court after the return from Denmark. Early in Part II, it is illustrated most finely in the poet's summary of the events intervening between Hygelac's death and Beowulf's accession to the throne: through his rejection of the crown and his protection of Heardred. This is the point of transition between the hero's role as retainer and his role as king. When the action of Part II begins, the devoted thane has become the devoted monarch, all of whose acts are motivated by his love for his people and by his recollection of their rulers who had been his kinsmen. Through all that has changed, the heart of Beowulf has not changed; and this constitutes the binding unity of the poem.

His heroic qualities—that is, the sum of all those qualities which make him what he is, not merely matchless strength and courage—are displayed most beautifully and significantly in personal relationships. These are the mainspring and the inspiration of his actions. The most important of all these relationships, from first to last, is that with his uncle Hygelac.

Although Hygelac appears in person only once, the poet manages to make him almost constantly felt throughout the poem. The hero himself is first mentioned not by name, but as *Higelaces þegn*; this, and *mæg Higelaces*, are the most frequent substitutions for the name *Beowulf* in Part I. Hygelac's name occurs 55 per cent as often as Beowulf's in Part I, and 69 per cent as often in Part II, where the requirements of alliteration do not materially affect its frequency.

More significantly, both the poet and his hero seem almost constantly preoccupied with Hygelac. In six of Beowulf's fifteen speeches Hygelac is mentioned tenderly and with deep affection; the poet also several times affirms or strongly suggests their mutual love. The story of Hygelac's last raid and death is told four times (once in Part I, three times in Part II)—more often than any other event; it is also briefly announced at the beginning of Part II. Each of the four accounts occurs at a highly dramatic moment; each has its peculiar emphasis, tone, and function.

Klaeber reminds us that here, and elsewhere as well, "different parts of a story are sometimes told in different places, or substantially the same incident is related several times from different points of view" (pp. lvii–lviii). This is a favorite narrative device of our poet's, not unlike the recurrence of a theme in music. But the exceptional prominence of the theme of Hygelac's death in *Beowulf*, the dramatic character of its use, and the emotion with which it is charged, justify us in regarding it as the equivalent of what we know in music as the *Leitmotiv*.

The poet's *Leitmotiv* was evoked by his concern for that balanced structure which Tolkien so clearly discerned. The young Beowulf is the hero as loyal thane; the old dragon-slayer is the hero as devoted monarch. And he was both these things because he was Hygelac's nephew. It was Hygelac's death which led to the overthrow of two peoples, both of whom Beowulf was concerned to save. It is Hygelac who supplies the *Leitmotiv*, which is the interwoven harmony of Hygelac's death and Beowulf's love for him.

Indeed, the poet makes much more of Hygelac, and of his relationship with Beowulf, than the main plot requires. Nothing in the *action* of Part I depends upon this relationship; only in Part II, in which the main action unfolds against the background of the Geatish wars, does Beowulf's kinship to Hygelac visibly affect his career. If the poet had presented it less richly, and had explained Beowulf's accession to the throne by a single statement of Hygelac's death, the main action could have been related quite as lucidly.

But so could the action of the *Odyssey* have been told without extensive treatment of the voyage of Telemachus; and the fortunes of its hero are not affected directly by the Greek poet's warm delineations of Nestor, Helen, and Menelaus. Both *Beowulf* and the *Odyssey* derive their main plots from folk-tale; and as W. P. Ker has said, "it is difficult to give individuality or epic dignity to commonplaces of this sort."[6] The poets were as conscious of this difficulty as the modern critics. The author of *Beowulf*, like Homer, recognized the necessity of grounding his hero's great actions firmly in place and time, and giving them emotional and ethical value through association with events and personages familiar and significant to the audience.

Indeed, our English poet goes beyond Homer in the constancy and purposefulness of his use of his hero's personal relations. It was not enough that Beowulf should display unequaled strength and courage in his victories over formidable monsters: the value of these exploits must be enhanced by the revelation of his deep and emotionally justified concern for those in whose interest he fought. Moreover, the demonstrations of his physical power and valor do not in themselves suffice to give Beowulf the roundness, the moral dimensions, and the human warmth of an epic hero. It is loyalty and unselfishness that make him unique as a hero, and constitute the essence of his heroic personality. These nobler attributes are exhibited—as they must be—in his relations with the other human personages of the poem: with Hrothgar and Wealhtheow; and most notably and constantly with Hygelac.

His associations with all the other persons of Part I (except, briefly, with Hygd) necessarily terminate with the close of the action of the first part; but his love and loyalty to his uncle rule his heart throughout his life; and Hygelac lives on to the end in both the poet's and Beowulf's recollection. Indeed, Hygelac dead is almost more alive than Hygelac living: nowhere is the poet so careful to express the impact of Beowulf's love for him upon the hero's emotions and actions as in the first two of the three reports of Hygelac's fall in Part II.

Outside the climate of the mutual love between these two, Beowulf would be little more than the monster-queller and marvelous swimmer of folk-tale. All the acts and events of his quasi-historical role in the epic flow from his relation to his uncle. It was as Hygelac's kinsman that he confidently pledged his own aid, and the military resources of the Geats, to Hrothgar and Hrethric; that he fought mightily in Hygelac's defense, and avenged him, in Frisia; that thereafter he refused the crown, acted as Heardred's protector, and as Eadgils' ally sought vengeance for Heardred; and that he himself became king. These details of his career are all revealed in direct connection with the first, and in the second and third accounts of Hygelac's fall.

The first report of Hygelac's end is given in the context of the feast in Heorot after Beowulf's victory over Grendel. Wealhtheow, who has perceived Hrothulf's ambition and is fearful for her sons, makes a moving appeal to Hrothulf's gratitude and loyalty. Then, knowing that conscience may weigh less than a crown, she turns to Beowulf, gives him a precious circlet, and asks his protection for her children. He withholds his answer until the hour of his departure; then (lines 1822–39) he promises his own aid, and Hygelac's military support, to Hrothgar against any foe, and offers Hrethric asylum at the Geatish court. That this speech and Hrothgar's answer (lines 1855–65) constitute an offer, and an acceptance, of a firm military alliance, is plain enough. If all had gone as Beowulf expected, Hrethric's life and crown could have been saved; and with a king who owed both to Geatish help once on the Danish throne, the Geats in turn might have had Danish aid against the Svear. But the poet's audience knew that Hrethric perished, and that Hrothulf usurped the crown; and the poet could not reverse the course of history. Therefore he carefully makes it plain, *before* Beowulf offers his support, that the Geats, though powerful at the moment of Beowulf's pledge, will be too weak to aid Hrothgar or Hrethric effectively in their hour of need. He has done this by telling us, immediately after Wealhtheow gives Beowulf the circlet, and just before her appeal to him, that Hygelac wore 'that neck-ring' on his last expedition, in which he and his host were destroyed. Hygelac's fall brings in its train Hrothulf's triumph and Hrethric's death; and with Hrothulf on the Danish throne, the Geats will be left isolated against the Svear.

The dramatic irony is deliberate and sharp. Against the major theme of Beowulf's triumph and the joy of the Danes in their deliverance from Grendel, there runs (to use Lawrence's figure) the counterpoint[7] of the tragedy of the Shieldings, which Beowulf confidently but vainly hopes to avert. This scene in Heorot, and its continuation in the last dialogue between Beowulf and Hrothgar, represent the poet's highest achievement in dramatic invention. Utilizing the known tradition that Geatish forces supported Hrethric in his unsuccessful resistance to Hrothulf, he avails himself of the traditional recollection of Hygelac's fall not only to account for Hrothulf's success and the future weakness of the Geats, but also to illustrate Beowulf's personal relations with Hygelac. The hero's last words to Hrothgar display his complete trust in Hygelac's support for whatever course of action he may propose. The poet's audience, recognizing the justice of this confidence, nevertheless knew, in this moment of recognition, that Hygelac's death would make it meaningless. It is grounded in the mutual love between Beowulf and his uncle, which has already been demonstrated in two earlier speeches by the hero, each uttered shortly before his combat with one of the monsters of the mere. In the first (lines 435–436, 452 ff.), Beowulf swears by his hope for Hygelac's continued love and favor that he will face Grendel without weapons, and implores Hrothgar, if he should fall, to send his corselet to Hygelac. In the second (lines 1482–87), just before he plunges into the mere, he asks that, in the event of his death, the gifts given him by Hrothgar be sent to Hygelac. These words bear testimony to his dependence on his uncle's trust and affection, as well as to his own great love for Hygelac.

The long scene at Hygelac's court, with which Part I concludes, carries farther the demonstration of their love, and displays it dramatically; it confronts us with the figure of Hygelac himself; and it prepares us for the concrete and striking evidences of Beowulf's devotion to Hygelac in Part II. In this scene the Geatish king speaks once: briefly, but nobly expressing his affection for Beowulf, his painful anxiety for Beowulf's safety in Denmark, and his thanks to God for his nephew's safe return. Beowulf in turn conveys the fullness of his admiration and love for Hygelac through his gift of the treasures bestowed on him by Hrothgar, and in the words that accompany it: 'These, O warrior king, I desire to transmit to thee, to give unto thee gladly. All comforts still come from thee; I have few close kinsmen, Hygelac, save thee!' (lines 2147–51).

The poet then dwells on Beowulf's utter loyalty to his royal uncle, and strongly asserts the close and reciprocal affection between them. The last lines of Part I emphasize Hygelac's munificence toward Beowulf, and appropriately recognize his own well-deserved rulership.

Thus, from Beowulf's first speech to Hrothgar to the end of Part I, the poet repeatedly stresses, both through the hero's mouth and in his own person as author, the beauty and strength of the bond between these two noble kinsmen. In the closing scene, moreover, he imparts to the figure of Hygelac a remarkable vividness: we see the Geatish king as a powerful and noble person, and perceive that Beowulf's admiring love for him is well deserved and ardently returned. The demonstration of this love through Beowulf's words and acts gives warmth and depth to the hero's personality, and an additional dimension to his actions. It is his strongest and most enduring emotion, and exerts its influence as long as he lives. In Part I, Hygelac is the center of Beowulf's world; in Part II, the recollection of Hygelac remains, a living, moving force, in his heart.

When the action of Part II begins, only Beowulf, out of all the persons of Part I, survives. But it is otherwise with Hygelac than with Hrothgar and Heardred: they are dead and forgotten; Hygelac lives on in our memory, and compellingly in Beowulf's. Hygelac's death has so weakened the Geats that, even with Beowulf, they are defeated by Onela. Only Beowulf stands between them and conquest. Because at last, after a fifty-year reign, he too must fall, and they with him, the second part of the poem is dark with the shadow of ineluctable doom. The aged hero is a symbol of his people: in him they live, and after him they perish.

The second narrative of Hygelac's fall occurs early in Part II (lines 2354b ff.), and stresses Beowulf's valor in Frisia, and its consequences.

Hygd offered him the throne; but he would not be lord to Hygelac's son, preferring to protect his young cousin until Heardred came of age to rule. Then Heardred too fell in battle; Beowulf became king, and took measures to avenge his cousin.

Here Beowulf's loyalty and love for Hygelac are set forth objectively, through the statement of his acts. His magnanimity toward Hygelac's son is motivated not only by his sense of duty toward the boy prince, but also by that same devotion to Hygelac which impelled him to defend his uncle to the last. It is an act of piety rooted less in obligation than in undeviating love.

The third report is in Beowulf's own words, and forms part of his long monologue (lines 2426–2537) spoken just before his challenge summons the dragon from its barrow. It is much more eloquent, and more subjective, than the other accounts. The old king, about to bid his men farewell, is without fear; but he is fey: *Wyrd* is 'immeasurably nigh'. Naturally, then, his thoughts dwell on the past: he recalls his youth, his love for his grandsire Hrethel and for each prince of Hrethel's line. He recalls Herebeald's fate, Hrethel's broken heart, and the swift attack by the Svear when they learned of Hrethel's death. He recounts Hæthcyn's fall at Ravenswood, and Hygelac's vengeful victory over Ongentheow; he speaks with strong emotion of the great love he had borne Hygelac, of his uncle's favors to him, and of his own devoted service. Always he had stood before Hygelac in battle; and so he means now to stand first in fight while sword and life shall last. So it had been 'ever since before the hosts I slew Dæghrefn, champion of the Franks, with my hands; not at all was he allowed to bring the precious breast-ornament to the Frisian king, but in the fight he fell, ... the grip of war crushed his breast, the pulsings of his heart.'

In this speech the poet lets his hero establish his place in the royal dynasty, and reveal his devotion to his kinsmen. Beowulf's reminiscences begin with a tender acknowledgment of Hrethel's loving care: 'I was seven winters old when the lord of treasures, kindly ruler of the people, received me from my father; King Hrethel protected and maintained me, gave me gifts and feasting, was mindful of kinship. Never in life was I a whit less dear to him ... than any of his children, Herebeald and Hæthcyn, or *my Hygelac*.' This 'my Hygelac' strikes the keynote of the speech: in recalling his kinsmen one by one, and all with deep and warm affection, Beowulf is yet thinking first and always of Hygelac. Therefore he does not need to speak his uncle's name again; when, sixty-six lines later, he declares: 'I repaid him for those treasures as occasion was granted me,' we know he is speaking of his service to Hygelac, who, living or dead, had always had his fondest love. Beowulf's loyalty and admiration for his uncle had thrice found utterance in Hrothgar's presence; they had filled his words and actions in Hygelac's hall; here they are most ardently stated at the focal point of his recollections of all his long-dead kinsmen. This speech is the strongest expression of human feeling in the whole poem; its climax is Beowulf's passionate resolve (lines 2497 ff.) to be worthy, in his last fight, of his beloved Hygelac. Old as he is, and king for fifty years, he is still, in his own heart, 'Hygelac's thane.' As Beowulf is the poet's hero, so Hygelac is Beowulf's.

The last account of Hygelac's fall (lines 2913b–21) is given briefly and objectively, by the Messenger sent by Wiglaf to announce that Beowulf and the dragon both lie dead. There will be no peace for the Geats, the Messenger predicts, once Franks, Frisians, and Svear hear of Beowulf's end: the Merovingian has had no love for the Geats since Hygelac's fateful raid. As Beowulf had done, the Messenger joins to his recollection of the catastrophe in Frisia an account of the great fight in which Hæthcyn and Ongentheow fell; but he makes much more of the battle in Ravenswood. This is proper, since it is the Svear who are soon to conquer the Geats. In the Messenger's narrative Hygelac looms large, as rescuer of Hæthcyn's broken men and conqueror of Ongentheow. This dual emphasis upon Hygelac's fall and his military greatness serves to point out that Hygelac's defeat and death were the primary cause of the decline of the Geats; and that Hygelac's overthrow of Ongentheow provided the motive, as Beowulf's end afforded the eagerly awaited opportunity or the Svear to fall upon and crush the Geats. The poet thus underlines the tragic irony of Beowulf's death in victory over the dragon, only more immediately fatal to the people he perished to save than were Hygelac's triumph over Ongentheow and his death in Frisia.

The narratives of Hygelac's fall and of the wars between Geats and Svear are so placed, and so managed, that they lend to the dragon-fight, and to the figure of the hero as king, a reality and a meaning stronger and deeper than the hero or the narrative of Part I achieves. The poet makes us aware, in Part II, that, because of Hygelac's end, the Geats can survive as a people only while Beowulf lives; and he has shown us, one by one, the critical stages in those wars which were to destroy them. The dragon-slaying is thus completely—and justifiably—encompassed by the traditional recollection of Geatish glory and of Geatish downfall. Through the story of each clash between Geats and Svear runs a darker thread, the tale of Hygelac's fall; and these stories enclose the main action. At only one point do they interrupt it, and then most briefly: the slaying of Eanmund by Weohstan, told in twenty-three lines, is introduced to motivate Wiglaf's loyal resolve to aid Beowulf against the dragon, and to explain the provenience of Wiglaf's sword.

Part II is more than the story of Beowulf's last heroic deed and death: it is also the story of the passing of that people whose last king he is. And these

two stories are inextricably fused; for the tragedy of Beowulf is the tragedy
of his people.

Throughout the poem, the author places in his hero's mouth, just before
each of his great exploits, a warm acknowledgment of his love for Hygelac.
Love and loyalty are, indeed, Beowulf's dominant traits: the essential quality
of his heroism is active, selfless *caritas*. Granted the courage and strength
which any hero must possess, the constant, instinctive illustration in thought
and action of loyal love toward lord and people makes of physical prowess
a means to consistently noble ends. Through the pervasive and climactic
representation of the relation between Beowulf and Hygelac the hero's
caritas is most clearly and convincingly revealed. The poet has enveloped
Beowulf's *Heldenleben* in the climate of his love for Hygelac; and thereby
he accomplishes a satisfying fusion of the monster-slayer with the king, of
the fabulous and the historical elements of the story, of subplot with main
action.

This envelopment binds the two parts of the poem into an inseparable
whole. The heroic ideal which Beowulf illustrates in each part, and as the
embodiment of which he lives and dies, is the projection of his character in
action; but it feeds on his love for Hygelac. Though he much exceeds the
measure of Hygelac, he draws strength from him. The young Beowulf lays
the fruits of his triumphs at his uncle's feet; the aged Beowulf, before his last
fight, makes his resolve to conquer or die a tribute to Hygelac's memory.
Through Hygelac's defeat and death, Fate deprived Beowulf (*hyne Wyrd
fornam*, line 1205b) of the power to save Hrethric, and made the extinction
of the Geatish nation inevitable once Beowulf was lost to them. Thus the
hero's victories are counterpoised by defeat; and his last and greatest victory
brings death and ruin I think, with Tolkien, that the poet meant to remind
us that this is life's way with men.[8] The most heroic life must close in death,
as Beowulf reminded Hrothgar; he who is permitted to 'achieve some share
of renown before death,' and to face his last hour with fortitude, conquers,
though he perishes. And however nobly man may strive toward noble ends,
unless those be God's ends, man strives in vain. But it is the courage to strive,
not success, which marks and ennobles the hero.

But the poet, who, as a good Christian, meant us to perceive this, was
also conscious of the pity of such success in failure. The tragic irony that is so
evident in the frustration of Beowulf's confident promise of aid to Hrothgar
and Hrethric is yet more pointed in Beowulf's outpouring of gratitude to
God that he has been permitted to buy with his death the dragon's treasure
for his people. The possession of that treasure brings with it a curse; and
his people, not knowing of the curse, express their love for their dead lord
by burying the treasure in his tomb. They know—for the Messenger has

forecast it plainly for them—that doom is soon to fall upon themselves; and rather than reap profit from their king's death they consign the treasure to the earth with him—thereby ensuring that his last wish also is frustrated. A doomed king has died to save a doomed people; and thus the harmonious interplay of main action and subplot reaches perfect fusion in the final scenes.

NOTES

1. Klaeber's edition, pp. li, cvii; Ker, *Epic and Romance* (2d ed.; London, 1922), pp. 90, 117, 160–161.

2. Tolkien, "Beowulf: The Monsters and the Critics," *Proceedings of the British Academy*, XXII (1936), pp. 271–272; Chambers, *Man's Unconquerable Mind* (London, 1939). pp. 68–69; Malone, "The Old English Period," in *A Literary History of England*, ed. Albert C. Baugh (New York and London, 1948), Bk. I, Pt. I, p. 94.

3. Gang, "Approaches to *Beowulf*," *Review of English Studies*, N.S., III (1952), pp. 1–12; Bonjour, "Monsters Crouching and Critics Rampant," *PMLA*, LXVIII (1953), pp. 304–312; Chambers, *op. cit.* (note 2, *supra*), p. 68.

4. Edition, pp. l–li, cxviii, cxx–cxxi.

5. Although the poet's allusions to the dynastic quarrels of the Shieldings (lines 1013–19; 1162b–68a; 1180b ff.; 1219–31) concern only Hrothulf's usurpation and the murder of Hrethric, he and his audience must have known of, and borne in mind, the later attack by Heoroweard (Hjörvarðr) on Hrothulf (Hrólf Kraki). This was certainly Chambers' view: see his *Beowulf: An Introduction*, pp. 29–30, 426–429, 448. It is, more-over, possible (I should think probable) that—as Chambers suggested in his revision of A. J. Wyatt's edition (*Beowulf with the Finnsburg Fragment*, Cambridge University Press, 1914, note to lines 82–85)—lines 82b–83a are an allusion to the burring of Hrólf's hall by Hjörvarðr, as lines 83b–85 allude to the fight at Heorot between Ingeld and the Danes under Hrothgar and Hrothulf.

6. *Epic and Romance*, p. 165.

7. *Beowulf and Epic Tradition*, p. 27.

8. Tolkien, *op. cit.* (note 2, *supra*), pp. 264–265, 274; cf. p. 260.

RICHARD J. SCHRADER

Succession and Glory in Beowulf

At the opening of *Beowulf* the poet celebrates the glory (*þrym*) and valor (*ellen*) of the ancient Danish kings (*þeodcyninga, æþelingas*).[1] For more than sixty lines he traces these qualities from their apparent beginning with Scyld Scefing to their culmination in Hrothgar, a great-grandson. This is the full Scylding line to that point, but the poem makes clear that there were earlier rulers of the Danes, presumably living before Sceaf, men such as Heremod and Hnæf. They are not mentioned until other themes require them; here the poet has established a *translatio gloriae* in which they have no part. The nature of the glory and the means of its transmission will have important consequences in Danish history (as presented in the poem), and similar ideas attached to succession appear in the Geatish section as well.[2]

The celebration of glory has such emphasis because human praise is the highest goal of the pagan characters, providing justification for individuals and a collective heaven for nations in a world where nearly all the apparent motion leads to dead ends. The poet may well have absorbed these lessons from the *City of God*, where Augustine contrasts earthly and heavenly (true) glory and speaks of pagans even more high-minded about the other things of this world than the Scandinavians of *Beowulf*:

From *Journal of English and Germanic Philology* 90, 4 (October 1991), pp. 491–504. © 1991 by the Board of Trustees of the University of Illinois.

21

Wherefore, when the kingdoms of the East had been illustrious for a long time, it pleased God that there should also arise a Western empire, which, though later in time, should be more illustrious in extent and greatness. And, in order that it might overcome the grievous evils which existed among other nations, He purposely granted it to such men as, for the sake of honour, and praise, and glory, consulted well for their country, in whose glory they sought their own, and whose safety they did not hesitate to prefer to their own, suppressing the desire of wealth and many other vices for this one vice, namely, the love of praise.... But since those Romans were in an earthly city, and had before them, as the end of all the offices undertaken in its behalf, its safety, and a kingdom, not in heaven, but in earth—not in the sphere of eternal life, but in the sphere of demise and succession, where the dead are succeeded by the dying [sed in decessione morientium et successione moriturorum]—what else but glory should they love, by which they wished even after death to live in the mouths of their admirers? ... For as to those who seem to do some good that they may receive glory from men, the Lord also says, "Verily I say unto you, they have received their reward" [Matt. 6: 2].[3]

1

After a destitute youth Scyld was a terrorizer of his neighbors. His glory (*weorðmyndum*, l. 8) was such that they were compelled to obey him (*hyran scolde*, l. 10) and pay tribute; that, emphatically, was a good king (l. 11). At death, he goes to the same Lord (*frea*, l. 27) that gave worldly glory to his son and successor, Beowulf Scylding (l. 16). It is a self-ordered funeral, like that which closes the poem, and he carries with him considerable treasure. As if in ironic compensation for the way he arrived (taking ll. 43–46 as litotes), all the pieces that are specified are war gear. Under a viking banner (*segen*, l. 47) he goes they know not where.

The interjected description of his son Beowulf adds that the people had suffered long from lordlessness before Scyld arrived, establishing a clear break with whatever had come before. God sent the young man to prevent a recurrence and gave him glory, which spread widely (*woruldare*, l. 17; *blæd*, l. 18). After summarizing the qualities of the good, if warlike, king, the poet has portrayed the worthy successor, a young man who uses his time as heir apparent to prepare for kingship (ll. 20–25). With his father out of the way—and the poet takes pains to underscore Scyld's passing (ll. 55–56)—the portrait resumes, but with few additional details except that this Beowulf was beloved (l. 54).

Even fewer lines are devoted to Healfdene, the next to rule the glorious (*glæde*, l. 58) Scyldings, and *his* children are merely listed. It is tempting to follow Klaeber's reconstruction (p. xxxvi) based on Scandinavian sources and assume that we are to understand that Healfdene was killed by Ingeld's father, Froda, chief of the Heathobards, but the poem is silent on the matter. We learn later that his son Heorogar succeeded him, then Hrothgar. Neither they nor Halga are seen as his avengers.

The field of view has progressively narrowed until the focus is exclusively on Hrothgar. Now it will open to describe his contributions prior to the coming of Grendel. To this point we have been given an outline of Danish history down to the poem's present. Outside this *Stammbaum*, which is an introduction that sets the standards by which to judge Hrothgar,[4] there is also in the poem a fragmentary prehistory which is not so glorious. The poet looks in two directions by having Hrothgar's scop celebrate Beowulf's triumph over Grendel with a mention of Sigemund's carrying off a dragon's treasure in a boat (ll. 895–97); though presumably not considered a Dane, he was known for his *ellen*-deeds (l. 900). Beowulf leaves Denmark with a boatload of treasure, and all of the dragon's hoard is buried with him when he leaves Geatland. The glory and valor shown in his climactic fight have ambiguous results, and the reburial of the treasure signifies the end of his tribe's glory, unlike Scyld's passing from the Danes.

The poet contrasts Sigemund with the notorious Heremod, whose *ellen* subsided (ll. 901–2) and who did not live up to his ancestral rank (*fæderæþelum*, l. 911). The poet's language makes it clear that he was a Danish king and predecessor if not father of Scyld.[5] He was ignored at the opening because the *translatio* begins when the Danish Beowulf succeeds the eponym, Scyld. Later on, Hrothgar himself elaborates on Heremod's offenses. He says that his Geatish rescuer will be a comfort (to *frofre*, l. 1707) to his people as Heremod was not to the Danes—and we recall the same phrase used of the former Beowulf (l. 14). Heremod was part of a disordered past outside the continuum of glory. Here the Danes are called Ecgwela's retainers for the only time, and in the next half-line Honor-Scyldings (l. 1710). I think that the balancing of the two is deliberate: Ecgwela is an unknown king, a "mythical" figure even to Hrothgar and part of a tradition before Scyld, as Scyld (only once) is son of the absent Sceaf (l. 4).[6] Heremod was forced into exile and killed (l. 1714), creating a lordless situation of the kind it was the function of Scyld to alleviate. (Bonjour goes so far as to claim that Heremod's death was followed by the very interregnum that Scyld ended [p. 7].) And when in power he would not reward the Danes for glory (*dome*, l. 1720).

To this same "mythical" time we should presumably assign Hnæf, slain at Finnsburg, and his father Hoc. Hnæf was a Danish chief sung about by Hrothgar's scop not long after the Sigemund–Heremod vignettes. Hnæf's people are called Half-Danes, Danes, and Scyldings, but their relation to the Danish royal house as it is presented in the poem is obscure.[7] For the scop it is a story that shows the vengeful Danes in a good light, but it is not told in his voice. It has been paraphrased and structured in such a way as to make prominent the sorrows of Hildeburh, Hnæf's sister, rather than to celebrate the revenge ethic.[8] In fact it is another tragedy of lordlessness (cf. l. 1103). It says of those on the pyre that their glory (*blæd*, l. 1124) was gone.

So the true line begins with Scyld. Fittingly, the first words about his great-grandson Hrothgar are that he was given success in war, glory (*weorðmynd*, l. 65) in battle, but this good king's retainers *eagerly* obeyed (*georne hyrdon*, l. 66). The warlike Scylding kings have sufficiently pacified the realm that a great meadhall can be built. None was mentioned for the Danes before this, and Scyld was instead known for destroying those of others (l. 5). That the glory of Hrothgar, at least, soon will end is made clear at once. Heorot will burn, probably during a feud with his son-in-law in a failed attempt to use marriage to keep peace.[9] And before that he must deal immediately with Grendel (l. *86*). He says at one point that prior to this invasion he was always able to protect his people (ll. 1769–76), maintaining the tradition started by Scyld.

For now his court is ideally ordered, reflecting the stability of the dynasty. To enter that court and be accepted by it, Beowulf must undergo a succession of challenges by persons of increasing importance. He is passed from one to another in an initiation that culminates in formal adoption, and so he enters Scylding history as if a Dane in the great tradition. First he encounters the coastguard, where the issue is whether these alien seafarers (ll. 254–55) are wanderers arriving in the style of Moses-like Scyld or march-haunting Grendel (l. 103). The coastguard wants to know their lineage, and Beowulf reveals the names of his uncle and father (ll. 252, 269–63). When satisfied, this servant (*ombeht*, l. 287) guides them (l. 292) to Heorot.[10]

There they must deal with another *ombiht* (l. 336), the herald Wulfgar. He too wants to know about their noble lineage (*æþelum*, l. 332), but feels that they come not as exiles but out of heart's greatness/glory (*higeþrymmum*, l. 339). With that, Beowulf finally discloses his name (l. 343). Hrothgar adds to the Geat's family tree when he supplies Beowulf's grandfather, telling Wulfgar that he indeed knows the recent history of that family (ll. 372–75) and bidding him to inform Beowulf that he knows his *æþelu* (l. 392). Wulfgar guides them in (l. 402).

Later on, after the formal introduction to Hrothgar, Unferth makes his problematical challenge. Among other things, he is disturbed that Beowulf's glory (*mærða*, l. 504) is greater than his, and among Beowulf's rejoinders is the charge that Unferth slew his own brothers (ll. 587–88), which the poet later confirms (ll. 1167–68). Even if this test is a formal flyting, it forces one to consider whether the Scylding heritage is sufficient to handle a military problem that involves not the destruction of a meadhall but the spiritual pollution of it. Beowulf's particular glory, soon to be engrafted onto that of the Danes, is that he alone can cleanse Heorot.

Finally, he meets Wealhtheow, who should be associated with these challengers. She makes no demands at this point, but her mead-dispensing precipitates Beowulf's vow (ll. 611–41). Her relevance to the process under discussion becomes clearer after the slaying of Grendel and the adoption of Beowulf, when Beowulf moves back through the same series of persons (or their equivalents) and out of Danish history. On this occasion she finds Hrothgar sitting with and trusting the suspicious Hrothulf and Unferth. Her function here is to make Beowulf aware that his adoption is not to be at the expense of the Danish royal line, which will in time have enough troubles from within. She properly addresses her husband first, enjoining him to leave the kingdom to their sons (ll. 1178–80), even though that kind of succession is not inevitable in the world of the poem.[11] Somewhat fitfully she trusts that Hrothulf would be a good regent (ll. 1180–83) and asks Beowulf to be kind in instruction, gentle in deeds to her boys (ll. 1219–20, 1226–27), that is, to take no more upon himself than what she expects of Hrothulf, citing the loyalty of the court about him as an (ironic?) example of what she means (ll. 1228–31). Later, Beowulf promises Hrothgar that he will protect his son (ll. 1836–39), and events prove that he had no designs on the throne.

Unferth (mentioned twice in passing after his challenge) reenters the action as a supporter of Beowulf in the encounter with Grendel's mother. He lends him a sword that had done *ellenweorc* (l. 1464), though he himself lost glory (*dome*, l. 1470) by not daring the venture himself. In that, he represents all the Scyldings, and the same might be said of the sword. It fails to help Beowulf, though he expected to work glory with it; for the first time its glory ceased (*dom*, ll. 1491, 1527–28). Beowulf returns it, with thanks (ll. 1807–12). He had already exchanged for it what may be the sword Hrothgar gave him for killing Grendel (ll. 1023, 1488–90).[12]

Beowulf does not reencounter Wulfgar, the *ombiht*, herald, and guide who came before Unferth in the prior (reverse) sequence. The only other *ombiht* is a Geatish attendant to whom Beowulf entrusted his sword before the fight with Grendel (l. 673). But another Danish hall-thane does appear on the night before Beowulf's departure (l. 1794). He guides him (l. 1795) not to another encounter but to bed.

So too the final meeting with the coastguard is entirely amiable. Beowulf gives him (or another attendant) a gold-wound sword (ll. 1900–1901). Perhaps, in challenging the fifteen Geats alone, the coastguard had shown more of the old glory than any other Dane Beowulf met. Like Scyld, the hero departs in a boat laden with treasure (ll. 1896–98), but he does not leave much hope behind.

The Danes are first made hall-less and then are lordless in their reversion to disorder. The Heathobard feud involving Hrothgar's son-in-law Ingeld will destroy Heorot, in the customary understanding of those early allusions to its burning. Beowulf imagines a scene (ll. 2032–69) like that which he heard Hrothgar's scop portray in the Finnsburg lay, where a man is goaded to take vengeance on the slayers of his lord. Beowulf cannot know the full outcome, but the poet evidently does. And then Hrothulf, by all indications, will take the throne after his uncle Hrothgar dies.[13] They were friends *then* (ll. 1019, 1164), when Beowulf visited. Wealhtheow expects that Hrothulf will be good to her boys *if* he remembers how well she and Hrothgar treated him when a child (ll. 1180–87). Beyond this "admirable subtlety," in Klaeber's words (p. xxxii), the poet does not go. No matter what happened in "real" history, he implies trouble ahead. If this does not fit facts exterior to the poem, then we should remember that he also makes Sigemund a dragon-slayer and contrives a demise for the Geats: poetic facts are made to serve themes. Further, it is significant that Hrothulf is not assigned the kind of glory he receives as Hrólfr Kraki in Scandinavian lore. The poet does not bother to detail the Danish succession, leaving us to infer that the *translatio* ends with Hrothgar—or Beowulf.

His first words to Hrothgar affirm that he is Hygelac's kinsman (l. 407), but he says less about his ancestry than what he told either the coastguard or Wulfgar. We could be meant to assume that he knows what Wulfgar would report, but it is also a gesture of courtesy, identifying himself with a formulaic phrase as a kind of verbal handshake with a man who knows him already—Hrothgar (in his first words) tells him without qualification why he had come (ll. 457–72). He is not reading the visitor's mind: all signs imply that Ecgtheow, Beowulf, and Hrothgar were well acquainted with each other. Beowulf came to return the favor performed for his father, when Hrothgar paid wergeld to end a feud at the very time he was consolidating his own power after the death of his brother Heorogar (ll. 465–69); the fates of the two families were linked thereafter.

For the first time, Hrothgar voluntarily gives control of the hall to another (l. 655), bidding him to remember glory (*mærþo*) and display mighty valor (*mægenellen*) (l. 659). These are the qualities that will make him worthy of association with the Scylding line laid out for us at the beginning. But Hrothgar already knows that only Beowulf, not any of the Danes, has them in sufficient measure to qualify for the task. Beowulf later says to his men that God will assign the glory (*mærðo*, l. 687) in the battle, and it is given to Beowulf (*guðhreð*, l. 819). The happy Danes speak of his *mærðo* (l. 857). They say that no one is more worthy of a kingdom (l. 861), though they do not find fault with Hrothgar, for "þæt wæs god cyning" (l. 863), and after the second fight Hrothgar will say the same thing about the young man's royal qualifications (ll. 1845–53). Both in their way are worthy Scyldings.

Hrothgar ratifies his honorary lineage by adopting him into a new kinship (*niwe sibbe*) while praising nonetheless, in Biblical terms, the woman who bore him (ll. 942–49). Hill has explored the complexities of the scene, noting that "Hrothgar first spiritually adopts Beowulf and then seems to offer the right of succession," signs of which are the four treasures; "Hrothgar offers something that falls between legal adoption and mere fraternal spirit."[14] That ambiguity—along with Beowulf's never indicating that he wants to take over and his stressing his loyalty to Hygelac upon returning home—is the poet's way of maintaining the *spiritual* nature of the succession.[15] Beowulf acknowledges the *ellenweorc* (l. 958) that brought this about, nicely pointing out that Grendel is *feasceaft* (l. 973). The reader can associate this with the original condition of Scyld (l. 7), the only times the word is used in this part of the poem: "feasceaft funden; he þaes frofre gebad" ([he was] found destitute; for that he received help). Not so for Grendel: "feasceaft guma frofre gebohte" (the destitute man [has not] bought help). Grendel has sunk back into the primordial disorder from which the Scyldings have always escaped thus far. Among the gifts Hrothgar gives Beowulf is a *segen gyldenne*, like the one bestowed on Scyld for his last voyage (ll. 47, 1021).

As he prepares to fight Grendel's mother, Beowulf reminds Hrothgar of the adoption, that is, that he is now fighting as his son (ll. 1474–79). The poet calls him a Scylding warrior—"freca Scyldinga" (l. 1563)—and the sense of that genitive plural is the same as in the appellation of his namesake, "Beowulf Scyldinga" (l. 53). Beowulf pointedly remarks that Hrothgar need no longer fear harm "from *that* side" (l. 1675), that is, *external* threats, once he has defeated Grendel's mother. Hrothgar responds by affirming that Beowulf's glory (blæd, l. 1703) has been established, that he will be a help (*to frofre*, l. 1707) to his people, the language used of Beowulf Scylding (ll. 14, 18). His advice includes a warning that Beowulf's present *blæd* of his might (l. 1761) will wane, which is why he should learn from the story of Heremod and from Hrothgar's own failure to protect his people. For now,

though, Beowulf is confident enough to promise help to the king if he
should be terrorized by his neighbors ("ymbsittend egesan þywað," l. 1827),
presumably the neighbors terrorized into submission by Scyld:

> egsode eorl[as] ...
> oð þæt him æghwylc ymbsittendra
> ofer hronrade hyran scolde. (ll. 6, 9–10)

That Beowulf takes his filial role seriously is reflected by the first
thing he reports to Hygelac about Hrothgar: "he seated me with his own
sons" (l. 2013; cf. ll. 1189–91). The first treasure he commands to be
brought in is the banner (l. 2152), as it was the first treasure Hrothgar gave
him (l. 1021). Another connection with dynastic matters is the armor he
likewise turns over (ll. 2155–62). He says that Hrothgar told him to tell
Hygelac that Heorogar, his older brother and predecessor, deliberately
passed over his own loyal son in giving the armor to him. It has not gone
to Hrothgar's natural sons, either. Now it passes to Hygelac as a permanent
reminder of the favor done for a Geatish exile at the time Hrothgar took
the throne. Unfortunately, Beowulf will never again have a chance to act as
a male peace-weaver for the Danes, as the succession evidently bypasses all
of Hrothgar's sons.

Beowulf's great opponents in Denmark may be thought of as an
opposing dynasty, remnants of another time and place of disorder. They too
have a pedigree, connecting them by a vague and metaphorical "thence" (l.
111) to the race of Cain: giants, elves, evil spirits. These physical progeny
were destroyed by the Flood; Grendel and his mother are their spiritual
heirs.[16] He is also the antithesis of Scyld. For instance, he comes at the end
of a line and not the beginning. A destroyer of his neighbors, he nonetheless
spares their meadhall, where he had total rule and fought against the right (l.
144). While "men knew not" where Scyld traveled in the afterlife, they know
not where Grendel goes here and now (ll. 50, 162). It is both a usurpation
and a parody of all the conquering that has gone on before. Fittingly, he is
feasceaft at his end (l. 973), not his beginning, and is succeeded by a parent,
not an offspring.

With the arrival of his mother we are given the same genealogy and
the same "thence" (l. 1265). The two are all the more mysterious and terrible
to the Danes for having no pedigree *they* know of (ll. 1355–57). Having
admitted ignorance of their ancestry, Hrothgar goes on unwittingly to reveal
their spiritual heritage by describing the hellish mere. The monsters' hall is
on the other side of the mirror. When they enter the Danish world it is to
fight against "the right." Since they are absurd inversions, it is not surprising

that (in a much-remarked role and gender reversal) mother is the successor and avenger of son.

Their world has relics of the antediluvian giants with whom they are associated. Whereas "old sword made by giants" is a reflexive formula in the later part of the poem (ll. 2616, 2979), it takes on real substance in the underwater lair, where Beowulf enters prehistory, outside any surviving lines of human descent. Beowulf uses such a sword (ll. 1558, 1562, 1679) when the gift from the Danish court fails. Its hilt then undergoes a *translatio*. Having already outlasted the giants and the Grendel clan, it now passes from Beowulf to Hrothgar (ll. 1677–86). The "origin of the ancient strife" is written on it (ll. 1687–93), along with the death of the giants, but that is another story Hrothgar does not know. In entering the modern world, the weapon has lost its edge; only its wisdom remains. So too the wisdom of Hrothgar is the chief relic of Scylding glory.

II

The Geatish succession, by contrast, is not as richly imagined, and an element of disorder obtains in all of it before Beowulf. The only figure named who might precede Hrethel is Swerting, the uncle or grandfather of Hygelac (l. 1203). The Geats of the story are most properly Hrethlings (l. 2960). Like Healfdene he has three sons and a daughter, and like Hrothgar he takes Beowulf into his family (ll. 2428–34). The long process seen in the first part, where Beowulf crowned and ended Danish glory, is here foreshortened in a series of disasters that brings Beowulf to the throne, when the history of disorder ends until the dragon arrives. Hrethel's son Hæthcyn accidentally kills his brother Herebeald, after which their father dies of grief and hostility with the Swedes ensues (l. 2472). Hæthcyn is killed by Ongentheow at Ravenswood when the Geats attack out of arrogance (l. 2926), leaving them lordless (l. 2935). Like a Scyld, Hygelac rescues them from that condition, arriving under viking banners (l. 2958). We already know that he will not live up to what is promised here, dying under a banner during another needless raid, his body and treasures passing (*gehwearf*, l. 1210) into the hands of inferior warriors.

Beowulf does not seize the kingdom; it "passed" to his control when Hygelac and his son Heardred died, as the sword "passed" to Hrothgar (*gehwearf*, ll. 1684, 2208). Hygelac's widow Hygd had wanted him to play the part of Hrothulf and displace his cousin when the king died, not trusting her young son's abilities (ll. 2369–72). But these *feasceafte* ones (l. 2373) could not prevail upon him to supersede Heardred, who rules until his death in the Swedish wars. Then it is Beowulf's natural turn.

The transition had begun long before, when Beowulf merged his part in Danish history with the future of the Geats on the occasion of his return. His recapitulation and his yielding of treasures to Hygelac are acts of obeisance. Also, Beowulf has "few [that is, no] near relatives" except for the king (ll. 2150–51)—a situation that anticipates his lonely end. The first thing brought in from Hrothgar's bounty is a banner (l. 2152), perhaps to be thought of as the one carried on Hygelac's fatal raid. A bit later he gives Hygd Wealhtheow's present of a necklace (l. 2172), which had already been associated with that venture (l. 1195). If the Hrethling dynasty is a story of decline, Beowulf's life has been one of increasing glory, from a youth who was thought worthless (ll. 2183–88) to one now given Hrethel's sword and enough land to make him an underking (ll. 2190–99). All of this is toward the end of the first part.

In the second, Beowulf is proud that none of his neighbors (*ymbesittendra*, l. 2734) had been able to oppress the Geats with terror (*egesan*, l. 2736). He founded new glory for the Geats, as had Scyld for the Danes, and prevented those surrounding him from repeating Scyld's viking depredations. The treasure buried with him included a golden banner (l. 2767), chronologically the last of these viking symbols in the poem, and what glory there is in the viking way for the Geats passed with him. His demise and, later, that of the Geats are owed to entanglement in two problematical successions. First, Beowulf becomes involved in the Swedish matter as king by helping the *feasceaft* Eadgils (l. 2393), grandson of Ongentheow, whom Hygelac's men had slain at Ravenswood. Eadgils and his brother Eanmund had fled the wrath of their uncle Onela (who, along with their father Ohthere engaged in slaughter of Geats at a time before Ravenswood [l. 2475]) and were protected by Heardred, Hygelac's son. Onela invaded, killing Heardred and Eanmund. With the aid of Beowulf's people, Eadgils returned to kill the king and take the throne. It develops that Wiglaf is carrying the sword of Eanmund, whom his father had slain; it was a reward from Onela (ll. 2602–19). The matter is complicated, difficult for anyone to take in at one reading (or hearing),[17] and even so the poet is careful to establish that there is a line, one that enters the poem's history with Ongentheow, though with the usual hint of a prehistory in the epithet Scylfing for the Swedes.[18] And again the Scylding pattern is reversed, with a destitute youth coming at the end of a line whose purpose in the poem is to rob the Geats of what little glory there is before and after Beowulf.

The second "succession" involves the dragon and a reenactment of the Danish adventure with new twists.[19] Like Hrothgar Beowulf had lived through many *ellenweorca* (l. 2399) beforehand, and his own hall is burnt (ll. 2324–27). His final *ellenweorc* (l. 2643) costs him his life, as Hrothgar's warning proves accurate. In one sense the dragon is the successor of Grendel, introduced in the same way ("oð ðæ an ongan," ll. 100, 2210) and ruling with the same power (*rixode/rics[i]an*, ll. 144, 2211), the only times those expressions are used. In another sense his career is the opposite of Beowulf's, *beginning* with a treasure barrow on a bluff by the sea (ll. 2241–43). He enters the poem as the successor of the "last survivor," guarding the hoard for three hundred years before a cup is stolen by a *feasceaft* man (l. 2285)—as with Eadgils, the sign of an ending about to occur. Only the lair has an eternal (*ece*) aspect to it, being the work of giants (ll. 2717–19) and surviving from Geatish prehistory like Grendel's antediluvian sword. The treasure, vainly cursed by men of old (ll. 3051–57), was meant to stay there until Doomsday (l. 3069), as was the dragon (l. 3083). In fact the gold is still in the ground, thanks to its burial with Beowulf, as useless to men as ever (ll. 3163–68).

The *translatio* of the gold had been wrongly continued by the thief, leaving Beowulf no choice but to fight its rightful guardian.[20] Anti-heroically, this wretch finds no ceremonial progression in his approach to Beowulf's throne (ll. 2281–83?, 2403–5) and remains nameless; like the earlier servants and not the hero, *he* does the guiding (l. 2409) when it is time to meet the dragon. This intruder from the deep past—not, like Grendel, a spiritual heir of anything—is the Geats' nemesis, and the end of the tragedy will be the primal terror worked by men like Scyld (*egesan*, l. 3154), as the female mourner rightly predicts, for all their praise of Beowulf's valor-work and glory (*ellenweorc*, l. 3173; *lof*, l. 3182).[21]

That will be the outcome of long-standing feuds, however, not their present lordlessness, for there is one last inheritor of Danish and Geatish glory. As Beowulf had "few [no] near relatives" when making his act of obeisance to Hygelac, so when, while dying, he passes regalia to Wiglaf (in lieu of a son [ll. 2729–32]), he remarks that Wiglaf is the last of their race, the Wægmundings (ll. 2813–14)—probably Swedes, but their relation to the Geatish royal family is unstated.[22] Wiglaf is also called a Scylfing (Swede) and a kinsman of the unknown Ælfhere, to cloud the issue further (ll. 2602–4), and his father had fought for the Swedes. In any event, having been informally adopted by Beowulf he stands in the same relation to the Hrethlings as Beowulf does to the Scyldings, the fifth, adoptive, and last true successor to the eponymous founder.[23] Beowulf's failure in his dying speech to predict disaster like the messenger or the female mourner is a judicious signal of confidence in Wiglaf and further evidence that he regards him as the next king.

However, Wiglaf's refusal to take a share of the treasure, magnanimously attributing the victory to Beowulf, is a way of burying all the glory of the Geats.[24] The tribe is now *feasceaft* in every sense. Its history from the beginning had been one of unwisdom[25] until Beowulf, who alone represented the same *þrymm* achieved by the Danes before Grendel intruded. The Danes had experienced ever-broadening glories, safe from external threats, while the Geats seem never uninvolved in feuds before Beowulf. His intervention in the Danish succession had happy results and represented a new pinnacle for those people. Similar interventions in Geatland only ensure the downfall of his own people, whose chaotic history compares poorly with that of the Danes.

NOTES

1. All quotations are from *Beowulf and the Fight at Finnsburg*, ed. Fr. Klaeber, 3d ed. (Lexington, Mass.: Heath, 1950). On the matter of why Danish genealogy might have interested an English audience, see Kenneth Sisam, "Anglo-Saxon Royal Genealogies," *Proceedings of the British Academy*, 39 (1953), 287–348; Alexander C. Murray, "*Beowulf*, the Danish Invasions, and Royal Genealogy," in *The Dating of Beowulf*, ed. Colin Chase (Toronto: Univ. of Toronto Press, 1981), pp. 101–11; Roberta Frank, "The *Beowulf* Poet's Sense of History," in *The Wisdom of Poetry: Essays in Early English Literature in Honor of Morton W. Bloomfield*, ed. Larry D. Benson and Siegfried Wenzel (Kalamazoo: Western Michigan Univ. Press, 1982), pp. 63–64; Robert T. Farrell, "*Beowulf* and the Northern Heroic Age," in *The Vikings*, ed. R. T. Farrell (London: Phillimore, 1982), p. 206.

2. Other treatments of themes relating to glory and succession include John Gardner, "Fulgentius's *Expositio Vergiliana Continentia* and the Plan of *Beowulf*: Another Approach to the Poem's Style and Structure," *PLL*, 6 (1970), 244, 253, 255–56, 260; Frank, pp. 55–56; Stephanie J. Hollis, "Beowulf and the Succession," *Parergon*, n.s. 1 (1983), 41, 44. On the imaginative history within the poem see also Robert T. Farrell, "Beowulf Swedes and Geats," *Saga-Book*, 18 (1972), 229; John D. Niles, *Beowulf: The Poem and Its Tradition* (Cambridge, Mass.: Harvard Univ. Press, 1983), pp. 179–96.

3. St. Augustine, *The City of God*, trans. Marcus Dods (New York: Random House, 1950), pp. 163, 165 (Book V, Chaps. 13, 14, 15); *PL*, 41: 158–60. For the relevance of *City of God* (Book V in particular) to the poet's conception of his pagans, see J. E. Cross, "The Old English Period," in *The Middle Ages*, ed. W. F. Bolton (London: Barrie & Jenkins, 1970), pp. 50–51; Bernard F. Huppé, *The Hero in the Earthly City: A Reading of Beowulf* (Binghamton: State Univ. of New York, 1984), p. 73. For Augustine's place in the tradition, see Maria R. Lida de Malkiel, *L'idée de la gloire dans la tradition occidentale*, trans. Sylvia Roubaud (Paris: Klincksieck, 1968), pp. 90–92.

4. See Adrien Bonjour, *The Digressions in Beowulf*, Medium Ævum Monographs, 5 (Oxford: Blackwell, 1950), pp. 1–11.

5. Klaeber, p. 164; Sisam, "Genealogies," p. 343; Murray, p. 106.

6. The Danes are also "Ing's friends" (ll. 1044, 1319). See Klaeber, p. xxxvii.

7. R. W. Chambers, *Beowulf: An Introduction to the Study of the Poem*, 3d ed. with a supp. by C. L. Wrenn (Cambridge: Cambridge Univ. Press, 1959), pp. 248–49; Kemp Malone, "Healfdene," *Englische Studien*, 70 (1935), 74–76.

8. Richard J. Schrader, *God's Handiwork: Images of Women in Early Germanic Literature*, Contributions in Women's Studies, 41 (Westport, Conn.: Greenwood, 1983), p. 42.

9. But see Norman E. Eliason, "The Burning of Heorot" (*Speculum*, 55 [1980], 75–83), for an emendation that shifts the reference in line 84 to Grendel.

10. Thomas A. Shippey is among those finding "no very clear use" in the poem for the coastguard–Wulfgar–Unferth sequence, looking to folktales for an explanation ("The Fairy-Tale Structure of 'Beowulf,'" *N&Q*, n.s. 16 [1969], 7–10). But see R. E. Kaske, "*Sapientia et Fortitudo* as the Controlling Theme of *Beowulf*," *SP*, 55 (1958), 430.

11. On the issue of primogeniture see Hollis, pp. 48 and 53, n. 13.

12. For Beowulf's return of the sword in lines 1807–12 I follow Shippey's reading (pp. 7–8, n.27) and not that of Klaeber (pp. 192–93, n. 1807), in which Unferth is giving it to Beowulf. Klaeber offers the suggestion about the exchange (p. 186, n.1488), but a sword is in the list of treasures turned over to Hygelac (ll. 2152–54) in the same order as received from Hrothgar (ll. 1021–23).

13. Another customary reading, but for the contrary notion that neither Unferth nor Hrothulf was necessarily treacherous, see Kenneth Sisam, *The Structure of Beowulf* (Oxford: Oxford Univ. Press, 1965), pp. 41, 80; and Gerald Morgan, "The Treachery of Hrothulf," *English Studies*, 53 (1972), 24, 33, 35.

14. John M. Hill, "Beowulf and the Danish Succession: Gift Giving as an Occasion for Complex Gesture," *Medievalia et Humanistica*, 11 (1982), 181, 184, 196, n. 19.

15. Regarding the imprecision of the adoption, Hollis observes that "it could be understood to mean no more than that, in a wholly metaphorical sense, Hrothgar recognizes Beowulf as the true heir to his greatness. At the other extreme, it can, evidently, convey that Hrothgar nominates Beowulf as his successor to the throne" (p. 41). She stresses that "*in the fictional world of the poem*, the bequeathing of a king's armour is a recognized means of signifying the heir to the throne" (p. 40; her italics). This understanding of the difference between poetic fiction and "real" history is akin to Michael D. Cherniss on the symbolic value of treasure in heroic poetry, in *Ingeld and Christ: Heroic Concepts and Values in Old English Christian Poetry* (The Hague: Mouton, 1972), pp. 79–101.

16. It makes little difference to my argument if the descent was more than spiritual, that some of these creatures survived the Flood. For the "Cain tradition" see David Williams, *Cain and Beowulf: A Study in Secular Allegory* (Toronto: Univ. of Toronto Press, 1982), Chap. 2.

17. For some problems connected with the Swedish wars and Beowulf's part in them, see Stanley B. Greenfield, "Geatish History: Poetic Art and Epic Quality in *Beowulf*," *Neophilologus*, 47 (1963), 213; J. E. Cross, "The Ethic of War in Old English," in *England before the Conquest: Studies in Primary Sources Presented to Dorothy Whitelock*, ed. Peter Clemoes and Kathleen Hughes (Cambridge: Cambridge Univ. Press, 1971), pp. 279–80; Norman E. Eliason, "Beowulf, Wiglaf, and the Wægmundings," *Anglo-Saxon England*, 7 (1978), 100.

18. Did the poet have the linguistic sophistication to realize that it originally may have meant "men of the [rocky] shelf" and was not a patronymic? The genealogical impulse was satisfied on an even smaller scale in the incidental reference to Offa: Garmund > Offa > Eomer, with Hemming (probably not an ancestor) in the background.

19. For another parallel, see John Gardner, "Guilt and the World's Complexity: The Murder of Ongentheow and the Slaying of the Dragon," in *Anglo-Saxon Poetry: Essays in Appreciation for John C. McGalliard*, ed. Lewis E. Nicholson and Dolores W. Frese (Notre Dame, Ind.: Univ. of Notre Dame Press, 1975), pp. 14–22.

20. See Cherniss, pp. 86–88.

21. The issue of whether the historical Geats were absorbed by the Swedes is not germane to my argument, but see Sisam, *Structure*, pp. 51–59; Farrell, "Swedes and Geats," pp. 257, 270–71; Adelaide Hardy, "Some Thoughts on the Geats," *Parergon*, 9 (1974), 27–39; Lars Gahrn, "The Geatas of *Beowulf*," *Scandinavian Journal of History*, 11 (1986), 111–13.

22. Speculation about the Wægmundings includes Farrell, "Swedes and Geats," pp. 240–44; and Eliason, "Wægmundings."

23. Scyld > Beowulf > Healfdene > Heorogar > Hrothgar > Beowulf; Hrethel > Hæthcyn > Hygelac > Heardred > Beowulf > Wiglaf. That Wiglaf really is to be thought of as Beowulf's designated successor is shown by Hill (pp. 184–85) and Hollis (pp. 39–40).

24. The gesture is well analyzed by Cherniss (pp. 92, 97–98).

25. See Kaske, pp. 440–46.

JOHN D. NILES

Locating Beowulf *in Literary History*

Faced with the problem of making sense of a poem like *Beowulf*—a poem from a very different epoch, composed according to stylistic criteria that differ markedly from those in fashion today—readers naturally want to ask "What does it mean?" Related to this question is a similar one favored by English professors, who like to take literary machines apart to see how they tick: "How does the poem mean?" Without neglecting either of these questions, neither one of which leads to simple answers, I wish to focus attention on a third one, that is not so frequently asked: *"What work did the poem do?"*

Putting the same matter in other words, what I propose to ask is "What are the cultural questions to which *Beowulf* is an answer?" This perspective involves, among other things, looking upon Anglo-Saxon heroic poetry as a discourse, in Foucault's sense of a corporate means for dealing with a subject and authorizing views of it. Adopting this stance, we can inquire how the poetic tradition of which *Beowulf* is an example served as one important means by which a culture defined itself, validated itself, and maintained its equilibrium through strategic adaptations during a period of major change.

Thanks in part to the impressive formalist scholarship of the past fifty years, we are accustomed to reading *Beowulf* as a superb work of art. The achievement of the broadly philological scholarship that has dominated the

From *Exemplaria* 5, 1 (Spring 1993), pp. 79–109. © 1993 Center for Medieval and Early Renaissance Studies.

academies within living memory has been to create this poem as an aesthetic object worthy of minute critical inquiry. Structuralist rage for order, patristic source-hunting, and oral-formulaic analyses of patterned phrasing have indeed extended our knowledge of the text, its filiations, and its internal systems of order. Paradoxically, the success of these forms of criticism may also have served to occlude our understanding of *Beowulf* as a socially embedded poetic act. As John Hermann has remarked,

> The problem is that it [i.e., the philological heritage] has been too successful; its very dominance keeps Old English studies from developing in new directions.[1]

Like Hermann and some other youngish scholars, as well as some old-school scholars of an historical bent, I suspect that the issue of understanding a poem of this kind cannot be resolved by philological or aesthetic investigations alone. That is not to say that such inquiries, if well conducted, will not form the basis of our understanding. They will. But the underlying issue is ontological, not aesthetic. To paraphrase Leo Spitzer,[2] what one wants to know is "Why did the phenomenon of *Beowulf* happen at all?"

Answering this question means reading the poem as a literary act with cultural antecedents and consequences. To begin with, we need to reconstruct an Anglo-Saxon context within which the poem and the fact of its textual existence make sense. I am not speaking of a "background," in the repudiated sense, but rather of an historical matrix in which the discourse of heroic poetry took place—whether in oral or manuscript form—and which this discourse had some power to shape, as well. As we proceed along these lines, eventually in the direction of assessing the poem's place in a larger cultural heritage that extends to the present day, we can proceed with indifference to earlier conceptions to the effect that *Beowulf* reflects the mentality of one specific group of people located in one time or place, or provides a clear window on early Germanic social institutions, or stands as an unambiguous statement of "heroic values," "Christian allegory," or any other monolithic abstraction. Instead, we can begin to read the poem as a site of ideological conflict, a complex work of art that responded to lively tensions, agreements, and disagreements in the society from which it came, just as its text has provoked many conflicting approaches in the last two centuries. Some readers, following Mikhail Bakhtin, have contrasted epic poetry to the novel, seeing the epic as a monologic genre that expresses a kind of party line.[3] This may be true of some epic poems. If so, I have not come across them. Much can be learned about *Beowulf*, I believe, by approaching it as a polyphonic work whose messages are contingent and sometimes contrary.

Rather than reflecting the static conditions of a single or simple age, *Beowulf* represents a broad collective response to changes that affected a complex society during a period of major crisis and transformation. To note only the most obvious of these transformations: by the time that this poem was put down in writing,[4] the English-speaking peoples of Britain had turned away from pagan beliefs and had embraced the teachings of Christianity. They had weathered the storm of Viking invasions and had established control of a mixed and somewhat turbulent Anglo-Scandinavian society. They were no longer competing against one another as separate tribes ruled by warlords but had developed a single kingdom, built largely on the Carolingian model and administered through coinage, written documents, and a state bureaucracy. The changes that affected the society to which *Beowulf* pertains were momentous, and by their workings the nation that we call England came into being.

In particular, the society to which *Beowulf* pertains was using writing, and not just oral poetry, to express an ideology capable of persuading people to be governed and rulers to govern well. To an extent that still seems remarkable no matter how familiar one is with this phenomenon, late Anglo-Saxon England excelled in book-making, and much of this book-making was in the vernacular. Whether the literacy that book-making presupposes was ever widespread among the laity, we cannot know with certainty.[5] By the time that *Beowulf* was written down, however, at least some of the secular aristocracy were no longer illiterates, relatively self-sufficient in their isolation from Mediterranean culture and, perhaps, indifferent or even hostile to the values that that culture represented. They were familiar with the use of poetry in English as a vehicle for Christian doctrine and a means of reinventing the Germanic past.

To see how these momentous events affect our reading of Beowulf, we should briefly place the poem into relation to the literary tradition that developed in post-Roman Britain once Germanic-speaking kings were in control of the land. I must apologize to my readers if this survey requires me to proceed over some well-worn ground; my only justification for doing so is that I shall find out a somewhat different path than others have taken.

When Britain was a Roman colony, many of its inhabitants were familiar with both the arts of literacy and the Christian faith. During the fourth and fifth centuries, for reasons not wholly clear, Roman Britain suffered an economic and administrative collapse that left it cut off from the mother country. Various forms of chaos and regression ensued until, according to tradition, the land was conquered by Germanic-speaking invaders from the North Sea coastal areas. The first of these warriors came as mercenaries. Others then migrated in great numbers, killing or enslaving the inhabitants and establishing their own kingdoms along ancestral lines. This is the account that the people of Anglo-Saxon England gave of their historical origins, at any rate, and most people of later ages have accepted it at its face value.

For archaeologists, the problem with this account is that there is little hard evidence for a large Germanic migration that led to the conquest of Britain. A Roman collapse there was, but a Germanic conquest? Maybe. There is much to be said for Richard Hodges's theory whereby the myriad regions of sub-Roman Britain evolved into the kingdoms of early Anglo-Saxon England rather than being suddenly replaced by them.[6] According to this theory, Roman Britain became progressively more and more Germanized rather than being conquered outright. Eventually a "Myth of Migration" then developed as a way of legitimizing the political interests that emerged in the post-colonial period, when warlords of Germanic stock or aspirations were intent on establishing their hegemony over a mixed population. In short, the Myth of Migration that was one of the Anglo-Saxons' controlling political ideas (as Nicholas Howe has shown)[7] was a projection of a desire on the part of many inhabitants of Britain for a distinguished non-Roman racial past. For better or worse, this desire happens to have been replicated by many people in England, Germany, and North America during the period from the late eighteenth to the earlier twentieth century, when the tide of Western racial consciousness reached its high-water mark in modern times.[8]

As Hodges notes, advocates of his theory must respond to the spiny question of why Latin and the Celtic languages were so fully eclipsed by the English language in Britain. Whether or not the theory is correct, and it will be debated for years to come, it has the attraction of drawing attention to the historicity of history; that is to say, the set of biases that make documents such as Bede's *Ecclesiastical History* and the annals of the *Anglo-Saxon Chronicle* untrustworthy as an account of "what actually happened." The theory is not contradicted by what we know of the human capacity for mythmaking. As Eric Hobsbawm and other historians have pointed out, there are few things more easily invented than a tradition that has existed since time immemorial.[9]

Whatever the right story of the decay and displacement of Roman institutions in Britain may be, the island soon became part of what Hodges calls a North Sea interaction zone. During the fifth, sixth, and seventh centuries, as new trade routes and intertribal connections linked the peoples of Britain with the other peoples fringing the North Sea, paganism of the Old Germanic type became increasingly the norm. Latin disappeared as the language of the ruling class. Germanic laws and customs took the place of Roman ones. The power of important leaders was displayed through the circulation of prestige goods as gifts and in the context of funerals, such as the spectacular seventh-century gravesites at Taplow and Sutton Hoo.

Most important for our present concerns, Anglo-Saxon kingship took on insular forms in a land that was once again yielding the impressive agricultural surpluses that translate into cash and loot. By the early seventh century, kings were constructing palaces, such as the one at Yeavering (Northumberland), that served as the focal points of their realms and the most visible expressions of their prestige. In royal milieus of this kind, cultivated poetry could flourish. From this time on, it is fair to surmise, stories relating to the Heroic Age, the half-mythical fourth- and fifth-century Age of Migrations, found a favored place in the repertory of singers vying for aristocratic patronage. Both then and now, people of noble status or ambitions have tended to have a weak spot for questions of lineage. Not only could heroic poetry express the ideology of current regimes, legitimizing structures of power through tales of dead ancestors. It could also satisfy the desire for origins (to use Allen Frantzen's phrase)[10] that anyone in Britain may have felt.

In this formative period, apparently, there developed a firm tradition of heroic poetry of the kind that Alcuin complains about, in his famous letter of 797, and that eventually found complex literary expression in *Beowulf*, *Waldere*, and the *Finnsburg Fragment*. During this period members of the ruling class had little use for books but possessed a well-developed literature without letters. They were familiar with runes but used them for practical rather than literary ends. Instead, in keeping with Old Germanic practice, they patronized songs that skilled poets performed aloud in celebration of kings and heroes.[11]

Too frequently, in the past, the study of the putative oral roots of texts that have come down to us in writing has been undertaken in a spirit of celebration of a golden childhood of the race from which literacy has lamentably cut us off. Work of this odor has a way of provoking an allergic reaction on the part of hard-nosed scholars who value both their own literacy and that of the Anglo-Saxons. Given the history of these debates, it is worth taking a moment to reconsider the oral matrix from which some of our extant texts are likely to derive.[12]

Understanding the literature that has emerged in a dominantly oral context, whether in the past or the present, is not an easy task. As Brian Stock has aptly remarked, "it may be asked whether, as literates,

we understand orality as anything but the opposite of literacy."[13] People
whose lives are deeply invested in Western educational institutions naturally
tend to understand illiteracy as nothing but deprivation, and this attitude
is reinforced by a host of governmental agencies. Today some people
even speak of "cultural literacy" as a synonym for broad-based humanistic
knowledge of the kind nice white people ought to have, while "cultural
illiteracy" is another term for unwashed ignorance. During the past hundred
and fifty years, as the disciplines of anthropology and folklore have emerged
into their modern forms, the search for the primitive or folk "other" has
sometimes been pursued as a foil for the dominant culture's quest for its
self-identity. Remnants of once-viable oral cultures have been folklorized to
indulge the nostalgia of the dominant society and to swell the pocketbooks
of entrepreneurs. Even good anthropological and folkloristic research has
sometimes been received in an atmosphere of colonialism or ethnocentrism,
so that just by employing the value-laden concepts of literacy and orality, in
Stock's view, "we thus run the risk of intellectual imperialism among peoples
that do not share our faith in the value of writing."

The fundamental and almost inevitable bias with which we favor the
written word can affect our ability to understand a poem like *Beowulf*, which
both is rooted in an oral culture and depicts one, in imaginary guise. If we
look upon an oral culture as lacking something that it should have in order
to be complete, we will not understand it as a working system with its own
efficacy and equilibrium.

The active tradition-bearer who is the heart of an oral tradition—its
motor, so to speak—is likely to have a recognizable style that sets him apart
from other performers.[14] When we look for that hypostatic entity that we call
"the tradition," in fact, what we find are just such creative individuals, each
with his or her own way of speaking or singing. As specialists in established
forms of oral expression, these people tend to be known and honored by
name in their communities. They are the makers of the tradition, not its
slaves, and their creativity is often manifest in a personal style that may
include a display of neologisms and original figures of speech, as well as an
ability to spin simple tales into complex, highly ornamented verbal displays.
The most gifted singer recorded by Milman Parry and Albert Lord in the
Balkans, Avdo Meðedović of the village of Obrov in eastern Montenegro,
was able to hear a song performed by a less skilled person, meditate on it
overnight, and perform the same song the next day at nearly three times its
earlier length, expanding the story with ornamental details of the kind that
were prized in this tradition: catalogs of names, descriptions of men, horses,
and weapons, detailed journeys, examples of direct discourse, evocations of
personal emotion on the part of actors, flashbacks in time, and the like.[15]

Fieldwork that I have undertaken with Scotland's travelling people in 1984, 1986, 1987, and 1988 reinforces this point. The person whom I have recorded at greatest length, Duncan Williamson of Argyll and Fife, is a connoisseur of oral traditions. He has made a lifetime habit of listening intently to other performers and absorbing their words, so that now, in his mid-fifties, he is a walking encyclopedia of verbal lore that he has learned from family members, crofters, fellow-workers, tramps, and friends. He has a larger repertory of songs and stories than anyone else whom I have encountered. Moreover, he has compiled full versions of songs that he learned from other people only in fragments; and when he learns a new story, he is likely to retell it at length, in his own fully ornamented style. When in the company of other singers, he is often able to help them when they falter, and in private he can be a sharp critic of other people's performances.[16] Through active, self-conscious, intelligent tradition-bearers like Međedović and Williamson, an oral culture realizes its full potential.

It would be a mistake to see such performers as isolated geniuses. An active tradition-bearer can only flourish when a community of like-minded individuals shares a body of lore and supports particular forms of verbal expression. The singer or storyteller tends to be a spokesman for accepted wisdom. His or her art is the art of perfecting known modes of expression and familiar themes, not inventing new ones. Gifted performers like these bring established genres to a fine point of expression, to the delight of those listeners who have competence in this medium. Oral literature can thus serve important functions of education and acculturation in the society in which it occurs. It tends to be one of the most important means by which children absorb the values of adult society and learn to pattern their behavior according to accepted norms. For adults, it confirms the gridwork of understanding that constitutes their knowledge of history, social structure, and moral action: in short, their culture.

The culture of early Anglo-Saxon England began undergoing the first of its crises of identity beginning in 597 when, according to Bede, missionaries sent by Pope Gregory the Great arrived in Kent to forge a new kind of colonial relationship between a set of Germanized kingdoms and what was now also a fairly thoroughly Germanized Rome. This missionary activity was both reinforced and threatened by the work of Irish monks in northern Britain. The relative speed with which the rulers of seventh-century Britain came to adopt Christianity—and adopt it systematically, not just as one of a number of competing cults—speaks of their desire for participation in a wider world of power and history than their Myth of Migration could provide.

Anglo-Saxon literature offers abundant evidence of a dynamic and sometimes contradictory accommodation of religious and temporal values during the period after the Conversion.[17] Perhaps more readily apparent than the new religion's effect on ethics was its impact on Anglo-Saxon concepts of identity. The proud pagan kings of sixth- and seventh-century Britain doubtless considered their domains to be "central" and "normal," as people like to do. With the Conversion, they were faced with an alternative perspective whereby they were peripheral members of a larger Christian community whose centers of physical and spiritual power were farther East, in Rome and Jerusalem. In this larger geographical context, purely Germanic customs were potentially aberrant. In like manner, Anglo-Saxon history could come to seem merely insular. One of the effects of the Conversion was to subordinate the Germanic past to the dominant history of the Mediterranean lands. The extended pseudo-genealogy that the West Saxon royal line invented for itself by the time of King Alfred is perhaps the most dramatic single manifestation of this tendency toward accommodation and subordination.[18] According to this new concept of history, the kings of Wessex no longer traced their lineage back to Woden and Geat as divine ancestors. Instead, these figures, now euhemerized, became intermediate links in a grand line of descent from Noah, hence from Adam. The Germanic tribes were thus welcomed to the family of the people of the Book, just as the Anglo-Saxon kingdoms became an outpost of Roman ecclesiastical organization. Germanic, Roman, and Biblical antiquity became three aspects of a single past.[19]

These cultural transformations were made possible through the mastery of writing, or what Jack Goody has called the technology of the intellect.[20] Writing made far-flung ecclesiastical organization possible. In time, it permitted the growth of a state bureaucracy to facilitate large-scale administration and finance. As Seth Lerer has discussed in depth, writing was a linking device that promoted complex cultural connections, as when Bede incorporated written documents such as papal letters into his *History* or when various Anglo-Saxon authors wrote glosses on Scriptural texts, glosses that in turn sometimes inspired later commentary.[21] By permitting knowledge to be accumulated in stable form in books and monastic libraries, the technology of writing fostered the growth of science, in partial displacement of magic. By calibrating time in the form of annals, writing made possible history in something like the modern sense, as opposed to legend or myth. It also allowed for the invention of literature as we know it today, with its allusive and densely intertextual character, as opposed to the poetry that was known only in face-to-face encounters.[22]

As Patrick Wormald has shown in an important attempt to set *Beowulf* within the aristocratic climate of early English Christianity, it would be a mistake to look upon Anglo-Saxon monks as a separate class with no worldly interests.[23] By birth as well as personal outlook, many monks had links with the secular aristocracy. Some noblemen seem to have looked upon certain monasteries as, in essence, their private domains, and abbots and priors were naturally drawn from the ranks of the upper class. Anglo-Saxon *boceras*, the bearers of literary culture, thus comprised an elite not only thanks to their knowledge, with its attendant power, but also through their social connections. This elite class may have had strong influence in the secular realm from early on. Certainly it did so by the end of the ninth century, once Alfred the Great, following the lead of King Offa of Mercia, had reorganized the West Saxon kingdom on the Carolingian model, with a strong emphasis on piety and the literate arts. By this time, the commonplaces of Latin learning had filtered through to all levels of the vernacular culture. But in the meantime, a major external threat had imperiled the continuity of life and letters in Britain.

It is no accident that we know of the defense of southern Britain from Viking marauders chiefly through a literary source, the *Anglo-Saxon Chronicle*, that seems to have been initiated with King Alfred's blessing. Like many canny statesmen, Alfred was aware of the political uses of literacy, and the *Chronicle* could be called the first piece of political propaganda written in English. Its annals for 871 to 896 consistently take a West Saxon perspective and show the king in a sympathetic and indeed heroic light. The same is true of the king's authorized biography, Asser's *Life of Alfred*, a work whose chief literary model was Einhard's *Life of Charlemagne*. Asser's book traces, among other subjects worthy of emulation, Alfred's tenacious efforts to learn to read, and it thereby helps document the revival of English learning and book-making for which this king is justly famed. Taken together, the literary translations from Latin into English that Alfred either sponsored, encouraged, or undertook in person represent, with the *Chronicle*, the first literary canon in English. Europe had not seen such a burst of literary activity since the age of Charlemagne.

Unlike Charlemagne, however, Alfred encouraged the growth of a kind of literacy that was previously of little importance in England and was virtually unknown elsewhere in Europe. This was literacy in the vernacular. To the extent that the ambitious program of education in English letters that he announced in the preface to his translation of Gregory's *Pastoral Care* was realized, it broadened the base of the pyramid of learning, making reading and writing less an esoteric exercise on the part of a clerical elite.[24]

Alfred's impressive accomplishments laid the foundations for a period that can justly be called the Tenth-Century Renaissance. This was a time of consolidation and growth in many spheres, not just the literary arts.

The story of the Danes in Britain during this period is largely one of accommodation and acculturation, as the Viking inhabitants of the Danelaw intermarried with the English, accepted the Christian faith, and took on positions of responsibility in both Church and state. With due attention to his quasi-imperial stature, as well as to the lustre that accrued to him from his triumph at Brunanburh in 937, Alfred's grandson Athelstan styled himself by such honorific titles as *basileus*, *imperator*, and *Angelsaxonum Denorumque gloriosissimus rex*.[25] By Athelstan's reign, for the first time, it is possible to speak of the English nation.

The flowering of literary arts during the tenth and eleventh centuries justifies our speaking of this period as a golden age of vernacular letters. In keeping with the literary program of his immediate predecessors, Athelstan had scribes at his disposal and accumulated an impressive number of manuscripts, which he distributed strategically as gifts.[26] In subsequent years, after old monasteries were reestablished and many new ones founded, all of them affected by the Benedictine Reform that was sweeping Europe during the second half of the tenth century, scribes produced a wealth of manuscripts written in both Latin and English. The great bulk of Old English writings that have come down to us, including the five great poetic codices that were inscribed about the year 1000, dates from this tenth- and eleventh-century period.[27]

How does the poem of *Beowulf* relate to these events?

To begin with, we should divide the question into two. First, what is the probable origin of the discourse, the collective heroic verse-making tradition, that finds textual expression in *Beowulf*? And second, what is the probable origin of this individual poem, in the shape that we now have it? Who wrote this text down, approximately when, and for what reasons?

The first question can perhaps be answered more readily than the second, and I have already given my thoughts on it in brief. Inasmuch as a well-defined tradition of heroic poetry was cultivated by the Anglo-Saxon warrior class, we can probably trace its origins to the period of growth and consolidation of the Anglo-Saxon kingdoms during the sixth to eighth centuries AD. In its basic formal characteristics, this kind of verse surely goes back earlier, to the sorts of songs that once circulated among Germanic tribes on the Continent. These early songs, however, must have differed markedly from the elaborate heroic poetry that developed in the halls of Anglo-Saxon kings. Blessed with wealth and occasional leisure, the Anglo-Saxons of the ruling class transformed memories or fantasies relating to the Age of Migrations into the stuff of a collective dialogue about history. They invented the Heroic Age as a legendary counterpart to their own era, one that chartered their own cherished institutions of kingship, thaneship, gift-giving, oath-swearing, and vengeance. They peopled this realm with shadowy chieftains—"Hengest," "Finn," "Offa," "Eormanric," and others, to cite examples only from *Beowulf*—whose names are attested in various and shifting ways in the genealogies of Anglo-Saxon kings. To these chieftains they added other lords and heroes whose names figured prominently in the oral history of the tribes of the North Sea rim: "Hygelac," "Sigemund," "Weland," "Hama," "Ingeld," "Ongentheow," and the like, again to cite examples only from *Beowulf*, leaving aside the whole panoply of names that are put on display in *Widsith* and *Deor* or that figure in the *Waldere* or *Finnsburg* fragments and other sources. Verbal portraits of this Age of Heroes served to express (or, perhaps, put into question) the ideology of a ruling class through a kind of poetry that was not history, but was a form of history. That is to say, this poetry reconstructed in imaginary form that period of the past that was felt to have the most direct influence on the present, or on what people wanted the present to be, or not to be.

As for dating *Beowulf*, we can begin with the certainty that the poem was composed during the three-hundred-year period between the "Cædmonian revolution" of the late seventh century and the time that our manuscript copy was written down, about the year 1000. In one sense or another, as part of a general movement by which songs were transformed into legible texts, the poem is a product of what German scholars have called *Verschriftlichung*,[28] a noun that sounds better in German than in its English equivalents "literarization" or "textualization." In order to narrow down the limits within which this specific act of textualization took place, let us give brief attention to the time when English poetry was first reified in writing.

Like most of the tales embedded in Bede's *History*, the story of Cædmon is a legendary account whose truth should not be confused with fact.[29] Whatever its factual bases may be, and it would be foolish to deny them altogether, the story functions as a myth of the coming of culture. According to widespread belief, important new elements of human culture are not made but given. They are the product of a gifted person's inspiration in a moment of isolation, when contact with divine power is made possible through prayer or dream.[30] The myth lends divine sanction to the cultural form or forms in question. In this instance, Bede's account of Cædmon serves as an origin myth for two related activities: the use of native verse to celebrate Christian themes, and the use of the technology of writing to record vernacular literature.

Although one still sometimes reads authoritative statements to the effect that one of the first tasks of St. Gregory's missionaries was "to destroy non-Christian mythology, along with the heroic poetry that could serve as a rallying point for a cultural tradition outside Christianity,"[31] such claims are fairly empty. Through euhemerizing the Northern gods, the missionaries did indeed manage to destroy them except as a racial memory, but heroic poetry is another matter. By following the example of Cædmon, Anglo-Saxon poets transmuted the medium of Old English verse into an instrument of Christian teaching and mental exploration. At the same time, by continuing to take their subjects from Germanic legendry as well as from Christian history, they salvaged what was salvageable from the historical ideas of their ancestors, not so as to compete with Christian faith but to bring this faith to more perfect expression, in terms that made culturally specific sense.

To begin with, Christian poets had to learn to sing the divine names. This is chiefly what "Cædmon's Hymn" consists of. But songs of praise were just the beginning. In time, poets learned to sing complex stories focussing on characters who shaped their thoughts and actions in accord with both heroic models and Biblical ones. In a poem like the Old English verse paraphrase of *Exodus*, Moses resembles a Germanic warlord. In a tale like *Beowulf*, correspondingly, the hero takes on Moses-like or Christ-like attributes.[32] The poetic tradition thus proved itself resilient, like any deeply entrenched cultural form. Far from being a static repertory of songs insensitive to a changing social and intellectual climate, Old English poetry remained culturally meaningful by adapting to the realities of the hybrid civilization, both Germanic and Mediterranean in its origins, that was now ascendant in Britain.

Literary histories published before the 1980s regularly state that *Beowulf* was composed not long after the Cædmonian revolution and probably during the eighth century, or the period of Bede and Alcuin, some time before the Vikings began their attacks. More recent scholarship has shaken this orthodoxy and has rekindled speculation that the poem derives from the Viking age, much nearer the date of the extant manuscript.[33] Although certainty in this matter may never be possible, I agree that there are good reasons for taking the poem as we have it as a product of the Tenth-Century Renaissance. As far as *Beowulf* studies are concerned, the Anglo-Scandinavian period is a time whose idea has come.

There are at least seven good reasons for locating *Beowulf* in the period of nation-building that followed the ninth-century Viking invasions. Other scholars may have other reasons for preferring either this date or an alternative one, but these seven points seem to me persuasive, when taken together.

1. *The role of the Danes.* The action of most of the poem is set in Denmark and serves as a showcase for the magnificence of the Danish court. Such an interest in things Danish is understandable after the Danes had settled in England in some numbers, but not before. In addition, the poet depicts the Danes in an ambiguous light. Some of them are admirable, though rather better at talking than fighting. Others practice cursed rites, drink more beer than is good for them, or (like Hunferth) have a way of blustering overmuch and stabbing one another in the back. Such an ambiguous portrait of the Danes fits the tenth-century period after the Viking wars had cooled, when many Danes, now converted to the faith, were being assimilated to the dominant culture.[34]

2. *The Scylding connection.* Near the beginning of *Beowulf* the poet calls prominent attention to the Danish king Scyld Scefing ("descendent of Scef") and his descendants, while twice, later, he draws attention to a Danish king named Heremod. The poem here either draws on or replicates the expanded West Saxon pseudo-genealogy that the West Saxon kings adopted by the time of King Alfred, under Viking influence. This genealogy included early kings named Scyldwa and Heremod, going back to a still more shadowy king Sceaf, "who was born in Noah's Ark." By the late ninth century, in other words, the genealogies of both Anglo-Saxon and Danish royal lines had been made to converge. The beginning of *Beowulf* thus celebrates an ancestral king of the English, not just of the Danes. The whole Grendel episode is thereby brought into relation to English history, which takes on a pan-Germanic aspect, and the kings of England are legitimized as rulers of both Anglo-Saxons and Danes.[35]

3. *Language and rhetoric.* With its well-developed vocabulary of religious experience, as well as its assimilation of commonplace Biblical and Latinate learning, the language in which *Beowulf* is composed shows strong affinities to that of other vernacular works that are most plausibly dated to the tenth century or thereabouts. Worth noting here are the vocabulary and rhetoric not only of poems chiefly secular, such as "The Wanderer" and "Widsith," but also of devout works in verse like "Judith," as well as late prose laws or sermons directed against pagan practices. Scholars who favor an eighth-century date for *Beowulf* have had notorious difficulty in accepting the authenticity of several overtly Christian passages that have a "late" feel to them.[36] The hypothesis of a tenth-century date eliminates this problem. In addition, certain skaldic turns of phrase in *Beowulf,* when taken in connection with the poet's sustained interest in things Scandinavian, suggest Norse influence from the post-Viking period."[37]

4. *Virtuous pagans.* While the *Beowulf* poet depicts the characters of his poem as pagans, as is historically accurate, he also presents at least some of

them as admirable persons. Both Beowulf and Wiglaf are models of courage. The aged Beowulf rules as a *rex justus*, pious and kind, somewhat nearer to the ideal of Augustine and Gregory the Great than one would predict of a Germanic warlord of the Heroic Age.[38] Many characters speak of God and His power, and at one point Hrothgar, another *rex justus*, delivers so sententious an address, couched in familiar homiletic phrases, that many commentators have referred to it as a "sermon." No authors writing in Latin during the eighth century portrayed the ancestral Germanic past in so favorable a light. Bede cast a cloak of silence over early Germanic legendry. Alcuin cried out against its influence in the monasteries. Only with the Alfredian renaissance do we see authors, writing now in English, seek to rehabilitate the materials of Germanic legendry for pious or didactic ends, as when Alfred, paraphrasing Boethius on the subject of mutability, laments "Where are now the bones of Weland?" The *Beowulf* poet's interest in virtuous pagans meshes with the Alfredian program of cultural reform, with its stress on the pious laity. The poem pertains to a stage of English culture when pagan Germanic lore no longer represented a threat to Christian spirituality, so that pagan Scandinavia could be used as the setting of a poem that addresses issues of salvation and spiritual evil.[39]

    5. *Old Norse analogues.* The only close medieval analogues to the *Beowulf* story are preserved not in English but in Old Norse.[40] *Hrólfs Saga Kraka* tells of the adventures of a certain Boðvarr, son of a person who was a man by night but a bear by day, who travels from Gautland (corresponding to the *Beowulf* poet's Geatland) to Denmark to stay at the court of king Hrólfr Kraki (corresponding to the *Beowulf* poet's Hrothulf, who in Danish tradition takes the place equivalent to Hrothgar's in *Beowulf*). There he humiliates Hrólfr's retainers and takes service with the king, then kills a beast who is described as "the worst of trolls." *Grettis Saga* follows a different plot but includes two passages that are remarkably similar to what we find in the Danish episode in *Beowulf*, once allowances are made for the difference between an aristocratic heroic poem and a domestic Icelandic prose saga. These passages represent the closest parallels to *Beowulf* to be found anywhere. Other Old Norse analogues are found in *Orms Þáttr Stórólfssonar* and *Samsons Saga Fagra*, among other texts. The existence of these parallels is enough to show that the story-pattern that underlies the Danish episode in *Beowulf* was fairly well known in Scandinavian lands during the post-Viking period, although not necessarily in other parts of Germania either then or at other times. The story-pattern could have travelled either way, but its relative popularity in Old Norse literature suggests that some early version of it travelled into England. There the *Beowulf* poet gave it heroic dress and elaborate ornamentation, in keeping with the habits of the kind of verse of

which he was a master. Interchange between Danish- and English-speaking inhabitants of England during the ninth or tenth century is not the only way of accounting for this shared story-pattern, but it is the easiest way.

6. *Three probable English allusions.* The poet makes much of three figures whose names would have set bells ringing in the minds of Anglo-Saxons: *Hengest*, the protagonist of a song that is performed to entertain the nobles in Heorot after Beowulf's first victory; *Offa*, king of the Continental Angles, whom the poet goes out of his way to praise in extravagant terms (lines 1945–62); and *Wiglaf*, the young warrior who ventures his life to go to the aid of Beowulf during the fight against the dragon. To take up each of these in turn:

(a) The Hengest of the scop's song bears the same name as the quasi-historical or pseudo-historical Hengest who, with his brother Horsa, in an account that goes back beyond Bede and the *Chronicle* to the history ascribed to Nennius, was one of the fifth-century founders of Anglo-Saxon England. This Hengest was honored as the ancestor of the kings of Kent. Apart from these two instances, "Hengest" ("steed") is not an Anglo-Saxon proper name. The fight of the *Beowulf* poet's Hengest against Finn is not datable, but it pertains to that part of the heroic past that shortly precedes the poem's present action. To take this Hengest to be the Hengest of the Migration Myth seems only natural.[41]

(b) The *Beowulf* poet's Offa bears the same name as the celebrated English king Offa who ruled Mercia from 757 to 796. In one document this latter Offa styled himself *rex totius Anglorum patriae*, "king of the whole land of the English," the first Anglo-Saxon king to claim so grand a title.[42] Offa of Mercia traced his ancestry back to the Continental Offa, who governed a territory (the old province of the Angles, in Jutland) that eventually fell under Danish rule. In later times the Danes, too, honored Offa as an ancestor and retold stories about him that they may have learned from English sources.[43] The poet's extravagant praise of the earlier Offa thus could serve as a compliment not only to the Mercians (or their political descendants), as has been often remarked, but also to the Danes as inheritors of Jutland and recent immigrants to Britain.

(c) The Wiglaf of *Beowulf* has no counterpart in early Germanic legendry. Perhaps significantly, however, he bears the name of an historical English king, the Wiglaf who ruled from 827 to about 840 as the last independent king of Mercia before it fell under West Saxon domination. The *Beowulf* poet ascribes to his Wiglaf a father named *Wihstan* and another ancestor named *Waegmund*. The Mercian Wiglaf had a grandson named *Wihstan* and a son named *Wigmund*. While the correspondence of names here does not match up in genealogical sequence, it amounts to more than the usual sort of alliterative chime between the names of blood-relations that one finds in poetry and history.[44] The collection of three such names in each of two families, one fictive and one historical, cannot be coincidence. While the quest for allegory in *Beowulf* has always proven vain, the search for culturally significant allusion is another matter. Very possibly, the poet's invention of a conspicuously heroic character named "Wiglaf," with these named ancestors, reinforces the oblique compliment to the royal family of the Mercians that many readers believe to be effected by the allusion to Offa.

If the passage relating to Offa does carry allusive force, then the poem dates from any time after Offa of Mercia stood in high repute. If the Wiglaf passages are allusive as well, then *Beowulf* was composed no earlier than the time of the historical Wiglaf's grandson, or the late ninth century. By this time Mercia had been absorbed into a larger political unity ruled by the West Saxon royal line. When taken together with other criteria for dating, the evidence of the Offa and Wiglaf passages points to (though it does not necessitate) a date for the composition of *Beowulf* during the earlier tenth century. In this connection it is worth remembering that Alfred's successors claimed descent from both Offas, as well as a right to Mercia, through Alfred's marriage to a lady of the Mercian royal line.

7. *The role of the Geats.* The poet is clear in specifying that the hero of the poem, "Beowulf," like his king, Hygelac, whom he succeeds to the throne, is a Geat. To what cultural questions is this tribal identification an answer? Few scholars have been concerned with this question lately. Editors have accepted that the Old English tribal name *Geatas* corresponds phonologically to the Old Norse tribal name *Gautar* (modern Swedish *Götar*), have noted that in Old Norse sources the Gautar inhabited a region corresponding to the southern part of modern Sweden, and have left the matter at that, with some speculative remarks concerning the date at which the Gautar were or were not absorbed into the Swedish nation and the possible connection of this historical event to the ending of *Beowulf*, with its predictions of tribal dissolution facing the Geats. But this is by no means the end of the matter. According to Bede's influential statement (*Ecclesiastical History* 1:15), Britain was settled by "the three most powerful nations of Germany": the Saxons, the Angles, and the Jutes (Latin *Iuti* or *Iutae*). The first two of these tribal identifications present no difficulty. The third has long been a puzzle, both to modern scholars and, apparently, to the Anglo-Saxons themselves. When Bede's Latin was rendered into Old English during the time of Alfred, the translator renders the name of this latter tribe as the *Geatas*—a name that sounds vaguely like *Iuti* or *Iutae* but means something different. This name, as Jane Leake has pointed out in a book whose impact on *Beowulf* scholarship

has not yet been fully felt, is not a miswriting; rather, the translator rationalized Bede's history in the light of current knowledge.[45] His rendering makes sense as an expression of mythical geography, for it is an anglicization of the Latin name *Getae*. The Hygelac who, in *Beowulf*, rules over the *Geatas* and dies at the mouth of the Rhine, appears in the *Liber Monstrorum* under the name of Chlochilaicus; and there (contrary to Gregory of Tours, who calls him a Dane) he is said to have ruled over the *Getae*. In the popular mind, as Leake has shown, the *Getae* were regarded as common ancestors of the Jutes, Danes, Goths, and Gautar. They stood in relation to these various tribes as an *Ur*-Germanic people of remarkable size and prowess. Their homeland was a great place for dragons, among such other marvellous inhabitants as the Amazons, cynocephali, anthropophagi, and sea-serpents who are described in *The Marvels of the East*, a work that directly precedes *Beowulf* in British Library MS Cotton Vitellius A. XV. When Alfred's translator interpreted Bede's *Iuti* or *Iutae* as the *Geatas*—just as when Alfred himself called Jutland *Gotland*, i.e., "land of Goths," when he interpolated into Orosius' *Universal History* a passage that tells of the journey of a Danish sailor past the coast of Jutland—he drew attention to this imagined link between the people of England and the storied tribes of the Scandinavian *heimat*. *Beowulf* thus shows some points of continuity with the historical and geographical writings that formed part of the Alfredian and post-Alfredian canon. By making his hero a Geat, the *Beowulf* poet indirectly shed lustre on the English people by shoring up their Germanic ethnic credentials. He also made clear how different the English had become—whether wiser, or simply diminished—from their grand and terrible Northern ancestors.

These then, in brief, are seven reasons for concluding that the orthodox eighth-century dating of *Beowulf* need not be accepted without question. No one of them is conclusive. Taken together, however, they point to a date for the composition of *Beowulf*, as we now have it, not earlier than the reign of Alfred and probably during the reign of one of his immediate successors, possibly Athelstan, who was chosen king by both Mercians and West Saxons in 924.

The question remains: why did someone, or why did some group of people, decide to go to the trouble and expense of committing to parchment what might seem, by strict devotional standards, a fairly "useless" secular poem like *Beowulf*?[46]

Looking just at the mechanics of writing, there are three chief possibilities: (1) *intervention by an outsider*, or collection of the poem from a poet skilled in the oral tradition by someone who was not the author; (2) *intervention by an insider*, or the writing down of the poem by a poet, skilled in oral composition, who was also trained in the technology of script; and (3) *literary imitation*, or deliberate literary composition in a manner that invokes or replicates certain features of the oral, traditional style. Present scholarly opinion seems to favor either the second or third possibility. I find the third one unattractive for reasons similar to those advanced by Irving, who has shown good stylistic and aesthetic grounds for reading *Beowulf* not as a lettered work sprinkled with oral formulas but rather as "a most distinguished descendant of a long and skillful oral tradition."[47] Although I would not rule out the second alternative, the manifest differences in subject, style, known sources, authorial voice, and artistic achievement that set *Beowulf* apart from such other Old English works as the signed poems of Cynewulf, who may well have been an author of such dual accomplishments, leave me skeptical of this approach. Instead, I would suggest that the first possibility—the model of Cædmon and the monks of Whitby, transposed to a secular key—may be the most likely. This claim calls for brief justification.

In a society where oral poetry is the norm, those poets who live within the tradition feel little impulse to write their songs or stories down. They do not need to write down poems to preserve them, because they and their audiences preserve them very well, thank you. This is what both they and their ancestors have been doing for years. The impulse to take down poems in writing comes chiefly from outside the oral culture, when another interested party happens upon the scene. The texts that result from this encounter are transmutations of the poetry into a different symbolic code meant for the eyes of people with literary training, and those people then do with such texts what they will. Examples of this kind of intervention into a tradition are to be found throughout the literature of modern anthropology and folklore: in the myths, legends, and charms that Malinowski collected from Trobriand Islanders or Sapir from California Indians, or the prose tales that fieldworkers allied with the Irish Folklore Commission recorded from Gaelic speakers in the west of Ireland, or the words and tunes that Cecil Sharp collected from rural singers in Somerset and the Southern Appalachians. Examples could be multiplied at will. Some epic poetry that has been published in recent years also falls within this category: the Finnish *Kalevala*, the Serbo-Croatian *Wedding of Smailagić Meho*, and *The Mwindo Epic* from central Africa certainly result from such a process of self-conscious collection, combined in the Finnish instance with a significant degree of rewriting and shaping. Some classicists accept that the Homeric epics are the result of a similar process of collection and reworking.[48] However hypothetical this suggestion must remain, it is a plausible one, and the length and artistic excellence of the Homeric poems do not count against it. Texts that result from an outsider's sympathetic engagement with an oral tradition, though highly mediated, are often long and of high quality, for they represent the collaborative efforts of a painstaking collector and the most gifted informants who can be found: the Međedovićs and Williamsons of an oral tradition, as it were. If all goes well, the text that results from oral dictation will be a "best" text that showcases the poet's talents.[49] It is often more complex, or more fully elaborated, or more clear and self-consistent in its narrative line, than a verbatim record of a primary oral performance would be, for it is the result of a purposive effort to obtain an impressive text that literate people will want to read. The editor of *The Mwindo Epic*, Daniel Biebuyck, notes that the version of this poem that he prints in his 1969 edition, and that he recorded from dictation, is not only by far the longest one he heard performed in the country of the Nyanga but also the "most comprehensive, most coherent, most detailed, and most poetic" of them all.[50] This is a version that Biebuyck specially commissioned, to the surprise of the poet, who was not accustomed to singing the episodes of this story as a continuous whole.

If my hypothesis carries weight, and the *Beowulf* poet was indeed a master of the aristocratic oral tradition who happened to be enlisted in an effort to reify this poem in the form of a material text, then what launched the material text into its existence was what can be called an *oral poetry act*. An oral poetry act is what happens when a collector asks a singer to perform a work not in its natural context, but rather in some special setting in the presence of a scribe, a team of scribes, a tape recorder, or some other secondary audience. The collector thus becomes a third factor in shaping the poem, after the poet and the primary oral audience, for he or she too has influence over what is performed. Like Hild and the monks at Whitby, the collector usually has a certain kind of poem in mind and may be indifferent to other, "irrelevant," kinds. He can specify that the poem is to be a summarized or a fully elaborated version. He may ask the poet to bring out certain aspects of his work and downplay others. Whether or not the collector has a clear literary agenda, the poet himself naturally wishes to please, especially if he is a professional who expects to be rewarded for his services in money or esteem. Any performer who is not a mere memorizer is used to reshaping materials to suit a particular audience and is unlikely to forego this habit for no good reason.

In these ways and in others, the presence of the collector affects the product of the oral poetry act. At first, this is a "scratch" version of the poem as it can be read by a textual community—that is, a group of readers who may or may not have much competence in the oral tradition, but who participate in an ongoing discourse about books.[51] If, later, a text comes to be distributed more widely, it will naturally be improved in ways that accord with the aims of the collector, the needs or desires of its readers, and the general conventions of written literature in the society in which it will be read. The meter may be smoothed out. Rhyme or other technical features may be made more regular. Non-standard or dialect forms may be replaced with standard ones or may be made more consistent. Gaps in the story may be filled in, errors or inconsistencies corrected, useless fillers deleted. Capital letters and punctuation may be added, lineation imposed, sectional divisions introduced, and so on. From beginning to end of this process of textualization, the collector thus becomes a collaborator in the act of poetry, not just a recorder of it. As the inventor of the text as it can be read in "hard copy," the collector makes myriad choices, whether consciously or unconsciously, that determine the character and readability of the product of his or her intervention into the realm of oral performance.

If the view that I am presenting has merit, then we do not have to read *Beowulf* as a literate island in a sea of much inferior oral poetry, as some scholars do, nor as the unmediated gift of an oral poet's inspiration, as some Romantically inclined scholars have done in the past. Rather it is a *tertium quid*: a unique kind of hybrid creation that came into being at the interface of two cultures, the oral and the bookish, through some literate person's prompting. The important thing to keep in mind is that, like all oral poetry recorded before the advent of advanced audio-visual technology, as Goody has reminded us,[52] the text of *Beowulf* would have been taken down outside the normal context of performance, in a situation where one or more outsiders were involved.

It would be vain, however, to speculate as to who wrote down the text, on what occasion. To the question "Why was the text of *Beowulf* written down?" perhaps only one good answer can be given, a negative one: "Why not?" By the end of the seventh century, the technology of writing down long poems was well in place in England. Literary models were there, in the form of Latin works like the *Aeneid* as well as vernacular ones like Cædmon's Biblical paraphrases. The important question to ask, perhaps, is "By what time did the reasons for *not* writing down a secular poem like *Beowulf* lose their force?"

As Roberta Frank has shown,[53] ecclesiastical opposition to poems about pagan antiquity seems to have cooled by the last years of the reign of Alfred the Great and the early years of the tenth century, roughly speaking. By this time, the climate of opinion about the Germanic past had shifted among monks and clerics to the point that songs about pagan Germanic heroes had ceased to seem either threatening or irrelevant. By this time, if not well before, songs about the pagan past had become infused with Christian values. Once this momentous shift of mentality and literary sensibility had occurred, someone in a position of power saw fit to preserve in writing the poem that we now call *Beowulf*. Whatever exact authority he or she wielded, this patron not only oriented his activities toward a Christian textual community, but also had some awareness of being part of that new political order that we now call the English nation. In company with other like-minded people, the patron knew or intuited that national ambitions could be legitimized in mythic terms through invocation of a common, pseudo-Christian, Anglo-Danish past.

In contemplating the place of *Beowulf* in literary history in terms like these, I do not claim to invalidate other approaches to the questions of date and origins. At most, I only hope to render such alternatives relatively unattractive, so that those scholars who advocate them may perhaps do so with less claim to authority. As Fredric Jameson has remarked, "Only another, stronger interpretation can overthrow and practically refute an interpretation already in place."[54]

One of the tasks of current Old English scholarship is the Jamesonian one of unmasking *Beowulf* as a socially symbolic act. Although its action is set in fifth- and sixth-century Scandinavia, the poem articulates a response to the two great sources of tension in English culture during the late sixth through the early tenth centuries: the integration of Germanic culture and Christian faith into a single system of thought and ethics, and the integration of all the peoples living south of Hadrian's Wall and east of Offa's Dyke into one English nation ruled by the West Saxon royal line.

Whether or not literature in general is produced through one or more ideological contradictions, as some modern theorists have held, it seems likely that *Beowulf* is the result of two major conflicts, each one of which was a lively cause of concern to Englishmen of the later Anglo-Saxon period. They can be paraphrased as follows. (1) "Our ancestors were great noblemen; our ancestors are damned." The first attitude could not simply be cast aside when Christian missionaries arrived to teach the need of salvation through Christ. *Beowulf* reveals a profound disquiet in regard to the orthodox doctrine that anyone not baptized into the faith is beyond redemption. (2) "The Danes are murderers and damnable heathens; the Danes are our trusted allies." The first attitude could not die out as soon as the descendants of the Viking invaders began to farm the land in peace, so that the second view could be safely announced. *Beowulf* shows how the impulse to honor the Danes and integrate their traditions with English ones was mingled with memories of a heathen people who had done their best to ravage English society and its centers of religion and learning over a period of some years. The poet's evocations of the magnificence of Hrothgar's court alternate with allusions to the damned rites that some of the Danes practice there (175–88) and to acts of fratricidal violence.

To put the matter a different way, we might say that when viewed in terms of its own culture, *Beowulf* is the projection of two great desires: (1) for a distinguished *ethnic* origin that would serve to merge English and Danish differences into a neutral and dignified pan-Germanism, and (2) for an *ethical* origin that would ally this unified race with Christian spiritual values. No matter that the heroes of Beowulf's day were unbaptized. Of their own free will, exercising the God-given power of reason, they recognized the controlling power of Providence in human affairs and had the wisdom and fortitude to fight against God's enemies on earth—or at least the more enlightened ones among them did, according to the poet's audacious fiction.

If this view is correct—and I must beg forgiveness for repeating this hedging rhetoric, for certainty in such matters must remain beyond our grasp—then for all its fictive and fantastic elements, *Beowulf* was a vehicle for political work in a time when the various peoples south of Hadrian's Wall were being assimilated into an emergent English nation. "Political" is perhaps too narrow a term for the work the poem does. For in reinventing the ancestral past in the light of Christian doctrine and the Danish presence, as well as in articulating a system of values appropriate to this task, the poem is a site where cultural issues of great magnitude and complexity are contested. Some of these issues, particularly the ones that involve the deadly opposition of the hero and the Grendel-kin, doubtless transcend the historical tensions of any one era and connect with bedrock contradictions that underlie civilization itself and its inevitable discontents.

To read *Beowulf* as I am suggesting is to read it as an exemplary specimen of the art of *homo narrans*, an art that has received much scrutiny in recent years. As folklorist and American Studies specialist Jay Mechling has pointed out,[55]

> Many respectable scholars, some of them giants in their special-
> ties, have turned away from positivist and formalist epistemolo-
> gies to an epistemology that sees reality as created, mediated, and
> sustained by human narratives. To accept this view is also to see
> that narratives are emergent, contingent, public, and contested;
> that they reflect interests (such as class, gender, race, age) and,
> therefore, that they are ideological and political, even when they
> seem not to be.

In keeping with this socially embedded way of looking at narrative, I suggest that *Beowulf* did much ideological work in its time. To be precise, we should not speak of this work as being done by the poem, but rather by its discourse, taken as the sum of poetic impulses of this kind. For however valuable *Beowulf* may be as a unique creation, it is still more important as an example—the only one that has happened to survive almost intact—of a type of literature that probably retained cultural centrality until fairly late in the Old English period, bearing the intellectual brunt of such social changes as occurred over time. In any period when philosophy and history function as aspects of poetry rather than claiming (even if speciously) the status of autonomous enterprises, poetry does the collective thinking of a people. Through poetry, issues of common concern in a society are thought through and are resolved in the form of stories. In such a medium, as Umberto Eco has said of the tradition of medieval scholastic thought,

> Innovation came without fanfare, even secretively, and developed by fits and starts until it was eventually absorbed within a free-and-easy syncretism.[56]

A task still facing *Beowulf* scholars is to define more exactly the nature of the syncretistic system of thought that underlies this narrative and lends it ethical and spiritual significance. Doubtless this task will never be complete, for, in attempting it, we are defining our own mentality as much as that of a distant historical period. Much is at stake when it comes to the study of origins, as recent scholarship has made us aware. As Edward Said has remarked,

> there is no such thing as a merely given, or simply available, start-ing point: beginnings have to be made for each project in such a way as to *enable* what follows from them.[57]

In early English literary history, questions relating to origins are also ones of character and potential use. "Is it oral or literary?" "Is it pagan or Christian?" "Is it Germanic or Latinate?" "Is it a part of English literature, or not?" "Is it *ours* or *theirs*?" One's answers to these questions are likely to reveal as much about one's own cultural investments as they suggest about a society and a literature that are now vanished beyond all power of recall, except in terms that make sense in our own consciousness. Precisely because the effort to understand the place of a work in literary history is itself an historically conditioned enterprise that almost cannot help but be bound up, whether implicitly or explicitly, with the aims of cultural critique,[58] the task should not be abandoned, however recalcitrant it may be.

NOTES

1. John Hermann, *Allegories of War: Language and Violence in Old English Poetry* (Ann Arbor: University of Michigan Press, 1989), 199.

2. Leo Spitzer, *Linguistics and Literary History: Essays in Stylistics* (Princeton: Princeton University Press, 1948), 3–4.

3. M. M. Bakhtin, *The Dialogic Imagination: Four Essays*, ed. Michael Holquist, trans. Caryl Emerson and Michael Holquist (Austin: University of Texas Press, 1981), especially the first essay, "Epic and Novel." For a critique of this aspect of Bakhtin's work as well as of Derridean deconstruction when applied to the realm of orality, see Ward Parks, "The Textualization of Orality in Literary Criticism," in *Vox Intexta: Orality and Textuality in the Middle Ages*, ed. A. N. Doane and Carol Braun Pasternack (Madison: University of Wisconsin Press, 1991), 46–61.

4. By "the time that the poem was put down in writing," I mean the time that our unique MS was written down, c. 1000 AD. Almost everyone agrees that this MS is a scribal copy. What is disputed is how long a poem we can meaningfully call *"Beowulf"* existed before this moment of copying. For reasons explained below, I see no reason to push the date of composition of the poem back before the tenth century, and the following discussion is based on this premise. Early-daters can still perhaps follow along with my discussion, granted that the poem continued in circulation through the tenth century.

5. The best overview of the subject is C. P. Wormald, "The Uses of Literacy in Anglo-Saxon England and Its Neighbours," *Transactions of the Royal Historical Society*, 5th series, 27 (1977): 95–114. Wormald sees no reason to think that cultured literacy ever became widespread among the laity. Two recent studies that finesse his conclusions are Susan Kelly, "Anglo-Saxon Lay Society and the Written Word," in *The Uses of Literacy in Early Mediaeval Europe*, ed. Rosamond McKitterick (Cambridge: Cambridge University Press, 1990), 36–62, and Simon Keynes, "Royal Government and the Written Word in Late Anglo-Saxon England," ibid., 226–57.

6. Richard Hodges, *The Anglo-Saxon Achievement: Archaeology and the Beginnings of English Society* (Ithaca: Cornell University Press, 1989).

7. Nicholas Howe, *Migration and Mythmaking in Anglo-Saxon England* (New Haven: Yale University Press, 1989).

8. On this topic see Reginald Horsman, *Race and Manifest Destiny: The Origins of American Racial Anglo-Saxonism* (Cambridge: Harvard University Press, 1981).

9. Eric Hobsbawm and Terence Ranger, ed., *The Invention of Tradition* (Cambridge: Cambridge University Press, 1983), esp. Hobsbawm's "Introduction: Inventing Traditions" (1–14).

10. Allen J. Frantzen, *Desire for Origins: New Language, Old English, and Teaching the Tradition* (New Brunswick: Rutgers University Press, 1990).

11. R. W. Chambers briefly reviews this heritage of oral poetry in his essay "The Lost Literature of Medieval England," *The Library*, 4th series, 5 (1925): 293–321. For the evidence from classical authors bearing on Germanic singers, see Jeff Opland, *Anglo-Saxon Oral Poetry: A Study of the Traditions* (New Haven: Yale University Press, 1980), 40–73.

12. For an overview of issues relating to the understanding of oral poetry see Ruth Finnegan, *Oral Poetry: Its Nature, Significance and Social Context* (Cambridge: Cambridge University Press, 1977). For a review of recent research in the fields of orality and literacy with particular attention to the medieval connection, and with citations to the relevant work of Eric Havelock, Walter Ong, Jack Goody, Michael Clanchy, Franz Bäuml, and other scholars, see D. H. Green, "Orality and Reading: The State of Research in Medieval

Studies," *Speculum* 65 (1990): 267–80. For a critique of Anglo-Saxon orality and textuality from a current theoretical stance, see Martin Irvine, "Medieval Textuality and the Archaeology of Textual Culture," in *Speaking Two Languages: Traditional Disciplines and Contemporary Theory in Medieval Studies*, ed. Allen J. Frantzen (Albany: State University of New York Press, 1991), 181–210 and 276–84.

13. Brian Stock, *Listening for the Text: On the Uses of the Past* (Baltimore: Johns Hopkins University Press, 1990), 9.

14. The influential concept of active and passive tradition-bearers goes back to the work of C. W. von Sydow, "On the Spread of Tradition," reprinted in his *Selected Papers on Folklore*, ed. Laurits Bödker (Copenhagen: Rosenkilde and Bagger, 1948), 12–13.

15. Albert Bates Lord, "Avdo Međedović, *Guslar*," *Journal of American Folklore* 69 (1956): 320–30, reprinted in his *Epic Singers and Oral Tradition* (Ithaca: Cornell University Press, 1991), 57–71. See also Međedović, *The Wedding of Smailagić Meho*, translated by Lord, vol. 3 in the series *Serbocroatian Heroic Songs*, collected by Milman Parry (Cambridge, Mass.: Publications of the Milman Parry Collection, 1974).

16. Some of Williamson's stories have been published from transcriptions of his tellings made by his American-born wife Linda: see *Fireside Tales of the Traveller Children* (1983), *The Broonie, Silkies, and Fairies* (1985), *Tell Me a Story for Christmas* (1987), *May the Devil Walk Behind Ye!* (1989), *Don't Look Back, Jack!* (1990), and *Tales of the Seal People* (1992), all published by Canonsgate, Edinburgh; *A Thorn in the King's Foot* (Harmondsworth: Penguin, 1987); *The Genie and the Fisherman and Other Tales from the Travelling People* (Cambridge: Cambridge University Press, 1991). Recordings from my Scottish fieldwork are on deposit in the American Folklife Center at the Library of Congress.

17. The best study of how this accommodation affected religious poetry remains Michael D. Cherniss, *Ingeld and Christ: Heroic Concepts and Values in Old English Christian Poetry* (The Hague: Mouton, 1972). Charles J. Donahue, "Social Function and Literary Value in *Beowulf*," in *The Epic in Medieval Society: Aesthetic and Moral Values*, ed. Harald Scholler (Tübingen: Niemeyer, 1977), 382–90, offers some brief but stimulating suggestions about how it affected *Beowulf*.

18. See Kenneth Sisam, "Anglo-Saxon Royal Genealogies," *Proceedings of the British Academy*, 39 (1953): 287–346. Michael Lapidge discusses these genealogies carefully in "*Beowulf*, Aldhelm, the *Liber Monstrorum*, and Wessex," *Studi Medievali* 23 (1982): 151–92, and holds that the extension from Geat back to Sceaf, and eventually to Adam, is a fabrication that "was done with Alfred's consent and arguably at his instigation" (187).

19. On this synthesis see Michael Hunter, "Germanic and Roman Antiquity and the Sense of the Past in Anglo-Saxon England," *Anglo-Saxon England* 3 (1974): 29–50.

20. Jack Goody, *The Interface Between the Written and the Oral* (Cambridge: Cambridge University Press, 1987), 59.

21. Seth Lerer, *Literacy and Power in Anglo-Saxon Literature* (Lincoln: University of Nebraska Press, 1991).

22. On this transformation, see Jeff Opland, "The Impact on English Literature of the Technology of Writing," in *Oral Literature in Context: Ten Essays*, ed. John D. Niles (Cambridge: D. S. Brewer, 1980), 30–43.

23. Patrick Wormald, "Bede, *Beowulf*, and the Conversion of the Anglo-Saxon Aristocracy," in *Bede and Anglo-Saxon England*, ed. Robert T. Farrell, British Archaeological Reports 46 (Oxford, 1978), 32–95.

24. On this process, see D. A. Bullough, "The Educational Tradition in England from Alfred to Aelfric: Teaching *Utriusque Linguae*," in "La scuola nell'occidente latino dell'alto medioevo," *Settimane di studio del Centro Italiano di studi sull'alto medioevo* 19 (1972), 2:453–94.

25. F. M. Stenton, *Anglo-Saxon England*, 3rd ed. (Oxford: Clarendon, 1971), 353.

26. Simon Keynes, "King Athelstan's Books," in *Learning and Literature in Anglo-Saxon England: Studies Presented to Peter Clemoes on the Occasion of His Sixty-Fifth Birthday*, ed. Michael Lapidge and Helmut Gneuss (Cambridge: Cambridge University Press, 1985), 143–201.

27. According to figures provided by Neil R. Ker, *Catalogue of Manuscripts Containing Anglo-Saxon* (Oxford: Oxford University Press, 1957), xv–xix, of the 189 major manuscripts written in Old English, all but eight are from the tenth century or later.

28. See Alois Wolf, "Die Verschriftlichung von europäischen Heldensagen als mittelalterliches Kulturproblem," in *Heldensage und Heldendichtung im Germanischen*, ed. Heinrich Beck (Berlin: De Gruyter, 1988), 305–28. For a discussion in English of some of the same issues, see Wolf, "Medieval Heroic Traditions and Their Transitions from Orality to Literacy," in Doane and Pasternack, *Vox Intexta*, 67–88.

29. Bede, *Ecclesiastical History* 4:24. For good comments on the story see Donald K. Fry, "The Memory of Cædmon," in *Oral Traditional Literature: A Festschrift for Albert Bates Lord*, ed. John Miles Foley (Columbus: Slavica Press, 1981), 282–93.

30. For some mythic and legendary parallels to Bede's account see Louise Pound, "Caedmon's Dream Song," in *Studies in English Philology: A Miscellany in Honor of F. Klaeber*, ed. Kemp Malone and Martin B. Ruud (Minneapolis: University of Minnesota Press, 1929), 232–39.

31. Northrop Frye, *The Secular Scripture: A Study of the Structure of Romance* (Cambridge: Harvard University Press, 1976), 20.

32. The first of the transmutations involved here is discussed well by Cherniss, *Ingeld and Christ*. On the second, note Gernot Wieland, "*Manna Mildost*: Moses and Beowulf," *Pacific Coast Philology* 23 (1988): 86–93.

33. See the articles collected in Colin Chase, ed., *The Dating of Beowulf* (Toronto: University of Toronto Press, 1981), as supplemented by Nicolas Jacobs, "Anglo-Danish Relations, Poetic Archaism, and the Date of *Beowulf*: A Reconsideration of the Evidence," *Poetica* [Tokyo] 8 (1977): 23–43; Kevin S. Kiernan, *Beowulf and the Beowulf Manuscript* (New Brunswick: Rutgers University Press, 1981); and other articles cited below, among other recent studies.

34. I have discussed this matter in *Beowulf The Poem and Its Tradition* (Cambridge, Mass.: Harvard University Press, 1983), 96–117.

35. See Alexander Callander Murray, "*Beowulf*, the Danish Invasions, and Royal Genealogy," in Chase, *Dating of Beowulf*, 101–11, and Audrey L. Meaney, "Scyld Scefing and the Dating of *Beowulf*—Again," *Bulletin of the John Rylands University Library of Manchester* 71 (1989): 7–40.

36. An example is Dorothy Whitelock, *The Audience of Beowulf* (Oxford: Clarendon, 1951), 77–78, following J. R. R. Tolkien, "*Beowulf*: The Monsters and the Critics," *Proceedings of the British Academy* 22 (1936): 294 (note 34).

37. Roberta Frank, "Skaldic Verse and the Date of *Beowulf*," in Chase, *Dating of Beowulf*, 123–39.

38. This point has been forcefully made by L. L. Schücking, "Das Königsideal in *Beowulf*," *Modern Humanities Research Association Bulletin* 3 (1929): 143–54, trans. as "The Ideal of Kingship in *Beowulf*," in *An Anthology of Beowulf Criticism*, ed. Lewis E. Nicholson (Notre Dame: University of Notre Dame Press, 1963), 35–49.

39. See the important article by Roberta Frank, "The *Beowulf* Poet's Sense of History," in *The Wisdom of Poetry: Essays in Early English Literature in Honor of Morton W. Bloomfield*, ed. Larry D. Benson and Siegfried Wenzel (Kalamazoo: Medieval Institute Publications, 1982), 53–65 and 271–77.

40. See Klaeber, *Beowulf and the Fight at Finnsburg,* 3rd ed. (Boston: D. C. Heath, 1950), xiv–xx; R. W. Chambers, *Beowulf: An Introduction to the Study of the Poem,* 3rd ed. (Cambridge: Cambridge University Press, 1959), 48–61, 138–92; G. N. Garmonsway, *Beowulf and Its Analogues* (New York: Dutton, 1971), 302–31.

41. For discussion of the question from two different perspectives, historical and mythological respectively, see Anton Gerard Van Hamel, "Hengest and His Namesake," in *Studies in English Philology ... Frederick Klaeber,* ed. Malone, 159–71, and J. E. Turville-Petre, "Hengest and Horsa," *Saga-Book of the Viking Society* 14 (1953–57): 273–90.

42. Walter de Gray Birch, ed., *Cartularium Saxonicum,* 3 vols. (London, 1885–93), 1:302, no. 214; for discussion see F. J. Stenton, "The Supremacy of the Mercian Kings," *English Historical Review* 33 (1918): 433–52.

43. Robert H. Hodgkin, *A History of the Anglo-Saxons* (Oxford: Clarendon, 1935), assumes that the Danes, in appropriating the province of Angel, "took over some of its Anglian folk-lore" (1:31); but the Danes' knowledge of traditions concerning Offa could also have come through the Danelaw.

44. Alois Brandl, "The Beowulf Epic and the Crisis in the Mercian Dynasty about the Year 700 AD," *Research and Progress* 2 (1936): 199–203, and George Bond, "Links between *Beowulf* and Mercian History," *Studies in Philology* 40 (1943): 481–93, both make this connection, but in the context of arguments too speculative to command assent.

45. Jane Acomb Leake, *The Geats of Beowulf: A Study in the Geographical Mythology of the Middle Ages* (Madison: University of Wisconsin Press, 1967), esp. 98–133. Leake brings into a new dimension a suggestion that was made by Elis Wadstein, "The *Beowulf* Poem as an English National Epos," *Acta Philologica Scandinavica* 8 (1933): 273–91. The reader is referred to Leake for details of the complex argument that I accept here in its main features, despite some lingering questions about the Gautar and why Leake is so uninterested in them. There is no reason to refute the objections of G. M. Smithers in his review article "The Geats in *Beowulf,*" *The Durham University Journal* 63 (1971), 87–103, for most of his arguments have no relation to Leake's main point about geographical mythology. Kemp Malone's peremptory dismissal, on phonological grounds, of any identification of the *Geatas* with the *Getae* (*Speculum* 43 [1968], 736–39) misses the point. Even if the Anglo-Saxons should not have made this identification, the evidence of *Beowulf* and the *Liber Monstrorum* is that they did so, and so we must reckon with their creativity.

46. The term "secular" is of course not wholly appropriate to a work like *Beowulf* that celebrates a kind of Christian hero, as is noted by Karl Brunner, "Why Was *Beowulf* Preserved?" *Études anglaises* 7 (1954): 1–5. Wormald, "Bede, *Beowulf,* and the Conversion," answers the question of preservation in his own way based on the assumption that *Beowulf* is pre-Alfredian and the work of a fully literate author. Here I present a different possibility based on a hypothesis that Wormald rejects, namely that the text of *Beowulf* has a close relation to the Anglo-Saxon aristocratic oral tradition. This claim rests on evidence (much of it stylistic) that I shall not try to present here. Many insights into the oral context of early Germanic verse are presented by Alain Renoir, *A Key to Old Poems: The Oral-Formulaic Approach to the Interpretation of West-Germanic Verse* (University Park: Pennsylvania State University Press, 1988). Edward B. Irving, Jr., *Rereading Beowulf* (Philadelphia: University of Pennsylvania Press, 1989), esp. 1–35, has cast his considerable authority behind the idea of an oral-derived *Beowulf* and uses this idea to make sense of many formal and aesthetic features of the poem.

47. Irving, *Rereading Beowulf,* 2. Understandably but still perhaps disappointingly, Irving does not engage with the issue of how the material text of *Beowulf* came into being.

48. See Albert Bates Lord, "Homer's Originality: Oral Dictated Texts," *Transactions of the American Philological Society* 94 (1953): 124–34, reprinted with slight revisions in his *Epic Singers*, 38–48.

49. The adjective "best" here refers to the collector's perspective, which represents that of a literate society. The collector's best text may be of no use whatever to the original audience.

50. Daniel Biebuyck and Kahombo C. Mateene, ed., *The Mwindo Epic from the Banyanga* (Berkeley: University of California Press, 1969), 19.

51. The notion of textual community is one that I am adapting from Stock, *Listening for the Text*, using "textual" in a narrow sense here to refer to the products of writing. The notion of literary competence, drawn from linguistics, has been discussed by Jonathan Culler in *Structuralist Poetics* (Ithaca: Cornell University Press, 1975), reprinted in *Reader-Response Criticism: From Formalism to Post-Structuralism*, ed. Jane P. Tompkins (Baltimore: Johns Hopkins University Press, 1980), 101–17. Oral heroic poetry is only a forceful instance of the general phenomenon whereby literature is made intelligible through systems of convention that make understanding possible. For a study of how members of Anglo-Saxon textual communities may have had some competence in oral poetry, see Katherine O'Brien O'Keeffe, *Visible Song: Transitional Literacy in Old English Verse* (Cambridge: Cambridge University Press, 1990).

52. Jack Goody, *Interface between the Written and the Oral*, xi.

53. Frank, *"Beowulf* Poet's Sense of History."

54. Fredric Jameson, *The Political Unconscious: Narrative as a Socially Symbolic Act* (Ithaca: Cornell University Press, 1981), 13.

55. Jay Mechling, *"Homo Narrans* Across the Disciplines," *Western Folklore* 50 (1991): 41–51, at 43.

56. Umberto Eco, *Art and Beauty in the Middle Ages*, trans. Hugh Bredin (New Haven: Yale University Press, 1986), 2.

57. Edward W. Said, *Orientalism* (New York: Vintage, 1978), 16, summarizing his own argument in his book *Beginnings: Intention and Method* (New York: Basic Books, 1975).

58. George E. Marcus and Michael M. J. Fischer, *Anthropology as Cultural Critique: An Experimental Moment in the Human Sciences* (Chicago: University of Chicago Press, 1986), make the same point about ethnography that I am making about literary history, which can resemble a kind of ethnography of the past.

SETH LERER

Grendel's Glove

Returning from his exploits at the Danish court, Beowulf comes home to Hygelac to tell of his adventures. He recalls events at Heorot, digresses on the moral implications of heroic action, tells the story of the Heatho-Bard feud, and presents abbreviated versions of the fights with Grendel and his mother.[1] The sequence of events he offers will be familiar to the poem's audience, and Beowulf himself announces that the struggle with the monster is a story not unknown (*undyrne*, 2000) to many of his potential listeners. The poem's audience will hear again of the hospitality of Hrothgar, the voracity of the monsters, and the success in underwater combat. That he had fought beneath the mere, he states again, is now a fact well known ("þe is wide cuð," 2135), and it would seem that Beowulf's own story offers little more than a review of what we, and his audience, already know.

But in the middle of the narrative, Beowulf proffers information neither we nor they have heard before. There is the naming of the first Geat killed, Hondscio (2076), and the description of Grendel's monstrous glove in which he was wont to put his victims (2085b–88). Moreover, in its protestations of excessive length and its self-consciousness of telling, Beowulf's story of the fight seems strikingly unlike anything he has performed before. Early-twentieth-century critics construed this episode as sharing in the legacy of Norse mythology, with Grendel's glove

From *ELH* 61 (1994), pp. 721–751. © 1994 The Johns Hopkins University Press.

hearkening back to the troll gloves of folktale.[2] Tolkein glossed over many of the details of the passage, noting only that "without serious discrepancy, it retells rapidly the events in Heorot, and retouches the account."[3] More recently, James Rosier found in the passage a complex pattern of wordplay that apposed the Geat's name—a transparent appellation cognate with the modern German *Handschuh*, "glove"—and the monster's *glof* in a punning set of references to the "play of hands" within the poem. The "identity of the missing thane," Rosier argued, "became artistically relevant" to the *Beowulf*-poet's thematic concerns with repayment, guardianship, and political control.[4] Building on Rosier's arguments, I have suggested elsewhere that Beowulf's speech to Hygelac's court represents a species of social entertainment: an attempt to turn heroic action and horrific violence into humor and self-deprecation, much like the self-accounts presented by the heroes of romance who, in turning past actions into present words, transfer a physical ordeal into conventions of poetic eloquence and thereby signal their return to civilization from the wilderness.[5]

I would like to reconsider some of these arguments here to assess Grendel's glove and Beowulf's narration from a different critical perspective, one shaped by recent scholarly and theoretical preoccupations with the body in archaic and medieval cultures. Such meditations on the body, both as the figuration of an epistemic site and as the historically definable locus of the social status of the self, have long acknowledged the controlling tension between wholeness and dismemberment. The marked or mutilated corpus has been taken as the focus of cultural understanding, the place where social organizations represent themselves both to their controllers and their controlled.[6] In *Beowulf*, such mutilated or dismembered forms become the foci for reflections on the poet's craft and on the place of imaginative fiction in society. The hero's story of the monster's glove, and its analogues and sources in Scandinavian mythology, offer a specific case of such self-reflection. More than a relic of a Northern legend, and more than a piece of narrative exotica, Grendel's glove comes to symbolize the meaning of the monster and the very resources of literary making that articulate that meaning.[7] It represents, in frightening yet also playfully enigmatic ways, the union of hand and mouth that defines the rapacious creature. It distills Grendel's grasp and gape into a piece of artifice, a thing of *cræft* and *orðonc*, that stands as the otherworldly alternative to those works of human craft that guard the body and the body politic from a potentially chaotic nature.[8] Grendel's glove is thus a literary rather than an archeological phenomenon: an object crafted out of ancient myth, narrative archetype, and social ritual. Its recollection offers Beowulf a narrative theatrics, a way of locating himself as both a comic and heroic figure in his entertainment before Hygelac's court. It offers us a riddle of representation whose solution takes us to the very workings of Germanic figurative diction.

Beowulf is in many ways a poem of the body.[9] Its actions celebrate that strength of sinew, mastery of breath, or power of the grip that define Beowulf as the victor over social challenge or monstrous invasion. Elaborate armaments and ornaments, while dressing and protecting the heroic form, more often fade into the background, or even fail, before the prowess of the victor or the wiles of the vanquished. The fight with the sea monsters during the swimming match with Breca, the combat with Grendel in Heorot, and the vanquishing of Grendel's mother in her lair, all center on the hero's maintenance of the intact body. By contrast, the results of these victories, and indeed, the consequences of non-Beowulfian encounters with such creatures, leave dismembered bodies. The poem's landscape is littered with ripped trunks, severed heads, and fragmentary limbs. Grendel's arm, Æscere's head, and the decapitated forms of the monster and his mother become the landmarks along which the poem's characters and its readers mark their progress towards heroic victory. And at the poem's end, when Beowulf's blade fails and his mail cannot save him from the dragon's fiery breath, it is a war of body parts that he loses, as the dragon's head-bone breaks the sword Nægling and the hero's own hand fails.[10]

To call *Beowulf* a poem of the body is, of course, to affiliate it with those traditions of the corporealized self that distinguish European heroic poetry from the Homeric epics to the *Song of Roland*. Indeed, many of the features I will attend to in the Old English poem—mutilation and dismemberment, the social expectations of physical violence, the cultural importance placed on eating, drinking, and their rituals—have long been seen as central to an epic world in which the hero and his victims share in the rites of self-display and bodily purification.[11] Part of my purpose in this essay, then, will be to locate Beowulf and Grendel in this world: to find in figurations of repast and sacrifice the legacy of Indo-European ritual and, furthermore, to locate in the hand and head, the mouth and belly, the emblems of what Pietro Pucci has called, writing on the *Iliad* and *Odyssey*, "heroic etiquette."[12] Such etiquette looks back to stories of the hunt and kill, and to the complex social legends that domesticated ancient violence into public ritual and shared religious action. Walter Burkert has detailed the manner in which each part of a sacrificial creature took on special meanings in these rituals: blood, flesh, viscera, bone, and skin all played a role in the propitiation of the gods and the feeding of their human subjects.[13] In the activities of offering and eating, and the myths which grew up to explain and to maintain them, Burkert finds models of society itself. Taboos of social interaction, hierarchies of class or function, and notions of the human interrelationship with the natural world are all encoded in the sacrifice. In tandem with this work, the group of researchers clustering around Jean-Pierre Vernant and Marcel Detienne in Paris have sought to understand "relationships between religion and society through inquiry focused on the phenomenon of sacrifice."[14] In the great myths of Dionysus and his slaughter, of Orpheus and his beheading, or of Thyestes and his dismemberment, as well as in the archetypal Homeric accounts of dining, these scholars have found tales both cosmogonic and sociogonic.[15] So, too, has Georges Dumézil and his later Indo-Europeanist heirs and critics.[16] The "general narrative" of creation, in which "a primordial being is killed and dismembered," comes to share in the accounts of social organization, as the body bears a broad relationship to both the structure of the universe and that of human society.[17] Analogies between, for example, the head and the heavens, the flesh and the earth, blood and water, are embedded in the myths of Indic, Iranian, Germanic, and the Greek and Latin peoples. Such stories as the killing, dismemberment, and burial of Romulus constitute veiled retellings of the story of creation while at the same time they domesticate, by rendering in literary form, the old brute practices of cultic sacrifice or social hunt.[18]

These narratives have, in addition to their cosmogonic and sociogonic purposes, a literary one as well, for bodies whole and broken lie at the center of many myths of poetry's own origins. The Old Norse legends of the mead of Odinn and the ritual dismemberment of Kvasir share a common Indo-European ancestry with the great myths of Sanskrit, Avestan, and Old Irish cultures.[19] Read together, they define what might be thought of as a bodily poetics: a conception of the birth of literary form out of the same shared ritual conventions as the birth of cosmic structure or of social life. The human body—marked and dismembered, reduced to its constituent elements or its disassembled limbs—is often taken as the site of allegory in the ancient traditions of literary speculation.[20] Metonymically or synechdochically, the body locates and explains phenomena of social life. It makes the processes of literary understanding part and parcel of the public apprehension of the self. To see the body as a world and the world as a body is not simply to metaphorize experience in corporeal terms (to live, say, in a body politic), but to experience the metaphorical as fundamentally corporeal. Poetic making is a matter of the body, as its parts and processes provide a visible, if not palpable, basis for figurative expression.[21]

This basis had, in fact, long been recognized by practitioners and theorists of the Germanic poetic tradition. The workings of the kenning, that distinctive marker of the figural and figurative, often hinge on bodily possession or adornment. So, too, does the Anglo-Saxon riddle with its predilection for rephrasing works of human artifice or natural creation as the objects of corporeal, if not sexual, human function.[22] The Old Norse skalds traditionally placed the body at the center of poetic imagination, as much of their metaphorics hearkened back to stories of the death of Kvasir and the genesis of poetry out of the liquid distilled from his broken form. As Carol Clover's reconstruction of the "skaldic sensibility" of medieval Scandinavian court poetry shows, the Old Norse skalds had generated their poetic lexicon and imagery out of the cosmogonic legends of corporeal dismemberment. To locate poetic performance in the breast and mouth, to find its inspiration in the figurative ingestion of Odinn's mead, is to link the body with the word.[23] So, too, Snorri Sturluson (1179–1241), in his syncretic codification of these traditions in his *Skáldskaparamál*, understood the techniques of transforming the human body and its parts into the terms of literary fiction. In this, an *ars poetica* of old Germanic culture, the myths of cosmic and social origin write allegories of poesis and interpretation. The body's parts, attributes, or possessions constitute the origins of kennings that characterize cosmic or meteorological phenomena. And, in particular, it is the parts and possessions of giants on which Snorri locates some of the most expressive of the kennings for the workings of the natural and social world.[24]

By finding Beowulf's announcement of Grendel's glove in the inheritance of this Old Norse poetics, I hope to do more than just reassess a source. Rather, I hope to illustrate the ways in which both *Beowulf* and Snorri draw on traditional accounts of bodily dismemberment and human ingestion to define the rituals of literary making. Both, I believe, present late literate reworkings of an older myth about heroic escape from the belly of the beast—a belly playfully defined as the enormous glove.[25] Read in tandem, these texts illustrate the workings of poetry itself, the mechanisms by which violent legends are transformed into courtly entertainment. But they also reveal the possible transgressions and violence barely hidden behind social rituals. If Beowulf is to be praised for his verbal prowess at Hygelac's court, it is at least in part because his tale shows how his bodily prowess had stanched a threat to social harmony. Now, in his brief story of the monster, the shattered body of Grendel and the whole returning body of the hero stand before us, side by side. Their bodies, like those of the creatures in the Old Norse legends, are the places where heroic action and poetic self-reflection come together. Grendel's glove and its Old Norse analogues share in these literary meditations, as they stand not only for the artifacts of the imagination but for the act of imaginative representation itself.

I

Perhaps the best known, and for my purposes the most apposite, of
Snorri Sturluson's collected stories is the narrative of Thor's adventures
towards the end of the *Gylfaginning*.[26] In response to Gylfi's inquiries about
the marvelous adventures of the Aesir, one of the gods proceeds to narrate
the experiences of Thor and Loki on the way to Utgarð, the hall of the
giants. The story (clearly a self-contained narrative unit) runs as follows.
Thor and Loki set out on a journey when they come to a farmhouse. Thor
sacrifices the goats with which he was traveling, cooks them, and invites the
farm family to a feast. Against the god's wishes, the family's son, Thjalfi, splits
the thigh bone of one of the goats to get at the marrow, and the following
morning, when Thor consecrates the bones and skins and the goats rise up
alive again, the lameness of one of them betrays the boy's misdeed. Fearful
of the god's visible anger, the family gives Thjalfi and his sister to the god
as bondservants, and together they set out for Utgarð. In the course of
their travels, they encounter the giant Skrýmir, into whose enormous glove
they accidentally wander; they reach the hall of the great giants, where
they engage in a series of contests, most of which center on feats of eating,
drinking, or social competition, and all of which they lose; and finally, having
been humiliated by the giants, they find themselves in the open air, the hall
having miraculously disappeared.

At first glance, the story of Thor and his goats bears a striking set of
resonances to the early rituals of the Indo-European peoples: "During the
evening Thor took the goats and slaughtered them, then had them skinned
and put into a cauldron. When they were cooked ...".[27] That his goats are
boiled (*soðit*) in a *ketil* goes back to the oldest European practices of sacrificial
cookery. Boiling in pots, as Burkert notes, is central to the rituals of early
Greek, Latin, and Hittite communities.[28] J.-L. Durand has shown that, for
the Greeks, the difference between roasting and boiling carried, in addition
to the ritual distinctions outlined by Burkert, a certain practical logic:
"Tough, freshly-killed meat that has been cut up ... is barely edible if it is
not boiled. For the Greeks, boiling is the most complete form of cooking."[29]
And Jan de Vries, while discussing Snorri's vignette from the perspective
of *Vegitationsriten*, nonetheless offers valuable analogues to the practice of
boiling the sacrificial animal in Germanic rituals.[30]

If Thor's boiling of the goats goes back to early European practice,
then his invitation to the family to share in the meal similarly resonates
with ancient patterns of communion. By transforming the sacrifice into an
act of social interaction, Thor initiates what Burkert would call "a circle of
participants ... segregated from the outside world."[31] The various activities

of killing, flaying, cooking, and distributing the meat mark out social hierarchies in which "each participant has a set function and acts according to a precisely fixed order." "The sacrificial community," Burkert continues, "is thus a model of society as a whole," where each individual has a certain role to play and certain taboos to avoid. It is precisely this question of taboo behavior which, as Burkert illustrates, defines sacrificial ritual as subject to "sacred laws" and, potentially, as disordering social and familial relations. In the case of Thor and his goats, it is Thjalfi who transgresses, cutting open the thigh bone to get at the rich marrow. It is not simply that Thjalfi has violated a general custom, but that he has taken for his own the piece of animal traditionally reserved as the god's portion. Burkert notes that, in many archaic rituals, "it is the bones, especially the thigh-bones, that belong to the gods," and he summarizes the research of critics and anthropologists on this matter:

> The bones are not to be used for the subsequent meal, so they are "consecrated" beforehand. The bones, above all the thigh bones and the pelvis with the tail, are put on the altar "in the proper order." From the bones, one can still see exactly how the parts of the living animal fit together; its basic form is restored and consecrated.[32]

In Snorri's tale it is Thor himself who restores and consecrates his once-dismembered and digested animals; it is not an act of cultural imagination but the testimony to his power as a god. When he beholds the lame goat, therefore, his intense anger has behind it the old rituals of thigh-bone sacrifice, and it is in the context of Burkert's formulation that we should take the measure of Thjalfi's crime. Beyond offering an insult to the god, his act violates the principles of social hierarchy and the patterns of a ritual designed to maintain order through correctly performed sacrifice. He transgresses a code of conduct fixed to social eating, and at the beginning of the Utgarð narrative, that transgression inaugurates a pattern of ingestive imagery central to the adventures.

Snorri tells tales of ritual and civilization. He draws on the deep myths of culture to illuminate the ways in which human society is centered on the structures of cooking, sacrifice, and communal eating and drinking. He offers what we might call fables of social ingestion: exemplary tales that show how food and its uses define men as men and gods as gods. His method, however, is to offer those tales as stories of transgression. Violations of ritual sacrifice and the conventions of the social meal predominate in the sequence of Thor stories. By turns comic and satiric, these tales map out the boundaries of acceptable human behavior. Snorri, in short, tells stories of threateningly bad table manners.

It is natural, therefore, that when the travelers encounter Skrýmir it should be hunger that motivates their actions and a feed bag that tests their strength. Now, having left the goats behind—and with them the communal rites of sacrificial control—Thor and his companions have only his knapsack (*kýl*) to bear their food, an unremarkable accoutrement that, even though it is the god's, does not seem to provide them with enough. Thor and his companions then find what they think is an open hall, and spend a night inside terrified by the loud roars and rumbles of the earth. Upon awaking in the morning, they encounter Skrýmir, who informs them that this hall is really his great glove (*hanzká*), and that what the travelers thought was an anteroom was in fact the glove's thumb. Then, after deciding to pool their resources into Skrýmir's provision bag (his *nestbagge*), Thor discovers this bag so tightly and so intricately laced that he cannot untie it and retrieve the food.

The transgressions of the table are transformed here from the potentially horrific moment with the goats into the comic deprecations of a dwarfish Thor. To a certain extent, Snorri is developing motifs learned from the older Eddic poems that depicted the god as the butt of insult. Passages in the *Harbarðzlioð* and the *Lokasenna* allusively remark on Thor's foolish encounter with the giant, and their similarities of phrasing have suggested to some scholars that behind the story of the glove is an extended narrative, a hypothetically envisioned ancient *Skrýmiskviða*.[33] In these poetic treatments Thor's adventures fit into the drama of the flyting, and here a disguised Odinn taunts the unsuspecting Thor as coward, fool, and dwarf before the giant called Fjalar.[34]

> Thor is brawny but not very brave:
> fear made you cram yourself into a glove's finger—
>   none would have thought you Thor;
> so great was your dread you didn't dare
> sneeze or fart lest Fjalar hear you.[35]

In the *Lokasenna*, Loki taunts the threatening Thor:

> You shouldn't talk of your travels eastward
>   to anyone alive!
> When you, great hero, hid in the thumb of a glove,
>   none would have thought you Thor.[36]

The myth that has been reconstructed from these texts has been understood to center on the god's reduction to the status of a dwarf. The picture of the giant's glove so large that one could hide in even its thumb has the feeling of a fairy tale, and together with the tone of insult in these stanzas, it suggests that the story is both a funny and an embarrassing one: a challenge to the power and the pride of a divinity.

When Snorri tells the story it becomes a comic fable of the threats to social eating detailed in the Utgarð story as a whole. Here, Thor enters with his traveling companions; here, it is they who are terrified and the god who is strong. And when Skrýmir explains that the "hall" they wandered into is in fact his glove, they are revealed not so much for their cowardice as for their stupidity. This, then, like the other vignettes that surround it, is a story of ingestion *and* interpretation. The god and his friends, hungry from lack of food, find themselves in a hall which is no hall. They safely exit from the glove, only to meet the giant and, in an inversion of this narrative's motif, confront a provision bag too tightly laced to open. Images of entry and enclosure, concealment and digestion, motivate these scenes, and they are funny in a way that the encounter with Thjalfi and the goats decidedly is not.

Thor and his friends are dwarfs not just in stature but in intellect, and the associations between rituals of eating and ideals of understanding is continued in the story of the god's encounter with the inhabitants of Utgarð. The first of their tests responds to Loki's boast that no one can eat faster than he can. But when a trencher is placed before him he cannot eat as quickly as Utgarð-Loki's servant, Logi, for while "Loki had left only the bones of his meat, ... Logi had eaten all his meat, bones and trencher into the bargain."[37] Then, after Thjalfi's loss in a race against someone called Hugi, Thor is challenged to drain the drinking horn. But after three huge swallows, Thor can only make a "slight difference" in the level of the drink. In lifting up the cat, and finally in wrestling with the old woman, Thor again fails, and in patient condescension, Utgarð-Loki finally explains the nature of the spells he had used to deceive the god and his followers.

Each of these scenes dovetails the public expectations of a social accomplishment with the private understandings of personification allegory. Racing and wrestling represent the forms of athletic competition sanctioned and regulated by the social order. Playing with the cat is, as Utgarð-Loki admits, a game for children, while the acts of eating and drinking emblematize social celebrations fitting for adult communities. But these contests are not what they seem. Perversions of social behavior, they make sport of dining conventions and celebratory play. Confronted with a horn that cannot be drained or an eater who consumes like wildfire, Thor and

Loki cannot compete fairly. They are trapped in a hall where the conventions of eating and drinking are upended. They are "civilized" figures confronted with aberrant practices, visitors to an enclosed space paradoxically outside the enclosures of society. Indeed, the very name "Utgarð" signals the paradox at work here. It can mean the hall out side, the *ut garð* in contrast to the *mið garð*, the middle yard or hall that constitutes the realm of men. Or, it may also mean the hall of those outside, the hall of the "other" and thus may present a parody of that dwelling of the gods themselves, *Asgarð*, the hall of the Aesir.[38]

In either case, Utgarð is a community in which the rules of social action do not apply, and if the drama of the Utgarð stories is the drama of food and play gone wrong, it is also one of understanding gone awry. Each moment in the narrative centers on a problem of interpretation, a decipherment of riddles in which Thor and his companions humorously fail to see an object or discern an individual properly. The servants of Utgarð-Loki are enigmas to the visitors, until the giant god reveals the transparency of their names and we, as well as Thor and his friends, soon know them as abstractions, habits of mind, or mythological beings. Utgarð is a community ruled by the laws of literature rather than of life. Its residents and visitors engage in rituals of social living that are not so much transgressive (as Thjalfi's handling of the goats was) as parodic. Indeed, what Utgarð parodies is allegory itself. The fact that Thor and his companions cannot see that Logi is "wildfire," Hugi "thought," and Elli "old age" signals that this is, at one level, a world of radical literalism, a world of personification allegory turned upside down, whose figures simply *are* the objects or conditions denoted by their names. By contrast, Utgarð-Loki's explanation that the cat is the Miðgarð serpent and that the drinking horn is the ocean depends on things that neither Thor nor we could possibly intuit. As the giant says, "The other end of the horn was in the sea, but you did not perceive that," and "that cat was not what it appeared to be."[39] Here, Thor has taken literally what is only later explained to be allegorical. He strides through a landscape of creatures that both demand and confound interpretation. In effect, he becomes a reader who consistently reads incorrectly, an interpreter manipulated into mistaking the real for the imaginary, and vice versa. As in the hollow of the glove, this hero loses himself and his friends in an adventure that is both a fantasy of ingestion and a lesson in allegory. That they escape is, in the end, testimony neither to his heroism nor his cunning, but to the consequence of a controlling—one might even say authorial—release.

The joke on Thor is thus a joke on us, a comic way of illustrating how figurative language works and, in turn, how the kennings and the idioms of poetry can playfully opacify a world of experience. We may think of these scenes in the *Gylfaginning* as dramatizing the concerns of the *Skáldskaparamál*, as they turn into narrative form the embedded allegories or metaphors of the poetic diction governing the Old Norse literary inheritance. One of the purposes of that work, as Snorri stated, was to educate the poet in the techniques of understanding "what is expressed obscurely."[40] "What is the rule for poetry without periphrasis?" Snorri will later ask. "To call everything by its own name."[41] Yet it is clear from Snorri's own account, and from the comprehensive catalogue of tropes and kennings, that the business of poetry lies precisely in *not* calling everything by its own name. The personification allegories of the contestants at Utgarð are but one form of such substitution, and in their encounters Thor and his companions act out an allegory of allegoresis. They represent, in other words, the reader of a metaphorically charged poetry, one confronted with the names of creatures who must stand for other things and, indeed, for whom the very idea of allegorical writing must be explained.

Snorri deploys these stories of sacrifice, communal dining, and comic ingestion to move from the cosmogonic and sociogonic to the hermeneutic and, thus, to locate these myths in the inherently corporeal basis of literary metaphorics. Such locutions as, say, Ymir's skull, flesh, and blood for the sky, the earth, and the sea, respectively, illustrate how the world of experience can be mapped onto the godly body.[42] By contrast, for example, calling the mouth "land or house of tongue or teeth," or calling the "upper limb" "the ground of weapons or shields, tree of shoulder and sleeve," or the "bow-forcer," present each individual human's body as itself both a cosmos and a lexicon of the imagination.[43] Each body contains all the parts that may describe the world; in turn, the things of the world may describe in full all of the body. Within these paradigms of a corporeal poetics, "Skrýmir's glove" may stand as something of a kenning in nascent form. Like those that take the objects of the world or the phenomena of meteorology and define them by the possessions of a creature, a kenning based on Skrýmir's glove distills the ritual impulses of the communal feast and the physical impulses of individual hunger. Bags become the image in which mouth and hand unite, and Skrýmir's *hanzka* comes to emblematize the monstrous nature of that union. Thor's escape from the glove is an escape from being eaten, an escape from the potentially horrific capture and ingestion by the giant. In the end, he comically survives, and the only thing that Skrýmir puts into his own *nestbagge* is the puny knapsack of the travelers.

Such an escape motivates Beowulf's account of his fight with Grendel when he comes home to the court of Hygelac. In his allusive narrative of hands and mouths lies both the matter and the mode of Norse mythmaking. We see the hero in his comic and instructive mode, a hero who, in telling his escape from Grendel's glove, gives us a story that defines the principles of literary representation for the poem itself. This is a story more Eddic than epic in its contours and its emphases, and I return to it now to suggest how it inscribes onto the body of the beast the poem's understanding of the allegorical in literary narrative.

II

Beowulf's concern with being eaten is voiced from the first of his narrative self-accounts at court. Challenging Unferth's version of the swimming match with Breca early in his stay in Heorot, Beowulf recounts not only his success in swimming but the attacks of the sea monsters. "Þrh mine hand" (558b), through my hand, he avers, he broke the grasp of a creature who had ensnared him. Having dispatched all of the monsters with his sword, he states:

> They had no joy at all of the feast, the workers of malice, that they should eat me, sit around a banquet near the sea bottom. (562–64)

At one level, Beowulf defines his victory as a success against the possible reversal of the norms of civilized human life. The feast and the hall, those loci of the social *gefea*, have been imaginatively transferred to those who would eat neither sacrificial animal nor prize of the hunt, but Beowulf himself. Their feast, their banquet, would not have taken place on the benches of the hall, but near the bottom of the sea. But, at another level, Beowulf introduces into the poem a motif central to the figurations of heroic success, and one that looks back, I believe, to the archetypes of the Thor stories. In Beowulf's victories—like those against Grendel and his mother—the hero's escape from being eaten is followed by his mutilation or dismemberment of the body of the creature who would have eaten him. During the match with Breca, the sea creatures have been wounded with the sword ("mecum wunde," 565b) and left stranded on the shore, their dead forms left so that they do not hinder any future voyages. "Yet," he states, "I came out of the hostile grip alive" (578). In this aside, Beowulf defines the trope of the heroic life: the escape from the grasp and swallow, from the hand and mouth, that testifies to the successes of the body's prowess and, furthermore, to the hero's necessary mutilation of those who would threaten to ingest him.

These tropes control the account of Beowulf's defeat of Grendel in his speech at Hygelac's court and, at first glance, these two performances seem very similar in tone and purpose. But they differ in detail. Beowulf's rejoinder to Unferth, for all its self-references, is unmarked by verbal play or literary enigmatics. When it is punctuated at all, it is with the gnomes familiar from the Anglo-Saxon wisdom traditions—gnomes that give a maximal and sententious, rather than a comic and elusive flavor to the telling.[44] At Hygelac's court, however, Beowulf's account is given to the trickery of pun and wordplay, interlace and allusion, that makes this performance a heroic one not in its recounting of events, but in its skill at presentation. It is, too, like the conquest of the sea creatures, a story of artifice; yet here that artifice is transferred from the body of the hero to the corpus of the beast. What helped save Beowulf when swimming against Breca was his body armor, "hard and handlinked" ("heard hondlocen," 551a). Beautiful as well as functional, it covers his breast "adorned with gold" ("golde gegyrwed," 553a). Such adornments may exemplify what Fred Robinson has seen as the protective and civilizing function of elaborate artifice in *Beowulf*. Here, the brute force of monsterly corporeality contrasts with the beweaponed and well-armed body of Beowulf himself, and it is clear that part of the poem's overall dynamics lies precisely in this contrast between the unadorned threatening chaos of the natural world, and the elaborate, artificial structures of a civic, social life that guards against it.[45] The body of the beast is always, it would seem, just that: pure body, unadorned and unprotected by the workings of craft.

It thus comes as a surprise to find, in Beowulf's returning speech, an item of distinctive craft attributed to Grendel's own possession.

> The glove hung wide open and weird, laced with cunningly
> wrought bands; it was completely adorned with works of artifice,
> the work of the devil, and made out of dragon skin. (2085–88)

Grendel's glove stands as something of an antitype to the protective, wonderfully magical creations that preserve the hero's body and his home. Laced up, *searobendum fæst*, it recalls the human works of skill (*searoponc*, 775) that kept Heorot together, bound fast in its iron bands during the fight with Grendel (773–75). As a work of personal artifice, the glove also recalls the near magic armor whose locked rings kept Beowulf safe (his *searofah* mail shirt, 1444), or the *searonet* that clothed his men (406). It also recalls the vision of Grendel's severed arm, hung up in Heorot as a *searowunder* for Hrothgar's men to see (920).[46]

Yet Grendel's glove is a grim work of horrific craft, a thing whose *orðonc* exemplifies neither the ingenuities of men nor the inherent artistry of God.[47] Unlike that armor, "golde gegyrwed," which saved Beowulf, this is a thing "eal gegyrwed" with a devilish skill. And unlike armor that would keep the human body whole, this is a monsterly accessory itself made of the pieces of another creature: dragon skin. Like Skrýmir's *hanzka* or his tightly laced-up food bag, Grendel's glove appears as a mechanism of the inhuman that can entrap the unsuspecting. Moreover, as that figurative version of the hand and mouth assembly that defines the monstrous, the glove stands for the gross processes of digestion that lie at the center of both the Grendel and the Thor stories. Much like the characters of the *Gylfaginning*, or, for that matter, much like the rapacious sea beasts who would make a meal of Beowulf, Grendel is a creature of unbridled appetite. His hunger motivates a cruelty that transgresses the most fundamental of social taboos—cannibalism—and makes him a being ruled not by the mind but by the mouth. Indeed, all that we know of Grendel and his kin (aside from the allusions to his genealogy and their potential exegetical resonances) is centered on the body parts that they use to eat: the massive hand that snatches men and the mouth that swallows them.

In the section of Beowulf's speech devoted to him, Grendel is a creature all of hands and mouth, and Beowulf's words construct an elaborate verbal interlace of these two body parts to reify the creature's features. It was, from the start he claims, a hand-fight (*hondræs*, 2072); the first Geat killed, now named Hondscio (2076), has a name that clearly resonates with the manual imagery of Grendel's threat. Grendel, too, is a *muðbona* (2079), one who can swallow up the lives of men, and whose own face is reduced to the synechdochic *blodigtoð* (2082). He grasps the hero with an eager hand ("grapode gearofolm," 2085), and while he would not leave Heorot empty handed (*idelhende*, 2081), it is his own empty hand that remains behind as a token of Beowulf's greater grip ("swaðe weardade / hand on Hiorte," 2098–99).[48] The image of the glove is thus, for the *Beowulf*-poet and for Snorri, a playful way of bringing together these two defining body parts. As a hand-shaped cavity that swallows men, the glove is both limb and mouth. It is as if these writers had both asked themselves a riddle: when is a hand like a mouth—or, perhaps, more in keeping with the spirit of the Exeter Book collection, what is it that looks like a hand but swallows like a mouth? Answer: a glove.

This notion of the glove as the solution to a riddle both complements my earlier suggestion that the giant's glove functions in Snorri's *Gylfaginning* as the core of a kenning and, furthermore, may help explain something of Beowulf's larger purposes and effects in his speech before Hygelac. The patterns of interpretive deception, word-play, and personification allegory operating in the Old Norse stories present striking parallels to the Hondscio/*glof* pun in the Old English. Both scenes transform the potentially horrific into comedy; both use the ruses of pun and transparent etymology to educate the audience in entertaining ways. "Hondscio" here is a joke, a contribution to the tame and reassuring retelling of Beowulf's story.[49] Far from Denmark, and distanced from his exploits, Beowulf transforms the terror of his experience into a form of social entertainment. The play on name and glove effectively dramatizes the horror of the Geat's death and the monster's appetite. It makes the story an acceptable social performance, one that will not—as Grendel's own disembodied head did—frighten men and queen (1647–50).

In one sense, then, Beowulf's verbal humor turns socially disruptive action into illustrative play. It enacts something of that tradition of *docere et delectare* later vernacularized for the Germanic tradition in Snorri's own *Skáldskaparamál*, when he offers his own compendia of kenning-compounds and allusive verses as both "scholarly inquiry and entertainment."[50] But, in another sense, Beowulf's wordplays and his references to Grendel's glove take us directly to the matter, as well as the method, of the Norse myths. These references, I believe, are to be construed as direct allusions to the vision of Thor the comic dwarf and to the flytings preserved in the *Harbarðzlioð* and *Lokasenna*. Confronted with a need to tell his own tale, Beowulf presents himself as something of a comic Thor, a hero on a journey filled with transparent names, monstrous objects, and enigmatic verbal challenges.

But, of course, unlike the misapprehending Thor, or the unfortunate Hondscio, Beowulf does not find himself in Grendel's glove. His escape is what makes him heroic; his actions take on a power and significance when shown against the foil of the Old Norse analogues. For the real point is that Beowulf presents a comic scene in order to define his heroism as a social performance. He presents a literary narrative of his actions that is not so much epic as Eddic—or to put it more precisely now, *skaldic*—in its pace, allusiveness, and verbal play. Faced with the request to tell of his adventures at the court, this Scandinavian hero performs a characteristically Scandinavian verbal act. He tells a pointedly allusive and succinct report, one that trades on not only a familiarity with Eddic tales of Thor and his escape from Skrýmir's glove, but one that relies on a certain courtly sensitivity to puns and wordplay and to the self-consciousness of poetic telling. His is a performance richly aware of its own performativity, a story interrupted with announcements either of intention or excuse. The opening claim, "Ic sceal forð sprecan," and the interruptive aside, "To lang ys to reccenne" (2093), announce, in effect, that Beowulf's narration will inform his audience less about the details of the struggle than about the hero's own skills at personal narration. We are not offered the horrific details of the fight; nor are we given a moral interpretation of its action in the gnomic terms that the *Beowulf*-poet, or Hrothgar, had earlier presented. Instead, what we get is entertainment, a self-conscious display of Beowulf's abilities to *sprecan* and an ironic aside when he knows that he may have spoken for "to lang."

These are what Carol Clover has identified as the key features of the "skaldic sensibility," the highly wrought, self-conscious literary style at work in Scandinavian courts from roughly the ninth through the eleventh centuries.[51] It is a style of first-person intrusiveness, a way of recapitulating familiar mythic or legendary matter not so much to recount their plots as to display the "poet's range of emotional response" to them. The skalds, as Clover puts it, turned the inheritance of myth "into a performance metaphor," spinning their stories of the origins of poetry and their displays of skill out of the myth of Kvasir and the many kennings generated by its tale of a broken and reconstituted body. The emphasis on wordplay, on what Clover calls the "ludic quality of skaldic poetry," is thus an integral part of this fascination with the origins and social function of poetic making.[52] More than showing off the skald's command of technique or archana, puns and allusions contribute to the thematic preoccupation with the limits of language itself. Skaldic performance, at its most extreme, pushes the resources of language to the point of near-incomprehensibility, as the proper understanding of the poem becomes akin to the solving of a riddle or the elucidation of a kenning.

In these terms, Beowulf's performance, while not nearly as elaborate as that of the professional skalds, does show us something of the verbal trickery at work in Scandinavian court versifying. It shows the hero in his courtly mode, a hero serving as his own best poet, one acutely conscious of the expectations of his audience to be both challenged and amused. The pun on Hondscio's name and the account of Grendel's glove thus function less as added details designed to enhance the realism of the monster's threat than as allusions calibrated to enhance the mythic quality of this self-presentation. They draw the poem's audience into the ambience of cosmogonic and sociogonic legends, recalling the comedy of Thor, the great myths of communal ingestion and bodily breakage, and finally, the ways in which Scandinavian poets relied on such myths both to display and reflect upon the nature of their verbal craft. Both *Beowulf* and *Gylfaginning* draw on the motif of the monster's glove to fix the point of contact between social ritual and literary habit. Both sets of stories offer tales of eating and its transgressions. Both use patterns of wordplay designed to illustrate the etymologies of certain terms and the centrality of verbal decipherment in the adventures of the hero and the teachings of an audience. They transform the stuff of ritual into the logic of comedy and the narrative of literary making.

Such transformations may enable us to reconsider Grendel's killing as a kind of sacrifice within the narrative and mythic archetypes that had developed out of the social rituals of bodily dismemberment and communal ingestion. Bones, skulls, and skins have always been, as Burkert notes, the stuff of the rites of purification, and the telos of the sacrificial act lies in the cleansing of the community. "Sacrifice transforms us," Burkert writes: "Killing justifies and affirms life; it makes us conscious of the new order and brings it into power."[53] So, too, does Beowulf's elimination of the monsters, an act defined throughout the poem as a cleansing. When he arrives in Denmark, he boasts that he will "Heorot fælsian" (432), and the narrator, introducing Grendel's severed arm as a token, states that the hero had indeed "gefælsod ... sele Hroðgares" (825–26). Wealhtheow, too, believes "Heorot is gefælsod" (1176), and when Beowulf kills Grendel's mother and severs her son's head, then the waters of the monster's mere are also "eal gefælsod" (1620). Finally, looking back over his adventures in old age, Beowulf himself remembers how he "sele fælsode ... at guðe forgrap" (2352–53)—that is, how he cleansed the hall and gripped Grendel completely to death. These acts are grounded in the verbal idiom of sacrifice. The verb used to describe them, *fælsian*, is the vernacular equivalent of such terms as *lustrare*, *purificare*, and *expiare*: Latin terms for the cleansing of the social self and the purification of that which has been defiled. As a place in need of such a cleansing, Heorot becomes the site of ritual, and Grendel's left-behind and returned body parts—the long bones of the arm assemblage and the skull of the severed head—become the tokens of this purification. *Fælsian* connotes in these contexts the act of dismemberment itself. Its repeated appearance in the poem signals that the killing of the monster necessarily requires the display of body parts, their communal beholding, and their understanding as the signs and tokens of the creature's death.[54]

Read in this way, the death of Grendel shares with the great myths of decapitation and dismemberment a resonance with the creation of the world and the establishment of culture. Like the many literary versions of the tales of Romulus, Thyestes, Dionysus, and Orpheus, this version of the death of Grendel relies on an ancient set of tropes to make a statement about the fragility of the human community and the power of literary narrative to bring individuals together into a shared awareness of their origins. If Grendel's killing partakes of the deep structures of ritual dismemberment, then much like Thor's goats or the older practices detailed by Burkert, the arm and head together should enable the beholder imaginatively to reconstruct the beast from which they came. Such reconstructions, as the story of the goats illustrated, had become part and parcel of the consecration of the slaughtered animal, and ultimately point towards the purification or cleansing of the community through sacrifice.

But the whole point of Beowulf's narration is that we *not* reconstruct—either physically or narratively—the severed body. The hand assembly is, throughout the poem, offered as fragment of the body left behind, a thing signifying, marking, or directing human action, emotional reaction, or interpretive response. Each thing, each part, becomes a symbol, a *tacn*.[55] The poem specifically identifies the head and arm as objects whose significance must lie beyond their bloody apparition.

> That was a clear sign when the battle-brave man set up the hand under the curved roof—the arm and the shoulder: there all together was Grendel's grasp. (833–36)

Beowulf, too, speaks in terms of tokens when he returns Grendel's head to Hrothgar.

> Behold, we have brought you this sea booty, son of Healfdene, man of the Scyldings, gladly, as a token of glory—what you look on here. (1652–54)

Similarly, in Beowulf's retelling before Hygelac, the hand is left as a *swaðe* (2098), a track or pathway.[56] Indeed, the word *swaðu* carries with it a whole host of hermeneutic resonances in Old English. In King Alfred's famous lament on the decline of English learning, for example, the word alludes to the example left by earlier English scholars: "Here one can still see their track, but we cannot follow after it."[57] And in the Exeter Book Riddles, the word refers to the tracks left by the pens and ink of the scriptorium: the "swaþu swiþe blacu" left by the pen and fingers of Riddle 51, or the "swaþe" made clear to the reader at the close of the last Riddle, number 95. The word *swaþu* in the Old English Riddles shares a semantic field with *last* (leavings, track, or pathway), and often appears paired with it.[58] Similarly, in *Beowulf*, the metrical construction of line 2098b, "swaðe weardade," is clearly modeled on (or part of the same formula as) the phrasing "last weardian" in Beowulf's original account of the battle to Hrothgar:

> Nonetheless, he left his hand remaining as a mark or track in order to save his life, the arm and the shoulder. (970–72)[59]

In Beowulf's telling, then, Grendel is symbolically dismantled into his constituent parts: not, as in the story of Thor and his goats, so that the hero can restore the body whole again in consecration, but so that they may remain as parts, safe in their symbolism and inactivity. They must remain as parts or objects, the *swaðu* of the hand or the *orþonc* of the glove, things for the delectation or interpretation of the viewer.

Beowulf's story is thus a profound enactment of and challenge to the mythic archetypes of heroic escape. On the one hand, it replicates the tenor of the comic Thor—transforms the heroic escape from death into comic exaggeration and glib wordplay. But, on the other hand, it recognizes that to cleanse (*fælsian*) the hall is not to bring the sacrificial body back to wholeness but to leave its shards and ornaments scattered across the landscape of the telling. Grendel must stay here, in the hero's self-reportage, as the synechdochic self: the bloody-toothed one, empty-handed, bearing a weird glove. All mouth and hand, he is reduced to trope and type—poeticized, as it were—according to the techniques at work in Old Germanic performance and later plotted out by Snorri. Though we have seen Grendel in his living body, but for the self-narrations of the hero he cannot come back to life. The horror of his grim rapacity must be displaced onto the glove: not body, but artifice.

If *Beowulf* is a poem of the body, it is, then, a poem of the fragmented and symbolized body. Grendel's severed head and arm are, much like the bladeless sword-hilt Beowulf recovers from the mere, symbolic remnants of a violent world. While they may once have threatened social life or cosmic order, they survive within the poem's telling as tame representations of a former horror. They are signs and symbols, figures for a violence that has gone on long ago.[60] The hand and head are thus not only objects in need of interpretation. They exemplify the symbolic itself, the building blocks of allegorical and mythic literature that facilitate the hero's display of his verbal skills and, in turn, the audience's understanding of the nature of poetic craft. The idea of the *tacn* or the *swaðu* is the idea of representation itself, of the display of symbols in the organization of narrative meaning. Beowulf's listeners at Hygelac's court—much like Thor and his companions or the deluded Gylfi himself in Snorri's tale—are confronted with strange names and odd inhuman things. To understand them is not just to crack the codes of allegory but to share in the successes of the social rituals of poetic performance. Such rituals are ultimately comic. On the one hand, they are funny, in that plays on name and etymology or visions of the dwarfish god defuse the tensions of a violent tale and make socially acceptable the recitation of a horrific battle. But they are also comic in a darker sense, one that, as Carolyn Walker Bynum has phrased it, "undergirds our sense of human limitation," and that, in its revelry in broken or disfigured bodies, shows us a narrative of human history where the "pleasant [has been] snatched from the horrible by artifice and with acute self-consciousness and humility."[61]

In effect, this is precisely what the courtly Beowulf has done. By drawing on the tropes and tricks of Scandinavian myth and verse, he snatches something, if not pleasant, then at least amusing from the horrible. That his report of the fight with Grendel says more about a piece of artifice than about the monster, and shows more of Beowulf's self-consciousness and humility than of his physical heroism, is fully in keeping with the comic flavor of his telling. But such comedy, as Snorri Sturluson had recognized, needs to be understood, and both the Old English poem and the Old Norse scholar spend considerable time seeking to educate their audiences in the techniques of that understanding. These techniques, as I have sought to illustrate throughout this study, represent the literary and intellectual end-product of a lengthy cultural process, one beginning with Old Germanic narratives of bodily dismemberment and alimentary ingestion that draw on deep structures of sacrificial ritual, and that have been elaborated into myths of sociogonic and cosmogonic epistemes. Beyond their applications as didactic works for the instruction of an audience or celebrant, these narratives also constitute a way of teaching something about figurative understanding. The inherent tendency of such narratives to reflect not only on the workings of allegory but on the corporeal foundation of allegoresis itself is what both Beowulf and Snorri have exploited. Old English and Old Norse poetic practices provide the larger paradigm for understanding the figure of the giant's glove—be it Skrýmir's *hanzka* or Grendel's *glof*—as a possible kernel of a kenning or a riddle: that is, as a possible mythological signifier for a natural referent that, in some sense, would participate in the narratives of a god's or hero's comic escape from captivity and ingestion. The many body parts that litter Beowulf's landscape thus come to function in an emerging corporeal poetics for the poem: a poetics of dismemberment, where sacrificial, social, and poetic ritual performances use the occasion of the separation of the body to give rise to public utterance.

Beowulf's conjuring of Grendel's glove, then, testifies to his command of the poetic resources of his culture. His performance is, in one sense, a social ritual: a fulfilling of a contract between the returning hero and the welcoming community for an account, both entertaining and instructive, of his adventures. It is, too, in another sense, a reflection on the problems of ritual itself: a recognition of the place that bodily dismemberment has in the deeper forms of cosmic, social, and poetic self-representation and explanation. To speak of a poetics of dismemberment, then, or to find in Beowulf's performance a commanding display of traditional materials and methods, is to speak of poetry itself and to see how the hero's literature takes the shards and fragments of dead bodies or inhuman artifacts and transforms them into reflections on the poet's craft and on the place of imaginative fiction in society.

NOTES

Earlier versions of this material were presented to audiences at Rutgers University (1989), the University of California at Berkeley (1990), and UCLA (1993). I am grateful to many in those audiences, especially to Joseph Nagy, John P. Herrman, and John Ganim, and to Mary F. Godfrey for the opportunity of directing her dissertation on a topic related to that of this study, "The Severed Head: Images of the Body in Old and Middle English Literature," Princeton University, 1992. In preparing this essay for publication, I have benefitted greatly from the detailed responses of Lee Patterson and the supportive suggestions of Nicholas Howe.

1. *Beowulf*, ed. F. Klaeber, 3d ed. (Boston: D.C. Heath, 1950), 1999–2162; hereafter cited parenthetically in the text by the line number. All translations from this text, as well as others, are my own unless specified otherwise.

2. Edward D. Laborde, "Grendel's Glove and His Immunity from Weapons," *Modern Language Review* 18 (1923): 202–4; Johannes Hoops, *Beowulfstudien, Anglistische Forschungen* 74 (Heidelberg: Carl Winter, 1932), 118.

3. J. R. R. Tolkien, "*Beowulf*: The Monsters and the Critics," *Proceedings of the British Academy* 22 (1936): 245–95, reprinted separately (Oxford: Oxford Univ. Press, 1958), 30.

4. James L. Rosier, "The Uses of Association: Hands and Feasts in *Beowulf*," *PMLA* 78 (1963): 8–14, especially his remarks on 11–12: "[The poet's] use of the words *hand* and *glof* in turn suggested, as he realized the appropriateness of particularizing Beowulf's lost companion, a Germanic equivalent—a form of *hantscuoh*—which he decided to adapt as a personal name, since as a compound it contributes to the hand motif and in a sense picks up or puns upon the allusion to the glove." See also the discussion in Mary F. Godfrey, "*Beowulf* and *Judith*: Thematizing Decapitation in Old English Poetry," *Texas Studies in Literature and Language* 35 (1993): 1–43, especially her remarks on 3–4.

5. Seth Lerer, *Literacy and Power in Anglo-Saxon Literature* (Lincoln: Univ. of Nebraska Press, 1991), esp. 183–94, which draws on the suggestive criticism of R. Howard Bloch on the conventions of heroic return and recitation (see *Medieval French Literature and Law* [Berkeley: Univ. of California Press, 1977], 198–202) and on the critical tradition surrounding Odysseus's return and self-disclosure to Penelope in the *Odyssey* (see Shiela Murnahghan, *Disguise and Recognition in the Odyssey* [Princeton: Princeton Univ. Press, 1987] and the scholarship summarized therein). Though the passages from *Beowulf* that I discuss here have not received much attention from modern critics, Beowulf's speech to Hygelac is commonly regarded as the closing gesture of the poem's first part. A representative formulation is that of Edward B. Irving, Jr., *Rereading Beowulf* (Philadelphia: Univ. of Pennsylvania Press, 1989), 153: "This scene occupies an important pivotal position in the narrative. It comes after the real end of the Danish portion at line 1887 and forms a strong epilogue to that section in its general tone, maintaining Part I's highly social atmosphere and its heavy stress on the royal political activity for which a hall is the proper venue. Beowulf's report is thus the last great hall-scene of the poem." Though offering a perceptive reassessment of the monsters in the poem from an anthropological perspective that complements my own, Ward Parks neglects to discuss Beowulf's own account of the fight with Grendel and, indeed, conflates the poet's first report of Grendel killing the unnamed "slæpendne rinc" (741a) with the later announcement by Beowulf that his name is Hondscio ("Prey Tell: How Heroes Perceive Monsters in *Beowulf*," *JEGP* 92 [1993]: 1–16, esp. 2).

6. For the philosophical and psychoanalytic inheritance behind this formulation, see the surveys of critical positions in Carolyn Dean, "Law and Sacrifice: Bataille, Lacan,

and the Critique of the Subject," *Representations* 13 (1986): 42–62, and Peter Stallybrass and Allon White, *The Politics and Poetics of Transgression* (Ithaca: Cornell Univ. Press, 1986). For historical approaches to the body's place in late antique and medieval social systems, see the following: Peter Brown, *The Body and Society: Men, Women, and Sexual Renunciation in Early Christianity* (New York: Columbia Univ. Press, 1988); Carolyn Walker Bynum, *Fragmentation and Redemption: Essays on Gender and the Human Body in Medieval Religion* (New York: Zone Books, 1991); John Boswell, *Christianity, Social Tolerance, and Homosexuality* (Chicago: Univ. of Chicago Press, 1980); Miri Rubin, *Corpus Christi: The Eucharist in Late Medieval Culture* (Cambridge: Cambridge Univ. Press, 1991). See, too, Sarah Beckwith, *Christ's Body: Religious Culture and Late Medieval Piety* (New York: Routledge, 1993), and the studies collected in "Boundary and Transgression in Medieval Culture," the special issue of the *Stanford French Review* 14 (1990), esp. Stephen G. Nichols, "Deflections of the Body in the Old French Lay," 27–50, and Milad Doueihi, "The Lure of the Heart," 51–68; and the highly influential article of Nancy Vickers, "Diana Described: Scattered Woman and Scattered Rhyme," *Critical Inquiry* 8 (1981): 265–79. For arguments and evidence enabling the construction of the Middle Ages as an "age of the body," see Linda Lomperis and Sarah Stanbury, eds., *Feminist Approaches to the Body in Medieval Literature* (Philadelphia: Univ. of Pennsylvania Press, 1993), esp. vii–xiv.

7. The only account of the glove that gestures in the broader critical directions I am positing here is that of Paul Beekman Taylor, "Grendel's Monstrous Arts," *In Geardagum VI* (1984): 1–12. Taylor reviews some of the Old Norse sources associated with the episode, as I do below, and recognizes that the glove-bag constitutes a work of "primeval cunning" (6); yet he is unconcerned with the larger function of the glove-episode either in the structure and meaning of Beowulf's speech as a whole or in the broader contexts of Germanic literary allegorical and narrative attitudes.

8. See the review of issues in Taylor (note 7), and the fundamental formulation of the role of artifice in Old English literature by Fred C. Robinson, *Beowulf and the Appositive Style* (Knoxville: Univ. of Tennessee Press, 1985). I have developed some of these approaches in *Literacy and Power* (note 5), in particular seeking to define the centrality of the term *orðonc* in the Old English Riddles (97–125).

9. Though *Beowulf* awaits a comprehensive assessment in the terms of the theory and history of the body sketched above, some gestures in this direction have been made by Godfrey (note 4); Janet Thorman, "The Body of the Mother in *Beowulf*," delivered at the Modern Language Association of America Convention, Chicago, 29 December, 1990; and by Gillian Overing, *Language, Sign, and Gender in Beowulf* (Carbondale: Southern Illinois Univ. Press, 1990), esp. 33–67. For an approach to Old English poetry that seeks to corporealize the idea of verbal performance itself, see Eric Jager, "Speech and the Chest in Old English Poetry: Orality or Pectorality?" *Speculum* 65 (1990): 845–59.

10. For a sensitive reassessment of these motifs in the poem, see Irving (note 5), 92–99.

11. See, for example, Charles Segal, *The Theme of the Mutilation of the Corpse in the Iliad* (Leiden: E. J. Brill, 1971); Pietro Pucci, *Odysseus Polutropos: Intertextual Readings in the Odyssey and the Iliad* (Ithaca: Cornell Univ. Press, 1987), esp. 157–90; Peter Haidu, *The Song of Roland and the Birth of the State* (Bloomington: Indiana Univ. Press, 1993).

12. Pucci (note 11), 171.

13. Walter Burkert, *Homo Necans: The Anthropology of Ancient Greek Sacrificial Ritual and Myth*, trans. Peter Bing (Berkeley: Univ. of California Press, 1983), esp. 1–82.

14. See the studies collected in Jean-Pierre Vernant, ed., *The Cuisine of Sacrifice Among the Greeks*, trans. Paula Wissing (Chicago: Univ. of Chicago Press, 1989), this quotation from Marcel Detienne, "Culinary Practices and the Spirit of Sacrifice," 1.

15. See, for example, Marcel Detienne, *Dionysos Slain*, trans. Mireille and Leonard Muellner (Baltimore: Johns Hopkins Univ. Press, 1979); Pierre Vidal-Naquet, *The Black Hunter*, trans. Andrew Szegedy-Maszak (Princeton: Princeton Univ. Press, 1986).

16. See in particular Georges Dumézil, *Gods of the Ancient Northmen*, ed. and trans. Einar Haugen (Berkeley: Univ. of California Press, 1973). For an extension and a powerful critique of Dumézil's methods and his legacy, see Bruce Lincoln, *Myth, Cosmos, and Society: Indo-European Themes of Creation and Destruction* (Cambridge: Harvard University Press, 1986).

17. Lincoln (note 16), 2.

18. See Lincoln, 42–43, working with reference to the interpretation in Burkert, "Caesar and Romulus-Quirinus," *Historia* 11 (1962): 356–76. Lincoln summarizes: "The distribution of Romulus's bodily parts is thus a mythic sociogony, describing the creation of a differentiated social order in which no *gens* could claim totality or absolute supremacy, but in which each had a role to play in the functioning of the city. Every meeting of the senate, therefore, was nothing less than a reassembling of the primordial totality, that is to say, a convocation of all the Roman *gentes* reunified the pieces of Romulus's dismembered body. At other times, however, as the gentes carried on their separate existence, Romulus's body remained scattered, and each adjournment of the senate repeated the dispersion of his bodily parts" (43). For bibliography on the myth and its interpretations, see 184–85. For an application of these paradigms to the narratives of beheading in Old English and Old Norse narratives, see Godfrey (note 4), 6–12, 34 n.26.

19. For nineteenth-century comparative philological accounts, see the bibliography assembled in Jan de Vries, *Altgermanische Religionsgeschichte*, 2 vols., 2d ed. (Berlin and Leipzig: Walter de Gruyter, 1956–57), 1:x–xlix. For more recent discussions of the origin of poetry in narratives of bodily dismemberment and the ingestion of the body's fluids, see the accounts in Dumézil (note 16), 20–25; Lincoln, 65–86, 196–97; Carol Clover, "Skaldic Sensibility," *Arkiv för Nordisk Filologi* 93 (1978): 63–81; Roberta Frank, "Snorri and the Mead of Poetry," in *Speculum Noroennum: Norse Studies in Memory of Gabriel Turville-Petre*, ed. Ursula Dronke (Odense: Odense Univ. Press, 1981), 155–70; and Godfrey (note 4), 7–10. In *Literacy and Power* (note 5), I argued that Bede's story of Caedmon similarly traded on these legends of ritual ingestion and shared poetic performance, contrasting them with the monastic traditions of *ruminatio* and the ideals of a Christian eucharistic ingestive imagery (see 42–48).

20. The idea of the human body as the site of allegorical imagination has been traced for a variety of literatures. For the coporealization of physical processes in what may be the originary allegorizing gestures of the Greek Scholiasts, see Felix Buffière, *Les Mythes d'Homère et la Pensée Grecque* (Paris: Belles Lettres, 1956), 85–132. For the traditions of an alimentary metaphorics in Late Antique and medieval literatures, see Ernst Robert Curtius, *European Literature and the Latin Middle Ages*, trans. Willard R. Trask (Princeton: Princeton Univ. Press, 1953), 134–36. See, too, Robert M. Durling, "Deceit and Digestion in the Belly of Hell," in *Allegory and Representation*, Selected Papers from the English Institute, 1979–80, ed. Stephen Greenblatt (Baltimore: Johns Hopkins Univ. Press, 1981), 61–93. The classic account of the political allegorics of the body is Ernst H. Kantorowicz, *The King's Two Bodies* (Princeton: Princeton Univ. Press, 1957). See, too, Jacques Le Goff, "Head or Heart? The Political Use of Body Metaphors in the Middle Ages," in *Fragments for a History of the Human Body*, part 3, ed. Michel Feher (New York: Zone, 1989), 13–26, and for later medieval civic and dramatic traditions, Mervyn James, "Ritual, Drama and Social Body in the Late Medieval English Town," *Past and Present* 98 (1983): 3–29.

21. Durling's remarks (note 20) succinctly sum up the position I am offering here: "The various models of the larger unity of humanity—the body of Satan, the body politic, the body of Christ—are all patterns in which individuals are contained as organs in the larger structures they only partly know. In these larger structures ... we are each allegorized beyond our knowledge and perhaps against our wills, contained by our limitations and our devices" (84).

22. Margaret Clunies Ross (*Skáldskaparamál: Snorri Sturluson's Ars Poetica and Medieval Theories of Language* [Odense: Odense Univ. Press, 1987]) has identified the principle of kenning-making as inherited and codified by Snorri as one in which "the base-word is the name of a possession, body-part, etc. of the determinant, which is a proper name, e.g., 'fire of Aegir,' 'meal of Frodi.'" A subset of this group is the kind of kenning in which "the relationship between the base-word and referent is often metaphorical, often mythologically sanctioned, e.g., 'storm of Odinn,' 'wheel of Hildr'" (95). In discussing this procedure at length, Clunies Ross concludes that "it is a tendency ... implicit in the entire Old Norse kenning-system" (145). For a provocative reassessment of the traditions of Anglo-Saxon riddling in this light, together with a review of the critical inheritance on the riddles, see Craig R. Williamson, *The Old English Riddles of the Exeter Book* (Chapel Hill: Univ. of North Carolina Press, 1977), esp. 23–28. For a discussion of the historical and structural links between riddles and kennings in ways that will bear directly on my later arguments, see John Lindow, "Riddles, Kennings, and the Complexity of Skaldic Poetry," *Scandinavian Studies* 47 (1975): 311–27.

23. Carol J. Clover (note 19), esp. 68–73.

24. See the discussion in Clunies Ross, *Skáldskaparamál* (note 22), on the term *nygerv-ingar*, literally "novelty" or "neologism," but in certain contexts explicitly concerned with allegorizations of body parts (see esp. 50, 76–77, 117, 132, 149–50). In his recent translation of the *Skáldskaparamál*, Anthony Faulkes renders Snorri's *nygervingar* as Modern English "allegory" in the discussion of kennings for the body parts head and limb (*Snorri Sturluson: Edda* [London: Dent, 1987], 153–54). For a discussion of the subtle range of connotations of the term *nygervingar*, as well as for an assessment of Snorri as a literary critic of skaldic verse, see O. D. Macrae-Gibson, "Sagas, Snorri, and the Literary Criticism of Scaldic Verse," in *Úr Dölum til Dala: Guðbrandur Vigfússon Centerary Essays*, ed. Rory McTurk and Andrew Wawn, Leeds Texts and Monographs, n.s. 11 (1989): 165–86. On Snorri's uses of the giants as "embodiments of the workings of nature," see Clunies Ross, 168. She also remarks on how the body parts of giants (for example, Iðunn's eyes and Aurvandill's toe, 171) and their possessions (for example, Hrugnir's whetstone, 171) figure prominently in Snorri's narratives as hearkening back to the older tradition of metamorphic narrative inherited from Ovid.

25. Though this is not the place to review extensively the debates on the dating of *Beowulf* (see Colin Chase, ed., *The Dating of Beowulf* [Toronto: Univ. of Toronto Press, 1981]) or Snorri's use of received and possibly orally transmitted poetry and myth, some statement of position is in order. By referring to *Beowulf* as "literate," I do not necessarily mean to deny the possibilities of the poem sharing in a larger European oral-formulaic tradition of composition. Instead, I refer to the poem *as it has survived* in the unique late-tenth- or early-eleventh-century manuscript copy, and in turn, how certain aspects of the poem's narrative may thematize its own modes of composition and transmission. For approaches to the institutional histories and ideologies controlling the scholarly discussion of these issues, see Allen J. Frantzen, *Desire for Origins: New Language, Old English, and the Teaching of the Tradition* (New Brunswick: Rutgers Univ. Press, 1990), esp. 179–200, and Michael Near, "Anticipating Alienation: *Beowulf* and the Intrusion of Literacy," *PMLA* 108

(1993): 320–32. For a valuable reconception of the historicity of Anglo-Saxon oral poetry and its transmission, see Katherine O'Brien O'Keeffe, *Visible Song: Transitional Literacy in Old English Verse* (Cambridge: Cambridge Univ. Press, 1990). For Snorri Sturluson's status as a literate compiler of traditional mythographic material and a synthesizer of Germanic popular and learned traditions of literary theory, see the general survey in John Lindow, "Mythology and Mythography," in *Old Norse-Icelandic Literature: A Critical Guide*, ed. Carol J. Clover and John Lindow (Ithaca: Cornell Univ. Press, 1985), 21–67, and the more specialized studies of Joseph Harris, "The Masterbuilder Tale in Snorri's *Edda* and Two Sagas," *Arkiv för Nordisk Filologi* 91 (1976): 66–101; Roberta Frank (note 19); Ursula and Peter Dronke, "The Prologue of the Prose Edda: Explorations of a Latin Background," in *Sjötíu Ritgerðir Helgaðar Jakobi Benediktssyni*, ed. Einar G. Pétursson and Jónas Kristjánsson (Reykjavik: Stofun Arna Magnussonar, 1977), 153–76; Arthur D. Mosher, "The Story of Baldr's Death: The Inadequacy of Myth in the Light of Christian Faith," *Scandinavian Studies* 55 (1983): 305–15; and the commentary in Snorri Sturluson, *Gylfaginning*, ed. Gottfried Lorenz (Darmstadt: Wissenschaftliche Buchgesellschaft, 1984). The only book-length survey of Snorri's work in English is Marlene Ciklamini, *Snorri Sturluson* (Boston: Twayne, 1978), a work which, however, has received a mixed critical reception (see Lindow, 33 and n.24).

26. Quotations from *Gylfaginning* will be from the selection edited by Anne Holtsmark and Jon Helgason, *Snorri Sturluson, Edda: Gylfaginning og Prosafortellingene av Skáldskaparamál* (Copenhagen: Ejnar Munksgaard, 1950), with translations (unless otherwise noted) from Jean I. Young, *The Prose Edda of Snorri Sturluson* (Berkeley: Univ. of California Press, 1954). Quotations from *Skáldskaparamál* will be from Finnur Jónsson, ed., *Snorri Sturluson Edda* (Copenhagen, 1900), with translations from Faulkes (note 24).

27. Holtsmark and Helgason (note 26), 49; Young (note 26), 69.

28. Burkert (note 13), 89–90, and the extended n.29 to texts and scholarship on the Greek, Latin, Hittite, and Germanic traditions.

29. J.-L. Durand, "Greek Animals: Toward a Typology of Edible Bodies," in Vernant (note 14), 87–118, this quotation from 103. See, too, Claude Lévi-Strauss, *The Origin of Table Manners*, trans. John and Dorreen Weightman (New York: Harper and Row, 1978), 471–93, who argues that the distinction between boiling and roasting signifies the difference between culture (that is, cooking with implements) and nature (cooking without).

30. Jan de Vries (note 19), 1:419 and n.1.

31. This and the following quotations in this paragraph are from Burkert (note 13), 37.

32. Burkert, 6, 13.

33. For the literary genealogy of Skrýmir, and the reconstructions of a legend surrounding his encounter with Thor, see Lorenz (note 25), 529–31; de Vries (note 19), 2:143–45; Detlef Brennecke, "Gab es eine *Skrýmiskviða*," *Arkiv för Nordisk Filologi* 96 (1981): 1–8; and Michael Chesnutt, "The Beguiling of Þórr," in McTurk and Wawn (note 14), 35–63 (who makes claims for the roots of this cluster of stories in the *Gylfaginning* in the traditions of Celtic mythology).

34. On the flyting as a genre and the critical appropriateness of that term, see Carol J. Clover, "The Germanic Context of the Unferp Episode," *Speculum* 55 (1980): 444–68, and Ward Parks, *Verbal Duelling in Heroic Narrative* (Princeton: Princeton Univ. Press, 1990). On the status of the *Harbarðzlioð* in this generic context, see Clover, "*Harbarðzlioð* as Generic Farce," *Scandinavian Studies* 51 (1979): 124–45, and the response of Marcel Bax and Tineke Padmos, "Two Types of Verbal Duelling in Old Icelandic: The Interactional Structure of the *Senna* and the *Mannjafnaðr* in *Harbarðzlioð*," *Scandinavian Studies* 55 (1983): 149–74.

35. Harbarðzlioð, in *Edda, Die Lieder des Codex Regius nebst verwandten Denkmalern,* ed. Gustav Neckel, 4th ed., rev. Hans Kuhn (Heidelberg: Carl Winter, 1962), stanza 26. Translation from Patricia Terry, *Poems of the Elder Edda* (Philadelphia: Univ. of Pennsylvania Press, 1990), 61.

36. *Lokasenna,* in Neckel (note 35), stanza 60. Translation from Terry (note 35), 82. I have altered Terry's translation of the last line of the *Lokasenna* stanza to make it echo precisely her translation of the third line of the *Harbarðzlioð* stanza, for the two lines in Old Norse are identical.

37. From Young (note 26), 73–74. The entire episode at Utgarð summarized here can be found on 73–78.

38. On the nature of Utgarð, and in particular, on the figure of Utgarð-Loki as either the transformed Skrýmir himself or as an antitype of Loki (who would thus be, in effect, the correspondingly named Ása-Loki), see the commentary and review of scholarship in Lorenz (note 25), 533–34.

39. Young (note 26), 78.

40. Faulkes (note 24), 64; Jónsson (note 26), 74.

41. Faulkes, 132. "Hvernig er ókend setning skáldskapar?—Svá, at nefna hvern hlut sem heitir" (Jónsson [note 26], 126).

42. "How shall the Sky be referred to? By calling it Ymir's skull and hence giant's skull ... " (Faulkes, 88; "Hvernig skal kenna himininn?—Svá, at kalla hann Ymis haus ok Þar af jotuns haus ...," [Jónsson, 90]); "How shall the earth be referred to? By calling it Ymir's flesh ... (Faulkes, 90; "Hvernig skal jorð kenna?—Svá, at kalla hana Ymis hold ... ," [Jónsson, 92]); "How shall the sea be referred to? By calling it Ymir's blood, ... (Faulkes, 92; "Hvernig skal sæ kenna?—Svá at kalla hann Ymis blóð ... ," [Jónsson, 92]).

43. See Faulkes, 153–54. For the former: "Munn skal svá kenna, at kalla land eða hús tungu eða tanna ... " (Jónsson, 145). For the latter: "Hond má kalla jorð vápna eða hlífa, við axlar ok ermar ... [and "allegorically," *í nygorvingum,*] ... bognauð" (Jónsson, 146).

44. As, for example, when he interrupts the narrative of his success with the statement, "Wyrd oft nereð / unfægne eorl, Þonne his ellen deah!" (572b–73) [Fate often saves the undoomed man when his courage is great].

45. "Where nature is malevolent and chaotic, artifice is reassuring.... The man-made wall, the road, the ship, the hall, the human clothing and armor are not only practically useful but also are comforting symbols of the ability of man, through skill and reason, to subdue and control the natural world.... The human essence is to be found in the artificial, and the works of men's hands not only express but actually help implement their desire for rational control" (Robinson [note 8], 71, 74). For a somewhat different critical perspective on the role of artifice and ornament in *Beowulf,* see Parks (note 5), 12–13.

46. On the range and meanings of *searo-* compounds in Old English see Paul B. Taylor, "*Searoniðas*: Old Norse Magic and Old English Verse," *Studies in Philology* 80 (1983): 109–25, and Stephen Barney, *Word-Hoard,* 2d ed. (New Haven: Yale Univ. Press, 1985), under the word *searu.*

47. I have discussed at length the semantic resonances of the word *orðonc* and the relationship between craft and verbal riddling signaled by this word and its compounds in *Literacy and Power* (note 5), 120–22, 185–87.

48. Head and hand are apposed again when Beowulf tells of his fight with Grendel's mother and the severing of *her* head:

> Þlær unc hwile wæs *hand* gemæne;
> holm heolfre weoll, ond ic *heafde* becearf
> in ðam guðsele Grendeles modor
> eacnum ecgum; (2137–40a; emphases added)

[For some time there was the sharing of hands to us (we were locked in hand-to-hand combat); the water welled with gore, and in the war-hall I cut off the head of Grendel's mother with a great sword.] Beowulf's unsuccessful encounter with the dragon also brings together the two terms. His sword sticks in the monster's head ("hyt on heafolan stod," 2679b), then breaks, and the poet comments that the hero's hand was too strong here ("wæs sio hond to strong," 2684b).

49. This and the following three sentences are adapted from my *Literacy and Power* (note 5), 184–85.

50. Faulkes (note 24), 64; Jónsson (note 26), 74.

51. Clover (note 25). See, too, the remarks in Lindow, "Riddles, Kennings, and the Complexity of Skaldic Poetry" (note 22), on the need for a courtly, initiated audience for skaldic wordplay and on the ways in which such wordplay "explores the semantic boundaries of Old Norse" (320). My claims for the affiliations between Beowulf's wordplay and the tricks of skaldic poetry, however, are by no means designed to efface the rich tradition of paronomasia in Old English verse. Puns have long been recognized as central to the enigmatic and the hermeneutic traditions of early English vernacular versemaking; see, for example, Fred C. Robinson, "The Artful Ambiguities in the Old English 'Book-Moth' Riddle," in *Anglo-Saxon Poetry: Essays in Appreciation*, ed. Lewis E. Nicholson and Dolores W. Frese (Notre Dame: Univ. of Notre Dame Press, 1975), 355–62, and Roberta Frank, "Some Uses of Paronomasia in Old English Scriptural Verse," *Speculum* 47 (1972): 207–26. My point here, rather, is that the specific combination of etymological name play and allusions to the giant's glove locate Beowulf's verbal fillips with the Norse traditions. My argument about Beowulf's performance also challenges the assumptions of Laurence N. De Looze, "Frame Narratives and Fictionalization: Beowulf as Narrator," *Texas Studies in Language and Literature* 26 (1984): 145–56, reprinted in R. D. Fulk, ed., *Interpretations of Beowulf* (Bloomington: Indiana Univ. Press, 1991), 242–50, who claims that Beowulf's first act of "fictionalizing" (that is, not simply inventing details and events but constructing a self-consciously shaped literary narrative) does not take place until his report of Haethcyn and Herebeald and the story of the father witnessing the hanging of his son (lines 2425–62a).

52. Clover, 64, 81.

53. Burkert (note 13), 16, 40.

54. Joseph Bosworth and T. Northcote Toller, *An Anglo-Saxon Dictionary* (London: Oxford Univ. Press, 1898), and T. Northcote Toller, *An Anglo-Saxon Dictionary Supplement* (Oxford: Clarendon Press, 1921), under *fælsian* and *gefælsian*. See, too, the discussion in Lars-G. Hallander, *Old English Verbs in -Sian* (Stockholm: Almqvist and Wiksell, 1966), 333–35, who suggests etymological links with other Germanic forms, positing a West Germanic adjective **faili-* or **failiia-* "faithful, secure, protected [in a religious sense?]" (335). The verb is restricted to poetry. In addition to *Beowulf*, it appears as follows in the poetic corpus (all line references are to the editions in George Philip Krapp and E. V. K. Dobbie, ed., *The Anglo-Saxon Poetic Records*, 6 vols. [New York: Columbia Univ. Press, 1931–53]): *Christ* (144, 320), *Fates of the Apostles* (66), and Riddle 83 (4). *Gefelsode* glosses *expiavit* and *fælsende* glosses *lustrans* in the glossaries preserved in British Library MS Cotton Cleopatra A.III (Hallander, 334). It appears to be the vernacular equivalent of *salvare* in the antiphon that stands behind the passage in *Christ* 143–44 (Hallander, 333 n.1).

55. For a review of the uses of the word *tacn* in the poem, with special reference to its application to the severed arm and head of Grendel in Beowulf's own accounts of his battles, see Godfrey (note 4), 1–5.

56. But E. B. Irving, Jr., notes that "the phrase *swaðe weardade* cannot be easily translated into modern English, but literally, of course, it means 'guarded [his] track,' and I

think it possible here that Grendel's right hand is represented as serving as a rear guard to cover his retreat" (*A Reading of Beowulf* [New Haven: Yale Univ. Press, 1968], reprinted as "The Text of Fate," in Fulk [note 51], this quotation from 183–84).

57. King Alfred quoted in Dorothy Whitelock, ed., *Sweet's Anglo-Saxon Reader*, 15th ed. (Oxford: Oxford Univ. Press, 1967), 6. For a discussion of the hunting imagery embedded in this passage, and its relevance to the larger political project of the *Preface* to the *Pastoral Care*, see T. A. Shippey, "Wealth and Wisdom in King Alfred's *Preface* to the Old English *Pastoral Care*," *English Historical Review* 94 (1979): 346–55, esp. his remarks on 348.

58. The word *swaþu* and its neuter equivalent *swæð* appear in the following Riddles (numbering, lineation, and solutions from George Phillip Krapp and E. V. K. Dobbie, ed., *The Exeter Book, The Anglo-Saxon Poetic Records*, vol. 3 [New York: Columbia Univ. Press, 1936]): Riddle 21 (6, 10, plow); Riddle 51 (3, pen and fingers); Riddle 75 (1, unsolved); Riddle 95 (12, perhaps riddle itself; Williamson [note 22] solves it as book). The phrase "on swape" means "behind" in Riddle 15 (25), as does the corresponding phrase "on last(e)" in Riddle 1 (51), Riddle 13 (11), and Riddle 72 (14). The compound *sweartlast*, "black-tracked," appears in Riddle 26 (11). For discussion of this imagery as it pertains to the riddles on the scriptorium, and their sources in the Latin *Aenigmata* of Aldhelm (*Aenigma* 59) and Eusebius (*Aenigma* 35), see Williamson (note 22), 294.

59. The phrase also reappears in line 2164, where it seems to mean "followed behind."

60. Much recent *Beowulf* criticism has evinced a fascination with the fragmentary, the symbolic, and the violent in the poem. For a variety of perspectives, see Marijane Osborn, "The Great Feud: Scriptural History and Strife in *Beowulf*," *PMLA* 93 (1978): 973–81; Gillian Overing (note 9), 33–67; Allen J. Frantzen (note 25), esp. 184–90; Near (note 25); and Parks (note 5). For such critics, too, the runically inscribed sword-hilt that Beowulf recovers from Grendel's mere and presents to Hrothgar (1687–99) serves as the nexus of the violent, the interpretive, and the cultural for the poem. Michael Near explicitly and eloquently associates the hilt with Grendel's head as constituting a "poetic network of literal and psychological submersions, private confines, silent figures, violent antitheses. Beowulf has reemerged from the recesses of Grendel's world with a speechless remnant most characteristic of the monster's inner isolation, his severed head, and the voiceless remnant of his unspoken language, the frozen text of the severed sword hilt" (325). My own contribution to this debate on the nature and function of the sword hilt was made in *Literacy and Power* (note 5), 158–94, and is qualified in "*Beowulf* and Critical Theory," in *A Beowulf Handbook*, ed. John D. Niles and Robert Bjork (Lincoln: Univ. of Nebraska Press, forthcoming), where I argue that Beowulf's recovery of the inscribed hilt serves as the narrative model for the modern critic's recovery of the "textualized" *Beowulf* from the recesses of oralist archaism and Tolkienian appreciation.

61. Bynum, "In Praise of Fragmentation: History in the Comic Mode" (note 6), 11–26; these quotations from 24, 25.

ANDY ORCHARD

Psychology and Physicality:
The Monsters of Beowulf

The central importance of the monsters in *Beowulf* has been underlined many times since J. R. R. Tolkien first highlighted their significance, arguing that in the struggles of Beowulf against his various monstrous foes the Poet wished to portray the noble image of 'man at war with the hostile world, and his inevitable overthrow in Time'.[1] Kenneth Sisam took a more sanguine view, suggesting that 'the monsters Beowulf kills are inevitably evil and hostile because a reputation for heroism is not made by killing creatures that are believed to be harmless or beneficent—sheep for instance'.[2] Both scholars, however, shared the now-common opinion that the monsters in *Beowulf* are crucial to the very structure of the poem, and in his investigation of larger rhetorical patterns in *Beowulf* John Niles similarly suggests that the poet produced a complex ring-composition focusing in turn on each of the three main monster-fights, which he characterises as 'the most important events of [the poet's] story'.[3] The same notion is implicit in Dorothy Whitelock's suggestion that the poem 'could easily have been delivered in three sittings'.[4]

Equally important, moreover, is the poet's clear intention to connect each of the three main monster-fights through shared themes and structure. As Sisam has noted, Beowulf's battle with Grendel is a one fall, one submission, and one knock-out bout, whilst the fight with Grendel's mother has quite a

From *Pride and Prodigies: Studies in the Monsters of the* Beowulf-*Manuscript*, pp. 28–57. © 1995 by Andy Orchard.

different pace.[5] Here we have a two-fall fight, with first the monstrous female, and then the man (quite literally) on top.[6] Likewise Beowulf tries two swords, and Grendel's mother two weapons also, her cruel knife (*seax*) and her hideous nails. The dragon-fight, by contrast, is in three rounds, clearly marked off by narratorial enumeration of each phase of the attack, as the dragon surges forward a second time (*oðre siðe*, line 2670) and a third (*þriddan siðe*, line 2688).[7] The level of difficulty experienced by Beowulf increases with each battle; Grendel causes comparatively few problems, whilst his mother, whom we are explicitly told had less terrible might (lines 1282–4), very nearly succeeds in killing Beowulf, and the dragon finally proves fatal. There is a commensurate increase in the amount of armoury brought to bear against the male (no weapons), the bestial female (two swords), and the serpent (two swords and a shield), as Beowulf steadily shifts from a primarily defensive role to an aggressive one, motivated to varying degrees in each of his battles by thoughts of glory, vengeance, and treasure.

These structural and thematic links between each of the three main monster-battles are underpinned by further parallels between successive conflicts which bind the individual episodes together. Thus Grendel and his mother are closely connected not simply by the family relationship between the monsters, but by their human shape, their cannibalistic acts, their shared dwelling, and their decapitation. Just as Grendel attacks Heorot by night, and fatally seizes Hondscio, so too does his avenging mother undertake a nocturnal raid to Heorot to carry off Æschere to his doom.[8] In the same way that Beowulf's wrestling-match with Grendel takes place within the confines of the hall, Grendel's mother comes to grips with Beowulf inside her own cavernous guest-hall.[9] Similar narrative parallels connect the episode of Grendel's mother and the dragon; in both it is the monster who initially is the aggrieved party, and who suffers loss; in both the monsters inhabit a waterside home, from which light shines; in both Beowulf requires two blades to despatch his foe; and in both Beowulf is accompanied by a group of retainers, only some of whom prove faithful.

Moreover, despite the clear antagonism between the worlds of monsters and men, there is, as in the *Passion of Saint Christopher* and *Judith* in the same manuscript, something deeply human about the 'monsters'. All are given human attributes at some stage, and the poet even goes so far as to evoke our sympathy for their plight. We might illustrate this first with reference to perhaps the least human of the monsters, the dragon.[10] When the unprovoked theft of treasure from the barrow by an unwelcome visitor is reported, we are presented with events from the dragon's perspective (*Beowulf*, lines 2287–9):

> Then the dragon awoke, strife was renewed; he hastened along the
> rock, the stout-hearted one discovered the footprints of the foe.

Here the stout-hearted one (*stearcheort*) is the dragon and the foe (*feond*) the human plunderer of his hoard. An exact reversal is seen in the dragon-fight itself, in which Beowulf, on the only other occasion in the poem on which the word is used, is described as 'stout-hearted' (*stearcheort*, line 2552), and the dragon is the 'foe' (*feond* line 2706). In the first instance we see things from the monster's point of view; the dragon is the aggrieved party. In a similar way our sympathy is evoked for Grendel's mother, driven to avenge the killing of her son by motives which would tug at the hearts of any Germanic audience. Her active engagement in the feud contrasts sharply with the passive impotence of other (human) mothers in the poem, notably Wealhtheow and Hildeburh, whose tale is told immediately before that of Grendel's mother herself.[11] Like the dragon Grendel's mother is seen as (at first) the victim of an unprovoked attack. Twice her journey is described as a 'sorrowful journey' (*sorhfulne sið*, line 1278; *siðode sorhfull*, line 2119), and we are offered the monster's perspective again. In the same way the poet explicitly mentions that Grendel's mother, like Hrothgar and Beowulf, ruled her mere for fifty years before she (like them) suffered at the hands of an unwelcome guest.[12] Her underwater dwelling is described in human, almost homely terms, as a 'roofed hall' (*hrofsele*, line 1515), albeit a hateful dwelling (*niðsele*, line 1513), and as a 'hall' (*reced*, line 1572) whose walls, like those of Heorot itself, were bedecked with weapons.[13] Likewise the dragon inhabits an 'earth-house' (*eorðhus*, line 2232) also described in the same language of the hall (*eorðsele*, lines 2410 and 2515; *eorðreced*, line 2719); the same word *dryhtsele* ('noble hall'), unattested outside *Beowulf*, applies equally to Heorot (lines 485 and 767) and the dragon's lair (line 2320).

But of all the monsters, it is Grendel who is most consistently depicted in human terms, particularly in the constant evocation of exile imagery to describe his plight.[14] He is, as successively fuller descriptions tell us, an 'unfortunate man' (*wonsæli wer*, line 105), a 'man deprived of joys' (*rinc ... dreamum bedæled*, lines 720–1; cf. line 1275), who 'wretchedly trod the paths of exile in the form of a man' (*earmsceapen /on weres wæstmum wræclastas træd*, lines 1351–2).[15] Twice he is described as *se mansceaða* (lines 712 and 737), in contexts which suggest that the poet may be playing on the two senses of the homographs *man* ('crime', 'wickedness') and *man* ('man'), especially since both terms are twice found linked by alliteration in *Beowulf*, notably on the first occasion on which the word *mansceaða* is employed (lines 110 and 712). Grendel is certainly 'the wicked destroyer', but he is also both 'the destroyer of men', and 'the man-shaped destroyer'.

Hrothgar makes a similar point concerning the human forms of both Grendel and his mother in his first description of them (lines 1345–57):

> I have heard the locals, my people, hall-counsellors, tell that they saw two such mighty wanderers in the wastes inhabit the moors, alien spirits, of whom one was, so far as they could most easily tell the semblance of a woman. The other wretched one whom, in past days, dwellers in the land named Grendel, trod exile-paths in human form, except that he was greater than any other man. They did not know of any father, whether any such had been begotten of secret spirits.

The physical manifestation of the wandering Grendel's extraordinary nature is his size: 'he was greater than any other man' (line 1353); little wonder that in the waterbound lair that Grendel shares with his mother, Beowulf should discover in his time of need a monstrous sword of suitable stature: 'the choicest of weapons, except that it was greater than anyone else could wield in battle-play' (lines 1559–61).[16]

Such a substantial enemy requires a hero of comparable greatness, and it is interesting to note that another third party, the coast-guard, gives his first impression of Beowulf himself in rather similar terms (lines 247–51):

> Never have I seen a mightier noble on earth, a warrior in armour, than is one of you; he is no hall-retainer made worthy with weapons, unless his appearance belies him, his peerless face.

An intriguing number of intimate links between Beowulf and his most famous foe may be suggested. We hear that in one of Grendel's raids on Heorot he had carried off thirty men (lines 122–3);[17] likewise Beowulf is described by Hrothgar as having the strength of thirty men in his hand-grip (lines 379–81), and in escaping from the scene of Hygelac's death he swims away carrying the armour of just this number of men (lines 2361–2).[18] In this same incident Beowulf is described as a 'wretched and solitary figure' (*earm anhaga*, line 2368), a term which might well have been used of Grendel, the 'wretch' (*earmsceapen*, line 1351) twice described as a 'solitary traveller' (*angenga*, lines 165 and 449).[19] So, Grendel on his murderous trips to Heorot is described as a 'hall-thegn' (*healðegn*, line 142), just like Beowulf and his men (*healðegnas*, line 719), and in their fighting both Beowulf and Grendel are linked as 'hall-dwellers', equally enraged (*yrre wæron begen, / reþe renweardas*, lines 769–70).[20] The fury experienced by both Beowulf and Grendel is a further factor which links the combatants; Beowulf waits for Grendel's arrival 'furious at heart' (*bolgenmod*, line 709), while the door of Heorot collapses at Grendel's touch 'since he was furious' (*ða (ha ge)bolgen wæs*, line 723); it might be noted that precisely the same reason is given for Beowulf's ability to overwhelm Grendel's mother in their first grappling (*þa he gebolgen wæs*, line 1539), and that throughout *Beowulf* the only figures who are described as 'furious' in this way (*gebolgen* or *bolgenmod*) are Beowulf, in each of his three monster-battles (lines 709, 1539, 2401, and 2550), Grendel (line 723), the monsters at the mere (line 1431), the fallen prince Heremod (line 1713),[21] and the dragon (lines 2220 and 2304). Beowulf, moreover, is described on his visit to the home of Grendel's mother as a 'hall-guest' (*selegyst*, line 1545), who in his encounter with the monster is 'despairing of his life' (*aldres orwena*, line 1565), much as Grendel the 'hall-thegn' (*healðegn*, line 142) in Heorot is equally 'despairing of his life' (*aldres orwena*, line 1002).[22] Beowulf fights monsters because only then is he well-matched. When he does face human champions, like the Frankish Dæghrefn, his methods are distinctly inhuman, one might almost say monstrous; Dæghrefn is simply crushed to death (lines 2498–508).

Again, it has often been noticed that the poet explicitly links Beowulf and the monsters that he fights by the description *aglæca* (or *æglæca*), for which Klaeber offers the creative series of translations 'wretch,' 'monster', 'demon', 'fiend', 'warrior', 'hero',[23] and which is used of Grendel (lines 159, 425, 433, 592, 646, 732, 739, 816, 989, 1000, and 1269), his mother (who is described as an *aglæcwif*, line 1259), the dragon (lines 2520, 2534, 2557, and 2905), the sea-monsters (line 556), and Sigemund the dragon-slayer (line 893).[24] In his account of Beowulf's descent into the monster-mere the poet uses the term ambiguously (line 1512), to designate either the monsters inhabiting the mere or (more likely) Beowulf himself, whilst during the description of the dragon-fight the poet speaks in one half-line of Beowulf and the dragon together as *ða aglæcean* (line 2592). Sherman Kuhn has suggested that the word *aglæca*, which occurs perhaps thirty-six times in extant Old English verse, derives from a very early borrowing of the prehistoric form of the Irish *óclach*, *ócláech*, and meant 'fighter', 'warrior'.[25] A perhaps more likely proposed etymology connects the first element of *aglæca* with a Gothic cognate *agis* ('terror', 'fright'), Old High German *egiso*, Old English *ege* and *egesa* ('awe', 'terror'),[26] and the second element with Old English *lacan* ('to move quickly').[27] The meaning of the term would therefore be 'the awe-inspiring one', 'the formidable one',[28] and this sense best answers to the sole example of the word in Old English prose, where Byrhtferth of Ramsey, with no apparent trace of irony, describes the Venerable Bede as *Beda, se aglæca lareow* ('Bede, the awe-inspiring teacher').[29] Whatever the precise connotations of the term, the fact that the poet employs the word to designate not only monsters but monster-slayers clearly underlines the linked contrasts between the worlds of monsters and men which run throughout the poem and the manuscript.

The conflict and comparison between monsters and men is far from being the only such thematic contrast which runs through *Beowulf*; Tolkien believed that the entire structure of the poem was predicated on the contrast between Youth and Age which is so apparent in Beowulf's own biography,[30] and such a technique of apposition, Tolkien argued, is implicit in the very structure of the Old English poetic line.[31] A similar kind of contrast has been perceived in the way in which the explicit action in *Beowulf* is matched by a graphic series of interior conflicts, leading Michael Lapidge to doubt that the poem can really be described as 'heroic' in any traditional sense,[32] while R. E. Kaske, by contrast, in highlighting the central importance in *Beowulf* of what he describes as 'the great heroic ideal of *sapientia et fortitudo*' ('wisdom and strength'),[33] underlines the differences between the physical and the psychological worlds which play such a large part in the poem, and are particularly important in the poet's developing depictions of the monsters.

The justly-celebrated portrayal of Grendel's approach to Heorot, which has been described as a 'hair-raising description of death on the march',[34] introduces just this distinction between the physical and the psychological worlds, as well as illustrating a number of the other contrasts raised, and deserves quotation as a fine example of the poet's art (lines 702–27):[35]

> Then there came in the dark night the shadow-walker stalking. The warriors slept, who ought to hold that gabled hall all except one. It was known to men that the fiendish [or 'sinful'] destroyer could not drag them under shadows against the Creator's will; but he, vigilant, in malice against the foe, awaited with swollen heart the joining of battle. Then there came from the moors, under misty slopes, Grendel approaching: he bore God's anger, the wicked destroyer intended to ensnare one of mankind in that high hall. He walked under clouds until he could most clearly perceive the wine-building the gold-hall of men, adorned with plate. That was not the first time that he had sought out Hrothgar's home; but never before nor afterwards in the days of his life did he come upon a harsher fate! Then there came travelling to that building the man deprived of joys. The door promptly sprang apart, secure with forged bands, when he touched it with his hands. The one intent on evil, since he was swollen with rage, tore open

the building's mouth. Swiftly after that, the fiend stepped onto
the decorated floor, advanced angry in spirit, from his eyes there
stood, most like aflame, an unlovely light.

What is most intriguing about this passage, as Alain Renoir has argued, is
the way in which the poet produces a growing sense of terror by offering
alternatively the viewpoint of the approaching monster and the waiting
warrior.[36] It is important to the purpose of the poem that up to this point
we can have no clear idea what Grendel looks like, since nothing in the
preceding verses has offered any substantial physical depiction at all; as
Michael Lapidge has argued: 'it is because the monster lies beyond our
comprehension, because we cannot visualise it at all, that its approach is one
of the most terrifying moments in English literature'.[37] Each repetition of
com (lines 702, 710, and 720) brings Grendel closer, a shadowy figure stalking
out of the darkness, away from the misty moors, and up to the hall. A similar
method of (in cinematographic terms) zooming in on the subject is employed
elsewhere in *Beowulf* to describe the approach of Beowulf and his men both
to Denmark, after their sea-voyage (lines 221–3),[38] and to Heorot, after
their trip to the monster-mere (lines 1623–44).[39] The same cinematographic
technique is employed elsewhere in the *Beowulf*-manuscript, notably in
Judith (lines 200–35), where the advance of the Jews into battle is ominously
depicted by repetition of the word *stopon* (lines 200, 212, and 227).[40]

Grendel is initially depicted here as a 'shadow-walker' (*sceadugenga*,
line 703), a description which recalls his earlier portrayal as a 'spirit' (*gast*,
cf. line 133) or 'death-shadow' (*deapscua*, line 160), and his later depiction
as an 'alien spirit' (*ellorgast*, line 807).[41] The word may well also signify, as
Stanley Greenfield has suggested, 'Grendel's outcast state, as one deprived
of God's light';[42] such a state is specified later in the same passage, with the
chilling statement that Grendel 'bore God's anger' (*Godes yrre bær*, line 711).
Indeed, the emotions of anger and malice are most explicit throughout this
passage;[43] the unspoken terror is implicit. But as Grendel comes closer to
Heorot, he becomes identified in successively more concrete and corporeal
terms. The precise sense of the term *s[c]ynscapa* (line 707) in this passage is a
matter for debate; the alliteration seems to demand the otherwise unattested
scynscapa,[44] deriving from the noun *scinna* ('sprite'),[45] and presumably
meaning 'demonic foe', a designation which, like his description both earlier
and later in the poem as a 'giant' or 'ogre' (*þyrs*, cf. line 426; *eoten*, line 761),
identifies Grendel with the wicked creatures of popular germanic legend,
but the manuscript clearly reads *synscapa*, as at line 801, a word which may
carry the double sense of 'persistent destroyer' or 'sinful destroyer'.[46] Like
s[c]ynscapa, the related term *manscaða* (line 712), which is used in turn of all

three of Beowulf's main monstrous foes,[47] carries a clear physical threat, and it is at precisely this point in the passage when we are first made conscious of Grendel's thoughts and impressions: he has intentions (*mynte*, line 712) and perceptions (*gearwost wisse*, line 715; *gesohte*, line 717; *fand*, line 719) of which we are increasingly aware as he approaches the hall. That Grendel is a sentient human(-shaped) being is made still more apparent when he finally reaches Heorot, and is described as a 'man', albeit one 'deprived of joys' (*rinc ... dreamum bedæled*, lines 720–1). As with his portrayal as a spirit and a sprite in this passage, the depiction of Grendel as a man is not unique; elsewhere he is described with a range of words which align him with men, such as *wer* (line 105), *guma* (lines 973 and 1682), *hilderinc* (line 986), and *hæleþ* (cf. line 2072).[48] What is important here is the effect; the threefold repetition of *com* marks off the passage into individual sections where we are progressively offered the perspective of the external narrator, the monster himself, and the people inside the hall, as Grendel glides closer, becoming ever more physically real and apparent until, ripping open the mouth of the hall in a fitting prelude to his own cannibalistic frenzy,[49] he stands, eyes blazing, on the decorated floor. What bursts into Heorot is not a nightmare,[50] but a monstrous terror made flesh. As Tolkien notes: 'in *Beowulf* the weight is on the physical side: Grendel does not vanish into the pit when grappled. He must be slain by plain prowess.'[51]

The description of Grendel's approach to Heorot introduces him as a physical character within the poem; previously he had been little more than a shadowy wanderer (*sceadugenga*, line 703), while subsequently we learn much about his physical traits, notably his enormous size (line 1353), so much so that it takes four men to carry his head (lines 1634–9), his steely nails (line 985), his feasting on human flesh and blood (lines 742–5), his habitat (lines 1345–72), and his invulnerability to iron weapons (lines 802–3 and 987–9).[52] Certainly his fight with Beowulf is undeniably physical. The hall is wrecked, joints crack, fingers burst, sinews spring apart, and Grendel, screaming in agony, flees.[53] The syntax and diction of the portrayal of the fight itself is suitably brisk and vivid, and serves to emphasise still further the link between the antagonists; as Katherine O'Brien O'Keeffe notes: 'not only does the poem predicate a connection between Grendel and the men he approaches, but as he comes closer to Beowulf, the language, syntax, and management of perspective in the scene blur the distinction between the two adversaries'.[54]

Grendel and Beowulf meet in an atmosphere in which the distinctions between man and monster have been deliberately obscured, and in a twilight domain where the mark of the assailant is measured as much in terror and anger as in corporeal harm. An identical contrast between the physical and psychological worlds is implicit elsewhere in the poet's depiction of the monsters, for example in Hrothgar's vivid description of the monster-mere (lines 1357–79):

> They dwell in a secret land, wolf-slopes, windy headlands, dangerous fen-tracts, where the mountain-stream goes down under the head-lands' mists, the flood under the ground. It is not far from here in the tally of miles, where that mere stands, over which hang frosty groves, a wood firm-rooted overshadows the water. There one can see each night a dreadful wonder, fire on the flood. No one lives so wise of the sons of men that knows the bottom. Even though a heath-stepper, driven by the hounds, a hart, strong in its horns, may seek the wooded forest, chased from afar, he will give up his life, his spirit on the brink, rather than plunge in to save his head; that is no pleasant place! From there the tumult of the waves rise up dark to the clouds, when the wind stirs up hateful storms, until the sky turns grim, the heavens weep. Now once again is a solution to he sought from you alone. You do not yet know the dwelling-place, the dangerous spot where you can find the sinful creature. Seek if you dare!

The poet adds further details to this picture in a later description of the expedition undertaken to the mere (lines 1408–17):

> Then the sons of princes passed over steep, rocky slopes, thin courses, narrow single tracks, unknown paths, precipitous crags, many dwellings of water-monsters; [Beowulf] went on ahead with a few wise companions to view the place: until suddenly he perceived mountainous trees towering over the grey rock, a joyless wood; water stood beneath, bloody and disturbed.

Richard Morris was the first to point out that this combined description is remarkably close to that found in Blickling Homily XVI,[55] where Saint Paul has a vision of Hell:[56]

> So Saint Paul was looking at the northern part of this world, where all the waters go down, and he saw there above the water a certain grey rock, and there had grown north of that rock very frosty woods, and there were dark mists, and under that rock was a dwelling-place of water-monsters and wolves; and he saw that on that cliff there hung in those icy woods many black souls, tied by their hands, and their foes, in the guise of water-monsters,

were gripping them like greedy wolves, and the water was black
underneath that rock, and between that cliff and the water was
a drop of twelve miles, and when the branches broke, the souls
who hung on those branches went down, and the sea-monsters
snatched them.

That several of the physical features of the home of Grendel and his mother
should match those of the Otherworld is scarcely surprising, given the
poet's constant identification of Grendel with demonic forces. Elsewhere
he is described as a 'fiend in hell' (*feond on helle*, line 101), a 'captive of hell'
(cf. *helle hæfton*, line 788), and a 'hellish spirit' (*helle gast*, line 1274); he and
his mother are together called 'devils' (cf. *deofla*, line 1680), while Grendel,
desperate to escape from Beowulf's clutches, is said to want 'to flee into
darkness, to seek the company of devils' (*wolde on heolstor fleon, /secan deofla
gedræg*, lines 755–6).[57] Many of Grendel's titles, moreover, recall those of
the devil, such as 'enemy of mankind' (*feond mancynnes*, lines 164 and 1276),
'God's opponent' (*Godes andsaca*, lines 786 and 1682), and 'ancient foe'
(*ealdgewinna*, line 1776).[58] More importantly, Grendel is called by the poet,
although not by the characters in the poem, a 'heathen' (*hæþen*, cf. lines 852
and 986), whose proper domain, in Christian eyes, is hell, as is made plain
by the poet's bald statement that 'joyless in the fen-refuge, he laid aside his
life, his heathen soul: there hell received him' (lines 850–2).[59] What makes
the association particularly striking are the verbal similarities between the
two descriptions in the homily and the poem, which have been noted many
times, and might be summarised as follows:[60]

Blickling XVI	*Beowulf*
þaer ealle wætero niðergewltað	ðær fyrgenstream … niþer gewiteð
	(lines 1359–60)
ofer ðaem wætere sumne hárne stán	fyrgenbeamas ofer harne stan
	(lines 1414–15)
of ðæm stáne awexene swiðe	ofer þæm hongiað hrinde bearwas
hrimige bearwas	(line 1363)
ðær wæron þystrogenipo	under næssa genipu (line 1360)
niccra eardung	nicorhusa fela (line 1411)
7 þæt wæter wærs sweart under	wæter under stod dreorig and
	gedrefed
þæm clife neoðan	(lines 1416–17)

Several scholars have seen a direct literary link between the two passages;[61]
debate has continued over whether the *Beowulf*-poet borrowed from the

Blickling Homily,[62] or vice versa.[63] Most recently the old notion that both authors were drawing on a third, intermediary, and vernacular source, originally favoured by Klaeber, amongst others,[64] has found increasing support; Charles D. Wright, in the course of a comprehensive discussion, considers a series of minor details in the descriptions in *Beowulf* and Blickling Homily XVI, and concludes that both authors were drawing independently on a vernacular version of the *Visio S. Pauli*.[65] Hildegard Tristram argues that the description in *Beowulf* 'is wholly traditional and probably borrowed from homiletic writings', but considers that the purely descriptive elements have been deliberately separated from their religious context,[66] and Wright concurs, noting of the *Beowulf*-poet that: 'while retaining the essential configuration, he divests particular elements of their explicitly eschatological reference by literalizing them: his "hell" is still in the north, because that is where the Danes live; his frosty trees, bereft of the souls that once were suspended from their branches, are left to "hang" over the water below; and his water-monsters have been exorcised of their demons'.[67] As we shall see, however, this is not the whole story, the poet of *Beowulf* also introduces eschatological elements into his description, albeit providing them with a naturalistic setting.[68]

In a similar way, it has been suggested that the description of the monster-mere can be compared to a vernacular poetic type-scene, fully integrated into Old English verse, which Donald Fry calls the 'Cliff of Death', and which he traces in three other poems, including 'four basic elements: cliffs, serpents, darkness, and deprivation, and occasionally wolves and wind'.[69] As an example of the theme, Fry cites the account from *Judith*, elsewhere in the *Beowulf*-manuscript, of the fate of Holofernes, who is despatched to damnation in the Old English poem immediately upon decapitation, in a scene which has no parallel in the Vulgate account (lines 111–21):

> The foul trunk lay dead behind, the spirit turned elsewhere under the deep cliff, and was there brought low, tied with torment for ever after, wound round with worms, bound with punishments, cruelly captive in hell-fire after death. He need not hope, enveloped in darkness, that he might pass from there, out of that worm-hall but he must dwell there forever henceforth without end in that dark home, bereft of hopeful joys.

The abrupt transition from Holofernes' tent in the midst of a desert plain, to a dark, seething hell of fire and serpents at the bottom of a cliff can be matched by remarkably similar descriptions of hell in *Christ and Satan* (lines

24–32, 89–105, and 132–6).[70] Of course, the account in Blickling Homily XVI demonstrates all of the same elements too, unless the *nicras* which the homily shares with Beowulf are held to be distinct from the more obviously serpentine 'multitude of worm-kin, wondrous sea-dragons' (*wyrmcynnes fela, sellice sædracan*, lines 1425–6) whom Beowulf and his men encounter at the mere.[71] But such an association would only serve to underline the essential terror of an imaginary and psychological landscape whose different physical features can scarcely be harmonised;[72] Eric Stanley memorably describes the scenery as 'a gallimaufry of devices, each of which is horrific in its associations'.[73]

It is clear that if the poet did borrow part of his conception of the monster-mere from a description of hell as given in a vernacular version of the *Visio S. Pauli*, he has overlaid the original with a number of extra details which lend extraordinary vividness, both physical and psychological, to his own particular depiction. In mentioning that each night a fire is seen on the turbid waters beneath the icy grove, the poet at once goes beyond the *Visio S. Pauli* (and Blickling Homily XVI), and aligns his own picture still further with a number of Insular visions of the Otherworld, where lost souls flit between fire and ice.[74] The particular collocation *fyr on flode* (line 1366) demonstrates further the artistry of the *Beowulf*-poet, who later on in the poem is able to exploit the same alliterative pairing both in his account of Beowulf's descent in the mere itself, when he emerges into the fire-lit hall of Grendel's mother (line 1516), and in Hrothgar's lengthy 'sermon' to Beowulf on his return from the mere, when he is warned of the insecurity of a prosperous earthly life, which can be cut short by a number of unforseen circumstances, including 'fire's grip and flood's surge' (line 1762).[75]

Outside *Beowulf*, combined reference to 'fire and flood' is largely restricted to homiletic prose, specifically apocalyptic visions of the end of the world.[76] In poetry the alliterative pair is found in the Paris Psalter (LXV.11), and in the eschatological *Judgment Day II* (line 166, rendering *fluvius ignivomus*),[77] where again the notion of mingled fire and flood seems particularly suited to Judgment Day themes, as, most spectacularly, in the following passage from *Christ III* (lines 972–88):

> So the greedy spirit searches through the depths; the ravaging flame casts down the high dwellings to the ground through the terror of conflagration; the widely notorious blast, hot and greedy for gore will destroy the whole world. Shattered city-walls will collapse outright; mountains will melt, and high cliffs, which kept the land safe against the floods, firm and stable bulwarks

against the waves, the breaking water. Then the death-flame shall
take every single creature, beasts and birds; the fire-dark flame
shall stalk the land, a seething warrior. Just as water had stirred
the floods, then in a sea of fire sea-fishes will scorch, stopped
from swimming, every sea-creature will fail and die, the water
will burn like wax.

The motif of the burning sea presented here is not very common, but clearly
signifies apocalypse; amongst Insular sources its occurrence has been noted
in the pseudo-Bede *Collectanea*,[78] as well as in several Irish texts, such as the
'Ochtfæochlach Choluim Chille'.[79] In a number of the prose accounts which
link the concepts of fire and flood, the punishing conflagration at the end
of the world is explicitly compared to the Flood which previously swept the
earth,[80] a notion which may ultimately derive from Luke XVII.26 (*Et sicut
factum est in diebus Noe, ita erit in diebus Filii hominis*);[81] Wulfstan makes the
point succinctly:[82]

> And truly just as the Flood came before because of sins, so too
> because of sins a fire will come over mankind and now the time
> is approaching very soon.

The image of apocalyptic cleansing flood and flame in the context of Grendel
and his mother is particularly appropriate; they were, after all, of the doomed
kin of Cain, whom God had purged in the Flood.[83]

Outside homiletic literature, reference to 'fire and flood' are notably
rare; in a land dispute of 968,[84] one party condemns the contentious property
to *fyre oððe flode*, rather than that it should pass to the other claimant, while,
more intriguingly, Cnut's second law-code (set down not long after the
compilation of the *Beowulf*-manuscript) explicitly forbids heathen worship,
which it defines as follows (11 Cnut V.1):[85]

> Heathen practices include the worship of devilish idols, heathen
> gods, the sun or moon, fire or flood, water-surges or stones or
> any kind of trees.

The description of Grendel's mere, combining as it does a number of
the natural elements (fire, flood, water-surges, stones, and trees) which
apparently lent themselves to animistic practice, is a most suitable dwelling
for a such a devilish and heathen spirit; as Richard Schrader has suggested:
'the imaginary scene in Beowulf is not hell itself but a place meant to suggest
the familiar locale of "devil-worship"'.[86]

In this context the possibility of influence from pagan Latin verse on the *Beowulf*-poet has also been raised with respect to the description of the monster-mere, particularly since almost every aspect of the portrayal can be matched elsewhere. Vergil gives a picture of a deep cave by a dark and turbulent lake in a gloomy grove no bird will fly over at the entrance to the Otherworld (*Aeneid* VI. 131–9, 236–42, and 296),[87] and elsewhere compares the fleeing pagan warrior Turnus to a stag pursued by a hound and trapped by a deep-banked river (*Aeneid* XII.749–55).[88] The pagan grove at Massilia is described by Lucan as dark and cold, with gore-spattered and snake-entwined trees where birds would not perch, and into which no wild animals would enter (*Pharsalia* III.399–425 and VI.642–51); Claudian depicts a dark and steaming lake at Aponus (*Carmen* XXVI), in whose depths from time to time can be seen 'ancient spears, royal offerings' (*veteres hastae, regia dona*), as well as a thick grove on the slopes of Etna filled with the victory-spoils of the gods, including giants' heads and the bones of huge serpents, where no Cyclops dares graze his sheep (*De raptu Proserpinae* III.332–56).[89] The works of Vergil and Lucan were certainly known and imitated in Anglo-Saxon England from the time of Aldhelm on; less compelling evidence may imply that some of Claudian's work was also available.[90] The direct or indirect influence of these poets on the *Beowulf*-poet may not be entirely out of the question, though the possibility is remote. The vigour of this Latin poetic tradition is perhaps further reflected in the closest analogue to part of the description in *Beowulf* that has been suggested to date: a much later Latin account of a magical lake into which no wild beast will enter, even if pursued by hounds, which is found in Alexander Neckham's *De laudibus divinae sapientiae*.[91]

Within the *Beowulf*-manuscript itself, of course, and ultimately derived from Latin tradition, we have yet another detailed description of a heathen sacred grove, in the *Letter of Alexander to Aristotle* (§36), where Alexander visits the sacred trees of the Sun and the Moon, and is told that:

> no drop of rain ever came in that land, nor bird, nor wild beast,
> nor did any poisonous snake dare to seek out the holy precincts
> of the Sun and the Moon.

The *Beowulf*-poet may have had a similarly marvellous grove in mind, although there, of course, there were serpents and dragons in abundance (lines 1425–6). Nor, as we shall see, is this the only aspect in which *Alexander's Letter to Aristotle* can be seen to match certain elements of the description of the monster-mere in *Beowulf*. On the edge of a large river full of undrinkable water in the wilderness, Alexander and his men find a cliff edged with huge and towering trees (§12);[92] marching along the river, they come to an island, but when some of Alexander's men attempt to swim across, disaster strikes (§15):

> And when they had swum about a quarter of the river, something terrible happened to them. There appeared a multitude of water-monsters [hippopotami], larger and more terrible in appearance than the elephants, who dragged the men through the watery waves down to the river bottom, and tore them to bloody pieces with their mouths, and snatched them all away so that none of us knew where any of them had gone. Then I was very angry with my guides, who had led us into such danger. I ordered that one hundred and fifty of them be shoved into the river, and as soon as they were in the water-monsters were ready, and dragged them away just as they had done with the others, and the water-monsters seethed up in the river as thick as ants, they were so innumerable. Then I ordered the trumpets to be sounded, and the army to head off.

The sudden appearance of this 'multitude of water-monsters' (*nicra mengeo*), which drag men down to the bottom, is intriguing partly because of the rarity of the term *nicras* in Old English, which, outside *Beowulf* and the *Letter of Alexander to Aristotle* is only found in a prose Life of St Margaret,[93] and in the account of the vision of Saint Paul in Blickling Homily XVI,[94] noted above, but also partly because in Beowulf's accounts of his own exploits, which include killing *nicras* (line 422), 'water-monsters' of the same kind attempt to drag Beowulf himself down to the depths (lines 553–75). Even the trumpets, which Alexander sounds to mark the end of the episode (§17), have an echo in the horns blown at the monster-mere in *Beowulf*, which, however, introduce the action there (lines 1423–5 and 1431–2).[95] Eventually, Alexander and his men are directed to a 'large lake' (*mere*), not far from human habitation,[96] thickly overgrown with trees, and infested with serpents and reptiles (§§16–18); the general resemblance to the monster mere is again intriguing. Still further parallels link the 'monsters' of *Beowulf* and the *Letter of Alexander*; at one point Alexander and his men are surprised by a fearsome creature attacking suddenly from the fens, which is impervious to any weapon, and which devours two of his companions with its sharp teeth (§27):

> Then all the land through which we passed was dried up and marshy, and canes and reeds grew there. Then there came suddenly out of the fen and fastness a beast, and the beast's back was

all studded with pegs like a snood, and the beast had a round head like the moon, and the beast was called *Quasi caput luna* ['moonhead', crocodile], and it had a breast like a sea-monster's breast and it was armed and toothed with hard and large teeth. And that beast slew two of my thegns. And we were unable to wound that beast with spears in any way nor with any kind of weapon, but with difficulty we beat it and subdued it with iron mallets and sledge-hammers.

What is particularly striking about this account, which in general terms might apply as well to Grendel, who is equally impervious to weapons (lines 801–4), is the description of the assailant coming 'out of the fen and fastness' (*of þæm fenne 7 of ðæm fæstene*), the more so since Grendel's own domain is described in exactly the same terms (*fen on fæsten*, line 104), in what is the only other example of the alliterative doublet extant in Old English literature. There is, as we have seen, orthographical and morphological evidence that the *Letter of Alexander to Aristotle* and *Beowulf* were both copied from the same exemplar;[97] other parallels of theme may strengthen the case for a still closer connection.[98]

Hrothgar's description of the monster-mere, then, whether drawn from the *Letter of Aristotle to Alexander* or from some vernacular rendering of the *Visio S. Pauli* (or both), may represent a significant blend of imported Latin and native germanic elements, the whole strongly influenced by the Christian homiletic tradition. In keeping with the wisdom and dignity which characterise his appearances throughout the poem, Hrothgar's longest speech to the victorious Beowulf on his return from the same monster-mere, bearing the grisly booty of the giant sword-hilt and Grendel's severed head (lines 1700–84), combines many of the same elements in much the same way. Ettmüller was the first person to describe the speech as a 'sermon',[99] and its very length and position at the heart of the poem have led a number of commentators to stress its importance in the wider structure of the poem; G. V. Smithers considered the passage 'a hinge on which the two halves of the poem are set'.[100] In fact Hrothgar's lengthy speech consists of much more than homiletic advice; Klaeber reckoned the speech 'conspicuous for the blending of heroic and theological motives',[101] and the 'sermon' has been sub-divided in various ways.[102] The opening undoubtedly establishes Hrothgar's authority as an old and experienced judge of the deeds of men (lines 1700–9), a theme to which he returns towards the end of his speech, where he muses on the length and success of his own career, before Grendel appeared on the scene (lines 1769–84).[103] But Hrothgar's is but the last of a series of *exempla* which warn of the dangers of complacency and overweening pride. After fulsome praise of Beowulf as a figure at the height of his powers, with considerable promise, Hrothgar posts a warning of the dangers ahead, by citing the case of Heremod, who at one time had seemed equally blessed (lines 1709–24):

> Not so was Heremod to the children of Ecgwela; he did not flourish for the happiness, but for the slaughter and massacre of the Danish people. Swollen with rage he shattered his hearth-companions, his close comrades, until he alone, famous prince, turned from the joys of men, even though mighty God had steeped him with the joys of strength and with powers promoted him beyond all men. Yet in his heart there grew a bloodthirsty spirit; he did not give the Danes rings according to judgment; joyless he endured so that he suffered pain for that struggle, long-lasting grief for his people. Learn from that, and recognise manly virtue. I, experienced in years, have uttered this speech for [or 'about'] you.

Just as the warning example of Heremod is invoked here, after Beowulf's great victory against Grendel's mother, so too his shadow is first raised after the fight with Grendel (lines 901–15). There it is stressed that Heremod had been the equal of Sigemund (as is Beowulf) before his temperament led him to the bad. Heremod's fate, to turn away in lonely exile from the joys of men, recalls that of Grendel himself, the more so since his exile takes place among giants, as Heremod, just like Grendel, passes 'into the power of enemies' (*on feonda geweald*, lines 808 and 903).[104]

Heremod is but one of a number of figures in Beowulf whose names carry psychological connotations remarkably appropriate to their characters, leading some commentators to see their plight as in some sense allegorical, and Müllenhof duly recognised in Heremod's activity the kind of zest for conflict suitable to one named 'war-spirit'.[105] Likewise, Kemp Malone demonstrated that the Geatish Queen Hygd ('sense') 'is consistently characterised in terms of her name',[106] while R. E. Kaske and Fred Robinson both contrast her sensibility with the rashness of Hygelac, her husband, whose behaviour they see defined by the sense 'instability of mind'.[107] The same implicit contrast between the physical and psychological worlds runs throughout the remainder of Hrothgar's 'sermon', a pivotal section of the poem, in which homiletic elements are rife, and which requires quotation in full (lines 1724–68):

It is wondrous to tell how mighty God, through his magnanimity deals out to mankind wisdom, land, and rank; he has control of all things. Sometimes he lets a well-born man's thoughts turn to pleasure, grants him in his homeland to possess the joys of the earth, a sheltering stronghold of men, makes subject to him areas of the world, broad kingdoms, so that he himself cannot in his folly perceive any end. He dwells in prosperity; not at all do old age or sickness harm him, nor does grim sorrow darken his spirit, nor does malice cause sword-hatred anywhere, but the whole world moves at his whim; he knows nothing worse until a portion of pride grows and flourishes; when the keeper sleeps, the guardian of the soul; that sleep is too sound, fastened with worries, the slayer very close, who shoots wickedly from his bow. Then under his covering he is struck in the heart with a bitter arrow, with the crooked commands of wonder of the accursed spirit: he cannot defend himself; what he has long held seems to him too little, angry at heart he grows niggardly, not at all honourably dispenses plated rings, but he forgets and neglects the world to come, the portion of glories that God, Ruler of Glory, had granted him. Finally it turns out that the frail body droops and falls doomed, and another succeeds, who doles out treasure recklessly, the ancient heirlooms of the warrior, does not reckon of terror. Guard yourself against that dread horror, my dear Beowulf, best of men, and choose for yourself the better part, eternal rewards; care not for pride, famous warrior! Now the glory of your might lasts for a time; but soon it will turn out that sickness or sword will separate you from your strength, or the fire's embrace or the flood's surge, or the bite of a blade, or the flight of a spear, or dreaded old age, or the brightness of your eyes shall fail and grow dim; finally it shall be that death, noble warrior, shall overpower you.

The implied contrast between worldly success and spiritual decay, between the physical world and the psychological, is explicit in the direct comparison between the 'portion of pride' (*oferhygda dæl*, line 1740) and 'portion of glories' (*weorðmynda dæl*, line 1752) which represent the changing fortunes of mankind, and here, after Beowulf has successfully defeated Grendel's mother, the poet reiterates the message implicit in the contrasting fortunes of Sigemund and Heremod (lines 874–915) or Hygelac and Hama (lines 1197–1214),[108] to which attention is drawn after Beowulf's defeat of Grendel; in each case the moral and didactic approach seems the same, an essentially exegetical technique familiar from vernacular homilies.

The style and content of Hrothgar's speech, moreover, may well owe something to homiletic technique.[109] As Peter Clemoes has pointed out, within the space of a few verses the poet employs no fewer than three alliterative couplings of synonymous or nearly-synonymous finite verbs: *weaxeð ond wridað* (line 1741),[110] *forgyteð ond forgymeð* (line 1751), and *forsiteð ond forsworceð* (line 1767), whereas only seven such pairs are found in the whole of the rest of the poem put together; such alliterative doublets were a frequent adornment of vernacular preaching from the earliest period.[111] Equally significant, perhaps is the reference to the 'soul's keeper' (*sawele hyrde*, line 1742), since the phrase is relatively rare in Old English, being largely confined to homiletic prose, where it is used on several occasions to describe Saint Michael in his role as psychopomp,[112] and no less than three times in the Old English translation of the *Visio S. Pauli*, in each case without warrant in the Latin.[113]

The sleep of such a 'guardian of the soul' is, of course, relatively commonplace within patristic and homiletic tradition; one author, for example, borrowing a motif from a Hiberno-Latin source,[114] notes that 'Almighty God teaches us vigils and prayers; the devil teaches us sleep and slackness'.[115] The 'slayer' (*bona*, line 1743), whose arrows cause such spiritual harm, is presumably to be identified with the devilish 'slayer of the spirit' (*gastbona*, line 177) to whom the poet disapprovingly notes the Danes sacrificing at their heathen shrines. The figure of the arrows of sin is doubtless ultimately indebted to the biblical rhetoric of Ephesians VI.11–16, the influence of which passage on Anglo-Saxon literature is remarkably widespread,[116] but it is still striking that the *Beowulf*-poet, by introducing the figure of the less than reliable 'guardian of the soul' come close to the extended homiletic treatment of the theme most fully explored by the author of Vercelli Homily IV (lines 308–10 and 337–42):[117]

> Then the devil has made a bow and arrows. The bow is made of pride, and the arrows are of as many kinds as man's sins ... Each day we have two guardians, and one comes from the heavens above, who is to establish a good example for us and teach us good virtues, and he has in his hand the shields which I mentioned earlier, and the sword, and he wants to defend us against the accursed devil, who comes from steely hell with his sharp arrows, with which to shoot us.

The 'bow of pride' described here seems remarkably close to the figure depicted in Hrothgar's 'sermon', whilst the notion of a 'guardian of the soul', both here and in the 'sermon', presumably derives ultimately from the biblical *custos animae* of Proverbs XVI.17 and XXII.5,[118] and indeed the extent to which both passages relate to the specific concerns of Hrothgar's 'sermon' is quite striking (Proverbs XVI.16–18 and XXII.4–6):

> posside sapientiam quia auro melior est et adquire prudentiam quia pretiosior est argento. semita iustorum declinat mala custos animae suae servat viam suam. contritionem praecedit superbia et ante ruinam exaltatur spiritum ... finis modestiae timor Domini divitiae et gloria et vita. arma et gladii in via perversi custos animae suae recedit ab eis.

> Possesse wisdom, because it is better than gold: and gette prudence, because it is more precious than silver. The path of the just avoideth evils: the keper of his soule kepeth his way. Pride goeth before destruction, and before ruine the spirit shal be exalted ... The end of modestie the feare of our Lord, riches and glorie and life. Armour and swordes in the way of the perverse: but the keper of his owne soul departeth far from them.

Apart from the general admonition concerning the value of wisdom and the dangers of pride alongside mention of the 'keper of [the] soule' (*custos animae*), the reference here to 'the feare of our Lord' (*timor Domini*) is intriguing in the context of the curious phrase in Hrothgar's 'sermon' in which we are told of a spiritual successor to Heremod who 'does not reckon of terror' (*egesan ne gymeð*, line 1757). Elsewhere in *Beowulf* the word *egesa* signifies 'terror',[119] but in this one passage may contain a sense approaching 'awe', as Vickrey has argued,[120] and can be compared not only with the phrase *timor Domini* from Proverbs already noted, but also in this context of a call to wisdom by the specific admonition in the Psalms that 'the beginning of Wisdom is the fear of the Lord' (*initium sapientiae timor Domini*, Psalm CX. 10). Certainly, precisely such a notion was adopted and underlined in various Old English homiletic texts, for example Vercelli Homily XII (lines 64–7):[121]

> Fear leads us from the inhabitants of Hell, and brings us to the kingdom above, and drives from us every folly, and instructs us in learning and understanding, and teaches us wisdom. That is fear.

By dealing sympathetically with the terror (*egesa*) implicit in the heroic life, the *Beowulf*-poet gently directs us to the benefits of Christian reverence (*egesa*), benefits which even a virtuous pagan, such as Heremod's generous successor, are, as we shall see, emphatically denied.[122]

In this context, of course, of Christian and heroic terminology apparently deliberately manipulated and obscured by the *Beowulf*-poet, the closing words of the poem, in which a eulogy to Beowulf is delivered in the course of what some have seen as a ceremony of pagan apotheosis (lines 3180–2) are particularly striking:[123]

> They said that he was of worldly kings the mildest to men, and the most gentle, the kindest to his people, and the keenest for fame.

The allusion to 'worldly kings' (*wyruldcyninga*, line 3180) effectively delimits the extent of Beowulf's endeavours, by its implicit reference to the heavenly king, knowledge of whom is denied to the dead hero, just as earlier in the poem Beowulf has twice been described as 'strongest in might in that day of this life' (lines 789–90),[124] in a twin reference which puts Beowulf firmly in his place, as it were: a hero of a bygone and strictly secular age.[125] In contrast to that secular praise, there may well be, as Mary P. Richards has indicated, a strongly religious flavour to the description of Beowulf as 'the mildest to men, and the most gentle' (line 3181), since the alliterative pair *milde ond monðwære* (or equivalent) is of rather frequent occurrence in Christian contexts, being used to describe, amongst others, Christ, Saint Neot, Bishop Eata, and the Archangel Gabriel.[126] There seems no good reason, however, to doubt that the same words can also be taken in a strictly secular sense, to denote, for example, praise for the prodigality of a generous prince,[127] and it is striking that in *Beowulf* itself Wealhtheow uses very similar terms to praise the Danes (lines 1228–31):

> Here is each warrior true to the other, mild of spirit, loyal to their lord. The thegns are united, a people fully prepared, the retainers have drunk [loyally]: they do as I bid.

That the same words denoting positive Christian virtues should seemingly be attributed to the pagan hero Beowulf only serves to underline the ambiguity of the final word of *Beowulf*, *lofgeornost* ('most eager for praise', line 3182), the dual associations of which were presumably equally apparent to Christian ears in the period when the *Beowulf*-manuscript was being copied.[128] The concept of *lof* ('praise') within *Beowulf* as a positive heroic and secular value to be gained by noble deeds is made clear by gnomic utterance both at the very beginning of the poem, when we are assured that 'it is by deeds of praise that one must prosper in every nation' (lines 24–5), and in the middle, during Beowulf's near-fatal conflict with Grendel's mother, when the poet notes that 'so must a man do who intends to gain long-lasting praise in war: he must have no care for his life' (lines 1534–6). The word *lofgeorn* and its morphological variants, however, are found only twelve times in the extant Old English corpus, of which the example in *Beowulf* represents the sole attestation of the word in verse. In prose, the term is found in three versions of a passage on the seven deadly sins by Ælfric,[129] once in the sermons of Wulfstan and once more in his *Institutes of Polity*,[130] and six times in the various versions of the Benedictine Rule.[131] In all these cases, the word carries unreservedly negative connotations.[132] By contrast, the word *domgeorn* ('eager for glory'), which occurs only five times, and always in verse, carries a positive sense on all occasions.[133]

The tension between Christian and heroic diction is, of course, fully exploited by a range of Old English poets, and several commentators have focused on a passage from the *Seafarer* which appears to suggest that worldly *lof* can have heavenly benefits (lines 72–80):[134]

> Therefore it is for all noble men the best memorial and praise of the living who remember him after death, so that before he must go hence, he should merit and achieve on earth by heroic deeds against the enmity of foes, opposing the devil, that the children of men may praise him afterwards, and his praise may live with the angels for ever and ever, the glory of eternal life, joy among the hosts.

This is but one of a series of passages throughout the *Seafarer* which consciously play on the twin sense of certain terms, both Christian and heroic,[135] most notably *drihten*, which in the space of three lines refers to lords both secular and spiritual.[136] Such passages amply demonstrate the way in which Anglo-Saxon audiences were well-attuned to the dual sense of certain terms, and to the twin values implied. Even while employing words like *milde*, *monðwære*, and *liðe*, which have morally positive senses in both Christian and heroic terms, it is surely striking that the *Beowulf*-poet uses the superlative form, which might presumably be thought more appropriate in a secular encomiastic context.

As for the superlative form of *lofgeorn*, the positive moral sense of which is far from clear in Christian terms, one might well compare the difficulties perceived by Bede in praising a mighty pagan who was 'most desirous of glory' (*gloriae cupidissimus*):[137]

His temporibus regno Nordanhymbrorum praefuit rex for-
tissimus et gloriae cupidissimus Aedilfrid, qui plus omnibus
Anglorum primatibus gentem uastauit Brettonum, ita ut Sauli
quondam regi Israeliticae gentis comparandus uideretur, excepto
dumtaxat hoc, quod diuinae erat religionis ignarus. Nemo enim
in tribunis, nemo in regibus plures eorum tetras, exterminatis uel
subiugatis indigenis, aut tributaries genti Anglorum, aut habita-
biles fecit. Cui merito poterat illud, quod benedicens filium patri-
archa in personam Saulis dicebat, aptari: 'Beniamin lupus rapax;
mane comedet praedam, et uespere diuidet spolia.'

At this time there was in control of the kingdom of Northumbria
a king who was most mighty and most desirous of glory,
Æthelfrith, who more than all the leaders of the English devastat-
ed the Britons, in such a way that he seemed comparable to Saul,
the one-time king of the Israelites, save only that he was ignorant
of divine religion. For none of all the ealdormen, none of the
kings, made more of their land, once the inhabitants had been
annihilated or subdued, either subservient to the English nation
or habitable to them. To him might properly be thought fitting
that which the patriarch, blessing his son in the person of Saul,
once said: 'Benjamin is a ravening wolf, in the morning he shall
devour the prey and in the evening he shall divide the spoil.'

The comparison with Saul is instructive; for his was no exemplary life, as
Eric Stanley has pointed out,[138] citing King Alfred's observations in his
translation of Gregory's *Pastoral Care*:[139]

Just as Saul, the king of the Israelites, earned that kingdom
through humility, and because of the prestige of that kingdom he
grew proud. For his humility he was raised up above other men,
and for his pride he was cast down.

Beowulf, like Æthelfrith (and Saul), a heroic king, and equally 'most eager
for praise' (*lofgeornost*), is, also, like Æthelfrith, a pagan, and no amount
of special pleading can save him: 'to be a heathen is sin enough'.[140] If, as
we have seen, there are close parallels to be drawn between the exploits of
Beowulf and those of the mighty monster-slaying heroes of the classical past,
like Alexander the Great, or (as we shall see) Hercules, then there are also
elements clearly drawn from biblical and patristic sources which hint more

darkly at the hell-fire and perdition that is the lot of all heathens. It may well be that from a Christian perspective the doubtless heroic Beowulf, in the closing words of the poem which celebrates his mighty deeds, like Alexander and Hercules, would seem damned with feigned praise.

NOTES

1. Tolkien, 'Beowulf, the Monsters, and the Critics', p. 260.

2. Sisam, *The Structure of 'Beowulf,'* p. 25.

3. Niles, 'Ring Composition and the Structure of *Beowulf*', p. 925; cf. Rogers, 'Beowulf's Three Great Fights', especially pp. 340–3. Others have proposed a much more complex structural patterning, notably Carrigan, 'Structure and Thematic Development in *Beowulf*', especially pp. 49–51; Leyerle, 'The Interlace Structure of *Beowulf*', especially pp. 15–17. For a useful review of suggestions concerning the structure of the poem, see Hume, 'The Theme and Structure of *Beowulf*', pp. 2–5.

4. Whitelock, *The Audience of 'Beowulf'*, p. 20; by comparison, Kemp Malone's rather stately reading of the entire poem, *'Beowulf' (Complete): Read in Old English by Kemp Malone*, 4 discs (Caedmon Records, TC 4001, 1967), takes just over four hours.

5. Sisam, 'Beowulf's Fight with the Dragon', p. 136.

6. See further the analysis of Nitzsche, 'The Structural Unity of *Beowulf*', pp. 293–4.

7. Cf. Sisam, 'Beowulf's Fight with the Dragon', p. 138.

8. Cf. Carens, 'Handscioh and Grendel', pp. 39–45.

9. See further below, p. 30.

10. The dragon is certainly the least human in terms of shape, notwithstanding the often-noted possibility, most fully argued by Tripp, *More about the Fight with the Dragon*, especially pp. 13–17, that, as in a number of Norse analogues, the dragon was originally a man transformed.

11. Cf. Nitzsche, 'The Structural Unity of *Beowulf*', pp. 290–2.

12. See further lines 1498 (Grendel's mother), 1769 (Hrothgar), and 2209 (Beowulf).

13. Cf. the description of the sleeping warriors in Heorot, immediately before the first visit of Grendel's mother: 'they set at their heads war-bucklers, bright wooden shields; there on the bench was easily seen, above each noble a towering helmet, a ringed corselet, a mighty spear' (lines 1242–6). Presumably a similar scene is envisaged in the monster mere, when Beowulf 'saw amongst the armour a victory-blessed sword' (line 1557).

14. See further the comments of Baird, 'Grendel the Exile', pp. 378–9; Greenfield, 'The Formulaic Expression of the Theme of "Exile" in Anglo-Saxon Poet', p. 205; Greenfield, *Hero and Exile*, p. 130.

15. The word *earmsceapen* may also be used to describe the dragon at line 2228; cf. Breager, 'Connotations of (*earm*) *sceapen*', pp. 327–30.

16. On this giant sword, see further below, pp. 111–12.

17. See further lines 1582–3.

18. See Puhvel, *'Beowulf' and the Celtic Tradition*, pp. 82–5, for an argument that the *Beowulf*-poet was influenced in his depiction of these episodes by Irish models.

19. On the description of Grendel as *angenga*, cf. Lapidge, *'Beowulf* and the Psychology of Terror', pp. 381–2.

20. Cf. Brodeur, *The Art of Beowulf*, pp. 231–3; Rosier, 'The Uses of Association: Hands and Feasts in *Beowulf*', p. 8.

21. On whom see further below, pp. 48–53.

22. Cf. Rosier, 'The Uses of Association: Hands and Feasts in *Beowulf*', p. 12.

23. Klaeber, ed., *Beowulf*, p. 298.

24. Cf. Gillam, 'The Use of the Term *aglæca* in *Beowulf* at lines 813 and 2592', pp. 145–69.

25. Kuhn, 'Old English *aglæca*—Middle Irish *ochlach*', pp. 213–30.

26. Cf. Huffines, 'OE *aglæce*: Magic and Moral Decline', pp. 71–81.

27. Mezger, 'Goth. Aglaiti "Unchastity", OE Aglæc "Distress"', p. 69; Lotspeich, 'Old English Etymologies', p. 1; Kuhn, 'Old English *aglæca*—Middle Irish *ochlach*', pp. 214–20; Lapidge, *'Beowulf* and the Psychology of Terror', pp. 380–1.

28. Cf. Dobbie, ed., *Beowulf*, p. 160.

29. Crawford, ed., *Byrhtferth's Manual*, p. 74/15; cf. Nichols, 'Bede "Awe-Inspiring"', pp. 147–8.

30. The contrast is most effectively stressed by Tolkien, 'Beowulf, the Monsters, and the Critics', for example, pp. 271–2.

31. Cf. Tolkien, 'Beowulf, the Monsters, and the Critics', pp. 273–4.

32. Lapidge, *'Beowulf* and the Psychology of Terror', pp. 373–4.

33. Kaske, 'The Sigemund-Heremod and Hama-Hygelac Passages', p. 489; Kaske, *'Sapientia et Fortitudo* as the Controlling Theme', especially pp. 423–8.

34. Brodeur, *The Art of 'Beowulf,'* p. 90.

35. The passage has been discussed many times; see particularly Brodeur, *The Art of 'Beowulf'*, pp. 88–94; Greenfield, 'Grendel's Approach to Heorot', pp. 275–84; Renoir, 'Point of View and Design for Terror', pp. 154–67; Storms, 'Grendel the Terrible', pp. 427–36; Irving, *A Reading of 'Beowulf'*, pp. 101–3; O'Keeffe, *'Beowulf*, Lines 720b–836', pp. 487–8; Lapidge, *'Beowulf* and the Psychology of Terror', pp. 383–4.

36. Renoir, 'Point of View and Design for Terror', pp. 160–5.

37. Lapidge, *'Beowulf* and the Psychology of Terror', p. 384.

38. Here the poet describes the successively more detailed view of approaching land from the sailors' point of view; 'they saw land, sea-cliffs shining, steep hills, broad sea-promontories' (lines 221–3). The term 'cinematographic' in this context was first suggested by Renoir, 'Point of View and Design for Terror', p. 162.

39. Cf. Rosier, 'The Uses of Association: Hands and Feasts in *Beowulf*', p. 12.

40. Cf. Campbell, 'Schematic Technique in *Judith*', p. 169. The passage in question is discussed with characteristic insight by Renoir, *'Judith* and the Limits of Poetry', pp. 147–8, although, somewhat curiously, the repetition of *stopon* is not discussed.

41. Cf. O'Keeffe, *'Beowulf*, Lines 702b–836', p. 486.

42. Greenfield, 'Grendel's Approach to Heorot', p. 280.

43. So in this short passage we learn of the vicious anger of Grendel (*bealohydig, gebolgen*, and *yrremod*, lines 723 and 726), Beowulf (*on andan / bad bolgenmod*, lines 708–9), and God (*yrre*, line 711).

44. Dobbie, ed., *Beowulf*, p. 151.

45. Cf. the collocation *scuccum* and *scinnum* ('demons and sprites', line 939).

46. Cf. O'Keeffe, *'Beowulf*, Lines 702b–836', p. 485, who points out that 'Grendel is described frequently by words compounded in *sin-* or *syn-*'.

47. Cf. above, pp. 31–3; the term *manscaða* refers to Grendel at lines 712 and 737, to Grendel's mother at line 1339, and to the dragon at line 2514.

48. See further above, pp. 30–1.

49. Irving, *A Reading of 'Beowulf'*, p. 104.

50. Cf. Lapidge, *'Beowulf* and the Psychology of Terror', pp. 383–5.

51. Tolkien, 'Beowulf, the Monsters, and the Critics', p. 280.

52. Lapidge, '*Beowulf* and the Psychology of Terror', p. 375.

53. One might contrast the very physical aspects of Beowulf's later adversary, the dragon, of which we are made aware long before the combatants clash. See further Sisam, 'Beowulf's Fight with the Dragon', p. 134.

54. O'Keeffe, '*Beowulf*, Lines 702b–836', p. 488.

55. Morris, ed., *The Blickling Homilies*, pp. vi–vii; the homily in question is in fact no. XVII in Morris's edition, but the fragment which Morris numbers XVI has been identified as a part of his Homily IV, causing a renumbering of Morris's Homilies XVII–XIX as XVI–XVIII. See further the facsimile by Willard, ed., *The Blickling Homilies*, pp. 38–40.

56. For the text, cf. Collins, 'Blickling Homily XVI and the Dating of *Beowulf*', p. 62; for the translation, cf. Malone, 'Grendel and His Abode', pp. 304–5.

57. Cf. Malone, 'Grendel and His Abode', pp. 298–9.

58. Whitelock, *The Audience of Beowulf*, pp. 10–11; Malone, 'Grendel and His Abode', p. 298.

59. Tolkien, 'Beowulf, the Monsters, and the Critics', pp. 278–80.

60. The list derives from Brown, '*Beowulf* and the *Blickling Homilies*', p. 908; cf. Collins, 'Blickling Homily XVI and the Dating of *Beowulf*', p. 65; Wright, *The Irish Tradition in Old English Literature*, p. 119.

61. A notable exception is Peter Clemoes, 'Style as a Criterion', p. 181, who argues against any such direct literary link, preferring instead to see the passages as reflecting oral and memorial traditions based on preached material.

62. Cf. Morris, ed., *The Blickling Homilies*, p. vii; Brown, '*Beowulf* and the *Blickling Homilies*', p. 909.

63. Collins, 'Blickling Homily XVI and the Dating of *Beowulf*', pp. 67–8.

64. Klaeber, 'Die christlichen Elementen im *Beowulf*', pp. 185–7; Klaeber, ed., *Beowulf*, p. 183; Hoops, *Kommentar zum Beowulf*, p. 164.

65. Wright, *The Irish Tradition in Old English Literature*, pp. 116–36, at pp. 133–6. For further indications that the author of Beowulfdrew on vernacular traditions ultimately drawn from the *Visio S. Pauli*, see further below, pp. 47–51.

66. Tristram, 'Stock Descriptions', p. 111.

67. Wright, *The Irish Tradition in Old English Literature*, p. 135.

68. See further below, pp. 42–5.

69. Fry, 'The Cliff of Death', p. 215.

70. Fry, 'The Cliff of Death', pp. 216–18.

71. The precise sense of *nicras* is uncertain; apart from *Beowulf* and Blickling Homily XVI the term is only found in the *Letter of Alexander* (§15) and in a prose Life of St Margaret (Cockayne, ed., *Narratiunculae anglice conscriptae*, p. 39), in both of which texts the required sense seems to be 'hippopotamus'. Cf. Davis, "'Hippopotamus' in Old English, p. 141; Fry, 'The Cliff of Death', p. 222. See too further below, pp. 234–5, 294–5, and 298–9. Hippopotami were certainly regarded as bestial, rather than serpentine, by the compiler of the *Liber monstrorum* (II.9 and II.17); it is possible that the *Beowulf*-poet meant to make a similar distinction in describing the *sædracan* and *nicras* as 'worms and wild beasts' (*wyrmas ond wildeor*, line 1430).

72. Cf. Klaeber, ed., *Beowulf*, p. 183; Lawrence, 'The Haunted Mere in *Beowulf*', p. 225, who states that 'it is impossible to reconcile all these [aspects of the description] so as to give a single consistent picture of natural scenery'.

73. Stanley, 'Old English Poetic Diction', p. 441; cf. Butts, 'The Analogical Mere', pp. 113–21.

74. Cf. Sims-Williams, *Religion and Literature in Western England*, pp. 243–72; Tristram, 'Stock Descriptions', p. 111.

75. The theme of the multiplicity of things which can cut short one's life is found, for example, in *The Seafarer*, lines 66–71, as well as in an earlier section of Hrothgar's 'sermon' (*Beowulf*, lines 1735–9), although in none of the parallel passages is there any mention of fire or flood, which appear to have been deliberately introduced by the *Beowulf* poet. See further, Gordon, ed., *The Seafarer*, pp. 42–3.

76. Most notably, of course, in the Old English version of the *Apocalypse of Thomas*, where a 'fiery flood' (*fyren flod*) is mentioned twice; cf. Willard, *Two Apocrypha in Old English Homilies*, pp. 4 and 6, and *Beowulf*, lines 1359 and 2128.

77. See further Caie, *The Judgment Day Theme in Old English Poetry*, pp. 194–5.

78. Printed by Migne, PL 94, col. 555: *quinta die ardebunt ipsae aquae ab ortu usque ad occasum* ('on the fifth day the very waters shall burn, from their rising until their fall'); Cf. Lapidge and Sharpe, *Bibliography of Celtic-Latin Literature*, no. 1257. See further Hill, 'The Old World, the Levelling of the Earth, and the Burning of the Sea', pp. 323–5.

79. Quin, ed., 'Ochtfæochlach Choluim Chille', p. 144; Biggs, *The Sources of Christ III*, p. 15.

80. Cf. the parallel passages from *Christ II*, lines 805–7 and *Judgment Day II*, lines 166–70; Caie, *The Judgment Day Theme in Old English Poetry*, pp. 194–5.

81. Cf. Matthew XXIV. 37; Heist, *The Fifteen Signs Before Doomsday*, pp. 27–9.

82. Bethurum, ed., *The Homilies of Wulfstan*, p. 122/7–9; cf. Napier, ed., *Wulfstan*, no. XLIII (*Sunnandæges spell*) 206/14–19 and 207/22–3; no. XLIV (*Sunnandæges spell*), 216/24–217/2.

83. See further below, pp. 58–85.

84. Recorded in Sawyer, *Anglo-Saxon Charters*, no. 1447, and Wormald, 'Anglo-Saxon Lawsuits', nos. 38–40.

85. Liebermann, ed., *Die Gesetze*, I, p. 312.

86. Schrader, 'Sacred Groves, Marvellous Waters', p. 81.

87. The similarities between this passage and Hrothgar's description of the mere are discussed by Haber, *A Comparative Study*, pp. 92–6; Renoir, 'The Terror of the Dark Waters', pp. 147–60; Andersson, *Early Epic Scenery*, pp. 145–59; Cornelius, 'Palus Inamabilis', pp. 321–5.

88. Cf. Schrader, 'Sacred Groves, Marvellous Waters', pp. 77–8, who also offers some other, less convincing, parallels.

89. Schrader, 'Sacred Groves, Marvellous Waters', pp. 78–9.

90. Orchard, *The Poetic Art of Aldhelm*, pp. 130–5, 139–41, and 152–5.

91. Rigg, '*Beowulf* 1368–72: An Analogue', pp. 101–2; Butts, 'The Analogical Mere', p. 118.

92. Particularly striking here is the emphasis in the Old English on the cliff edge (*On þære ea ofre stod hreod 7 pintreow 7 abies þæt treowcyn ungemetlicre gryto 7 micelnysse þy clyfe weox 7 wridode*), which has no parallel in the Latin. On the alliterative doublet *weox 7 wridode*, which occurs in *Beowulf*, line 1741 in the form *weaxeð ond wrideð*, see Clemoes, 'Style as Criterion', p. 180, and below, pp. 132–3.

93. Cockayne, ed., *Narratiunculae anglice conscriptae*, p. 39.

94. Davis, '"Hippopotamus" in Old English', pp. 141–2.

95. In both cases, the effect of the horn-blowing is to make the assembled troop sit down. Whilst such an action is quite natural for Alexander and his men, who promptly begin to eat, the action of the foot-soldiers accompanying Beowulf is decidedly curious, and may indicate that here the *Beowulf*-poet is the borrower. For an alternative

explanation of the horns, see Braswell, 'The Horn at Grendel's Mere: *Beowulf* 1417–41', pp. 466–72.

96. Cf. the proximity of the monster-mere in *Beowulf* to Heorot (lines 1361–2): *nis þæt feor heonon / milgemearces þæt se mere standeð*.

97. See above, pp. 2–3.

98. See further below, pp. 132–9.

99. Ettmüller, ed., *Beowulf*, p. 136; cited by Stanley, *In the Foreground: 'Beowulf,'* p. 240.

100. Smithers, 'The Meaning of *The Seafarer* and *The Wanderer*', p. 8; cf. Goldsmith, *Mode and Meaning in 'Beowulf'*, pp. 183–209.

101. Klaeber, ed., *Beowulf*, p. 190.

102. Cox, Cruces, p. 132; Maeber, ed., *Beowulf*, p. 190; Hansen, 'Hrothgar's "*Sermon*" in Beowulf', p. 62.

103. Müllenhof, 'Innere Geschichte', pp. 213–14, believed that the two parts of the speech were entirely incompatible, and ascribed the first to his hypothesized interpolater B, as cited by Stanley, *In the Foreground: 'Beowulf'*, p. 241.

104. See further Blake, 'The Heremod Digressions in *Beowulf*', p. 282.

105. Müllenhof, *Beowulf*, p. 51; Klaeber, ed., *Beowulf*, pp. 162–3; Robinson, *The Tomb of Beowulf*, pp. 212–13.

106. Malone, 'Hygd', p. 358.

107. Kaske, '"Hygelac" and "Hygd"', pp. 200–6; Robinson, *The Tomb of Beowulf*, pp. 213–17.

108. Cf. Kaske, 'The Sigemund-Heremod and Hama-Hygelac Passages in *Beowulf*', pp. 491–4.

109. See, for example, Hansen, 'Hrothgar's "sermon" in *Beowulf* as Parental Wisdom', pp. 54–6.

110. Cf. the parallel doublet *weox 7 wridode* in the *Letter of Alexander to Aristotle* (§12) in the Appendix below, pp. 232–3. See further above, pp. 44–5.

111. Clemoes, 'Style as a Criterion', pp. 180–1; cf. Klaeber, ed., *Beowulf*, p. 192.

112. See, for example, Bazire and Cross, ed., *Eleven Old English Rogationtide Homilies*, III.144–5, p. 53.

113. Healey, ed. *The Old English Vision of St Paul*, lines 91, 104, 131; pp. 67 and 69. Such links further strengthen the possibility that the *Beowulf*-poet was influenced by a vernacular rendering of the *Visio S. Pauli*, cf. Wright, *The Irish Tradition in Old English Literature*, pp. 132–4.

114. Wright, *The Irish Tradition in Old English Literature*, p. 244.

115. Healey, ed. *The Old English Vision of St Paul*, p. 325, lines 79–80; cf. Fadda, ed. *Nuove omelie anglosassoni*, p. 169, lines 72–3, who, however, reads *slæw* for *slæp*. See also Assman, ed. *Angelsächsische Homilien und Heiligleben*, XIV.106–7, p. 168: *deofol of lareð slæpnesse and sent us on slæwðe*, and Wright, 'Docet Deus, docet diabolus', pp. 451–3.

116. Cf. Hermann, *Allegories of War*, pp. 39–42.

117. Scragg, ed., *The Vercelli Homilies*, pp. 102 and 104; cf. Wright, *The Irish Tradition in Old English Literature*, pp. 260–1.

118. Cf. Klaeber, ed., *Beowulf*, p. 192.

119. The simple form *eg(e)sa* occurs in various morphological forms in lines 276, 784, 1827, 2736, and 3154; the compounds *gledegesa* (line 2650), *ligegesa* (line 2780), and *wæteregesa* (line 1260) are also attested, all bearing the same basic sense of 'terror' or 'horror'.

120. See further Vickrey, '*Egesan ne gymeð* and the Crime of Heremod', pp. 295–300.

121. Scragg, ed., *The Vercelli Homilies*, p. 230.

122. See further below, pp. 170–1.

123. Robinson, *The Tomb of Beowulf*, pp. 3–19; the text I have adopted here is that given by Richards, 'A Reexamination of *Beowulf*, ll. 3180–3182', p. 165.

124. Cf. lines 196–7 (*mægenes strengest / on þæm dæge þysses lifes*), or the description of the death of Grendel *on ðæm dage þysses lifes* (line 806).

125. See further Robinson, *'Beowulf' and the Appositive Style*, p. 54; Frank, 'The *Beowulf* Poet's Sense of History,' pp. 54–5.

126. Richards, 'A Reexamination of *Beowulf* ll. 3180–3182', pp. 165–7. Her evidence can be greatly supplemented: I note around twenty collocations of the two words.

127. This is a common meaning for the cognate adjective *mildr* in Old Norse verse; see further Wieland, '*Manna mildost*: Moses and Beowulf', pp. 86–93.

128. Cf. Richards, 'A Reexamination of *Beowulf* ll. 3180–3182', pp. 163–7; Rosier, 'The Two Closings of *Beowulf*', pp. 1–6.

129. Skeat, ed. *Ælfric's Lives of Saints*, I, p. 356, line 302; Morris, ed., *Old English Homilies*, p. 297; Warner, ed., *Early English Homilies*, p. 17, line 19.

130. Bethurum, ed., *The Homilies of Wulfstan*, Sermo 10c, p. 207/128; Jost, ed., *Die 'Institutes of Polity, Civil and Ecclesiastical'*, p. 262.

131. Schröer, ed., *Die angelsächsischen Prosabearbeitungen den Benediktinerregel*, pp. 18/18, 54/9, and 55/3; Schröer, ed., *Die Winteney-Version den Regula S. Benedicti*, pp. 71/22 and 73/9. The word *lofgeorn* also occurs in the appropriate place in the variant texts of the vernacular Rule in Durham, Cathedral library, B. IV.4 and London, British Library, Cotton Tiberius A. iii; see further Frank and Cameron, ed., *A Plan for the Dictionary of Old English*, no. B.10.3.2, and Venezky and Healey, *A Microfiche Concordance*. On *lofgeorn*, see further below, pp. 56–7.

132. Cf. Stanley, 'Hæthenra Hyht in *Beowulf*', pp. 147–9.

133. Cf. *Andreas*, line 693, 878, 1308; *Elene*, line 1291; *The Wanderer*, line 17.

134. See further Tolkien, 'Beowulf, the Monsters, and the Critics', pp. 280–7; Richards, 'A Reexamination of *Beowulf* ll. 3180–3182', pp. 166–7.

135. Greenfield, 'Attitudes and Values in *The Seafarer*', pp. 18–20.

136. Cf. Gordon, ed., *The Seafarer*, pp. 26–7.

137. Colgrave and Mynors, ed., *Bede's Ecclesiastical History*, p. 116; a footnote suggests that 'the phrase "most eager for glory" reminds one of the OE word "domgeorn" used in such Anglo-Saxon poems as *The Wanderer* and *Judith* [*sic*] to describe the typical heroic warrior. The whole chapter may well be influenced by some lost heroic poem celebrating the deeds of Æthelfrith.'

138. Stanley, 'Hæthenra Hyht in *Beowulf*', p. 148.

139. Sweet, ed., *King Alfred's West-Saxon Version of Gregory's 'Pastoral Care'*, I, p. 112.

140. Stanley, 'Hæthenra Hyht in *Beowulf*', p. 150.

EDWARD B. IRVING JR.

Christian and Pagan Elements

Although *Beowulf* deals with ancient Germanic stories and heroes clearly dating back to a time before the Anglo-Saxons or their Continental cousins were converted to Christianity, in its style throughout its narrator and characters seem entirely comfortable with the conventional Christian phrases found elsewhere in Old English poetry, phrases deferring at all times to a recognizably Christian order. There are references to God's creation of the universe, the story of Cain, Noah's flood, devils and hell, and the Last Judgment. At least since 1951, when Dorothy Whitelock's influential *The Audience of Beowulf* appeared, readers have generally agreed that the poet of the text we have was a Christian composing for a Christian audience. Many scholars, and perhaps most ordinary readers, have simply accepted this odd blend of pagan story and Christian teller as perhaps illogical and somewhat puzzling in purpose and implications, but nonetheless the way the poem is. To many other scholars over the years, however, the combination of pagan and Christian elements has seemed a problem demanding clearer resolution.

We ought first to clarify our key term, since *pagan* is a word used in at least three different senses in discussing this problem: the literal, the vestigial, and the ethical. The first sense is the most precise, since it refers to the actual practices and beliefs of a pre-Christian religion in which

From *A* Beowulf *Handbook*, ed. Robert E. Bjork and John D. Niles, pp. 177–192. © 1998 by the University of Nebraska Press.

Germanic peoples participated. For a general account of this religion, see
Owen (1981), Wilson (1992; largely archaeological evidence), Polomé
(1989), and Niles (1991). *Beowulf* contains descriptions of pagan religious
rituals. Most striking are the three accounts of pagan funeral rites, of a kind
known to be frequently condemned by Christian authorities: there is an odd
version of a ship burial (odd since the funeral ship is not buried in a mound
but pushed out to sea) in the funeral of Scyld (26–52), a ceremonial pyre for
the casualties in the Finn Episode (1107–24), and Beowulf's own cremation
funeral at the end (3134–82), all three rites accompanied by rich grave goods.
Discovery in 1939 of a sumptuous ship burial, almost certainly a royal one,
at Sutton Hoo in the former kingdom of East Anglia, datable within a few
years of 625, and thought by some to be the tomb of King Rædwald, has
provided a clear picture of the nature of such pagan funerals on English soil,
a picture consonant with the descriptions in *Beowulf*, so much so that some
have tried, though without any striking justification, to tie this archaeological
find directly to the poem (see Frank 1992, and, for a full account of the find,
Bruce-Mitford 1975–83; see also Pearson, van de Noort, and Woolf 1993
and, for a recent discussion of the possible relation of *Beowulf* to East Anglia,
Newton 1993).

Then at one point (and one point only, in 175–93) the Danes, despairing
of any other remedy for Grendel's attacks, are said to engage in the actual
worship of heathen gods, for which the poet roundly condemns them, though
realizing with some sympathy that they cannot help their ignorance. Though
the Danes of the poem (and indeed all its characters) were pagans both before
and after this event, we never otherwise see them engaging in actual worship
of any kind (though they may voice vaguely Christian-sounding expressions of
gratitude to God), no pagan gods are ever referred to elsewhere, and there is
no other explicit mention of their being pagans.

Thus, this curiously isolated passage, the so-called Christian Excursus,
was early seized on by scholars who saw it as an obvious reader's interpolation
(e.g., Ettmüller 1875), perhaps an outburst of offended piety touched off by
some earlier version's more offhand reference to pagan worship. The passage
is out of keeping with the dominant strategy of the poem, which might be
summed up as "let's assume these old heroes were much like us in their
beliefs." Those sensitive to tone will note that in style the passage very much
resembles the language of Old English religious and homiletic texts but has
few stylistic parallels elsewhere in *Beowulf* itself; one such parallel might be
the description of the curse on the dragon treasure (3069–75), curious in that
it describes a pagan curse in unmistakably Christian language.

A second "pagan" area is less clearly defined and may be the least
important in the controversy, though it was much investigated in earlier

years when there was great interest in turning up every trace of paganism. Much of it, perhaps most of it, is what we might call fossil paganism, where an expression we can now identify as originally pagan has been preserved in a poetic formula that may well have lost any such specific meaning. The Germanic gods live every day now in the names of the days of the week, but no one notices it. Like an attic, language, especially the highly stereotyped language of Old English verse, preserves much forgotten lumber. For instance, warriors in *Beowulf* wear helmets with images of boars on them (303b–06a). The boar was an animal sacred to the Germanic god Freyr, and thus its image was once seen as powerful protection, but probably later Anglo-Saxon poets merely inherited a verbal convention that saw boar images as appropriate for heroes' helmets and had no special thought of Freyr. Brief references to magic spells and "battle runes" ("onband beadurune," 501a) probably fall into the same category (but for the persistence of some pagan practices even in late Anglo-Saxon England, see Wentersdorf 1981). Doubtless some of the much-discussed phrases concerning Wyrd or Fate, especially when it seems to be personified, were also such fossil expressions, and not evidence for any still viable religious beliefs in a god or goddess of Fate (the curious should consult references to wyrd in the glossaries, and see Phillpotts 1928 and Kasik 1979). There is not enough evidence to conclude that the hanged son for whom the old father mourns, in the famous passage in Beowulf's last long speech (2444–59), had been hanged as a human sacrifice, as some have speculated; he might simply have been executed by royal command for some crime. But the recent discovery of mutilated bodies, perhaps hanged, surrounding what might have been a large tree in the cemetery at Sutton Hoo does make the possibility of human sacrifice among the pagan Anglo-Saxons seem more vivid.[1]

The account of the mysterious arrival by boat of the child Scyld Scefing and his ceremonial departure after death seems to be derived from a pre-Christian myth, perhaps an important fertility myth. R. D. Fulk (1989) believes it to be a genuine pagan myth preserved in oral tradition and thus evidence of the antiquity of *Beowulf*. But the story is certainly not offered here as an object of living belief, indeed, any suspicion of such pagan taint is removed by having the Christian God himself deeply involved in the sending of Scyld to the Danes' rescue (12–17; see the comments of Osborn 1978, 973–74).

Another pagan institution that may have left an important imprint on the poem (though a difficult one to detect) is the "cult of kingship" described by Chaney (1970; see also Swanton 1982; Bauschatz 1982; T. Hill 1986; Rollason 1989). In this view of royal sacral authority, the Anglo-Saxons typically blended pagan and Christian beliefs, but such details as the representation of Scyld as "luck-bringing" savior, the rather priest-like role of

King Hrothgar, the emphasis placed on King Beowulf's burial mound, which seems almost to be constructed for his people to venerate, even the depiction of God as above all a royal figure, all may be powerful pagan themes that were, as Chaney makes clear, modified and continued by the church, for instance, in the veneration of militant royal saints like Edmund and Oswald. For a general consideration of Germanic modifications of Christianity, see Russell (1994).

A third sense of *pagan* lies in the realm of ethics and morality, and this is the area that has caused the most argument. Here matters might often be clarified if we used terms like *secular* or *non-Christian* (or possibly *Germanic* or *heroic*) for *pagan*, since we clearly do not know enough about truly pagan ethics, the explicit recommendations of pagan priests, for example, to talk reliably about the subject.

The fundamental ethical code of the poem is unmistakably secular: it is the warrior code of the aristocracy, celebrating bravery, loyalty, and generosity, with the hero finding his only immortality in the long-lasting fame of great exploits carried out in this world. It is not fundamentally different from the code found in Homer's *Iliad*. Katherine O'Brien O'Keeffe (1991) provides a good summary of the values of this code. In later Scandinavian mythology, a similar code is sanctioned by the warriors' god Odin (Woden in Old English), who rewards his followers with a place in Valhalla, but we cannot assume that such beliefs were current among Anglo-Saxons, though they sometimes thought it important for their kings to claim descent from Woden (doubtless thinking of him as an ancient hero rather than as a god). The code could clearly have gone on existing, however, without such elaborate supernatural sanctions—as in fact it did.

In certain strict Christian contexts, on the other hand, some of these secular virtues can be seen as vices: especially pride in the frank display of strength and the open pleasure taken in material wealth. Wealth was to the Germanic people ordinarily a positive value, a symbolic measure of a man's worth (see Leisi 1952–53 and Cherniss 1972), but in Christian thinking wealth led too quickly to the deadly sin of avarice. And it was always the case that strict Christians might elect to view these pagans, however obedient they may have been to their own code, as ignorant of the true God and thus having before them only the prospect of damnation.

Before we conclude too hastily, however, that such a secular heroic code is incompatible with the ethics of Christianity, as some have done, we should remind ourselves that a very similar heroic ethic coexists famously with noisily explicit Christianity in other early-medieval heroic poems like *The Song of Roland*. There the Frankish heroes cheerfully alternate mass with massacre, the supposedly noncombatant Archbishop Turpin stoutly cleaves pagan knights in twain, and Roland himself glories in his pride, only sporadically aware of any higher responsibility than to the heroic code involving himself, his fellows in the comitatus of the Twelve Peers, and the Emperor Charlemagne. If in some sense Roland is condemned for his reckless secular pride, he is also loved for it, or there would have been no point in composing the poem or celebrating its hero.

The history of this controversy over "Christian and Pagan" is long, complex, and central to succeeding interpretations of the poem; every general essay on *Beowulf* has been obliged to deal with the problem. I should trace the course of the discussion briefly before focusing on recent attempts to reconcile the apparent polarities.

The earliest nineteenth-century readers of *Beowulf*, most of them northern Europeans, were involved in the Romantic search for national origins and in a revolt against Mediterranean traditions; hence they tended to welcome, and exaggerate, any pagan elements as authentically Germanic and to discount the Christian elements. In his prefatory remarks to the first edition of *Beowulf*, Thorkelin (1815b) had such readers in mind when he wrote: "Some will claim this epic cannot be genuine since it is full of Christian doctrine concerning the one and only God." Thorkelin believed the poem to have been composed by a Danish poet and then imported to England and slightly Christianized, possibly by King Alfred. "Nothing in this poem, I venture to say, would smack of Christianity had mention not crept in, à la Alfred, of the brothers Abel and Cain and his descendants, the Jutes or giants, those destroyed by the Flood, and of the satyrs and monsters. To these intrusions, if you like, add the lament about the Danes' ignorance of God, their worship of Odin, and the pagan spirits doomed to hell" (Thorkelin 1815b).

Ten Brink in 1883, to choose one instance of these early paganizers, speaks of the poem as being based on "the myth of Beowa, the divine hero who overcame the sea-giant, Grendel.... He is essentially Frea [i.e., Freyr] in a new form, the bright god of warmth and fruitfulness."[2] It will be noted that here the initial story of Scyld and Beow or Beowa (a name, most commentators now assume, converted erroneously though understandably by some scribe or editor into "Beowulf ") is jumbled together with the main plot of the poem, a common practice in earlier years, with the hero Beowulf being identified with the old god Beow(a). To such readers *Beowulf* seemed a self-consistent and gloriously "pagan" poem by a "folk" poet, but a work that had subsequently been tampered with by Christian scribes and interpolators. This way of thinking accorded with then prevalent ways of reading the Homeric poems as layers of different versions, interpolations, and revisions, in a process that tended to obscure the purity of some earlier, more primitive, and thus more valuable ethnic expression. In the case of *Beowulf*, it was sometimes believed that, before its scribes copied such inflammably pagan material, the church had to add some "Christian coloring" (to use a now famous phrase) to mask and justify the process (see Blackburn 1897; Chadwick 1907; Moorman 1967).

There were certainly precursors of Christian interpretations of the poem, but for this century we might focus on Klaeber, who published in 1911 and 1912 a series of articles that studied and documented the Christian elements in the poem responsibly and in great detail. He made the indisputable claim that the so-called Christian coloring was not laid late and lightly on the surface but was worked deeply into the very tissue of the poem at every point and could not be surgically removed without the death of the patient, and his majestic and universally admired edition of the poem (1950a) stressed the same point. The student will find Klaeber's own summary in the section of the introduction to his edition entitled "The Christian Coloring" (xlviii–li). It should be agreed by all that, like Klaeber, we can deal responsibly only with the single text we have, even though we are of course free to speculate about possible earlier versions of the poem, whether written or in purely oral form, that might have been less Christian or not Christian at all (for interesting speculations about such earlier strata, see Stevick 1963).

A few others (Schücking 1929a; Du Bois 1934) joined Klaeber in stressing these Christian elements, but it was Tolkien's renowned essay of 1936 that somewhat paradoxically started a powerful new wave of Christian interpretation—paradoxically because Tolkien made much of later pagan Scandinavian mythology, especially the Final Battle and Defeat, Ragnarok, the Twilight of the Gods, as a source for the pessimistic tone of the poem, at the same time seeing the poet as a mature Christian who would have viewed the world of the poem as "heathen, noble, and hopeless (265)." Nowadays, there is more skepticism than Tolkien felt about whether the Anglo-Saxons themselves even knew of such a final battle, since it is only recorded several centuries later in Iceland (van Meurs 1955). Still, the emotional similarity holds true enough: both the poem and the later Scandinavian eschatological myth must be seen as profoundly tragic in tone.

A still fairly cautious and temperate Christian view was that of Marie P. Hamilton in 1946: she envisioned a poet, influenced by Augustine's *City of God*, who saw signs of God's grace operating in pre-Christian Scandinavia, with the poem showing "the Germanic tradition ennobled by the new theology, as by a light flashed backward into the heroic past" (309). A similarly moderate attempt to deal with the likelihood of the poem being fundamentally Christian, though in a severely limited way, was that of

William Whallon in 1962, who held that the poet displayed "a primitive form of Christianity" and saw Beowulf and Hrothgar as Christians of the poet's own kind, though having only "a slight grasp of Christianity as we understand it" (82).

But 1963 can be remembered for several much more radically Christian interpretations. In 1951, D. W. Robertson Jr. had included the poem within his all-embracing Augustinian frame of reference as a poem dealing with *caritas* and its opposite *cupiditas*, in an article that led to the movement often named "Robertsonian." In 1960, Margaret E. Goldsmith published "The Christian Theme of *Beowulf*" and continued along the same lines in several articles culminating in her 1970 book, *The Mode and Meaning of Beowulf*. She finds teachings of Augustine and Gregory in Hrothgar's "sermon" (1770–84) and views the poem as a kind of Christian historical novel, with selected bits of paganism deliberately laid on as "local color," such as the references to fate or Wyrd. Of the hero, she writes: "As king, we admire his strength and fortitude. As man tempted, we share his agony of spirit. As soul aberrant from truth, 'reflected against the stainless mirror of the real,' we can only pity him. For he is supremely brave, supremely heroic in suffering, and supremely wrongheaded" (1963, 83). In the same Brodeur festschrift, E. G. Stanley (1963) writes of the certainty of Beowulf's damnation in the eyes of any Christian poet and severely judges the hero's final moments in these Christian terms: "He is a pagan, virtuous, all but flawless. His flaw being this, that ignorant of God he, in the hour of his death, could think of nothing other than pelf and a cenotaph; avarice and vainglory" (203). Still, this "flaw" is immense in any serious Christian context and overshadows whatever pagan virtues the hero may have revealed; the fundamental verdict on Beowulf is crushingly negative. The influential anthology of critical studies edited by Lewis E. Nicholson also appeared in 1963; most of its articles simply start from the assumption that *Beowulf* is an explicitly dogmatic Christian poem.

Another series of short articles published in 1964 and 1965 by Stanley, and later collected in 1975 as *The Search for Anglo-Saxon Paganism*, recounts, often amusingly and with copious quotations, the stubborn and long-lasting attempt by many scholars and critics, extending well into this century, to deny utterly the Christian nature of poems like *Beowulf*. The quotations tell their own undeniable and embarrassing story, but Stanley's study has since often been used by others to accuse any contemporary scholars who refuse to read *Beowulf* as an orthodox Christian tract of being as pigheaded and self-deluding as the older paganizers. This seems an inappropriate extension of Stanley's useful research.

The assertion that *Beowulf* is a seriously didactic Christian poem was now being restated by many scholars (see, e.g., Kaske 1968), and took several forms. An early interpretation was to identify the hero with Christ and to read the poem as an allegory like book 1 of Spenser's *Faerie Queene*, where the Christ figure Saint George also slays a dragon (Cabaniss 1955; McNamee 1960b). This view now seems to have been generally discarded, but another attempt to preserve Beowulf as a basically good and moral hero within a Christian framework is the "noble heathen" approach. For this, one must first posit a more tolerant form of Christianity than we usually find in the early Middle Ages.

Such an attitude is to be found in the more liberal Irish attitude toward noble heathens among their ancestors that has been stressed by Charles J. Donahue; it is a known fact that Irish missionaries had much to do with converting the northern English (Donahue 1950, 1977; see also McCone 1990). But Anglo-Saxonists have unfortunately always been slow to accept the reality of any important influences from the Celtic cultures, and, although this view is a tempting one, it has not attained general acceptance. Taking another approach, Larry D. Benson (1967) pointed out that the Anglo-Saxon missionaries to the Continent in the seventh and eighth centuries felt great sympathy and admiration for the yet unconverted Franks and Frisians and that the poem's positive attitude toward its heathen characters might have reflected that context.

More recently, scholars have brought in the analogy of the Icelandic sagas, in which the action often takes place before the conversion of Iceland about the year 1000 and where pagan characters may be represented as unquestionably admirable. A well-known example would be Gunnar Hamandarson in *Njáls saga*, a noble and glamorous warrior, co-hero with Njal in the saga, who lives and dies a pagan and is given pagan burial. After discussing such Old Norse parallels, Lars Lönnroth (1969) states that "the whole drama of *Beowulf* seems to be based upon a conflict between noble and monotheistic pagans, dwelling in a world of light and order, and godless heathen monsters" (1969, 7). Richard North (1991) deals chiefly with Icelandic works in discussing "pagan words and Christian meanings"; he sees Gunnar as sympathetic in almost Christian terms.

Such are some of the defenses offered for Beowulf's character, but it has also been under heavy attack from some of the Christianizers, who claim that, far from being a figure of Christ, Beowulf is an active sinner who deserves damnation not merely for the unlucky technicality of being unconverted but for his own evil deeds. Margaret Goldsmith has already been mentioned in this context. Her book of 1970, its footnotes thick with Biblical and patristic references, accuses Beowulf of two deadly sins, pride in recklessly volunteering to fight the dragon alone and cupidity in longing for the dragon's treasure, and similar accusations have since been echoed by others.

Two examples of more recent books taking a more moderate "exegetical" view are Huppé (1984) and Dahlberg (1988). Huppé views Beowulf as not so much actively evil as helplessly "caught in the iron circle of heroic error" (38) and sees the conclusion as demonstrating the failure of the "ancestral way" of the English (40). Dahlberg, who is heavily Augustinian in his developing of a Christ-centered theory of kingship applicable to the poem (26–35), finds in it a "sense ... of constant uncertainty and apprehension" (35). Like Robinson (1985), he stresses what he sees as the poet's careful critical distancing from pagan ideals and behavior.

Aside from often occasioning truly major distortions of the poem's meaning, such interpretations usually demand that we see the poet as a serious cleric, if not a theologian, and his or her audience as one familiar with many patristic niceties. But many studies of this exegetical school tend to be ominously more full of claims like "the audience would instantly have recognized" and "any Anglo-Saxon Christian would know" than full of any evidence for such knowledge. The charge of arguing in a circle is often brought, fairly, against this kind of interpretation. Since the poem is assumed to have hidden meanings, it must have had readers who could recognize them. But such hidden meanings may be visible only to the faithful.

Arguments that introduced a Latin vocabulary into the discussion by that very fact tended to tilt the interpretation of the poem noticeably toward a Latin/Christian/literate context, rather than a secular/Germanic/oral one. Such arguments were those of Bloomfield (1949–51) who wished to see the name *Unferð* as being a translation of *Discordia* and the poem thus resembling Prudentian allegory, and of Robert E. Kaske (1958), who insisted on using the Augustinian terms *sapientia* and *fortitudo* in a long (and quite valuable) critique. But the Anglo-Saxons had plenty of words of their own for these two qualities (Kindrick 1981). Fitting *Beowulf* into such Latinate contexts inevitably makes it seem more "Christian" than it may actually be; unfortunately, we have no equivalent oral/heroic "documents" to support the poem's other components, because such documents never existed.

Opposition to the more extreme Christian interpretations has been steady and sometimes acrimonious. John Halverson (1966) attacked some of the articles in the Nicholson anthology, maintaining that *Beowulf* "is primarily a secular poem with a secular hero" (275) and holding that one may be "suspicious of glowing claims about the thoroughness and sophistication of Anglo-Saxon Christianity" (276). In the following year, Charles Moorman published "The Essential Paganism of *Beowulf*," asserting that the principal Christian elements (which he lists as allusions to free will, Hrothgar's sermon, Beowulf's moderate behavior and gratitude to God, and assigning the troll Grendel to the race of Cain) are all quite peripheral to the main story itself, in which the "pagan" features (listed as pessimism, a sense of unyielding fate, the heroic code, the praise of heroism, and the celebration of prowess and courage) are central. G. V. Smithers (1970) also speaks of the poet's interjecting of some Christian values into the poem but holds that it is the inherited pagan heroic ethos that matters.

Michael D. Cherniss (1972) sounds many of the same notes in a longer work, its title, *Ingeld and Christ*, an allusion to Alcuin's famed remark, *Quid Hinieldus cum Christo?* (what does Ingeld have to do with Christ?), allegedly reproving the monks of Lindisfarne for listening to secular poetry about the pagan hero Ingeld, a minor character in *Beowulf* (see also Levine 1971). It has been recently argued with some force, however, that Alcuin's letter was not intended for monks at Lindisfarne or elsewhere but directed at a more secular "mixed" audience at a bishop's feast (Bullough 1993). In countering the attribution of covetousness to Beowulf, Cherniss spends much time explaining the positive or heroic Germanic concept of treasure visible in the poem, where it is used to define honor and worth, with no ironic undertone.

Before we venture some tentative conclusions on this controversy, we should first be sure we get everything we can in the way of evidence out of the poem itself, with as few preconceptions as possible. Some years ago (Irving 1984), I made a modest attempt to do so and will summarize a few conclusions. I used a rough quantification of what are generally accepted as Christian references: biblical allusions; references to "Metod" and "Dryhten" and the like; allusions to hell or the Last Judgment. To give a better sense of relative densities, I counted single words, so that "ece" and "Dryhten" registered as two units rather than as a single phrase (for an earlier study of the Christian language of the poem, see Batchelor 1937).

One important finding was that lines 1–1887 of the poem contain one hundred forty-two such references while lines 1888–3182 contain only thirty-six—that is to say, there is one Christian reference for every thirteen lines in the Danish part of the poem and one for every thirty-six in the Geatish part. Several possible reasons for the difference suggest themselves. The most thoroughly Christian speaker of the poem, Hrothgar, is absent in part 2; he averages twice as many Christian references as the narrator in the poem as a whole. Then too the symbolic structure of part 1 is amplified in Christian terms in a way that part 2 is not: it is in part 1 that Grendel is said to be descended from Cain, associated with devils, and either resident in or destined for hell, and it is here that the pious Hrothgar thanks God for sending his champion in the person of Beowulf. But the final fight with the dragon is never put in symbolic terms like these, though prolonged and strenuous attempts have been made by a number of exegetes to relate him to Satan, the great dragon mentioned in chapter 12 of the Book of Revelation.

If the difference between the two parts in this respect is significant, any full account of the Christian/pagan problem might then have to deal fairly and separately with both parts of the poem. It seems likely that the version of *Beowulf* we have may have been patched together from two or three earlier stories. If so, it seems plain that the Danish story (or perhaps two stories: "Grendel" and "Grendel's Mother") was given a much more thorough Christian treatment than the final story of Beowulf's death fighting the dragon. Why this uneven distribution of Christian references remained in the final composite version is unclear. Osborn offers one possible reason: "There is no need for further scriptural references after the two kinsfolk of Cain have been destroyed" (1978, 979). One may even speculate that the final poet believed that, whatever his heroic virtues, the pagan Beowulf's death had better not be surrounded by too much Christian language, lest it raise awkward questions.

In the same study, I concluded that the kind of Christianity that *Beowulf* displays is distinctly limited: not so much primitive (though critics may once have seen it as the Christianity of those recently or barely converted) as either deliberately or unconsciously tailored to the dimensions of heroic poetry. Thus, God is not associated with prayers, angels, saints, and miracles (or with the never-mentioned Christ) but is the great and austere King of Heaven, perpetually at war with an evil force of trolls and demons and using the heroic power of Beowulf to accomplish his ends. Preserving the safe and brightly lit human world God has created is clearly a moral goal, but the means he uses are less spiritual than physical. Yet the vitality of this royal, monotheistic God is genuinely felt in the poem; we can still respond to its presence today. In 1984 I wrote: "God is truly felt as a living presence only at those moments when we feel the surges of heroic power in Beowulf. In this special sense the hero is indeed God's agent, for he is the only way we can be aware of God and of how he acts in the world of men we know" (18).

The "mixed" or "blended" nature of the poem is now agreed on by almost everyone, but scholars differ in how to describe it or account for it—and will always continue to do so, in the absence of more knowledge. One way to explain it is to posit some kind of mixed audience. In 1978, the historian Patrick Wormald published an important study of such a mixed audience (see also Wormald 1991). He amasses much evidence to argue that the early Anglo-Saxon church was heavily secularized, with churches and monasteries often the property of aristocratic families, whose members became bishops and monks. He concludes that Christianity "had been successfully assimilated by a warrior nobility, which had no intention of abandoning its culture, or seriously changing its way of life, but which was willing to throw its traditions, customs, tastes and loyalties into the articulation of the new faith" (1978, 57). Thus, a poem like *Beowulf*, which celebrated the greatness of their noble ancestors, would be exactly what representatives of such a secularized culture would demand and would produce. Members of this kind of audience might refuse flatly to concede that their traditional heroes were unworthy of respect or even of some form of salvation. Wormald's view has received support from Lapidge (1982) and Niles (1983, 115; 1993c, 146), among others.

Other readers have made much of a more subtle kind of mixture within the poem itself, namely, the unmistakable contrast in tone between the exultant Danish section, where so much is achieved, and the deep sadness and sense of loss of the last section on Beowulf's death. They tend to take this sense of loss as a form of Christian message. Earl (1982) sees the poem as a statement of deep and necessary mourning (in the psychiatrist's sense) for a great heroic past now irrevocably destroyed by the coming of the new faith. Benson (1967), Frank (1982a), and Robinson (1985), as well as others, view the poem as a kind of historical novel, similar to the Icelandic sagas, in which a conscious and painstaking effort is made by a Christian author to recreate the pagan heroic world, perhaps chiefly to show its limitations as well as its appeal. Thomas D. Hill (1986) echoes Hanning (1974), who speaks of the gloom deriving from "history as yet unillumined by the promise of redemption" (86).

Yet it should be pointed out here that there are readers in our own post-Christian century who have never seen history so illumined and may feel themselves perfectly at home with the "existential" gloom and bleakness of Beowulf's last end. They may find it simply a realistic view of mortal life. They may believe that, like other epic heroes, Beowulf goes in unflinching courage, in the words of Wallace Stevens, "downward to darkness, on extended wings."

This kind of blending of the two traditions, where a work produced in an unmistakably Christian context seems able to tolerate large admixtures of the secular with no sense of incongruity, is not easy to describe. A bold but not entirely persuasive attempt to describe in serious philosophical terms the kind of universe the poet envisions is that of James Earl (1987). His title suggests his basic approach: "Transformation of Chaos: Immanence and Transcendence in *Beowulf* and Other Old English Poems."

The better-known recent attempt of Fred C. Robinson (1985) to define such blending, however, seems to me misguided and unsuccessful, perhaps because he tries so hard to eliminate the very incongruity rather than accepting it as a fact of the poem. While Robinson acknowledges the secular side of the poem, describing it as the poet's wish to honor "lost ancestors" (13), the very word *lost* can be pushed a little farther into meaning *damned*, and we are not surprised to find that he holds to most of the usual "exegetical" interpretations as well (e.g., the dragon = Satan, the characters are "lost eternally").

Robinson tries to resolve these flat contradictions between "heroic" meaning and theological demands by assuming an extraordinary number of puns and deliberate double meanings, where a word or phrase is ostensibly "pagan" but is also sending hidden "Christian" meanings to the audience. Thus, the poet is seen as constantly wigwagging secret messages to his Christian audience over his characters' heads. Robinson here resorts to a desperate expedient, since such punning is no feature of the oral-derived style. It is rather a way of reading inherent in the Latin exegetical tradition of interpretation, where the nut of any word must be forcibly cracked to extract the church's kernel.

Finally, and perhaps most important, the tone he attributes to the poem seems entirely inappropriate: the poet is shown as constantly pointing to, or perhaps gloating over, the pitiable or pathetic condition of the benighted characters. This is in no way the *Beowulf* most of us think we know.

Yet Robinson's approach is a valid attempt to deal with the problem of a double audience, though his method is not successful. Earlier scholars apparently did not really discriminate clearly between what the fictional characters know and what (Christian) knowledge seems to be shared by poet and audience. A fine place to see this distinction is the scene where Hrothgar examines the hilt of the giant sword Beowulf has just brought up from the depths of Grendel's mere.

> Hrothgar spoke, looked at the hilt, the old relic, on which was
> written the beginning of the long-ago struggle, when the flood,
> gushing ocean, struck the race of giants (they suffered terribly);
> that was a nation alien to the Lord; for that the Ruler gave them
> their final reward through the surge of water.
> (1687–93)

Does Hrothgar read this biblical story? Represented on the hilt (written? carved in runes [the "runstafas" of 1695]? just possibly [the word *writan* has this meaning] drawn as a picture?) is the story from Genesis 6:1–2, describing the "giants on the earth in those days"; mention of them immediately precedes God's decision to destroy all life in the Deluge. A *post hoc, ergo propter hoc* logic can easily see the Flood as directed specifically at the giants. We must say that Hrothgar is here quite illiterate. It is impossible for him to "read" this story, as it was impossible at the beginning of the poem for the assembled Danes in Heorot to "hear" the story of Cain and Abel the poet tells us as a natural sequel to the scop's account of Creation, which the Danes *did* hear. (For further discussion of this aspect of the poem, see Osborn 1978).

John D. Niles has spoken in several places (1983; 1991) of the "tempering" of the strong secular themes of the poem with Christianity, a better way to describe what happened. Something like this takes place, but we may still feel a certain uneasy incongruity. We have a classic example of such strange pairing in the Franks Casket, where a panel showing Weland, a pagan hero of a tale of bloody vengeance, as offering a vessel made of a skull to his captors nestles symmetrically beside one showing the Magi offering gifts to the Christ Child. Did an Anglo-Saxon examining the casket feel that these were similar gifts, both part of equally powerful and interesting stories from the past? So the artist seems to suggest; there is no indication in the *picture* that the Christian story is to be favored. We can never answer that question with any assurance, but it is likely that the Anglo-Saxon's answer would not be ours.

But we should return to safer ground in our own time. Though it is currently unfashionable to assert that literary works are founded on some basic and apparently universal aesthetic principles, I believe they are so founded and that such principles can be applied to *Beowulf*. Since I have tried to carry out this application at some length elsewhere (Irving 1968, 1989), I will here mention only one of the simplest of such inductively derived principles: what a poet talks about and gives full attention to well over 95 percent of the time is what he or she is interested in and what the poem is chiefly about, and thus it is what readers and critics should give their attention to.

From this point of view, *Beowulf* is, in overwhelming mass, an admiring account of heroic action, focused with special intensity on a single figure (there is nothing in the poem that is not directly related to Beowulf), and a somewhat less admiring account of the heroic world in which action takes place. This overwhelming mass, the towering bulk of the poem, has been ignored or brushed aside by those who have clung to the now moribund view of the poem as flat-out Christian sermon; they concentrate on a tiny number of details widely scattered in the poem—surely making up no more than 1 percent of the poem. But it is simply wrong to let details wag the dog.

Yet it would be fair, and an appropriate conclusion that will bring us back closer to the words of the poem, to look at some of these hot spots of past discussion of our topic, these hooks on which so much has depended.

One famous spot is Hrothgar's "sermon" (1700–84). Calling his speech a sermon may prejudge the issue, of course; the term was originally jocular, before the humorless took it over. Hrothgar's chief point is that we should all remember that we are vulnerable to fate and death or we will suffer dire consequences, a valid warning that might be made by any Christian or any pagan. Some readers (e.g., Stanley 1979, 62) have taken the speech to be a theme statement of which the poem is almost an exemplification, but the actual warning is so broadly couched and all embracing that it is hardly a real theme, though appropriate generally to any work with a gloomy ending. It might have been a real theme if Beowulf had turned arrogant or believed he would never die, but that never happens. It is true that Hrothgar's sermon contains some notably Christian imagery (of the evil spirit shooting arrows to wound the sinner), but this agrees with Hrothgar's usual preaching tone and the high ratio of Christian language in his speeches. Furthermore, Hrothgar may not be entitled to make a theme statement about the poem's main business (the nature of heroism), since he is not at all the hero of the poem (for unheroic aspects of his character, see Irving 1989).

A second hot spot is the phrase "ofer ealde riht." News is brought to Beowulf that the dragon has destroyed his royal hall. His reaction is as follows:

> For the good one that was grief in the breast, greatest of sorrow-
> ful emotions; the wise one believed that against old law he had
> bitterly angered the Ruler, the eternal Lord. His breast welled up
> inside with dark thoughts, as was not his custom.
> (2327b–32)

This seems to be the only time Beowulf feels himself estranged from God's purposes or support, however briefly. He concludes at once that this must be because he has offended God in some way, "against old law." Is that phrase, "ofer ealde riht," a reference to a Christian law (see Goldsmith 1963, 78), or the "old law" of the Old Testament, or "natural law," or a pagan law (Moorman [1967] thinks it might be the heroic code itself), and if so, what does it mean here? Might it just mean vaguely "in a wrong way" in a formulaic phrase dating back to the oral stage of poetry? We cannot furnish certain answers to these questions. It is certainly hard for us to see how Beowulf has had anything to do with the dragon's sudden attack. Beowulf may blame himself for it (he is a super-responsible king, and it happened under his administration), but if we blame him, we turn the whole poem from then on into something it so very clearly is not—a conventional study of crime and punishment rather than a moving tale of a hero's last battle and courageous death.

An even more problematic passage occurs immediately after Beowulf speaks his last words to Wiglaf.

> For the old man, that was the last word from his inner thoughts,
> before he chose the pyre, the hot hostile flames; from his breast
> his soul went to seek the judgment of the righteous.
>   (2817–20)

The last two words occur elsewhere in clear religious contexts and normally refer to the favorable judgment made on the virtuous at the time of their death, usually implying their admission to heaven (see Greenfield 1985). Here Beowulf's body is said to "choose" the flames of the pagan pyre; his soul, however, escapes this fate and travels to find "the judgment of the righteous." But if he is not a Christian, how can his soul enter heaven? This question can be answered either by exerting very considerable pressure on the phrase "soðfæstra dom" or by putting up with the inconsistency of what is implied. In the first case, the phrase *might* be forced to mean the opinion of good secular men (though why would his *soul* seek that?), rather than God's judgment, but that would be a distortion of ordinary meaning. In the second case, we must accept the poet's casual assumption that so good and great a king obviously deserves heaven, if anyone does—whatever ecclesiastical bureaucrats may say. Earlier we were told that King Hrethel of the Geats "chose God's light" when he died (2469). The phrases slide neatly and quietly into place; poet and audience seem to agree that these are the appropriate and expected phrases for the death of good men—unless you are talking about extreme cases of wickedness, like those who fall back on worshiping idols (178b–83a) or like Grendel, hell dwelling, man eating, Cain descended (805b–08). They unmistakably go to hell, and, in the heat of the flyting between them, Beowulf predicts the same destination for the brother slayer Unferth (588b–89). Obviously, the virtuous—the *soðfæst*—Beowulf cannot go where those people go, and his soul goes somewhere. It goes to heaven. Yet perhaps it is also just as true that his "pagan soul" is placed in the barrow up above the sea in the course of a pagan's funeral and wins the pagan's reward of eternal fame on earth. We may be looking at the paradox of the Franks Casket once again.

Examples like these reveal a few of the underlying reasons for the long controversy over the poem's religious dimension. Apparently a consensus is now forming, or has formed, on the subject: namely, that *Beowulf* is at all points a smooth *blend* of pagan/secular elements with Christian ones, with its chief purpose to express and celebrate the heroic ethic (see, e.g., John 1974; Tietjen 1975; Earl 1983; Niles 1983). Many believe that the poem is a "swan song," a conscious memorial tribute to a vanished, or vanishing, culture, and this is certainly what the historical context would suggest it might be, but people may differ on what that implies. Some share the views of Hanning (1974, 99): that the poem is "a devastating commentary on the hero, and the history, of an age possessed of grandeur but denied the knowledge of Christ from which alone could come understanding and control of its destiny." Here Hanning's word *devastating* seems to throw the emotional balance quite off; nothing in the poem devastates this hero. Others would insist that so strong a statement of ultimate Christian meaning is merely what some think *should be* in the poem, but in fact is not. It is necessary to say at the end of this discussion that such differing *personal* beliefs are unlikely ever to be fully reconciled with each other. And so there will be no end to this discussion.

It hardly needs pointing out, finally, that the Christian/pagan question is tightly connected to other problems dealt with elsewhere in this volume. I will mention here only the unsolved problem of dating the poem. To simplify greatly, we are most likely to find a Christian poet interested in stories from a pagan past in either of two periods: in the time well after the conversion of the English but before the Viking invasions, roughly in the eighth century; or in the later Benedictine revival period of the late tenth and early eleventh centuries, when so many manuscripts were being produced, including the *Beowulf* manuscript. Looking at the problem strictly from this chapter's standpoint, in favor of the earlier period are these factors: the oral tradition is fresher and stronger and the stories are better remembered and admired; some generations have passed since the conversion, but memories or traces of paganism are still present; courts like that of King Offa of Mercia, with some imperial pretensions, or aristocratic monasteries like those described by Wormald have arisen that might furnish suitable "mixed" audiences, with a strong interest in celebrating a heroic past (see Howe 1989). In favor of the later period are these factors: an apparent urgent need to incorporate the culture of the newly converted Danish settlers, who had brought along their own stories of Scylding heroes, into a united national epic tradition; Alfred's well-known encouragement of vernacular literature; enough distance from the pagan English past to enable a poet to recreate it sympathetically; perhaps keener awareness of classical epics like the *Aeneid* as models for a long heroic poem; possibly even new infusions of stylistic features from Old Norse poetry. On these grounds alone, however, we can make no firm decision about the date.

NOTES

1. At a session of the Medieval Institute at Western Michigan University in 1993, Martin Carver, director of the Sutton Hoo archaeological project, suggested (with great tentativeness) such an interpretation of the evidence.

2. Quoted in Calder 1981, 214. The reader is referred to this valuable outline of the earlier criticism of Old English poetry, especially up to 1870, and to similar surveys of criticism relevant to this chapter by Rollinson (1973), Donahue (1977), and Short (1980b). George Clark (1990, 13–21, 45–46) has as excellent and up-to-date summary of the matter.

JOHN D. NILES

Myth and History

Anyone delving into the annals of *Beowulf* scholarship will find examples
of the mythic fallacy, or what Walter J. Ong has called "the myth of myth"
(1962, 131–45). This is the conviction that primal stories underlie features of
a literary text and give this text its chief significance and value. These master
narratives, or myths, are believed to derive from a deeper or more elemental
source than the text in question, whether this source is located in the remote
past or the unchanging human psyche.

Myths in this sense are unlike allegories in that they are not normally
encoded in texts by authorial design,[1] nor is their presence announced through
transparent labels (such as Christian and Faithful meet Mr. Money-love
while fleeing the City of Destruction). Scholars must infer their presence in
a given literary work by probing its plot, patterns of imagery, and the like as
well as through the study of names and their possible etymological meanings.
To discover a myth in a text is a privileged scholarly enterprise that naturally
lends that text added value, if not an almost magically therapeutic force, for
myths are commonly thought to express enduring wisdom about the human
condition. Texts come and go; myths are thought to be coherent and to have
high truth value. Myths are therefore prized in and of themselves as well as
being of heuristic use as keys that will unlock the secrets of literature. To
put the matter another way, the typically modern condition of *amythia*, or a

From *A* Beowulf *Handbook*, ed. Robert E. Bjork and John D. Niles, pp. 216–232. © 1998 by the
University of Nebraska Press.

139

world stripped of its myths (to use a term favored by Loyal D. Rue [1989]), is a post-Nietzschean spiritual wasteland from which escape must be found if human culture is to survive.

While the quest for secret meaning in *Beowulf* has often gravitated toward myth, whether of a pagan or a Christian kind,[2] it has also turned to history. With no less energy than the myth seekers, scholars of a historicist orientation have scrutinized the text and ransacked external sources either to provide a real-life identity for the characters and tribes who figure in the poem or to locate features of its landscape and plot in the actual world. A historicist fallacy has thus arisen side by side with the mythic fallacy, whether in tandem with it or opposed. History, like myth, assumes a high truth value for those who believe in it. Just as some critics use the poem as a means of discovering a "myth to live by," others respond more vibrantly to the complex and tragic history that they believe to be secretly woven into *Beowulf* than they do to the plain story itself.

Beowulf begins with a genealogical prologue that sets the main action of the poem against the background of Danish dynastic history from the time of Scyld Scefing, the eponymous ancestor of the Scyldings, to that of Hrothgar, his great grandson. Since Scyld is generally taken to be a mythical king while Hrothgar is thought to be historical, readers must soon confront a question posed by Claude Lévi-Strauss in the context of North American Tsimshian myths: "The problem is: where does mythology end and where does history start?" (1978, 38). The reader's desire to distinguish between two different modes of past time, the fabulous and the factual, runs headlong into the obstacle of the storyteller's blank refusal to admit such distinctions. Such an impasse naturally spurs reflection as to how adequate the reader's categories are.

Lévi-Strauss's question has an obverse side—"Where does history end and where does mythology start?"—that is worth posing for its bearing on the poem's main plot. This plot takes us from the shadowy land of the herds people, the "Geats," to Hrothgar's brightly lit Denmark, then back again to "Geatland," with stops at two fabulous locales, Grendel's mere and a firedrake's barrow. Again and again in the history of *Beowulf* criticism, scholars have tried to convert the more fabulous elements of this plot into the terms of a myth whereby a godlike savior or Everyman-like hero is pitted against adversaries suggestive of primeval chaos, death, or the unconscious. Alternatively, the poem's putatively historical elements have been taken as factual and, indeed, as amounting to a master narrative, myth-like in its functions,[3] that explains one or more features of either the Scandinavian or the Anglo-Saxon past.

Treading such slippery turf, and unsure that anyone among us has unmediated access to the truth about the past, some contemporary historians no longer claim that a firm distinction between myth and history either can or should be made. In his *Mythistory and Other Essays* (1986), William H. McNeill describes the task of the historian as a never-ending process of "historiographical myth making and myth breaking." At its best, in his optimistic view, the process of historiography results in "ever-evolving mythistories [that] become truer and more adequate to public life" (20).[4]

It was chiefly to combat the entrenched habits of naive historicist thinking that J. R. R. Tolkien went out of his way in 1936 to defend the narrative text of *Beowulf* ("the monsters," in his synecdoche) against the trivializing gestures of academic criticism ("the critics"). For Tolkien, the question of the historicity of the elements of *Beowulf* was a distraction from the text as an example of magnificent fiction. Tolkien initiated a revolution in *Beowulf* studies that continued strong through much of the century. Historicist claims about *Beowulf* have still been heard, but by being presented as facts, not interpretations, they have stayed outside the precincts of criticism. Only in the past ten or fifteen years, thanks in part to controversy concerning the date of the poem, have the biases of positivist historicism and literary aestheticism been challenged strongly enough for a fresh critical approach to *Beowulf* to emerge. This approach, which as yet has no name but is associated with the New Historicism,[5] focusses less on issues of historicity or literary value *per se* than on questions of how a given text serves as an agent of social ideology, a means of collective self-fashioning, and a participant in period-specific tensions and tropes.

My purpose in the main body of this chapter is to review selected examples of first mythic and then historicist criticism of *Beowulf*, having now briefly set them into a wider context. I will then briefly offer reasons for regarding the poem *as* a myth or, better, as an example of mythistory: that is, as a narrative that, by telling about a formative period of the ancestral past, served the Anglo-Saxons as a charter for contemporary institutions of kingship and thaneship while also reinforcing a wide range of culturally-specific beliefs and values. Skepticism is my keyword here, however, and I will conclude by suggesting reasons to question some aspects of the argument that I myself have posed.

I. THE QUEST FOR MYTH

The term *myth* means many things to many people. Notoriously, the word covers a range of meanings that extends from "sacred narrative" or "the highest form of truth" to "false idea" or "lie."[6] When used in a scholarly context, it is usually a neutral term denoting a story about gods, heroes, and the like, set in ancient times, viewed as true, and serving to explain important features of the natural world. Although the term appears often in *Beowulf* criticism, it is seldom defined. Although often used neutrally, sometimes it has been used in the approving sense that it carries in Jungian psychology; *myth* then refers to an archetypal story, akin to dream, that encodes a message relating to personal spiritual growth. Sometimes this positive connotation spills over to the former usage, as if it were by nature a good thing for a poem, novel, or play to have a mythic dimension, or as if one were showing something final about it when one demonstrates that it resembles a myth.

It is now over a century and a half since Karl Müllenhoff (1849a, 1889), inspired by the nature mythology that was then in vogue, offered a meteorological interpretation of *Beowulf* that was in keeping with late Romantic ideas concerning the character of primitive literature. According to Müllenhoff, *Beowulf* was a symbolic drama whose action signified human beings' struggle for existence in a hostile physical environment over which they had little control. Nineteenth-century scholars looked for traces of primitive nature myths in *Beowulf* with results that varied with each investigator (for reviews of this scholarship, see Klaeber 1950a, 25, and Chambers 1959, 46–47). The appeal of Müllenhoff's approach to *Beowulf* was due partly to its invocation of a specific northern geography.

Müllenhoff found it essential that the main action of *Beowulf* takes place in the North Sea coastal zone in and around Jutland, the ancestral homeland of the Angles. Grendel, Grendel's mother, the dragon, and the Breca episode all represent personifications of the North Sea in its devastating storms and floods. Since there is a seasonal aspect to the strife of sea versus land, calm weather versus storm, the hero's death represents the demise of the sun in winter, while the winning of the dragon's hoard signifies that the resources of the whole vegetative kingdom have been secured for human benefit for another year. The whole story is thus a localized myth of the seasons. How did what was originally a legend featuring a local hero figure (*Localsage*) come to take on the characteristics of myth? Müllenhoff found the answer to this question in onomastics: the adventures that the poet ascribed to the Geatish warrior Beowulf were attached to him by mistake, for they once properly pertained to the agricultural god *Beaw* or *Beow*, who is introduced into the poem under the erroneous name "Beowulf" (18 and 53). The Anglo-Saxon poem preserved a primitive myth in displaced and somewhat garbled form.

Müllenhoff's theories were the orthodoxy of their day. Nature myths were so arbitrarily defined that they could not well be refuted, only ignored. It was thus predictable that as new intellectual movements emerged during the early decades of the twentieth century, the mythographic impulse began to fall of its own weight to earth. Still relevant to *Beowulf* studies are the devastating criticisms that W. W. Lawrence leveled against Müllenhoff and other mythologists (1909; 1928, 129–60). As Lawrence saw, readings of *Beowulf* as a displaced nature myth left themselves open to charges of *a priori* methods and reductive thinking. Their main disadvantage was that they stifled inquiry. By chasing phantoms of the prehistoric imagination, such theories explained little about the particulars of the poet's account of the hero's specific conduct in Denmark and his homeland.

The waning of nature mythology did not mean the end of the mythological impulse in *Beowulf* criticism. Given that *Beowulf* is the only early Germanic epic on a secular theme to have survived virtually intact, and taking into account also its many marvelous features and its apparent indebtedness to an ancient folktale pattern (Panzer 1910), scholars inevitably have continued to search the poem for evidence bearing on early myths and cults. In addition, some critics have developed new models for the understanding of *Beowulf* based upon the search for psychological archetypes.

Some of the mythic connections that have recently been posited pertain specifically to Germanic terrain. The ravens that feed on the dead, for example, are thought to be reflexes of Odin's birds (Huntley 1981). The rites of drinking and cup bearing in Heorot have been likened to the nurturing of the tree Yggdrasil, one of the central activities of the Norns (Bauschatz 1982, 85–116). The Danish hero Hengest, featured in the scop's song of Finn and Hengest, has been linked, with his brother Horsa, to early Germanic and Indo-European myths of divine twins (Turville-Petre 1953–57; Joseph 1983). The Heathobard chief Froda has been found to be a displaced figure of the god Frey (Ebenauer 1976). The poet's allusion to the story of the arrival of Scyld as a helpless foundling has been linked, by a circuitous path, to tales of the Eddic giant Bergelmir and the Estonian agricultural deity Pekko (Fulk 1989; cf. Neckel 1910). According to Karl Schneider (1986), the whole poem is based on a putative Germanic creation myth about a Primary God, otherwise figured as a hermaphrodite giant named Hegil, who sacrificed himself for the sake of the cosmogony. Schneider's neopaganism runs the risk of burlesque in that he finds that "Cædmon's Hymn" too was composed in honor of Hegil, who is none other than the ithyphallic giant carved into the chalk hill at Cerne Abbas. Helen Damico (1984) has advanced complex etymological arguments to support the claim that Wealhtheow, Hrothgar's queen and a cupbearer in Heorot, has a vestigial relation to the valkyries of ancient Germanic belief. She arrives at a composite speculative portrait whereby Wealhtheow is imagined as "a female of noble birth, southern in origin, who undergoes a period of enslavement" and who also has martial and priestly qualities (64–65). Any of the studies mentioned in this paragraph are open to the same criticism as Müllenhoff's: by ignoring the possibility that a pagan myth may adopt a different semiotic code when taken up by a

Christian author (see Clunies Ross 1989, 8–9), they still tell us little about *Beowulf* as a literary creation. At best, such arguments can shed light on the complex matrix of myth and rite from which the poem developed.

Other connections between *Beowulf* and Old Norse myths known from the *Elder Edda* or Snorri Sturluson's *Prose Edda* have been argued from time to time, although never with definitive results, partly because of the difficulty of knowing if authors and audiences in Anglo-Saxon England were familiar with the Norse myths in question. The chief of these connections are the accidental slaying of Herebeald by Hæthcynn, a tragedy that has been likened to Baldr's death; the relation of the ending of the poem, with its images of impending desolation, to the Norse concept of Ragnarok; and the resemblance of Beowulf as dragon slayer to Thor, particularly with regard to that god's combat against the Midgard Serpent.

The Baldr connection, raised repeatedly in the critical literature (see Klaeber 1950a, xli n.5; also Nerman 1913a, 70–71; and Neckel 1920b, 141ff.), has a sound linguistic basis in that the second element in the name of Hrethel's son *Herebeald* is cognate with Old Norse *Baldr*, while the first element in the name of Herebeald's slayer *Hæðcyn* is cognate with Old Norse *Høðr*, Baldr's slayer. Herebeald and Baldr die in analogous ways—Herebeald is killed by an errant arrow, Baldr by being struck with a thrown dart—and each death inspires great grief and desolation. A vestigial connection to the myth is therefore plausible, yet the link remains delicate. The reason Baldr is grieved so intensely is that he is the fairest of all the gods, while nothing is said about Herebeald's appearance. All nature grieves for Baldr, while it is the aged Hrethel alone who suffers suicidal grief for Herebeald. The Norse myth is a fully elaborated story that features Loki's treachery and disguise, Baldr's lavish ship cremation, and Hermoð's arduous journey to Hel, three themes that have no analogues in the Herebeald episode from *Beowulf*. While the myth of Baldr may be echoed vestigially in the poem, it has been altered almost beyond recognition.

Some readers of *Beowulf* have followed Tolkien (1936) in linking the last part of the poem, with its warnings of impending warfare and tribal dissolution, to the Norse concept of the end of the world in a final combat of gods and men against the hostile hosts of monsters. Since one cannot be sure that the myth of Ragnarok was known to the Anglo-Saxons, those who pursue these traces must postulate that the myth as told in *Vǫluspá* is early and pan-Germanic in origin rather than being a late development influenced by Christian concepts of apocalypse. Ursula Dronke (1969), accepting *Vǫluspá* as early, argues that the *Beowulf* poet's account of the building of Heorot is based on pagan creation myth; she finds in both sources the theme of a menaced creation faced by approaching destruction. Paul Beekman Taylor

(1966) argues that the poet develops a three-fold parallel between Heorot, the whole created earth (as in the Christian myth of Genesis), and Asgard (as in the cosmogonic myth related in *Vǫluspá*). Pagan and Christian myths thus reinforce one another. The connection between *Beowulf* and Norse myth remains impressionistic, however, for the ending of *Beowulf* falls short of apocalypticism. The funeral of a beloved leader, one who sacrificed his life to defend his people, is attended by expressions of grief that spring in part from fears of worse days to come. In other words, things are as they should be, dramatically speaking. One would not have wanted the Geats to rejoice at this moment. The muted ending of *Beowulf* confirms the note of pessimism that permeates this philosophical poem throughout, lending the dragon episode in particular a melancholy air. To look beyond this pessimism for echoes of pagan myths is to shift into an associative realm where Wagnerian strains prevail.

Ever since N. F. S. Grundvig praised *Beowulf* as "a heroic poem of Thor" (1820, 1), critics have wanted to see the hero of the poem as a displaced figure of the great warrior god of Norse mythology. Both Dronke and Taylor point out parallels between Beowulf as dragon slayer and Thor as slayer of the Midgard Serpent, a connection that was urged by Müllenhoff (1889, 4) despite its inherent incongruities on the side of both the dignified hero and his scaly, apparently nonaquatic opponent. Freshening up the Thor connection and turning it to new ends, Seth Lerer (1994) has recently argued that in the passage telling of Grendel's marvelous dragon-skin glove, the *Beowulf* poet trades on his audience's familiarity with the Eddic tale of Thor's escape from the giant Skrýmir's glove, at the same time as he presents an unconscious reflex of an ancient pattern of ritualistic dismemberment. Counting against conscious allusion is the same problem already cited: claims about literary debts run up against the difficulty of knowing whether the Eddic myths were known to the Anglo-Saxons. As for a connection to ancient rites, such arguments remain impressionistic in the absence of evidence concerning what such rites were and who practiced them, when and where.

Given the origins of *Beowulf* in the Isle of Britain, it is natural that the Celtic realm too, with its rich array of myths, should be searched for parallels to the story. The search has met with only partial success. In a book that draws on a set of previously published articles, Martin Puhvel (1979) postulates Celtic origins for such features of *Beowulf* as the unusual might of Grendel's mother, the hero's marvelous swimming prowess, the "sword of light" that the hero wields against the demoness, and the subsequent melting of that giant blade. Although the parallels are fairly close and their sum total impressive, they remain somewhat disjointed, for there is no one myth or even one coherent body of myth to which the poem can be related. Puhvel deals in isolated motifs only, and these can surface in folk literature of all description.

Going beyond Germanic and Celtic mythology to a deeper European past, some scholars (like Lerer, discussed above) have found evidence linking *Beowulf* to myths or rites that are believed to be embedded either in the Indo-European tradition or in a more capacious ancient context. Studies by Joseph Fontenrose, Albert B. Lord, and Alvin A. Lee are cases in point.[7]

In his *Python: A Study of Delphic Myth and Its Origins* (1959), Fontenrose casts his comparative net widely enough to catch both Beowulf and Thor in it as Germanic manifestations of a basic and far-flung story pattern celebrating the victory of a divine or semidivine hero figure over a dragon or chaos demon who guards a life-giving spot. Only a loose fit can be found between the local contours of *Beowulf* and the general pattern that Fontenrose isolates, however. Working in a similar mode, Lord (1980) has made the more cautious claim that *Beowulf* includes vestigial elements of two narrative patterns that play a major role in various ancient epics. These are a pattern of the hero's "withdrawal, devastation, and return," including the death of a surrogate figure, and a hero's escape from a male monster and thwarting of a female monster who wishes to keep him in an otherworld locale. Lord's arguments have the attraction of accounting for features of the text that might otherwise go unexplained, like the necessity of Hondscio's or Æschere's death. Although his line of investigation is intriguing, his comparisons are based on too small a body of evidence to be compelling. In a recent article (1993), Lee has revived a type of mythological criticism that is associated with Northrop Frye and that Lee developed in his earlier *The Guest-Hall of Eden* (1972). Lee sees the poet as drawing obliquely on Christian myths of Creation and Doomsday to create an image of Heorot as *imago mundi*, brilliant but destined to fall. If the dominant myths here—"the myth of a hero destroying monsters that attack by night from beyond the light-filled human centre" and "the myth of the death of the hero and the return to chaos" (1993, 202)—have features in common with Christian doctrine, Lee still sees no symbolism at work in *Beowulf* but rather a merging of mythic conceptions in a poem that came to life in a no-man's land stretching between pagan and Christian belief.

One claim about *Beowulf* that has surfaced persistently during the second half of the twentieth century is that the poem is indebted to ancient rites of passage or, alternatively, an ancient hero pattern, whose ultimate source is a set of archetypes in the unconscious mind. The controlling ideas of this neomythological school first surfaced in a note published by S. F. Johnson (1951); they have been argued subsequently, with variations, by a small parade of critics, including Carl Meigs (1964: Hrothgar is a sacral king, Beowulf a healing quester, Wiglaf a re-emergent savior), Jeffrey Helterman (1968: Grendel is the hero's shadow self, while Wealhtheow and Grendel's mother represent two aspects of the Great Mother), Terry A. Babb (1970: the poem is a combat myth telling of creation and dissolution), Janet Dow (1970: the poem mirrors initiation rites, symbolic of psychological processes, so as to reaffirm man's place in the cosmic rhythm of all nature), A. Margaret Arent (1969: the poet secularizes ancient mythic motifs and cult practices that are based on universal patterns buried in the human psyche), Amy Page and Vincent H. Cassidy (1969: the poet tells of a man-god who is sacrificed for the universal good), John Miles Foley (1977: Hrothgar and Grendel represent two opposing aspects of the Good/Terrible Father, while the hero represents the ego involved in a deadly Oedipal struggle), and Michael N. Nagler (1980: the poem embodies a hero-quest archetype portraying the victory of a savior over the forces of chaos). In a similar vein but with impressively detailed anthropological support, Stephen O. Glosecki (1989) has gathered evidence linking *Beowulf* to accounts of shamanic initiation. For Glosecki (1989, 152–210), *Beowulf* includes reflexes of many ancient initiatory elements: the hero as "hcalcr" and "apprentice shaman," Grendel as a "disease spirit," the hero's byrnie as symbol of his link to "a mythic father initiator," and the descent through Grendel's mere as entry to "a dangerous dreamtime."

All these studies, even Foley's and Glosecki's, could be called essentially Jungian in inspiration, whatever other factors they may stir into the soup (a dash of Freud, a large chunk of Eliade, a shake of Joseph Campbell, an old chestnut deriving from James Frazer or Jessie Weston). The appeal of Jungian approaches to literature is their apparent ability to explain so much that is important; their drawback is their reductive and totalizing method. For Jungians, a story is taken to be an expression of certain archetypes lodged deep in the human psyche. The meaning of the story is revealed when these archetypes and their relations are named. Since archetypes are prelogical, they cannot be explained rationally but surface only in symbolic form in myths, dreams, fairy tales, and the like. There is no need to prove their existence; it is enough to know that individuals have access to them through the work of interpreters. Thus we arrive at the role of the literary critic as analyst. The reader of literature, like the hero, is involved in an initiatory journey that arrives, to no one's surprise, at the desired end of spiritual satisfaction.

This is essentially the method that Helterman, Babb, and Dow employ and that the other critics cited above implicitly rely on. Grendel is taken to be Beowulf's shadow self. The physical combat between these two fearsome opponents is taken to represent an inner struggle between two opposed psychic principles, one of which is associated with our moral being, the other with those dark impulses that civilized people normally suppress (Freud's ego or superego and id, respectively, whether or not these terms are invoked). To approach *Beowulf* in this manner is to read its action as a psychomachia whereby fearsome antisocial impulses threaten to overwhelm consciousness but are ultimately overcome and integrated into an expanded self. Foley (1977) takes this argument and converts it to communal history: the integration in question was a cultural one for the Anglo-Saxons as a people.

There remains a question as to whether such studies as these, with their broad and familiar categories of opposition, tell us much that is specific about either the contours of this literary text or the mental world of the people who made it. Any approach to *Beowulf* that reduces a long, involuted narrative action into a single pattern of initiation or a single clash of demiurges is missing too much. If a reading has nothing to say about a variety of matters that were of importance to the poet, to judge from the number of lines he devotes to them—the logic of the feud, for example, or the protocol of gift giving, or issues of dynastic succession, or the demands of leader-thane loyalty, or problems that are inherent in the institutions of exogamy, fosterage, or wergild—then again, it is missing too much. Perhaps the most important question relating to any Jungian approach to *Beowulf* is not "Is it a true account of the poem?" but "Is it a complete enough account of the poem's particulars to satisfy our desire for period-specific, socially-grounded understanding?"

In the end, the neomythological school that was active during the period from 1950 to 1990—roughly the period of the Cold War, as it happens—cannot be refuted. Like the nineteenth-century school of nature myth to which it at times adverts, it can only fall to ground of its own weight at such time as it ceases to offer answers to the kinds of questions that critics are increasingly inclined to ask.

II. THE QUEST FOR HISTORY

Beowulf has always been taken as a poem that includes history. Few people, however, have paused to contemplate what history means when filtered through a literary work of this character. Most of the debates about historicity that have dominated prior scholarship are posed in terms foreign to the conceptual world of the Anglo-Saxons. When historians ask chronological questions from oral tradition, as David P. Henige has remarked in his *The Chronology of Oral Tradition: Quest for a Chimera* (1974, 1), they are usually seeking information that those sources were never designed to provide. Even when historians turn from chronology to genealogy and try to ascertain basic facts about a person's ethnic identity, no agreement from their sources may be forthcoming, for the legalistic distinction between "historical fact" and "useful and commonly accepted idea about the past" may be a foreign one except to certain technicians of the written word.

During the period that followed the modern discovery of *Beowulf*, critics were chiefly interested in appropriating the poem so as to magnify one or another nation of Europe through what the poet had to say about the early history of the Germanic peoples. Scholars thus posed such questions as "Where was Heorot located, and when and how was it destroyed?" "Who are the *Geatas*?" "Who are Hygelac, Ongentheow, Onela, and the other kings who are prominently named in the poem?" and "When were the *Geatas* wiped out by the Swedes?" Among the debates that ensued, none was fiercer than the one concerning the tribal identification of the *Geatas*: Are they Jutes? Are they Goths? Are they the tribe known in Old Norse as Gautar and in modern Swedish as Götar? Neither the Geatish Question, as it might be called given its former prominence, nor any other debate concerning history admitted the possibility that modern concepts of time, space, and historical truth may not apply to a poem of this character.

There is a delightful quaintness about the nationalistic biases that inspired some of the Old Historicism of that time. Who today, for example, would call *Beowulf* a German heroic poem that happens to have been preserved in an Anglo Saxon copy, as H. Leo did in 1839? Or who would venture the confident assertions that Daniel H. Haigh makes in his 1861 study *The Anglo-Saxon Sagas: An Examination of Their Value as Aids to History*? Here we learn that the action of *Beowulf* was localized in northern England. The hall Heorot (or *Hart*) really once stood at *Hartlepool*, near Durham. The Scylding kings lived here, hard by the coast of Northumberland, while Ingeld held a principality in York. As for Grendel, he was no monster. That was the poet's hyperbole. He was a man, an outcast who ranged freely in the wastes of that region.

Local boosterism of this kind is easy to dismiss. But to what extent do historicist fallacies still govern the current understanding of *Beowulf*?

Chiefly because no historical prototype can be found for the poem's hero, great excitement attended the discovery that the name of the hero's uncle—Hygelac, king of the Geats—corresponds phonologically to the Chochilaicus, king of the Danes, who figures in the chronicle of Gregory of Tours and in the anonymous *Liber Historiae Francorum*. A network of events known only from *Beowulf* is thus set into an absolute chronology ranging from the accession of Healfdene ("445," according to Klaeber, 1950a) to the death of Hrothulf ("545").

It is worth stressing that no date is part of the fabric of the poem itself. In the poem, the past is the past. The narrative action takes place "in

geardagum" (in days of old), not in the kind of history that is the creation
of annalists and chroniclers. And yet Klaeber is so driven by a sense of
chronological exactitude that he even invents a character who is found
necessary on temporal grounds. This is Hygelac's "first wife," whom Klaeber
introduces into Geatish history because of his belief that the wife that the
poet does attribute to Hygelac, Hygd, must have been too young to have
been the mother of the princess who was given in marriage to Eofor as a
reward for Eofor's killing of Ongentheow (1950a, xxxviii). If one sets out to
subtract mythological ghosts like Beaw from the text of *Beowulf*, one would
also be advised to subtract historical ghosts such as this bride.

Just as Klaeber encourages a chronological fallacy, calibrating the
Beowulf poet's past so as to impose the rhythms of a metronome on it, he
contributes to a cartographic fallacy as well. Every advanced student of *Beowulf*
is familiar with the map entitled "The Geography of *Beowulf*" that Klaeber
includes as part of the front matter of his edition (1950a, viii). Nowhere
in the poem are spatial relations spelled out with anything resembling the
specificity of this map, with its gridwork of Greenwich-meridian latitude and
longitude, its exact charting of the coastlines of Scandinavia and Germany, its
location of Heorot on the isle of Zealand, and its prominent labeling of the
homeland of the *Geatas/Gautar* in what is now southern Sweden. Nowhere
does the *Beowulf* poet tell us where either Heorot or the land of the Geats is
located. He speaks of both Danes and Geats as inhabiting lands that border
on the sea but omits telling us what lands or what sea or seas he is thinking
of: the North Sea, the Kattegat, and the Baltic, we assume, but these are our
names, not his. Nor does the poet say whether the Geats lived north, south,
east, or west of the Danes. One geographical detail he does provide has
caused discomfort among critics, for again and again he states that a body of
water separates the Geats from the Swedes, who must seek them out "ofer
sæ" (across the sea), "ofer sae side" (across the wide sea), "ofer heafo" (across
the open sea), or "ofer wid wæter" (across the wide waters). These statements
are awkward if the Geats are taken to be the Gautar. The poet's claim about
a sea voyage must then either be taken as a reference to inland seas—not a
very convincing explanation either philologically or nautically—or treated as
a mistake. A less arbitrary response is to take the Geats as one of a number
of tribes who figure in what Leake (1966) has called the "geographical
mythology" of *Beowulf*.

Historicist fallacies concerning *Beowulf* are hard to kill. Hrothulf's
supposed treachery comes first to mind. Lawrence (1928, 73–79) offers the
following summary of the story of Hrothulf as the central element of a tale
that might be called "The Fall of the House of Hrothgar." To paraphrase his
theory:

The immediate danger confronting the Danes is the incursions of the demon Grendel. But the king faces troubles more serious than this. His sovereignty, won by disregarding the legitimate successor, Heoroweard, is challenged by his scheming nephew Hrothulf, aided, it would appear, by his treacherous counsellor Unferth. Hrothulf usurps the throne, but he is not to go unpunished. The rightful heir to the throne, Heoroweard, wins the crown by slaying Hrothulf in his own hall.

Here we have the elements of a fiction, constructed from scattered sources, that has been repeated so often that it has come to take on the semblance of fact. Lawrence is idiosyncratic in believing that Hrothgar assumed the throne unfairly and that Heoroweard eventually avenged this insult by killing Hrothulf. His speculations about Hrothulf's schemes and crimes, however, have become firmly entrenched in the critical literature (see, e.g., Malone 1927, 269; Hoops 1932b, 153; Klaeber 1950a, xxxii; Chambers 1959, 25–29; Brodeur 1959, 153–57; Bonjour 1965, 30–31).

Although Kenneth Sisam attempted to exorcise the ghost of Hrothulf's treachery (1965, 80–82), the notion of Hrothulf's blood guilt and usurpation has remained unaffected by the *Beowulf* poet's failure to provide information about such crimes. Nor does any other source mention Hrothulf's guilt; it is entirely a product of critical extrapolation from a few lines of text (1013–19, 1163–65) that can just as well be taken to refer to something completely other than Hrothulf's supposed usurpation. An outsider to the realm of *Beowulf* criticism might here suspect an example of the ironic fallacy—the idea that two literary meanings are better than one, especially if one of them is sardonic.

A second historicist notion that has become entrenched in the critical literature is the idea that the ending of *Beowulf* refers to the literal annihilation of the Geats, who are the Gautar of southern Sweden (an identification that is essential to this view). In a classic example of the tragic fallacy—the notion that tragedy is the highest form of literature, especially when it is based on *hamartia*, or the fatal flaw of a high-ranking person[8]—Beowulf's death is taken to be the prelude to the extinction of the Geats as a people, and this supposed catastrophe is then blamed on the rash judgment of Beowulf himself. The hero's fatal flaw is his "understandable, almost inevitable pride" (Leyerle 1965, 89.; cf. Goldsmith 1960, 1963, 1964, 1970; and Huppé 1984, 40). Entranced by the lure of high tragedy, and giving literal value to dire prophecies made by several speakers near the end of the poem, scholars too numerous to mention have taken these prophecies as relating to history and have dated the actual destruction of the Geats to one or another period before the poem was composed. Lawrence (1928, 85–106), elaborating on the theory, speculates that the defeat of the Geats, whose leaders at that time were Heardred and Wiglaf (!), spurred the development of legends concerning a fictive savior named Beowulf and hence led to the creation of our epic. This is guesswork run riot. As both Sisam (1965, 51–59) and Robert Farrell (1972, 28–43) have noted, critics have spun out such theories in the absence of historical evidence either that the Gautar disappeared at any time during the first millennium or that their eventual absorption into "greater Sweden" was the result of wars of conquest. The modern equation of the *Geatas* with the Gautar rests almost exclusively on the phonological correspondence of these names, together with some *Götterdämmerung*-style thinking.[9]

In a similarly speculative mood, some critics have succumbed to the temptation to extrapolate from the poet's narrative and wonder what happened in history after the narrative of *Beowulf* leaves off. Where did the wretched Geats go, once driven in exile from their homeland? Chambers (1959, 400), repeating a hypothesis raised by F. Rönning (1883) and varied by Malone (1925) and Girvan (1935, 80), suggests that a group of Geatish exiles crossed the sea to Angeln, there to sing nostalgic lays about the great days of the Geatish kingdom; the Angles then migrated to Britain with these stories in tow, hence the existence of our *Beowulf* as an epic poem incorporating what is believed to be reliable Geatish history. Thomas Hill has recently helped keep such imaginings alive (1986, 46–47). While Geatish refugees have no place in James Earl's thinking, Earl bases a theory of the poem and its deep motivating psychology on three aligned ideas, each one of which is open to question (1991; 1994, 46–47, passim). These ideas are that the historical Geats suffered annihilation long before the poem was composed, that the fall of the Geats is symbolic of the death of civilization, and that the death of civilization (as in *Vǫluspá*) was a controlling myth for the Anglo-Saxons. Earlier I raised the problem of using the Norse concept of Ragnarok to explicate features of *Beowulf*. Going one step further than other critics, Earl weds northern apocalypticism to a historicist fallacy concerning the Geats and their destruction. The result, though eloquently argued, seems to mirror more closely the Freudian anxieties of the nuclear era than the orthodox Christian doctrines of the world that produced *Beowulf*.

Chasing a related will-o'-the-wisp, some critics ask: "What happened to the wretched Danes who went into exile once Hrothulf had done his dirty work?" In his recent *The Origins of Beowulf and the Pre-Viking Kingdom of East Anglia*, Sam Newton looks into the connections between Wealhtheow, her son Hrothmund, and their tribe the Helmings or Wulfings, on the one hand, and Anglo-Saxon kings of the East Anglian royal line, on the other. He finds that the East Anglians cultivated a foundation legend—now lost, like so much else—that told of their descent from Wealhtheow's line of Scylding kings (1993, 77–132). This guess leads to a special theory of the poem's composition: it was produced in East Anglia (Sutton Hoo country) during the first half of the eighth century (1993, 133–45). Meditations of this kind thus move seamlessly from supposed dark hints of treachery in *Beowulf,* to a master narrative about history, to a theory of the poem's genesis, with all that such theories imply.

Arguments like these could not well be advanced without the aid of maps. As cartographers are aware, however, no map is neutral; each one encodes a way of looking at the world. By defining one group's boundaries and relations to other groups, maps can be a valued means of naturalizing that group's sense of identity (and, sometimes, its hegemonic ambitions or pride of place).

Gillian R. Overing and Marijane Osborn's recent *Landscape of Desire* (1994) is a case in point. Here the authors report on a sailing expedition they undertook from Sweden to Denmark in an effort to retrace Beowulf's route from his homeland to Hrothgar's court. Any attempt to map the spatial itinerary of a character from ancient legend—an Agamemnon, an Odysseus, a Beowulf—itself runs the risk of taking on some of the qualities of myth. Since Overing and Osborn have no doubt that "the *Beowulf* poet had a sound sense of the history and material culture of the period of his poem" as well as sound nautical knowledge, they are able to project into space a definite homeland for the Geats, who are revealed to be a subgroup of the Gautar dwelling along the coast of western Sweden in what is now the province of Bohuslän. The authors' desire is focused so exclusively on medieval Scandinavia that there is no place for Britain on their maps. Their geographical conclusions are made poignant by the tragic fallacy that plays over nearly all historicist readings of the poem. The Geats suffered tribal dissolution, and Geatish exiles—here, sorrowing women—carried the story of this tragedy abroad, perhaps to the very headlands visited by the authors. This is a book self-consciously, artfully, full of daydreams and salt spray. Even if it cannot place its readers a yardarm closer to Hronesness, it can at least provide temporary vicarious respite from the dry winds of amythia.

In sum, those who turn to *Beowulf* in search of hard knowledge about the past may be asking it to provide more information than it can yield. A more productive question to ask is: "What use does the poet make of the elements of an imagined past?" This is the question that Bonjour raises again and again in *The Digressions in Beowulf* (1950), a book that remains valuable precisely because the author analyzes the poem's episodes and digressions as examples of narrative art rather than trying to use them to uncover facts about history. The same is true of Stanley Greenfield's nuanced discussion of the poet's use of Geatish history to establish epic breadth and a tragic mood in part 2 of the poem (1963a). Paradoxically, studies of the historical elements in *Beowulf* are likely to be most productive when they are willing to let history go.

III. THE POEM AS MYTH AND AS RECALCITRANT TEXT

The landscape of myth criticism is littered with the bones of dead theories. Wherever one looks in this lunar dreamscape, one stumbles across elements of the unreal: weather gods, Terrible Fathers, chaos demons, rites of passage, ritual dismemberments, shamanic dream travel, phallic swords, uroboric wombs, and the like. A dim light suffuses everything with an eerie glow. The aura of the holy is enhanced by reeking altars dedicated to Jung, Frazer, or other High Gods of modern mythography. The ground is otherwise bare. What a relief to return to that other land of heart's desire, the landscape of history! This ground at least seems brightly lit, with reassuringly familiar contours. But look: what monstrous people inhabit it! Wherever one turns, one finds cutthroats, schemers, backstabbers. Intrigue leads to usurpation, usurpation to vengeance, vengeance to disaster, murder, annihilation. It is a land where nothing seems to happen but treachery and death. Still, at the core of all these mythic or historical accretions, the poem remains what it has always been: a grand, magnificently ornamented account of heroism and devotion, of proud acts and of loss that strikes to the heart.

How are we to read *Beowulf*, then, if the search for its historical contents seems only another manifestation of the search for its underlying myths?

One response to this question may be to reconceive of *Beowulf* as a poem that did work in its time as both a product and an agent of complex cultural transformations. What is of primary interest from this perspective is not the *historicity* of its narrative, in the sense of its capacity to yield hard information about the past, but rather its *mythicity*, in the sense in which that term has been introduced.

It is not wild speculation to suppose that the discourse of heroic poetry, as a special instance of what Robert W. Hanning has called "heroic history" (1974), subsumed some of the functions of myth for the Anglo-Saxons. Myths, in the neutral sense of sacred narratives about the actions of gods and heroes *in illo tempore*, are commonly understood to have the function of "chartering" a society's institutions while validating certain culturally specific attitudes and beliefs.[10] They can do cultural work in their own time and place by projecting current ideology back into the past and associating it with founding figures. In a manner similar to myth, a heroic poem like *Beowulf* may have provided Anglo-Saxons with a model for current institutions of kingship and thaneship, a means of validating power relations among Saxons, Mercians, Danes, and other groups, and a justification for a wide range of attitudes and values about such matters as kinship obligations, the need for generosity on the part of kings and loyalty on the part of thanes, the dangers of greed and unchecked violence, and the sacredness of one's word. As should go without saying, myths can also establish emphatic differences between the present world and the more primitive world of the past. The setting of *Beowulf*—Denmark and adjoining regions of Northern Europe during the Heroic Age of the Germanic peoples—lent itself well to the mythopoeic impulse, for this was regarded as the point of origin for the English people, the pagan Egypt for their Christian Canaan.

As I have stressed, this remote setting was a country of the mind. In defiance of modern chronology, its various legendary inhabitants—Hrothgar, Hygelac, Ongentheow, Ingeld, and the rest—rubbed shoulders with one another regardless of when they "really" lived according to latter-day reckoning. Beowulf creates its own history, chronology, and geography that are operative only within the confines of the poem and that cannot be related directly to anything outside it. No one can navigate this country using the latitude and longitude of Greenwich meridian space, for, as Nicholas Howe has remarked, the poet thinks of Germania "less as a region to be mapped than as one to be evoked" (1989, 143). The lands of the Danes, the Geats, the Swedes, and the other tribes that are mentioned in the poem are nowhere set into clear relation to one another. Routinely, these tribes are separated from one another by a sea, and the coastlines along which they live have headlands. *Sea* is a trope that indicates distance, not just water. *Headlands* denotes a political border or threshold, not just a range of promontories. Those utterly conventional geographical details are the only ones the poet chooses to give.

Ancient Germania as it figures in *Beowulf* was a vague *then*, not a *now*, a capacious *there*, not a *here*. Its inhabitants were people of extraordinary size, strength, and courage who were *those legendary ones*, not *us*; and yet from those people we have derived much of our character, or so the origin myth affirms. The Germania of *Beowulf* has what Robert Kaske has called a "strangely Old Testament tone" (1958, 273), as if it were a northern counterpart to the biblical past of Moses and Abraham (see also Tolkien 1936, 28; Wieland 1988). The ancient Continental homeland of the English was a site where huge and unruly forces clashed under the watchful eye of God. The kings and heroes of this realm were not just more wealthy, more courageous, more generous, or more ferocious than the people of subsequent generations; several of them were literally gigantic, as Hygelac was reputed to be and as the young Beowulf seems to impress the Danish coastguard as

being (247b–49a). By invoking this imagined realm of the past, the Anglo-
Saxons saw themselves reflected as if in a convex mirror, far larger than life.
As Howe has suggested, through *Beowulf*—and, surely, through other poems
like it that did not happen to survive—they were able to give flesh to one
of their cherished ideas, that there once existed an Old Dispensation of the
Germanic peoples before their migration to Britain and their conversion to
the Gospel of Christ had transformed the terms of their existence.

As one can see, the response I am suggesting to the question "How
shall we approach *Beowulf*?" invokes yet another master narrative: the
story of how the English became English, in the full sense of that term.
There are dangers in this approach as well. To add another item to a list of
fallacies that now includes the mythic, the historicist, the chronological, the
cartographic, the ironic, and the tragic, this critical impulse could be called
the nationalist fallacy. Those critics who flirt with it tend to assume that the
idea of nationhood (or, at least, a generalized sense of nationalistic pride and
identity) was as important to the inhabitants of medieval Europe as it is to
most people today. Motivating such research is the central faith that *Beowulf*
derives from a time and place when what historian Benedict Anderson (1983)
has called an "imagined community" was under construction, so that the
poem must have some relation to a story that has England as hero. Perhaps
the idea of nationhood was important to high-ranking persons living in the
poet's day. Perhaps it was not. Most people of that time, even if they lived in
the tenth century, may often have felt more passionate about local issues and
loyalties than about national ones.

The nationalist impulse in *Beowulf* criticism springs from the conviction
that encoded in the narrative of *Beowulf* is a set of allusions to well-known
figures from the English past (Niles 1993a, 98–101): Hengest, the founding
father, particularly of the kings of Kent; Offa the Great, contemporary of
Charlemagne and ruler of a powerfully united Mercia; his grandson Wiglaf,
the last king of an independent Mercia before that kingdom became absorbed
by the kings of Wessex; Wealhtheow, the queen whose family seems somehow
wrought up in East Anglian traditions; the Geats themselves as one of the
three founding tribes of England, according to the West Saxon translator of
Bede. It should go without saying that every one of these allusions must be
inferred. The poet never mentions England directly. Even if these inferences
are justified, the wish to find them so should be seen as one manifestation
of a current scholarly desire for a *Beowulf* that relates to the period of nation
building that followed, step by step, once King Alfred had gained moderate
success in his wars against the Danes.

We are left with a curiously recalcitrant text. Despite all efforts to
unlock its meaning, it has remained equally resistant to mythomania and

historicist ferreting. Perhaps in no other area of *Beowulf* studies is the truth clearer that literary meaning, as defined by the critics, is a product of literary theory rather than of literature itself. Understandably, few critics of *Beowulf* have been willing to take it at its face value, as an epically elaborated account of how a certain warrior named Beowulf, nephew of the king of the Geats, ventures to Denmark to free that kingdom from the depredations of two cannibalistic giants, then meets his death in combat against a dragon after having ruled in his homeland for fifty years. That, plus a great deal of lore and legend about the Germanic past, is what the poem is about: not solar heroes, not Ragnarok, not initiation rites, not the passion of Christ, not the struggles of the human psyche, not any of the other subjects discussed in this chapter. If we insist on discovering hidden meaning in *Beowulf*, we may be forgiven for wishing to anchor our appreciation for that poem in a master narrative that seems to us worthwhile. Anyone, after all, may at times feel an undeniable urge to swim in that ocean of stories, that bath of primal narrative elements, out of which this particular work emerged when a gifted poet gave it firm shape. We will spin out such theories, all the same, at the risk of having them seem quaint to future eyes.

NOTES

1. There are many exceptions to this generalization, especially in the modern period with the appearance of such works as Eliot's *The Waste Land* and Joyce's *Ulysses*.

2. The role of Christian myth or allegory in the poem will not be my concern here, as that topic is treated by Alvin A. Lee in chapter 12 ("Symbolism and Allegory").

3. Compare Lévi-Strauss (1978, 42–43): "I am not far from believing that, in our own societies, history has replaced mythology and fulfills the same function."

4. McNeill chooses not to address a contrary, equally plausible view: that the process of historiography can result in ever more firmly-entrenched errors, as long as those errors are adequate to public life.

5. A brief orientation to work of this character is provided by the anthologies edited by Veeser (1989, 1994).

6. For a set of essays illustrating chiefly anthropological approaches to myth, see Dundes (1984); for literary uses, see Ruthven (1976) and the essays included in Vickery (1966); for approaches from the perspective of sociology and oral history, see Samuel and Thompson (1990). This last book plays a variant on the title of a well-known book by Joseph Campbell (1972), the foremost contemporary practitioner of Jungian approaches to myth. Lewis (1976, 121) has stated succinctly why one word, *myth*, can carry such a wide range of meaning: "Myths proclaim great truths by telling great lies!"

7. I shall leave aside David Bynum's study *The Daemon in the Wood* (1978), for Bynum's interpretation of the "two trees" of *Beowulf* (analogous to the two trees in the Garden of Eden) hinges on a philological error: *wudu* in lines 1364 and 1416 means "woods," not "a tree."

8. Here I am using the phrase *tragic fallacy* in a manner that is deliberately somewhat tangential to that of Joseph Wood Krutch in an essay of that title (1970). For him, the

term denotes the false ascription of the name *tragedy* to mundane modern dramas of a melancholy nature. His own essay exemplifies the term as I am using it, to denote critics' quasi-religious veneration for Aristotelian models of tragedy as the highest form of literary art.

9. There is one other reason to accept that equation, however: the fact that Bǫðvarr Bjarki, the counterpart to Beowulf in the analogous part of the Old Norse *Hrólfs saga kraka*, is identified as one of the Gautar. For discussion, see Chambers (1959, 54–61).

10. Functionalist accounts of myth are associated above all with Bronislaw Malinowski (e.g., 1926, 1932, 1935). Malinowski has been criticized, however, for minimizing the extent to which myth can adapt in response to social pressures.

SCOTT DeGREGORIO

Theorizing Irony in Beowulf:
The Case of Hrothgar

If the conspectus of scholarly opinions in the new *A Beowulf Handbook*[1] serves as any indication, the question of irony in *Beowulf* is as vexed a problem as any other associated with the poem. This recent collection makes explicit what many have perhaps suspected for some time, namely that there is little scholarly consensus on this matter. Reading through the *Handbook*'s essays, one sees this lack of consensus in the markedly mixed attitude the contributors show towards the term: some employ it liberally and with confidence, while others view it with open distrust. So it is, for instance, that while T. A. Shippey sees in the studies of William Lawrence, Adrien Bonjour, Arthur Brodeur, John Leyerle and "the whole post Leyerle school of 'fatal contradiction' critics" a productive tradition of interpretation underwriting an "'ironic' view of the poem now well established,"[2] John Niles by contrast notes a general tendency in past interpretations of *Beowulf* to succumb to the pitfalls of "the ironic fallacy—the idea that two literary meanings are better than one, especially if one of them is sardonic."[3] The stakes in such disagreements transcend mere quibbles over terminology. In any account, the question of irony will turn on the substantive and dynamic topics of phenomenology of language, linguistic usage, and the production of meaning, and the assumptions we bring to each of these.

From *Exemplaria* 11, 2 (Fall 1999), pp. 309–343. © 1999 Pegasus Press, University of North Carolina at Asheville.

Such issues, however, have figured marginally in previous discussions of irony in *Beowulf*, and in this respect the *Handbook*'s treatment of irony follows precedent. These earlier treatments by and large have either argued that Beowulf deploys irony of one kind or another,[4] or alternatively have expressed great hesitancy over whether this could be so (often because of an insistence upon *Beowulf* as oral-derived poetry, which I shall address later),[5] but neither approach has addressed the slippery issue of what irony means.[6] This is, in a sense, understandable. "Anyone who tries to define irony is asking for trouble,"[7] as Beryl Rowland has written. Such prudent side-stepping of the issue is I think largely responsible for the present fogginess surrounding the question of irony in *Beowulf*. Medievalists have tended to think of irony in very narrow terms. Classical and medieval rhetorical theory had customarily defined irony as a trope in which one word was substituted for another of opposite meaning.[8] This definition, which has remained the pervasive one throughout the term's history, is effectively based upon the definition of irony as antiphrasis, "the use of a word or phrase to convey the idea exactly opposite to its real significance."[9] There is, to be sure, nothing wrong with this definition; oftentimes irony does work within the tight framework of a semantic switching of opposed meanings. Problems arise, however, when it is supposed that irony in a literary context must always work along these narrow lines. Indeed, I suspect that the conclusions such a restricted view of irony imposes on *Beowulf*—that the poem consistently legitimizes meanings opposite to those explicitly stated, that the poet/singer was intentionally criticizing the story's characters, etc.—may be at least partly responsible for the circumspection some have shown toward ironical perspectives on the poem. Yet acknowledging irony in *Beowulf* need not entail such conclusions, forced as they are by too narrow a conception of how irony operates.

By interrogating the conceptual limitations established by the tradition of reading irony as mere semantic inversion, recent attempts to theorize irony have brought alternative models to light which can be of great use for thinking through the question of irony in *Beowulf*. In her recent book *Irony's Edge: The Theory and Politics of Irony*,[10] Linda Hutcheon departs from a host of commonplace assumptions about irony: that irony results from the intending ironist alone who encodes a hidden meaning for an audience; that irony has to do solely with the decoding of that hidden meaning; that ironic meaning involves the effacing of one meaning for another; and above all that such meanings can always be construed antiphrastically as the use of a word or phrase to convey a meaning exactly opposite to its established significance. What she proposes instead is a less author-centered, less antiphrastic, more hermeneutic model for understanding irony. Author-centered approaches are problematic because they fail to account for the obvious fact that ironies exist which may not have been intended.[11] In such cases, the intentionality of the interpreter in creating meaning plays as constitutive a role as the ironist's in making irony happen. But in contrast to the view that irony is the product of the inferring interpreter alone,[12] Hutcheon suggests a middle path, one which privileges neither the author nor the interpreter, but which locates irony somewhere between them, "in the dynamic space of the interaction of text, context, and interpreter."[13] One consequence of this move is to put language front and center, and it is precisely this emphasis on how irony unfolds on the semantic level of the signifier that offers special interpretive purchase for approaching *Beowulf*.

According to Hutcheon, what makes irony semantically distinctive from other forms of figurative language is its inclusive, differential, and relational nature.[14] Irony is "inclusive" because, rather than rejecting a said for an unsaid meaning, it incorporates or "includes" both the said and the unsaid into a genuine relationship of plurality; it is "differential" because, strictly speaking, the meanings thus engendered form a relationship of difference rather than of antiphrastic opposition or logical contrariety; and it is "relational" because it is the bringing together, the playing off of these different meanings against each other, which produces the irony. By emphasizing these aspects of irony, Hutcheon demonstrates that ironic meaning is dynamic and plural, in conscious contrast to the view that posits an oversimplified and unnecessary reduction of irony to some kind of unitary meaning via antiphrastic inversion. Irony's inclusive, relational, and differential semantic structure effectively undermines this view by shifting the focus away from fixing meaning around an exclusive, stable binary opposition, to mapping it instead onto an oscillating path between meanings. One could summarize the difference between these positions by saying that, whereas the former envisages irony as a static trope moving toward semantic closure in the legitimization of a single, usually derogatory, unstated meaning, the latter sees it as a dynamic oscillation between the said and the unsaid which encourages us to see ironic meaning as the unresolved interplay *between* different meanings.

This emphasis against monologic closure, however, runs counter to previous treatments of irony in *Beowulf*.[15] Richard Ringler's New Critical reflections on dramatic irony in Grendel's final attack on Heorot work to uncover "an elaborate structure of ironies,"[16] each functioning in a clear and unambiguous way to underline the discrepancy between Grendel's intention and his fate at the hands of Beowulf. In contrast to Hutcheon's insistence on the instability of ironic meaning, Ringler domesticates irony's nuanced potential for semiosis by putting it at the service of the balanced structure of the literary artifact, as the New Critical aesthetic demands.

Similarly, Elizabeth Liggins's treatment of irony and understatement detects ironies of various kinds operating in the poem, but always as a result of the poet's "finely controlled sense of irony," used to give the poem a "duality of perspective" and "depth and subtlety."[17] Far from compounding the complexity of the work, however, these features are said to contribute to "the structure of the poem" and even to reflect a "significant part of the poet's philosophy."[18] Such approaches take away with one hand what they give with the other, finding in irony both a surplus of meaning and the means by which to control, contain, and explain it. In doing so, they miss what is central to Hutcheon's model, namely irony's capacity to frustrate semantic closure by keeping alive the field of competing significations at its core. In this connection, Daniel O'Hara's definition of irony as "the power to entertain widely divergent possible interpretations—to provoke the reader into seeing that there is a radical uncertainty surrounding the processes by which meanings get determined in texts and interpreted by readers,"[19] captures what is at stake in Hutcheon's model and what, by contrast, many treatments of irony in *Beowulf* have de-emphasized.

I suggest that the poem's characterization of Hrothgar through narrative action, speech, and especially epithets provides a particularly clear instance of this model of irony. To my knowledge, this configuration of features has not been an object of scrutiny before. Scholars interested in Hrothgar have tended to focus on the epithets in isolation from other modes of characterization, insisting that the honorific phrases so liberally applied to him throughout the poem should everywhere be taken at face-value. "They are not at all ironic,"[20] writes Edward Irving, echoing the view of John Hill, who claims that "the poet is not ironic ... in his appellations for Hrothgar and the Danes, those keen-sighted, valiant warriors."[21] These conclusions reflect scholarly perceptions of the nature of epithets in the poem as a whole, as represented by formalist and especially oral-formulaic interpretations. Part of my objective in this article is to question the assumptions behind these views, but it will be best to return to this task later, after I have reviewed the relevant material from the poem, and presented my reading of it. The central observation which needs to be made now is that critics such as Irving and Hill appear to understand irony in terms of the antiphrastic model, by which irony is an exclusive, binary trope that legitimizes and secures a single, negative meaning. The stated, literal meaning—here, that Hrothgar is a good king—is erased by and replaced with an ironic, diametrically opposite meaning, namely that Hrothgar is a bad king. The scholarly conversation around Hrothgar has, interestingly, long been fixated on the question of whether the poem presents him in a positive or a negative light,[22] revealing the same tendency to binaristic, either/or thinking which has characterized critical assumptions about irony.

In contrast to this strain of thinking, my analysis of the epithets and other modes of characterization applied to Hrothgar relies neither on an antiphrastic model of irony, nor merely concludes that Hrothgar is an inept king. Rather, an understanding of irony akin to Hutcheon's model affords me a practical tool for analyzing a discursive matrix in the poem centered on a conflict between different kinds of language or voices, which hitherto has gone unnoted. The conflict I see here is essentially one between a panegyric language on the one hand and the narrative action of the poem on the other, which embodies other voices in tension with that panegyric language. The panegyric force of the epithets encourages us to adopt an idealized, socially specified view of Hrothgar. The epithets repeatedly call attention to his prowess, wisdom, and other kingly attributes, and in this way bring to mind the network of social obligations and roles which he, as the ruler of the Danes, is obliged to fulfill. Scholars often point out that such epithets are notable for their appropriateness to narrative context, as if they were a veritable ground zero of standard, unambiguous heroic phraseology.[23] But in some cases, it is equally clear, the obverse is true. At certain moments the epithets seem incongruously applied to Hrothgar, submerged as they are within narrative contexts or flanked as they are by competing voices with which the panegyric voice of the epithets is clearly at variance. This voice is not always co-extensive with the poem's narrative action. The two often pull in different directions, resulting in a conflict of perspectives or meanings which I read as ironic—not because one perspective or meaning erases or subverts another, but precisely because such semantic reconciliation never occurs. Rather, an interplay of viewpoints remains which, I argue, can be profitably discussed with reference to Hutcheon's idea that irony in fact thwarts such closure by keeping vying perspectives and meanings before us without shutting them down. I hope to make this evident in what follows by examining three categories of epithets, those concerning protectorship, prowess, and wisdom, with an eye towards accentuating their immediate narrative contexts and the effect these contexts have upon them.

* * * *

The first section of *Beowulf* (1–2199)[24] constructs through a finely wrought texture of expression an image of Hrothgar as the protector and guardian of the Danes. Within this span of text he is called *folces hyrde* once (610), *helm Scyldinga* three times (371, 456, 1321), and *eodor Scyldinga* twice (428, 663), the sense in each case being quite literally "protector of the Scyldings."[25] Less frequent but equally pertinent designations include *leodgebygean*, "protector of the people" (269), *East-Dena eþelwearde*, "keeper of the lands of the East Danes" (269), and *rices weard*, "guardian of the kingdom" (1390). These titles evoke an explicitly heroic model of Germanic warrior kingship, based upon the ideals of martial power and heroism.[26] In particular, they call straight to mind the king's obligation to protect and sustain his people. A king was the protector of the *folc*, a role secured by his success in war and possession of a large *duguð* or warband. Protectorship itself of course had many facets, but in an heroic context its primary connotation involved physical protection from invading tribes. Though he need not always be the most powerful warrior of his warband, the king's own valor and prowess were crucial to this role. In leading his men into battle, he too must demonstrate his own martial capabilities, both to ensure victory and to set, by his own actions, a model of heroic excellence to be imitated. Defeat was not deemed an option, still less any form of cowardice, over which death itself was to be preferred. As the Old English *Maxims I* puts it, "Courage belongs to the bold, a helmet to the brave, and always the least reward to the mind of the deserter."[27]

But while terms such as *folces hyrde* and *eodor Scyldinga* generate these expectations, there is a pervasive sense that, in practice, Hrothgar fails to fulfill them. Upon first meeting him, it is true, we are told that to Hrothgar

> ... was granted success in war, glory in battle, so that his retainers willingly obeyed him, until the young warriors became a mighty war-band.
> 64–67

And directly after this we learn of the building of Heorot, generally considered his most significant accomplishment in the poem, and one which certainly reveals his desire to protect and sustain his people. But this image of a powerful Hrothgar begins to fade almost immediately, being overlaid by other elements in the narrative. Shortly after Grendel's first attack, for instance, we encounter a very different image of Hrothgar, hardly one which squares with his social position as *hyrde*:

> The renowned king, the hero proven in past times, sat in sorrow, the mighty one suffered, felt grief for his thanes when they beheld the track of the hateful one, of the accursed creature.... It was a long time, a span of twelve winters, that the lord of the Scyldings endured adversity, all woes, great sorrows.
> 129–49

Although the epithets *aeþeling ærgod,* "the hero proven in past times," *ðryðswyð,* "the mighty one," and *wine Scyldinga,* "lord of the Scyldings," in this passage clearly wish to sustain our perception of Hrothgar as a protector of his people, the narrative action offers little corroboration. The point, to be sure, is not just that Hrothgar appears powerless here, but that he appears powerless amidst a dense collocation of honorifics stressing his might and fame. The combination cannot but strike us as incongruous. Though heroism itself is entirely absent in this scene, the language of heroism enshrined in the epithets persists, if anything idealizing itself, in lieu of its absent subject. For our purpose, however, the central insight about this incongruity between panegyric voice and dramatic situation is that it is not construable in terms of strict antiphrastic opposition; the meaning of the passage cannot be reduced to the unitary irony that Hrothgar is a coward. If there is irony in the way these voices play off each other, it is best described not as determining a fixed meaning, but as precipitating a friction between meanings whose coexistence is shot through with semantic openness. Hrothgar appears simultaneously as idealized protector and helpless king; the irony, I am suggesting, lies precisely in this simultaneity, in the fact that the text establishes *and* maintains different viewpoints, rather than somehow reducing them to the unitary affirmation that Hrothgar is a coward. It is, to employ Hutcheon's categories, an irony amply distinguished by its relational, differential, and inclusive character, marked as it is not by opposition and reduction, but by encompassing plural significations within a shared context.

Something more perhaps needs to be said at this point regarding my use of the word context, for it has an extensive pedigree in discussions of irony, and I employ it with a slightly different register than that established by New Critical usage, developed predominantly by Cleanth Brooks. In his well-known 1951 essay "Irony as a Principle of Structure," Brooks defined irony as "the *obvious* warping of the statement by the context."[28] By this he meant that it is above all context "which endows the particular word or image or statement with significance,"[29] and which functions as the principle mechanism in leading the reader to what, in *The Well-Wrought Urn,* Brooks called "that recognition of incongruities"[30] which he considered essential to irony. But it must be borne in mind that for Brooks such incongruities eventually take shape and become intelligible in "the structure of meaning which is the poem,"[31] being in the end part and parcel of its organic totality. Hutcheon's model, by contrast, militates against a formalist reception of the text, envisaging no such resolution. The whole point for Hutcheon is that, far from shutting down the recognition of incongruities and range of meanings associated with it, irony's nature is to keep these alive and in flux, complicating any straightforward response to the text. Context in her theory thus comes much closer to the sense given to the term by Mikhail Bakhtin in *The Dialogic Imagination*, a work which deeply informs Hutcheon's reflections on irony, as she acknowledges. Like Brooks, Bakhtin places great emphasis on the need to situate words in concrete contexts, within the larger wholes to which they belong. But in his framework of the "dialogized" or multi-voiced text, that whole is not an overarching structure which makes all else intelligible, but an incessant conflict occurring between different voices or specific uses of language as a result of the specificity conferred upon them by their context. In Bakhtin's words,

> The authentic environment of an utterance, the environment in which it lives and takes shape, is dialogized heteroglossia, anony-mous and social as language, but simultaneously concrete, filled with specific content and accentuated as individual utterance.[32]

An utterance's "environment" (i.e. its context) is here, then, precisely what counteracts closure and preserves its "dialogized heteroglossia," Bakhtin's master trope for the sense of tension originating from the constant struggle between mutually contending voices in a text.[33]

The more nuanced potential of a Bakhtinian understanding of context stems from the fact that it is not just sensitive to incongruities within a text, but considers them irresolvable and keeps them in play, thereby preserving a text's multivalence or, in Bahktin's formulation, its "polyphonic" (i.e. multi-voiced) character.[34] This emphasis on mutually contending voices is apparent in *Beowulf* in the way panegyric phrases such as *folces hyrde* and *eodor Scyldinga*, considered as one voice, run up against what the narrative says of a mourning Hrothgar, a separate voice that does not undercut so much as rub up against the voice constructed by the epithets in a way suggestive of competing perspectives and uncertainties about how to interpret them.

A similar dynamic is present in the way the epithets rub up against the voice of Hrothgar himself, which, far from reinforcing his role as protector, seems only to widen the gap further. In his first speech to Beowulf, for instance, Hrothgar laconically acknowledges his humiliation as signified in the shattering effects of Grendel's attacks, the most pitiful being the destruction of his warband:

> "It brings pain to my heart when I tell anyone what Grendel has brought upon me with his scorn-filled thoughts, his hostile attacks, humiliation in Heorot. My hall-troop, war-band, has been decimated; fate has swept them off into Grendel's terror. Easily may God thwart the savage assailant's deeds! Many times

> warriors drunk with beer have boasted over the ale-cups that they
> would meet Grendel's attack with grim swords in the beer hall.
> Then, in the morning, when the daylight shone forth, this mead-
> hall was a hall drenched with blood, all the bench-floor soaked
> with gore, a bloodstained hall. I possessed fewer loyal men, dear
> warriors, for death had consumed them."
>   473–88

Neither the content or tone is easily reconciled with the notion of
protectorship. The note struck in this sustained lament is one of humiliation
(*hynðo*), and despair. Powerless, Hrothgar can only mourn and hope for
some kind of divine intervention, clear in his knowledge that neither he
nor his men, whose efforts to defeat Grendel have failed utterly, can effect
a remedy for their dire situation. But in this respect, Hrothgar's mention of
his *oretmecgas* and the hall stained with their blood only begs the question
of Hrothgar's own lack of action in the fight against Grendel. The efforts of
his men may be fruitless, but they at least exhibit a capacity for heroic action
which the aged king himself no longer possesses. The contrast, however
subtle, thus serves to underscore Hrothgar's inaction and, by implication,
his fundamental inability to discharge the office of *hyrde* so prominent in the
epithets.

The same tension between Hrothgar's words and the ideal of
protectorship established by the epithets appears in a later speech:

> "It was not long ago that I did not expect to see relief from any
> of my miseries, when the best of houses stood defiled with blood,
> gory from swords, a far-reaching agony for each of my counsel-
> ors, for each of those who did not expect that they could ever
> defend the people's fortress from its enemies, from demons and
> evil spirits."
>   932–39

Hrothgar admits here, for instance, that before Beowulf's arrival his attitude
was one of pure resignation, which envisaged no *bot* for salvaging the *husa
sedest*. He had, in short, tacitly accepted defeat, abandoned through his own
hopelessness the very role which he, as *hyrde*, was obliged to fulfill. However
much the epithets may ideally configure him as the guardian of his people,
the Hrothgar the narrative depicts departs from such an ideal.

Similar incongruities may also be observed regarding the virtue of
prowess. Here again the epithets build up a concrete image and attendant
expectations of Hrothgar as a courageous warrior who, like Scyld Scefing,

fears no enemy and is set on victory. Thus he is called *guðrof*, "famed in
battle" (608), *sigerof kyning*, "king famed for victory" (619), *hildedeor*, "the
battle-brave one" (2107), and *ðryðswyð*, "the mighty one" (131). The problem
posed by these epithets parallels that of Hrothgar as *hyrde*. How is the idea of
Hrothgar as *hildedeor* and *guðrof* to be squared with the image of a powerless
king mourning incessantly? Here too one can find instances of epithets
being incongruously applied to the king in odd narrative moments. Thus,
just after wishing Beowulf luck before he fights Grendel, Hrothgar is shown
heading off to seek the bed of Wealhtheow, an episode often cited by critics
who berate the king for his feebleness. My interest here lies rather in the
recognition of a panegyric voice in differential relationship to the nature of
the dramatic situation itself. The passage in question reads:

> Then Hrothgar, the protector of the Scyldings, left the hall
> with his band of warriors; the war-leader wished to seek Queen
> Wealhtheow as a bed-fellow.
>   662–65

As before, the scene combines a panegyric voice, in this case one stressing
both the ideals of protectorship (*eodur Scyldinga*) and martial prowess
(*wigfruma; gedryht*), with a dramatic situation hardly harmonious with it. The
one fixes our attention on the king as a protector and warleader, the other on
his present incapacity to discharge these functions in practice.

In this connection, one fact regarding the ideal of martial prowess is
worth considering. At no point does the narrative proper show Hrothgar
engaging in combat. We are told that he once achieved *heresped* (64) and
wiges weorðmynd (65), but what we see is an older Hrothgar whose earlier
martial achievements are now bygone glories. Hrothgar himself confirms
this impression, for the single glimpse we do catch of him fighting occurs,
tellingly, not in the narrative proper, but within Hrothgar's memory, when
he learns of the death of Aschere.

The incident takes place immediately after Grendel's mother,
seeking to avenge her son, attacks Heorot, wreaking utter havoc but
killing only a single Dane, Aschere, Hrothgar's closest friend and most
prized counselor. Beowulf is summoned forthwith to hold counsel with
Hrothgar, who, realizing that Beowulf has not yet learned of the attack,
breaks into a speech of lamentation for his dead friend. "Ne frin þu æfter
sælum" he cries,

> "Do not ask about joy. Sorrow is renewed for the Danish people:
> Aeschere is dead, Yrmenlaf's elder brother, my counsellor and my

adviser, my close comrade when we used to defend our heads in
battle, when foot-soldiers clashed, beat on boar-figures."
1322–28

The lament recalls the time when Hrothgar and the now slain Aschere
fought side by side as comrades (*eaxlgesteallas*), and defended each other
from the enemy. The temporal implications of the first *ðonne* strongly color
our perception of this shaft of recollection: though we catch a glimpse of
the great prowess glorified by the epithets here, the adverb signals that such
prowess belongs to the past, a past which survives now only in Hrothgar's
memory.[35] Thus the final words in this speech ("Now once again help lies
in you alone," 1376–77) place the burden of retribution on Beowulf, whose
ensuing admonition that Hrothgar ought to replace sorrow with vengeance
(1384–89) suggests that Hrothgar's fixation on the past has had the effect
of hampering action in the present. The prowess which once would have
allowed him to take up the task of avenging Aschere's death himself has all
but disappeared, despite its prominence in the epithets used to characterize
him.

As a final instance we might consider the attribute of wisdom, for which
again there is a prominent strand of epithets running through the poem.
These in the main are clustered around the words *snotor* and *wis*, which serve
as the basis for a number of titles. Thus Hrothgar is called *snottra fengel* "the
wise prince," twice, (1475, 2156), *se snotera*, "the wise one," twice, and *snotor
guma*, "the wise man" (1384), and *snotor hæleð*, "the wise warrior" (190),
each once. Similarly, he is also called *wisa fengel* "the wise prince" (1400),
once, and *se wisa*, "the wise one," twice (1318, 1698). If, however, we include
references to old age as well (under the assumption that wisdom and old
age are synonymous), a host of other epithets deserves mention: *frod cyning*,
"the old king" (1306), *wintrum frod*, "old in winters" (1724, 2114), *ealdum
infrodum*, "the old wise man" (1874), *eald ond anhar*, "old and very gray"
(357), *blondenfeax*, "the gray-haired man" (1873), and *harum hildfruman*, "the
gray-haired war-leader" (1678). Whatever ones we include, the honorific
epithets abundantly emphasize Hrothgar's wisdom.

But it is not just the epithets that sustain our sense of Hrothgar's
wisdom. Unlike the claim to prowess, palpable instances do exist in which
Hrothgar exhibits wisdom in practice, the most obvious being his so-called
sermon (1700–1784). Yet, although the acuity of Hrothgar's sermonizing
against the dangers of greed and pride can hardly be denied, certain incidents
in the poem problematize our perception of Hrothgar's wisdom. The
excessive grief that Hrothgar displays over the death of Aschere, for instance,
merits the following rebuke from Beowulf:

"Do not grieve, wise warrior. It is better for a man to avenge his
friend than to mourn greatly. Each of us must experience the end
of life in the world. He who can should strive for glory before
death: that is best for the warrior after he has gone from life. Get
up, guardian of the kingdom, let us go quickly to look on the
track of Grendel's kinswoman."
   1384–91

As in previous examples, so here an epithet fits uncomfortably within the given
dramatic context. Despite Beowulf's addressing the king as *snotor guma*, "wise
man," Hrothgar appears for the moment to have become so overwhelmed
by grief that his great wisdom has been neutralized. As George Clark has
pointed out, while Hrothgar's grief is of course readily understandable in
human terms, the extent of his surrender to it violates the standard of heroic
behavior.[36] Thus it is that Beowulf must remind the sorrowing Hrothgar of
the proper, heroic response to his friend's death, pulling the king back from
his grief-stricken reflections to the need for swift retribution. It is as if the
wisdom which of itself would have impelled Hrothgar to such a response has
momentarily disappeared.

    Two other instances in the poem relating to Hrothgar's wisdom strike
me as equally problematic. These, however, do not feature a tension between
epithet and immediate narrative context, as in the previous example. Rather,
they focus on a broader contrast between the king's reputation for wisdom,
as proclaimed by the epithets generally, and particular decisions Hrothgar
himself makes. First, it seems curiously at odds with Hrothgar's wisdom that
dishonored and potentially treacherous figures such as Unferth and Hrothulf
sit in honor at Hrothgar's court, instead of someone like Aschere.[37] Though
critics have sought to defend both Unferth and Hrothulf from excessively
negative views, neither character is wholly unproblematic. From Beowulf,
we learn that Unferth is both a kin-slayer and a coward (587–597),[38] while
Hrothulf is at least potentially implicated in some future treachery which will
befall the Danes (1014–19).[39] However one wishes to interpret these details,
the very implications they raise, whether true or not, create uncertainties
about the state of Hrothgar's court and, by extension, the king's own wisdom.
No epithets stressing Hrothgar's wisdom appear in either the Unferth or
Hrothulf scenes; but the appearance of such epithets elsewhere in the poem
is prominent enough to point up the incongruous relation between panegyric
voice and dramatic action as it pertains in the poem more generally. And
indeed, here, in the case of Hrothgar's associations with the curious figures
of Unferth and Hrothulf, that relation appears to remain in tension.

A similar tension marks Beowulf's account of Hrothgar's attempt to end the long-standing feud between the Danes and the Heathobards by marrying his daughter Freawaru to Ingeld, the Heathobard prince and son of King Froda. Again, in contrast to the voice of panegyric praise extolling Hrothgar's wisdom (the speech includes a score of such epithets), the narrative makes it clear through other voices that his plan for peace will fail, and with grim results. The first and most obvious voice is Beowulf's. When asked, upon his return to Geatland, to provide an account of his battle with Grendel, Beowulf gets only a short way before digressing into an extended reflection upon Hrothgar's plan to marry Freawaru to Ingeld. It is significant that he emphasizes the fact that Hrothgar hopes the marriage will bring an end to the cycles of conflict between the Danes and the Heathobards. As Beowulf tells Hygelac:

> "Young and gold-adorned, she is betrothed to the gracious son of Froda. The lord of the Scyldings, the guardian of the kingdom, has arranged this, and deems it a wise act of policy that, with this woman, he might settle their portion of deadly feuds, of conflicts."
> 2024–29

Beowulf's comment that Hrothgar considers his plan "a wise act of policy" invokes the ideal of wisdom consistently proclaimed by the epithets. But it quickly becomes apparent that Beowulf's intention is not to extol Hrothgar's great wisdom. On the contrary, his reason for mentioning Hrothgar's plan is to point out its futility, convinced as he is that

> "In any nation, the deadly spear seldom rests for long after a man has been slain, even if the bride is good."
> 2029–31

To underscore his point, he goes on to imagine what the likely outcome will be when, during the marriage festivities, the Heathobards behold Danish warriors wearing treasure which they plundered from them in battle. The sight, Beowulf forecasts, is sure to spark bitter memories in those who can still recall the death of their kinsmen:

> "Then at the beer he who beholds the treasure will speak, an aged spear-warrior who recalls everything, the spear-death of warriors—grim is his heart. Distraught in his mind, he will start

to provoke a young warrior through the thoughts of his heart, to awaken the evil of war, and will speak this word: 'Can you, my friend, recognize that sword, the precious blade, which your father bore in battle his last time in armor, where the Danes cut him down? ... Now here some son of his slayers walks in the hall, proud of the weapon, boasts of the murder, and carries the treasure that should rightly belong to you.'"
      2041–56

Compelled to take vengeance on their kin-slayers, a Heathobard will slay a Dane, the peace will be broken, and the feud reinstated with a renewed thirst for blood. "Þy," Beowulf concludes,

"Therefore I do not consider the loyalty of the Heathobards, their part of the peace brought about by the marriage, to be without deceit towards the Danes, their friendship fast."
      2067–69

Of course, Beowulf's dim prediction could be ignored as groundless speculation, were it not that material elsewhere in the poem corroborates his prediction as one that will be borne out in fact. This is made clear at an early point in the narrative, in a cryptic allusion that completes the poet's account of the building of Heorot. The great hall, we learn, will one day be destroyed by fire because of a feud between a father-in-law and a son-in-law:

The hall stood tall, high and wide-gabled; it awaited the hostile flames of hateful fire; the time was not yet at hand for sword-hate between son-in-law and father-in-law to arise after deadly hatred.
      81–85

Caution has recently been recommended concerning how one extrapolates from cryptic allusions such as this one;[40] but that Hrothgar and Ingeld are meant is beyond doubt, the *ecghete* being the obvious extension of the *wælfæhð* (2228) mentioned in Beowulf's report to Hygelac.[41] As it turns out, then, Hrothgar's wise act of policy not only fails; worse, it leads to the destruction of Heorot, the social pillar supporting the society of the Danes. To be sure, there is nothing inherently foolish in Hrothgar's attempt to bring about peace through the alliance. On the contrary, his intentions are fully noble, meant to further the welfare of his people. But the idealizing voice of the epithets thus tells only half the story. Other voices and perspectives create an interplay of viewpoints which the text nowhere reduces to unanimity.

The connections among my three examples should be clear. Consistently, as we have seen, the narrative action of the poem impinges precisely on those ideals associated with the Hrothgar epithets, thereby creating a confrontation of perspectives unreconciled by the poem itself. Neither the meaning of the lines nor our affective response to it can be reduced to a stable or tidy opposition.[42] We may indeed sympathize with Hrothgar in knowing that his alliance with the Heathobards will fail, but this affect—or any other—is not synonymous with the meaning of the episode, which remains complexly plural. Since there is no one voice to speak of in the poem, but only voices, meaning cannot be unitary but remains dialogic, existing within a field of possibilities whose parameters are defined by the frictions within and interrelations between the various perspectives at stake. The Hrothgar epithets, we have seen, lie right at the center of this dynamic, and hence are not the stable, unproblematic formulas they are often taken to be. This has, however, remained the prevailing critical view of epithets in *Beowulf* for some time, and in the pages remaining I should like to look more closely at the reasons characteristically adduced in support of this view, and to point out their limitations.

In his 1882 dissertation *Die Synomyma in Beówulfsliede*, Karl Schemann gave the first detailed treatment of epithets in *Beowulf*. Far from ironic, Schemann found them to be adequate indicators of the character traits of the figures to whom they are assigned. Thus enshrined in the Hrothgar epithets he found the essence of the Danish king's character: "Hrothgar's character is portrayed with a great deal of warmth in all parts of the poem. All are united in their commendation of his noble virtues as a ruler and of his far-reaching reputation."[43] Years later Klaeber argued with far greater explicitness against the idea that irony could possibly inhere in the epithets. In a 1905 article he repudiated Thomas Arnold's view that the term *Sigescyldingas* (597) must surely be ironic, objecting that epithets in *Beowulf* are always used mechanically without regard to the specific situations in which they appear, and that the poet himself did not care for irony: "Hroðgar is, without question," so he concluded, "the *helm Scyldinga*, though he cannot protect his men."[44] While Klaeber's dismissive treatment of the conditioning role of context has not gone unchallenged,[45] his arguments against irony harmonize readily with more recent scholarly views, themselves equally suspect about irony in *Beowulf*. Thus, in a recent treatment of regal epithets in *Beowulf*, Hiroto Ushigaki has argued (in terms reminiscent of Schemann) that such epithets relate "in one way or another to characterization" and everywhere reveal "our poet's constantly positive and sympathetic attitude."[46] On this view the Hrothgar epithets thus present "the image of a perfect and ideal king, endowed with all manly and kingly virtue."[47] There is no discrepancy between voices here, only a direct and problem-free characterization of heroic attributes.

The oral-formulaic approach to *Beowulf*,[48] though arriving at much the same conclusion as the formalists, adduces a very different set of reasons against associating irony with the epithets, derived ultimately from the notion that an insurmountable divide lies between oral and literature culture.[49] How this affects the "literature" of each culture has been described in detail by Walter Ong in an essay entitled, interestingly enough, "From Mimesis to Irony: The Distancing of Voice."[50] Ong's premise is that the differences between mimesis and irony aptly capture the differences between oral and written literature, and provide a conceptual trajectory for charting the move from one to the other. Oral cultures are mimetic, he argues, because

> the entire oral noetic world relies heavily, even fundamentally, on copying not just nature but oral utterance itself in its manage- ment of knowledge.

Oral storytelling for this reason depends on

> stringing together preexistent, imitable formulary elements ... including epithets, standard parallelisms and oppositions, ken- nings, set phrases, and all sorts of other mnemonic or recall devices.[51]

Now, because this kind of storytelling is always participatory, taking the shape of a "live interaction between a speaker and his audience,"[52] one of its most salient characteristics is that it "cannot readily achieve the distance from life which complex irony demands"[53]—a distance which Ong associates above all with writing. The transmutation of the spoken word into a visual representation introduces a tendency toward objectification which, in Ong's view, effectively dissolves orality's mimetic fusion of speaker, utterance, and hearer.[54] What it leaves in its stead is a vast gap, an ever-shifting and profoundly indeterminate set of relations between utterer, text, and reader, which for Ong is the very stuff which makes irony possible. Cultures without writing may on occasion, he admits, use the kind of irony derived from "conveying truth by asserting its opposite," but

> its use there is severely limited. Oral cultures appropriate knowledge ceremonially and formulaicly, and their verbalization

remains basically conservative and in principle directly account-
able to hearers.... Oral cultures want participation, not questions.[55]

Before even approaching a given oral work, then, the oral-formulaist
could on theoretical grounds find reasons to reject its association with
irony. Irony belongs within the sphere of literate culture. The oral work, by
contrast, inhabits a preliterate world free from irony's disruptive influence,
where community and spontaneity—rather than absence and ratiocination—
provide the measure for an almost Edenic conception of language. As a
result, those who scrutinize the phraseology of an oral work for irony are
doing no more than *mis*interpreting it according to literate standards. One
encounters this argument frequently in *Beowulf* criticism,[56] often couched in
the claim that epithets and formulas are chosen not for sense but for metrical
or alliterative usefulness.[57] The very act of oral composition precludes
a more sophisticated role for the formulas. How could the performing
scop have time to set up intricate and subtle meanings, and how could the
listening audience ever register them?[58] Others have argued that it is not
the scop so much as the whole oral tradition itself which determines the
epithets' meaning. Every particular use of an epithet, according to this
view, automatically invokes a larger "extrasituational network of meaning"
authorized by oral tradition, part of whose function is to elide the "gaps of
indeterminacy" surrounding certain uses of epithets or formulas.[59] In this
way, the certifying and laudatory force found in most occurrences of the
formula *þæt wæs god cyning* can neutralize the ironic potential in a given use of
it, as when it is suddenly applied to Hrothgar after Beowulf defeats Grendel
(see 862–63).[60]

In my view, the formalist and the oral-formulaic approach to the
epithets and the question of irony are hampered by the same problems.
Both assume that linguistic complexity is always a matter of control and that
meaning, be it ironic or otherwise, is always a matter of what is intended.
While there is no denying that formulas such as *þæt wæs god cyning* possessed
inherited traditional meaning, it does not follow from this fact that an
audience would always and everywhere be able to register only that meaning.
This would be to presume that tradition legislates and controls all meaning,
so that there are no meanings outside of it; and, worse, that language itself
is univocal and unitary and somehow purged of its potential for ambiguity.
Tradition certainly has the capacity to valorize certain meanings over
others. But to say that it can in every instance vaporize all ambiguity so as
to guarantee that a predetermined meaning—and this meaning alone—will
be automatically comprehended is to miss language's inherent capacity for

semiosis.[61] If, as is clearly the case, the poet's application of the *þæt wæs god cyning* formula to Hrothgar at lines 862–63 ("ne hie huru winedrihten wiht ne logon, / glædne Hroðgar, ac þæt wæs god cyning") sits awkwardly in the context of the narrative and therefore seems to pose what Foley calls "rather sizable 'gaps of indeterminacy,'"[62] then that indeterminacy may be significant in itself, for us as for earlier audiences. Smoothing it over in the name of some transcendent, tradition-authorized frame of reference only elides the specificity of this particular use of the formula, and erases the ambiguity thus created between this and its more traditional meaning.[63] That tension is clearly operative here, as it is in the Hrothgar epithets, too.

On the other hand, to say that the Hrothgar epithets could not possibly be ironic because the performing scop never would have had the time to so present them to a listening audience, who in turn never would have had at their disposal the distance necessary to perceive them as ironic, is to frame the issue of irony explicitly in terms of intention—of an encoding ironist who plants the irony, and of a decoding audience who uncovers it.[64] By this logic, irony is possible only if the scop consciously intended it. Yet, as I pointed out earlier, serious problems attend this way of thinking about irony. Irony comes about in complex and multiple ways, sometimes only in the poet's mind but sometimes in the audience's interpretation, and only sometimes in the combination of the two. The audience cannot be tagged "passive consumers or 'receivers' of irony," when in fact they too, as Hutcheon emphasizes, "make irony happen by [an] ... intentional act, different from but not unrelated to the ironist's to be ironic."[65] This is not to say that an ironist's intentions are never important, only that "The ironist is not the only performer or participant and, therefore, the responsibility for ironic communication (or its failure) is a shared one."[66] The fact that a scop might reel off formulas with little conscious reflection, then, does not in itself militate against the possibility that certain formulaic expressions might produce irony. The governing issues here will pertain as much if not more to the complexities of audience response and, perhaps above all, to language's dynamic capacity for plural meaning. As William Whallon commented long ago, discussing the artistic potential of formulas, "Time-servers though the periphrastic expressions are, they may nevertheless be handsome or ironic or humorous."[67]

The question to ask, therefore, is not whether the scop would have had enough time to frame the epithets ironically, but whether the social matrix for his language was complex enough to enable an audience to see in the use of an epithet more than one perspective, shades of register or nuances in meaning and possible tensions inhering between them. Talk of multiple perspectives and nuances in meaning is bound to strike some as yet another "literary" superimposition on the poem's supposed orality. But I would hesitate to use such terms. At stake here is not a rigid choice between orality or literacy. *Beowulf*'s debt to orality can hardly be denied; but the orality of the poem, it is equally clear, can be known only on the level of textual effect. There is no clear-cut line between oral and written in *Beowulf*, the poem is a product of both.[68] If anything, what this symbiosis suggests is that Ong's model reifies literacy by distinguishing it too sharply from orality, and that some of the distinctions he makes as a result of too firm a distinction are therefore not so firm and fast as he would have us conclude. Certainly the idea that before writing irony didn't exist warrants suspicion. Ong here attaches far too much importance to the idea that distance and objectivity are *the* preconditions which bring irony into existence. Again, the mistake results from seeing irony as the product of the intending ironist alone, who is the one distanced from his audience by the intrusion of writing.[69] Irony, however, depends equally upon a myriad of other factors—not just upon ironists, but upon interpreters, contexts, and above all upon the capacities for multiple meaning inherent in the dynamics of language itself. To project onto *Beowulf* a now lost and unrecoverable notion of an oral language somehow resistant to irony is to project onto it a language stripped of its capacity for richness, depth, contradiction, difference, ambiguity, and the host of other features involved in the creation of meaning—features, indeed, which so manifestly mark the language of *Beowulf*. These features do not suddenly appear in language with the invention of writing. They are inherent in all language, oral or written, as is the capacity for irony.

I have argued that there is indeed room for talking about irony in *Beowulf*, in ways which need not necessitate overdetermined views about the poet's intentions, nor disavow the poem's oral origins. We have seen that questions of intentionality and orality have impeded scholarly understanding of whether and to what extent irony operates in the poem, and that a viable way around these obstacles may be to adjust our understanding of irony—not, to be sure, because it is convenient to redefine a term until it fits whatever one wants it to, but because the prevailing views of irony which have dominated discussion of the poem are far too narrow and conceptually distorting. My inquiry has centered on the poem's characterization of Hrothgar because, as I see it, there is no clearer test-case in *Beowulf* for illustrating the multivocal concept of irony which has been the focus of this article. The panegyric epithets are part of a poly-perspectival matrix that contributes to the poem's decidedly ambiguous characterization of Hrothgar. Their honorific edge represents him one way, the poem's narrative action portrays him another. I am hardly the first to note that Hrothgar's is a mixed portrait. What *is* new is my suggestion that the ambiguity surrounding Hrothgar is truly ambiguous, that, here, there are plural perspectives which remain plural, rather than eventually be given clarity and unanimity by the poem's structure, theme, surrounding traditions, or any other elucidating framework. A dialogic concept of irony provides a way of talking about plural meaning, a way of seeing the gap in the poem between panegyric language and narrative action—a gap which develops on the poem's own terms—as open-ended and complex, as meaning not one thing, but many simultaneously. As others have convincingly shown, open-endedness indeed characterizes all of *Beowulf*,[70] the restriction of my scope largely to the panegyric voice of the Hrothgar epithets is in no way intended to counter this claim, but only to theorize one particularly cogent localization of this open-endedness where none was thought to exist before.

NOTES

An earlier draft of this study was read at the 1997 Kalamazoo International Medieval Congress. I would like to thank Toni Healey, Roberta Frank, Patrick Conner, George Clark, Timothy Boyd and especially David Townsend for their suggestions and encouragement.

1. *A Beowulf Handbook*, ed. Robert E. Bjork and John D. Niles (Lincoln: University of Nebraska Press, 1997).

2. T. A. Shippey, "Structure and Unity," in *A Beowulf Handbook*, 170.

3. John Niles, "Myth and History," in *A Beowulf Handbook*, 227. Similar disparities over irony are implicit elsewhere in the *Handbook*, as in the counterpoint George Clark's liberal use of the term ("The Hero and the Theme," 271–90) gives to Ursula Schaefer's reservation over "the difficulty of ascertaining whether particular diction is meant to produce comic or ironic effects" (108).

4. Richard N. Ringler, "*Him Seo Wen Geleah*: The Design for Irony in Grendel's Last Visit to Heorot," *Speculum* 41 (1966), 49–67; T. A. Shippey, *Beowulf* (London: Edward Arnold, 1978), 54–38, repr. in *Interpretations of Beowulf: A Critical Anthology*, ed. R. D. Fulk (Bloomington: Indiana University Press, 1991), 194–205; Harry E. Kavros, "The Feast-Sleep Theme in *Beowulf*" *Neophilologus* 65 (1981), 120–28; Elizabeth Liggins, "Irony and Understatement in *Beowulf*," *Parergon* 29 (1981): 3–7; E. G. Stanley, *In the Foreground* (Cambridge: D.S. Brewer, 1994), 66–67; Pauline E. Head, *Representation and Design: Tracing a Hermeneutics of Old English Poetry* (Albany: SUNY Press, 1997), 111–12.

5. John D. Niles, *Beowulf: The Poem and Its Tradition* (Cambridge: Harvard University Press, 1983); Edward B. Irving, Jr., *Rereading Beowulf* (Philadelphia: University of Pennsylvania Press, 1989), 13–15.

6. To my knowledge there is no in-depth study of irony in *Beowulf* in Old English literature in general.

7. Rowland, *Essays on Chaucerian Irony*, ed. Beryl Rowland (Toronto: Toronto University Press, 1985), xv.

8. The earliest recorded use of the Greek *eironeia* is found in Plato's *Republic*, where it is applied to Socrates by one of his victims, and meant something like "a smooth, low-down way of taking people in" (D. C. Muecke, *Irony* [London: Methuen, 1970], 14). Aristotle's treatment of the term in his *Ethics* and *Rhetoric* teased out of this association with Socrates the following two senses: irony as a form of showing contempt (*Rhetoric* 1379b),

and irony as a form of self-deprecation (*Ethics* 1127b). It is in Cicero's elaboration of the latter as *urbana dissimulatio* that the notion of stating the opposite to the intended meaning begins to take shape: "Urbana etiam dissimulatio est, cum alia dicunter ac sentias, non illo genere, de quo ante dixi, cum contraria dicas" (*De oratore* 2.67.269, ed. Augustus S. Wilkins [Amsterdam: Adolf M. Hakkert, 1962], 366; see also Quintilian, *De institutio oratoria* 8.6.44–54, where irony is classed as the kind of *allegoria* in which contraries are shown). By the fourth century, the Pseudo-Aristotelian *Rhetorica ad Alexandrum* could state the idea more explicitly: "Irony is saying something while pretending not to say it, or calling things by the opposite of their real names" (trans. W. S. Hett [London: Heinemann, 1936], 21). From here it is a small step to Donatus's "ironia est tropus per contrarium quod conatur ostendens" (*Ars grammatica* 3.6, in *Grammatici latini*, ed. Heinrich Kiel [Hildesheim: Georg Olms, 1961], 4:367–402), which provided the basis for later formulations. Cf. Isidore, *Etymologiae* 1.37.23; Bede, *De schematibus et tropis* 2.2.12. See Dilwyn Knox, *Ironia: Medieval and Renaissance Ideas on Irony* (Leiden: E.J. Brill, 1989), for an extended treatment of medieval conceptions of irony. For general historical accounts of irony from ancient Greece to the twentieth century, see Norman Knox, "Irony," in *Dictionary of the History of Ideas: Studies of Select Pivotal Ideas*, ed. P. P. Wiener (New York: Scribner, 1973), 2:626–34; and Joseph A. Dane, *The Critical Mythology of Irony* (Athens: University of Georgia Press, 1991).

9. Richard A. Lanham, *A Handlist of Rhetorical Terms* (Berkeley: University of California Press, 1991), 93.

10. Linda Hutcheon, *Irony's Edge: The Theory and Politics of Irony* (New York: Routledge, 1995).

11. Examples of such approaches are Wayne C. Booth, *A Rhetoric of Irony* (Chicago: Chicago University Press, 1974); Dennis H. Green, *Irony in Medieval Romance* (Cambridge: Cambridge University Press, 1979); Simon Gaunt, *Troubadours and Irony* (Cambridge: Cambridge University Press, 1989).

12. For this view, see for example, Umberto Eco, *A Theory of Semiotics* (Bloomington: Indiana University Press, 1976); Daniel O. Nathan, "Irony and the Artist's Intentions," *British Journal of Aesthetics* 22 (1982): 245–56; Stanley Fish, "Short People Got No Reason to Live: Reading Irony," *Daedalus* 112 (1983): 175–91.

13. Hutcheon, *Irony's Edge*, 58. On intentionality and irony see chapter 5, 116–40.

14. The following explication of these features draws freely from Hutcheon, *Irony's Edge*, 57–88.

15. Exceptions do exist, however. Although generally circumspect in his remarks on irony in the poem, T. A. Shippey does allude to irony's capacity to heighten our "inability to judge plain statements" (*Beowulf*, 35). See also Gillian Overing, *Language, Sign and Gender in Beowulf* (Carbondale: Southern Illinois University Press, 1990), whose remarks on irony (see especially 51–52) tie in with her view of *Beowulf* as an open-ended text.

16. Ringler, "The Design for Irony in Grendel's Last Visit," 66.

17. Liggins, "Irony and Understatement," 3, 6, 7.

18. Ibid., 5.

19. Daniel O'Hara, review of Derrida, *Of Grammatology*, in *Journal of Aesthetics and Art Criticism* 36 (1977): 362, quoted by Alan Wilde, *Horizon of Assent: Modernism, Postmodernism, and the Ironic Imagination* (Philadelphia: University of Pennsylvania Press, 1987), 6–7.

20. Irving, *Reading Beowulf*, 50. Unlike most critics, who hold that Hrothgar's depiction is either positive or negative, Irving in this book offers a more nuanced reading of Hrothgar's characterization, revising his view, as he acknowledges (49), from his earlier

opinion in *A Reading of Beowulf* that Hrothgar is wholly admirable. He speaks, in terms analogous to the ones I employ, of a "double point of view" (47) deriving from the poem's characterization of Hrothgar as simultaneously noble and impotent. Yet he refuses to see this in terms of irony because the oral-derived nature of the poem is, he believes, incompatible with irony (a view I will criticize in this article). Instead, he prefers to understand this "double point of view" as a common mode of characterization in oral-derived poetry, and as a result shuts down the uncertainties and ambivalence this double point of view precipitates.

21. Hill, "Hrothgar's Noble Rule: Love and the Great Legislator," in *Social Approaches to Viking Studies*, ed. Ross Samson (Glasgow: Cruithne, 1991), 169. The same conclusion is reached by Gary D. Schmidt, "Unity and Contrasting Kingships in Beowulf," *Concerning Poetry* 17 (1984): 4; and Hiroto Ushigaki, "The Image of 'God Cyning' in *Beowulf*: A Philological Study," *Studies in English Literature* (Tokyo) 58 (1982): 63–78, whose article provides, as far as I know, the most thorough examination of the Hrothgar epithets. Ushigaki never explicitly claims that the Hrothgar epithets are devoid of irony, though he implies as much in treating them as transparent, wholly unproblematic indicators of Hrothgar's character, which he describes as "perfect" and "ideal" (70). I will return to his work.

22. The roots of this debate can be traced to the 1930s with Levin L. Schücking's *Heldenstolz und Würde im Angelsächsischen, mit einem Anhang: Zur Charakterisierungstechnik im Beowulfepos*, 42.5 (Leipzig: S. Hirzel, 1933), and Arthur E. Dubois's "The Unity of Beowulf," *PMLA* 49 (1934): 374–405; both argued that Hrothgar is guilty of pride. This view received support from later critics of a Christian orientation, particularly Paul F. Baum, "The *Beowulf* Poet," *PQ* 39 (1960): 389–99, repr. in *An Anthology of Beowulf Criticism*, ed. L. E. Nicholson (South Bend, Ind.: University of Notre Dame Press, 1963), 353–65; and Margaret E. Goldsmith, "The Christian Perspective in *Beowulf*," *CL* 14 (1962): 71–80, repr. in Nicholson, 373–86. With Robert E. Kaske, "*Sapientia et Fortitudo* as the Controlling Theme of *Beowulf*," *SP* 55 (1958): 423–56, repr. in Nicholson, 269–310, the charge of pride was joined by the charge of impotence, which remains widespread today, e.g. Edward Peters, *The Shadow King Rex Inutilis in Medieval Law and Literature* (New Haven: Yale University Press, 1970), 96–100; Carmen Cramer, "The Voice of Beowulf," *Germanic Notes* 8 (1977): 40–44; Albert B. Lord, "Interlocking Mythic Patterns in Beowulf," in *Old English Literature in Context*, ed. John Niles (Cambridge: D.S. Brewer, 1980), 137–42; John D. Niles, *Beowulf: The Poem and Its Tradition* (Cambridge: Harvard University Press, 1983); René Derolez, "Hrothgar King of Denmark," in *Multiple Worlds, Multiple Words: Essays in Honour of Irène Simon*, ed. Hena Maes-Jelinek et al. (Liège: University of Liège, 1987), 51–58; E. B. Irving, Jr., *Rereading Beowulf*, and his earlier article "What to do with Old Kings," in *Comparative Research on Oral Traditions: A Memorial for Milman Parry*, ed. John Miles Foley (Columbus, Ohio: Slavica, 1987), 259–68; George Clark, *Beowulf* (Boston: Twayne, 1990), 106–8. In contrast to these negative assessments, J. R. R. Tolkien's brief remark that Hrothgar represents "a Christian English conception of the noble chief" offers a kind of counterpoint which later critics have developed. See his landmark essay, "*Beowulf*: The Monsters and the Critics," *Proceedings of the British Academy* 22 (1936), 245–95, repr. in Nicholson, 51–103. For developers of his view, see Henry B. Woolf, "Hrothgar," *Louisiana State University Studies*, Humanities Series, 5 (1954), 39–54; John Leyerle, "Beowulf the Hero and the King," *MÆ* 34 (1965) 89–102; A. P. Campbell, "The Decline and Fall of Hrothgar's Danes," *Revue de l'Université d'Ottawa* 45 (1975): 417–29; Raymond P. Tripp, Jr., "The Exemplary Role of Hrothgar and Heorot," *PQ* 56 (1977): 123–29; and J. M. Hill, "Hrothgar's Noble Rule."

23. For examples of this argument, see Thalia P. Feldman, "Terminology for 'Kingship and God' in *Beowulf*," *Literary Onomastic Studies* 2 (1975): 100–115; Hiroto Ushigaki, "Image of 'God Cyning'"; Fred C. Robinson, *Beowulf and the Appositive Style* (Knoxville: University of Tennessee Press, 1985); and Paul Beekman Taylor, "The Epithetical Structure of *Beowulf*," *Neuphilologische Mitteilungen* 91 (1990): 195–206.

24. All citations are from *Beowulf and the Fight at Finnsburg*, ed. Fr. Klaeber, 3rd ed. (Boston: D.C. Heath, 1950), by line number. Translations throughout are my own.

25. Hrothgar is also called *eodor Ingwina* (428). See Klaeber, ibid., xxxvii n6 and George Jack, *Beowulf: A Student Edition* (Oxford: Clarendon Press, 1994), 88, for an explanation of the phrase. The information presented here is drawn from *A Concordance to Beowulf*, ed. J. B. Bessinger, Jr., programmed by Philip H. Smith, Jr. (Ithaca: Cornell University Press, 1978). Klaeber, appendix 2, 270, provides a list of all the terms applied to kings in the poem.

26. The issue of kingship in *Beowulf* is admittedly a complex one. Here I am interested strictly in the ideals enshrined in the Hrothgar epithets, which critics unanimously agree suggest a Germanic warrior model of kingship; see, for example, Feldman, "Terminology for 'Kingship and God,'" 100–115; Ushigaki, "Image of 'God Cyning,'" 63–78; Barbara Raw, "Royal Power and Symbols in *Beowulf*," in *The Age of Sutton Hoo: The Seventh Century in North-Western Europe*, ed. M. O. H. Carver. (Woodbridge, Suffolk: Boydell Press, 1992), 167–74; and Michael J. Swanton, *Crisis and Development in Germanic Society 700–800: Beowulf and the Burden of Kingship*, Göppinger Arbeiten zur Germanistik 333 (Göppingen: Kümmerle, 1982), especially 81–108. Swanton's remarks on the historical applicability of the poem's heroic vocabulary are salutary: "The question of how far we may deduce from the 'heroic' vocabulary of *Beowulf* an 'heroic' structure in contemporary society is problematic, inasmuch as an ancient 'pagan' Germanic situation has to be described in terms which are subsequently used to accommodate quite different Christian concepts" (29). Consequently, my comments here should be understood as limited strictly to the fictional world of the poem. See, however, the recent discussion of Peter Clemoes, "Kingship in *Beowulf* and kingship in practice," in *Interactions of Thought and Language in Old English Poetry*, Cambridge Studies in Anglo-Saxon England 12 (Cambridge: Cambridge University Press, 1995), 3–67, which establishes several illuminating correlations between the depiction of kingship in the poem and the actual practice of kingship in early Anglo-Saxon England. For further discussion of kingship in the poem, see Levin L. Schücking, "Das Königsideal im *Beowulf*," *Bulletin of the Modern Humanities Research Association* 3 (1929): 143–54, trans. in Nicholson, *Anthology of Beowulf Criticism*, 35–49; George Clark, *Beowulf*, 43–58; John M. Hill, *The Cultural World of Beowulf* (Toronto: University of Toronto Press, 1995), 85–107; Thomas D. Hill, "Scyld Scefing and the 'Stirps Regia': Pagan Myth and Christian Kingship in *Beowulf*," in *Magister Regis: Studies in Honor of Robert Earl Kaske*, ed. Arthur Groos (New York: Fordham University Press, 1986), 37–47; A. E. C. Canitz, "Kingship in *Beowulf* and the *Nibelungenlied*," *Mankind Quarterly* 27 (1986): 97–119; David G. Allen, "The Coercive Ideal of *Beowulf*," in *Literary and Historical Perspectives of the Middle Ages*, ed. Patricia W. Cummings, Patrick W. Conner, and Charles W. Connell (Morgantown: West Virginia University Press, 1982), 120–32. General studies of kingship in Anglo-Saxon England which make reference to *Beowulf* include William A. Chaney, *The Cult of Kingship in Anglo-Saxon England: The Transition from Paganism to Christianity* (Manchester: Manchester University Press, 1970); J. M. Wallace-Hadrill, *Early Germanic Kingship in England and the Continent* (Oxford: Clarendon Press, 1971); Barbara Yorke, *Kings and Kingdoms of Early Anglo-Saxon England* (London: Seaby, 1990).

27. *The Exeter Book*, ed. G. P. Krapp and E. Van Kirk Dobbie, ASPR 3 (New York: Columbia University Press, 1936), 163. On the heroic ideal, see the thoughtful summary by Katherine O'Brien O'Keefe, "Heroic Values and Christian Ethics," in *The Cambridge Companion to Old English Literature*, ed. Malcolm Godden and Michael Lapidge (Cambridge: Cambridge University Press, 1991), 107–25, and the salutary critiques by Rosemary Woolf, "The Ideal of Men Dying with Their Lord in the *Germania* and in *The Battle of Maldon*," *ASE* 5 (1976): 63–81, and Roberta Frank, "The Ideal of Men Dying with Their Lord in *The Battle of Maldon*: Anachronism or *Nouvelle vague*," in *People and Places in Northern Europe, 500–1600. Essays in Honour of Peter Hayes Sawyer*, ed. Ian Wood and Niels Lund (Woodbridge, Suffolk: Boydell Press, 1991), 95–106.

28. Cleanth Brooks, "Irony as a Principle of Structure," in *Twentieth Century Criticism: The Major Statements*, ed. William J. Handy and Max Westbrook (New York: Free Press, 1974), 60; see also his earlier essay, "Irony and 'Ironic' Poetry," *College English* 9 (1948): 231–37, from which this one is expanded. On Brooks's theory of irony, see Paul A. Bové, "Cleanth Brooks and Modern Irony: A Kierkegaardian Critique," *boundary* 2 24 (1976): 727–59, repr. in *Destructive Poetics: Heidegger and Modern American Poetry* (New York: Columbia University Press, 1980), 93–130; and Dane, *Critical Mythology of Irony*, 149–58.

29. Brooks, ibid.

30. Brooks, *The Well-Wrought Urn: Studies in the Poetry of Structure* (New York: Reynal & Hitchcock, 1947), 191.

31. Brooks, "Irony as a Principle of Structure," 61.

32. Bakhtin, "Discourse in the Novel," in *The Dialogic Imagination*, trans. by Caryl Emerson and Michael Holquist, ed. Michael Holquist (Austin: University of Texas Press, 1981), 272. Cf. 276:

> The word, directed toward its object, enters a dialogically agitated and tensioned-filled environment of alien words, value judgments and accents, weaves in and out of complex interrelationships, merges with some, recoils from others, and intersects with yet a third group: and all this may crucially shape discourse, may leave a trace in all its semantic layers, may complicate its expression and influence its entire stylistic profile.

33. David K. Danow, *The Thought of Mikhail Bakhtin: From Word to Culture* (London: Macmillan, 1991), 51–52. See pages 32–33 for an explanation of Bakhtin's understanding of context.

34. Thus my stress on contending voices in *Beowulf* owes a good deal to Bakhtin's theorizing. However, here I am interested in Bakhtin's dialogism only to the extent that it helps to clarify my understanding of irony. At a 1988 Kalamazoo Symposium on the Sources of Anglo-Saxon Culture, Glory Dharmaraj attempted a wider application of Bakhtinian poly-vocality to *Beowulf* in a paper entitled "*Beowulf* and Bakhtin: A Study in the Interplay of Voices." Her essay has not yet been published.

35. Another passage which sustains this impression occurs in the account of Hrothgar's court which Beowulf gives to Hygelac, when he offers the following description of the Danish king.

> There was song and mirth. The old Scylding, having learned many things, recounted stories from days past. At times the one brave in war struck the glad wood, the harp's joy; at times he told tales, true and sad; at times the great-hearted king related strange tales according to custom; at times, again,

bound with age, the old warrior mourned for his youth, his battle-strength.
His heart surged within when he, old in winters, recalled everything.
2105–14

The image of the old king reflecting on the *gioguðe* and the *hildestrengo* he
once possessed, which causes his heart to surge within him (*hreðer inne weoll*),
points similarly to the immateriality of his prowess. For him, it exists only as
something to be remembered.

36. Clark, *Beowulf*, 105–6.

37. This incongruity is noted too by Schmidt, "Unity and Contrasting Kingship," 5,
but only in passing.

38. The negative reading of Unferth, based largely on an allegorical interpretation of
his name, was first proposed by Martin W. Bloomfield, "*Beowulf* and Christian Allegory:
An Interpretation of Unferth," *Traditio* 7 (1949–51): 410–15, repr. in Nicholson,
Anthology of Beowulf Critcism, 155–64. Similar negative views have been proposed by
James L. Rosier, "Design for Treachery: The Unferth Intrigue," *PMLA* 77 (1962): 1–7;
Adelaide Hardy, The Christian Hero Beowulf and Unferth Pyle," *Neophilologus* (1969):
55–69; Fred C. Robinson, "Personal Names in Medieval Narrative and the Name of
Unferth in Beowulf," in *Essays in Honor of Richebourg Gaillard McWilliams*, ed. Howard
Creed (Birmingham, Ala.: Birmingham-Southern College, 1970), 43–48; and Robert
S. Ginger, "The Unferth Perplex," *Thoth* 14 (1974): 19–28. For a range of rebuttals to
the negative view, see Adrien Bonjour, "*Beowulf* and the Snares of Literary Criticism,"
Études anglaises 10 (1957): 30–36; Norman E. Eliason, "The Þyle and Scop in *Beowulf*,"
Speculum 38 (1963): 267–84; J. D. A. Ogilvy, "Unferth: Foil to Beowulf?" *PMLA* 79
(1964): 370–75; Ida M. Hollowell, "Unferth the Þyle in *Beowulf*," *SP* 73 (1976): 239–65;
Geoffrey Hughes, "Beowulf, Unferth and Hrunting: An Interpretation," *ES* 58 (1977):
385–95; Patricia Silber, "Unferth: Another Look at the Emendation," *Names* 28 (1980):
101–11; Norma Kroll, "Beowulf: The Hero as Keeper of Human Polity," *MP* 84 (1986):
117–29; Brian Daldorph "Mar-Peace, Ally: Hunferð in *Beowulf*," *Massachusetts English
Studies* 10 (1986): 143–160; R. D. Fulk, "Unferth and His Name," *MP* (1987): 113–27;
and Irving, *Rereading Beowulf*, especially 36–47.

39. While the literature on Hrothulf is not nearly as voluminous as Unferth material,
it is marked by the same split between positive and negative accounts. Kenneth Sisam, *The
Structure of Beowulf* (Oxford: Clarendon Press, 1965), 34–38, 80–82, and Gerald Morgan,
"The Treachery of Hrothulf," *ES* (1972): 23–39, have used Scandinavian sources to clear
Hrothulf of the charge of treachery, seemingly apparent in lines 1017–19: "Heorot within
was filled with friends: the Scylding-people then knew not of wicked deeds," and lines
1164–65: "they were still at peace at that time, each one true to the other," where the
adverbs *þenden*, "then," and *gyt*, "still," would seem to indicate a future time when the
Danes would know of treason and when Hrothgar and Hrothulf would not remain true to
each other. Yet, as Jack holds in his recent edition of the poem (*Beowulf: A Student Edition*,
98), those sources are considerably later than and distinct from *Beowulf*. Jack alerts us further to the independent account of Hrothulf's slaying of Hrothgar's son Hrethric in Saxo
Grammaticus's *Gesta Danorum*; for analysis, see R. W. Chambers, *Beowulf: An Introduction
to the Study of the Poem* (Cambridge: Cambridge University Press, 1959), 26–27.

40. John D. Niles, "Myth and History," in *A Beowulf Handbook*, 218–32.

41. The relation of these two passages is generally acknowledged, despite the fact that
there is no absolute proof linking them. Lines 81–85 do not mention Hrothgar and Ingeld

by name; but that they are meant can be supported on at least three counts: 1) lines 81–85 link coherently with lines 2024–69 which corroborate the relationship between Hrothgar and Ingeld as well as posit strife between them; 2) Saxo Grammaticus and other traditions attest to the basic outlines of the story (see G. N: Garmonsway et al., *Beowulf and its Analogues* [London: J. M. Dent, 1968), 155–206, 241–47); and 3) *Widsith* 45–49 mentions a battle between Hrothgar and Ingeld which occurs, tellingly, at Heorot:

> Hrothwulf and Hrothgar, nephew and uncle, held peace between themselves for a very long time, after they had staved off the tribe of the Wicings and demolished the vanguard of Ingeld and cut down the force of the Heathobards at Heorot.

(*Exeter Book*, ed. Krapp and Dobbie, 150–51.) However, the fact that *Widsith* does not mention the destruction of Heorot by fire has seemed a strange omission. Norman E. Eliason, "The Burning of Heorot," *Speculum* 55 (1980): 75–83, has cited this and a number of philological difficulties in lines 81–85 against the view that they allude to the feud between Hrothgar and Ingeld. Yet the conventional reading can be defended against Eliason on a number of grounds: the account in *Widsith* is obviously not intended as a comprehensive description of the battle, and even though an event as remarkable as the destruction of Heorot would seem to merit mention, we ought not to be surprised by its omission; moreover, Eliason's own proposal that line 84 should be emended so that it be understood as referring to Grendel's attack is problematic for any number of reasons (e.g., Grendel is not a fire-breathing monster; Heorot survives Grendel's attack); and finally, although the manuscript calls for emendation of some kind, Eliason's interpretation requires more severe emendation (i.e., adding words such as *dorste* and *þe*) than the conventional reading, without improving the sense. See Klaeber, *Beowulf*, 129–30, n82–85; and *DOE*, s.v. *aþumswearian*.

42. On the affective dimensions of irony, see Hutcheon, *Irony's Edge*, chapter 2, 37–56.

43. "Hróðgâr's Character wird in allen Teilen des Gedichtes mit vieler Wärme ges childert. Alle sind darin einig, seine hohen Herrschertugenden und seinen weithin sich erstreckenden Ruhm zu preisen." Schemmnn, *Die Synonyma im Beówulflied mit Rüchsicht auf Composition und Poetik des Gedichtes* (Münster diss., Hagen 1882), 72. Yet, interestingly, Schemman did not let his optimistic view of the Hrothgar epithets go unqualified: "Wenn Hróðgâr ein Krieger und ein Held genannt wird, so kann sich das höchstens darauf beziehen, dass er sich grossen Kriegsruhmes erfreut Als Held tritt er uns im Gedichte gerade nicht entgegen" (72; "When Hrothgar is called a warrior and a hero, at most this can be based upon the great reputation in warfare which he enjoys. In the poem, he does not exactly confront us as a hero"). My translations.

44. Klaeber, "Studies in the Textual Interpretation of *Beowulf*," *MP* 3 (1905–6): 247; Arnold, ed., *Beowulf: A Heroic Poem of the Eighth Century* (London: Longmans, Green, & Co., 1876), 43 n597.

45. William Frank Bryan, "Epithetic Compound Folk-Names in *Beowulf*," in *Studies in Philology: A Miscellany in Honor of Frederick Klaeber*, ed. Kemp Malone and Martin B. Ruud (Minneapolis: University of Minnesota Press, 1929), 120–34; and William Whallon, "The Diction of *Beowulf*," *PMLA* 76 (1961): 309–19.

46. Ushigaki, "Image of 'God Cyning,'" 70, 71.

47. Ibid., 70.

48. The scholarly literature on oral-formulaic theory is voluminous. For extensive bibliography, see J. M. Foley, *Oral-Formulaic Theory and Research: An Introduction and*

Annotated Bibliography (New York: Garland, 1985); for an historical survey, see Foley, *The Theory of Oral Composition: History and Methodology* (Bloomington: Indiana University Press, 1988). For detailed Old English-specific bibliography and historical survey, see Alexandra Hennessey Olsen's two-part article "Oral-Formulaic Research in Old English Studies," *Oral Tradition* 1 (1986): 548–606, and 3 (1988): 138–90. I note here only a few of the central studies in the field of Old English not mentioned elsewhere in my article: Francis P. Magoun, Jr., The Oral Formulaic Character of Anglo-Saxon Poetry" *Speculum* 28 (1953): 446–67; Albert B. Lord, *The Singer of Tales* (Cambridge: Harvard University Press, 1960); Robert D. Stevick, "The Oral-Formulaic Analyses of Old English Verse," *Speculum* 37 (1962): 382–89, repr. in *Essential Articles for the Study of Old English Poetry*, ed. Jess B. Bessinger, Jr. (Hamden, Conn.: Archon, 1968), 393–403; Jeff Opland, *Anglo-Saxon Oral Poetry: A Study of the Traditions* (New Haven: Yale University Press, 1980); Alain Renoir, "Oral-Formulaic Context: Implications for the Comparative Criticism of Medieval Texts," in *Oral Traditional Literature: A Festschrift for Albert Bates Lord*, ed. John Miles Foley (Columbus, Ohio: Slavica, 1981), 416–39; J. M. Foley, *Traditional Oral Epic: The Odyssey, Beowulf, and the Serbo-Croatian Return Song* (Berkeley: University of California Press, 1990). Oral-formulaic theory's concern with epithets derives largely from Milman Parry's thesis *L'épithète traditionnelle dans Homère: Essai sur un problème de style homérique* (Paris: Les Belles Lettres, 1928), trans. and repr. in *The Making of Homeric Verse: The Collected Papers of Milman Parry*, ed. Adam Parry (Oxford; Clarendon Press, 1971), 1–190. See William Whallon, *Formula, Character, and Context: Studies in Homeric, Old English, and Old Testament Poetry* (Washington, D.C.: The Center for Hellenic Studies, 1969), for a comparative study of epithets in Homeric and Old English poetry.

49. The idea is a staple of anthropologically inspired treatments of orality and literacy. See Marshall McLuhan, *The Gutenberg Galaxy: The Making of Typographical Man* (London: Routledge & Kegan Paul, 1962); Jack Goody and Ian Watt, "The Consequences of Literacy," in *Literacy in Traditional Societies*, ed. Jack Goody (London: Cambridge University Press, 1968); Walter J. Ong, *Orality and Literacy: The Technologization of the Word* (London: Methuen, 1982; repr. Routledge, 1988), and "Before Textuality: Orality and Interpretation," *Oral Tradition* 3 (1988): 259–69. The cognitive and social determinism deriving from a sharp distinction between oral and literate societies has been challenged extensively. See, for example, Ruth Finnegan, *Literacy and Orality: Studies in the Technology of Communication* (Oxford: Basil Blackwell, 1988), and her two earlier articles "How Oral is Oral Literature?" *Bulletin of the School of Oriental and African Studies* 37 (1974): 52–64; "What is Oral Literature Anyway? Comments in the Light of Some African and Other Comparative Material," in *Oral Literature and the Formula*, ed. Benjamin A. Stolz and Richard S. Shannon (Ann Arbor. Center for the Coordination of Ancient and Modern Studies, University of Michigan, 1976), 127–66. In *Literacy and Orality* (13), Finnegan states that

> Much of the plausibility of the 'Great Divide' theories has rested on the often unconscious assumption that what the essential shaping of society comes from is its communication technology. But once technological determinism is rejected or queried, then questions immediately arise about the validity of these influential classifications of human development into two major types: the oral/primitive as against the literate/civilized.

For a related argument, see Charles O. Frake, "Did Literacy Cause the Great Cognitive Divide?" *American Ethnologist* 10 (1983): 368–71.

50. Ong, "From Mimesis to Irony: The Distancing of Voice," *Bulletin of the Midwest Language Association* 9 (1976): 1–24, repr. in *Interfaces of the Word: Studies in the Evolution of Consciousness and Culture* (Ithaca: Cornell University Press, 1977), 272–302. All references are to the latter.

51. Ibid., 284.

52. Ibid., 277.

53. Ibid., 289.

54. Ibid., 283: "Writing and print distance the utterer of discourse from the hearer, and both from the word, which appears in writing and print as an object or thing."

55. Ibid., 288–89.

56. E.g., Robert P. Creed, "On the Possibility of Criticizing Old English Poetry," *TSLL* 3 (1961): 98, where Creed states that "We should not praise a particular passage for its singularity of phrasing"; and John Niles, "Toward an Anglo-Saxon Oral Poetics," in *De gustibus: Essays for Alain Renoir*, ed. John Miles Foley (New York: Garland, 1992), 360, where Niles affirms the "bookish" nature of irony and its predilection toward a "detachment" uncharacteristic of oral narrative as mentioned in Ong. See also Niles, *Beowulf: The Poem and Its Tradition*, 146, 198, and especially 201, for further caveats against irony. For an attempt to cut a middle path between the oral and literate camps of interpretation, see Foley, "Orality, Textuality, and Interpretation," in *Vox intertexta: Orality and Textuality in the Middle Ages*, ed. A. N. Doane and Carol Braun Pasternack (Madison: University of Wisconsin Press, 1991), 34–45.

57. The root of the idea comes from Parry's discussion of "ornamental" epithet in *L'épithète traditionnelle*, 22. See Robert P. Creed, "The Making of an Anglo-Saxon Poem," *ELH* 26 (1959): 446, rpt. in *Essential Articles*, ed. Bessinger, 363–73. See Stanley B. Greenfield, "The Canons of Old English Criticism," *ELH* 34 (1967): 141–55, for a criticism of Creed's view.

58. Irving, *Rereading Beowulf*, 13. This line of thinking contributes to Irving's ultimate conclusion that the Hrothgar epithets are "not at all ironic" (50).

59. John Miles Foley, *Immanent Art: From Structure to Meaning in Traditional Oral Epic* (Bloomington: Indiana University Press, 1991), 6–9. This feature of oral art Foley's coins its "traditional referentiality," which he defines as "the invoking of a context that is enormously larger and more echoic than the text or work itself, that brings the lifeblood of generations of poems and performances to the individual performance or text. Each element in the phraseology or narrative thematics stands not simply for that singular instance but for the plurality and multiformity that are beyond the reach of textualization" (7). See also Foley, "The Implication of Oral Tradition," in *Oral Tradition in the Middle Ages*, ed. W. F. H. Nicolaisen (Binghamton: CEMERS, 1995), 31–57.

60. The example is Foley's, *Immanent Art*, 212–13.

61. A similar claim for tradition's capacity to control and resolve semantic ambiguity is made by Fred Robinson in *Beowulf and the Appositive Style*, although his concern, of course, is with Christian rather than with oral tradition. Robinson skillfully demonstrates how the poem's use of apposition is everywhere marked by a "quality of implicitness or logical openness" (14); but in the final analysis he concludes that this quality is everywhere controlled and eventually dispelled by the larger, intervening traditional ideology of Christian belief, which sees no ambiguity in acknowledging the damnation of pagans. The plurality of meaning so forcefully opened up by apposition is, in the end, shut down by tradition. For a response to Robinson's view which, like my interpretation of the epithets, reasserts the open-ended nature of the poem's language, see Overing, *Language, Sign, and Gender*, 7–11, 16, 34.

62. Foley, *Immanent Art*, 212.

63. See Stanley B. Greenfield, "The Formulaic Expression of the Theme of 'Exile' in Anglo-Saxon Poetry," *Speculum*, 30 (1955): 200–206, repr. in *Essential Articles*, ed. Bessinger, 352–62, where Greenfield defines the "originality" of conventional formulas as "the degree of tension achieved between the inherited body of meanings in which a particular formula participates and the specific meaning of that formula in its individual context" (205).

64. The main objection to this position in the past has focused not on intention but instead on the idea that formularity is not compatible with artistry. See Larry D. Benson, "The Literary Character of Anglo-Saxon Formulaic Poetry," *PMLA* 81 (1966): 334–41, repr. in *Contradictions: From Beowulf to Chaucer: Selected Studies of Larry D. Benson*, ed. Theodore M. Anderson and Stephen A. Barney (Brookfield, Vt.: Scholar Press, 1995), 1–14; Donald K. Fry, "The Artistry of *Beowulf*," in *The Beowulf Poet: A Collection of Critical Essays*, ed. Donald K. Fry (Englewood Cliffs, N.J.: Prentice Hall, 1968), 17; Stanley B. Greenfield, *The Interpretation of Old English Poems* (London: Routledge & Kegan Paul, 1972); Godfrid Storms, "The Subjectivity of the Style of *Beowulf*," in *Studies in Old English Literature in Honor of Arthur G. Brodeur*, ed. Stanley B. Greenfield (Eugene: University of Oregon Press, 1963), 171–86. However, in "Homer's Originality: Oral Dictated Texts," *Transactions of the American Philological Association* 84 (1953): 124–34, Lord had addressed this charge, arguing that oral-formulaic theory does not hold that orality and artistry are incompatible. See J. M. Foley, "Literary Art and Oral Tradition in Old English and Serbian Poetry," *ASE* 12 (1983): 183–214, for a related argument.

65. Hutcheon, *Irony's Edge*, 118.

66. Ibid., 123.

67. Whallon, "The Diction of *Beowulf*," 310. See also Donald K. Fry, "Formulaic Theory and Old English Poetry," in *International Musicological Society, Report of the 13th Congress, Berkeley, 1977* (Kassel: Bärenreiter, 1981), 172; and Richard W. Lewis, "*Beowulf* 992a: Ironic use of the Formulaic," *PQ* 69 (1975): 663–64. However, these arguments for irony's compatibility with the highly conventional and formulaic language of Old English poetry remain the exception, not the rule.

68. Thus I agree with Allen Frantzen, "Writing the Unreadable Beowulf: 'Writan' and 'Forwritan,' the Pen and the Sword," *Exemplaria* 3 (1991): 356: "However oral it may be, *Beowulf* is deeply written and already read; it is not a poem of transition from one culture to another, but a poem of many simultaneous states."

69. Ong, "From Mimesis to Irony," 288: "Irony has become a focus of concern today for creative writers and critics alike as the person who produces an utterance has been more effectively distanced from the person who takes in the utterance. This distancing has been effected by writing and, much more, by print."

70. Overing, *Language, Sign, and Gender*; Frantzen, "Writing the Unreadable Beowulf"; James W. Earl, "Beowulf and the Origins of Civilization," in *Speaking Two Languages: Traditional Disciplines and Contemporary Theory in Medieval Studies*, ed. Frantzen (Albany: SUNY Press, 1991), 65–89, repr. in *Thinking About Beowulf* (Stanford: Stanford University Press, 1994), 161–88.

PHYLLIS R. BROWN

Cycles and Change in Beowulf

In our postmodern world appreciation of literary style, structure, and
theme involves more than a confidence that art recreates in microcosm a
Christian God's creative ordering, patterning, and hierarchizing and more
than a pessimism grounded on a belief that really there is no God, no order,
no pattern and that hierarchies are always artificial and oppressive. For many
the reader's responsibility to construct a "sensible" interpretation or read a
text with or against critical fashion has displaced authorial prerogative. One
especially important effect of reader-centered theory's ascendancy has been
critical awareness of the profound impact a reader's own knowledge base
and beliefs have on interpretive acts. Thus a critic's condition of existential
angst may lead him to see similar suffering in literary characters; one of
the great powers of literature is to reflect the world as we would have it
be. More specifically, readers experiencing a sense of futility and doom in
the face of late twentieth-century political and social turmoil have often
valued the epic Beowulf for its skill in creating a powerful sense of futility and
doom, believing Beowulf's death signals the end of a Heroic Age. This essay
argues that a fuller understanding of some cultural systems contributing
to medieval spirituality in the early Middle Ages, transmitted to us for
the most part through patristic writings, opens up different possibilities
for late twentieth-century readers' interpretation of the cycles and change

From *Manuscript, Narrative, Lexicon: Essays on Literary and Cultural Transmission in Honor of
Whitney F. Bolton*, ed. Robert Boenig and Kathleen Davis, pp. 171–192. © 2000 by Associated
University Presses, Inc.

189

in *Beowulf*, especially the poem's ending. Competing with the apocalyptic view is the possibility that dramatic reversals continue—for better and for worse—beyond Beowulf's death, beyond the end of the poem, beyond the poet's death, the audience's death, and the reader's death—until the end of time—in ways that seem meaningless unless readers provide their own understanding of the patterns.[1]

In the early Middle Ages, cultural systems, including spirituality, were far from monolithic; nevertheless, Gregory the Great is generally named as the original expositor of a distinctly medieval spirituality, a dubious honor in the eyes of those who prefer to skip over the "Dark Ages." Typical of this mode is Robert Barr's account of theology's "wane and demise" in the sixth, seventh, and eighth centuries in Western Europe: Barr credits writers of the late-patristic era at best with compilation and transmission.[2] In contrast, more recent scholarship, notably Carole Straw's *Gregory the Great*, explores with great care and respect the ways in which Gregory builds on earlier theologians, departs from some and returns to others, and the important ways he has contributed to modern spirituality.[3]

Particularly relevant to a study of cycles and change in *Beowulf* are Gregory's papal achievements and his writings about ways in which the divine expresses itself in the world of mortals. Straw writes,

> As pope, Gregory attempted to accommodate the Church to the world and yet to purify the Church from secular corruption. Even as the Papacy assumed greater responsibilities in the secular realm—maintaining the supplies of food and water, paying soldiers, negotiating treaties, administering estates, and systematizing charitable operations—Gregory still sought to preserve the Church from the pollution of secular values.[4]

His policies responded to the immediate needs in Italy, where political and economic changes resulting from the dominance of the Germanic kings, especially the arrival of the Lombards in 568, manifested themselves in a kind of social revolution: "the rapid formation of a new military aristocracy that came to dominate society at the expense of the civilian senatorial aristocracy, the conflation of civilian and military authority and administration that eventually enhanced the military elite."[5] He urged, "*Age quod agis!*" ["Do what you can do!"] and never abandoned an ideal of Christian empire uniting disparate peoples.[6] According to Straw, for Gregory

> Reaching the other world is much simpler now because it is so immediately present. Union with God is eminently attainable:

one can even cling to the light inwardly at the same time one is busied outwardly in secular affairs. As the spiritual and carnal boundaries are broken for body and soul, this world and the next, so too the boundaries between the self and others weaken, the social unity is intensified. Each individual exists only as a member of the larger, transcendent body of Christ, which is political and social as well as religious; a delicate hierarchy preserves the right order and harmony of the universe.[7]

Gregory apparently saw beyond simple binary oppositions of pagan and Christian, good and evil, to more complex relationships that simultaneously offered greater opportunity and greater responsibility for each human individual.

Theological beliefs such as Gregory's go a long way toward helping twentieth-century readers see the cycles and change in *Beowulf* from a Christian as well as a pagan perspective and thus appreciate more fully the *Beowulf* poet's commingling of Christian and pagan elements.[8] Gregory's theology especially challenges a widespread belief that Christian doctrines expressed in other Anglo-Saxon writings contribute to *Beowulf*'s sense of futility because all non-Christians, no matter how virtuous or heroic, were damned. Much late-antique theology supports the argument for damnation. By the late fourth and early fifth centuries, Peter Brown shows, "In the Christian church, the spiritual dominance of the few was made ever firmer and more explicit by a denial of ease of access to the supernatural that would have put 'heavenly' power in the hands of the average sinful believer." Augustine, Brown points out, wrote in book ten of his *Confessions*, "surely all life on earth is a temptation," and Abba Poimen passed on Anthony's saying, "The greatest thing that a man can do is to throw his faults before the Lord and to expect temptation to his last breath."[9] This ascetic worldview, already evident in the papal renunciation of Origen's belief that God's grace was sufficient even to save Satan himself, was fundamental to calling heretical Pelagius's belief "man could take the initial and fundamental steps toward salvation by his own efforts, apart from Divine grace."[10] Such a grim reality for Christians suggests futility for pagans.

However, other currents of thought coexisted with the Christian awareness of the enormity of human sinfulness. Thus Brown concludes *The Making of Late Antiquity* with the remark, "Throughout that debate [on the holy], we meet men and women who held doggedly to an obscure intuition, with which they grappled in a language top-heavy with the presence of the supernatural: in a poignant search for some oasis of unalloyed relationships between themselves, they made plain that what human beings had marred only human beings could put right."[11] Similarly, R. A. Markus warns that readers must "look deeper than Augustine's more polemical statements on secular history and its writers" to understand Augustine's complex understanding of the relationships between secular and sacred history.[12]

Augustine's writings present not only the grim view that humanity had entered an unregenerate old age just prefatory to the second coming; he also, according to Markus, saw "a more fundamental duality between the period of promise [the prehistory of Christ] and that of fulfilment [after Christ's incarnation]."[13] Moreover, as W. F. Bolton has shown, four centuries later Alcuin's writings incorporate complex attitudes toward secular and Christian history. Thus Alcuin's admonition "If your forefathers ... because they did not hope as it was right to hope, suffered what we read in the history ... and perished in the desert because of hardness of heart; much more [*multo amplius*] are such things as befell them to be feared by you" is in a sense balanced by his exclamation, "But even in the histories of the ancients it is read that almost everywhere in the cities there was asylum as a refuge for criminals. And this was among the pagans! How much more among Christians, for the sake of mercy, should the churches have their honor in the rescue of fugitives?" Pagans function as positive *and* negative examples for Christians. Bolton goes on, "So also the poem asks *quanto magis*—if Beowulf was virtuous, how much more should Christians, in the grace of the new covenant, strive to be so."[14] As Bolton suggests, Beowulf's heroism and virtue are only negative when compared to Christ's heroism and virtue in a reductive way. I will build on Bolton's discussion of Alcuin and *Beowulf* to argue that awareness of human virtue as well as of sin contributes to the poem's worldview. To downplay the textual evidence that the hero Beowulf has achieved something beyond a pagan, hopeless, eschatological end—a lesson in futility—is to deny a large part of what makes the poem great and what made Christianity attractive to many during the Anglo-Saxon period.[15]

Gregory the Great, writing and working in circumstances very different from Augustine's fourth century and Alcuin's eighth, expresses belief in a world whose "invisible reality exists alongside the visible reality it sustains and determines."[16] According to Straw,

> Gregory is apt to spell out just what God's possibilities are: good fortune and prosperity can mean either election or abandonment; but then so can misfortune and adversity. In any individual case, the outcome of God's actions may be unknown, but the general principles of God's dispensation are known, and proper human action can be prescribed. In so labeling the possible meanings of

God's dispensation, Gregory systematizes the unknown and draws
a clear map to guide the pilgrim's return to his homeland.[17]

These Gregorian ideas are fundamental to the sixth- and seventh-century
Christianization of Britain undertaken by Augustine of Canterbury and to
Bede's understanding of it expressed in his *Ecclesiastical History*. Both the
sense of futility associated with knowledge of human sinfulness and Gregory's
confidence that virtuous human action can be directed and understood in
light of the general principles of God's dispensation are pertinent to an
understanding of *Beowulf*. Tempering the indisputable elegiac tone of the
poem is a Christian confidence that virtuous behavior can alter the course of
events in the world for the better while Christians await the second coming.
In this light, diction and theme relating to cycles and change in *Beowulf*
suggest more than the tragic end of the Heroic Age.

   The poet says early on that the Danes know only the "hæþenra hyht"
(179) ("hope of the heathen"), and specifies,

> They knew not the Lord,
> the Judge of our deeds,   were ignorant of God,
> knew not how to worship   our Protector above,
> the King of Glory.[18,19]
>   (180–83)

However, immediately after specifying the futility of pagan practices, the
poet contrasts the fire's embrace with God's embrace:

> Woe unto him
> who in violent affliction   has to thrust his soul
> in the fire's embrace,   expects no help,
> no change in his fate!   Well is it with him
> who after his death-day   is allowed to seek
> the Father's welcome,   ask His protection!
>   (183–88)

The futility emphasized by critics interpreting the final section of the
poem, especially Beowulf's death, and the prognostications of doom for the
Geats, is carefully contextualized by the poet for an audience that has been
taught the benefits of Christian faith and revelation.[20] An examination of
structure, theme, imagery, diction, and character—especially of Beowulf and
Wiglaf—reveals that the poet's treatment of change, especially reversals in
fortune, creates an undercurrent of confidence in the potential for individual

choice and virtuous behavior to counteract forces of destruction, both natural and supernatural, much as Christianity offers postlapsarian mortals the opportunity to reverse the effects of sin through a combination of faith and good works.

The poem's structural intricacy provides an appropriate context for the thematic and theological complexity. Theodore Andersson writes of the poem, "The *Beowulf* poet, located between the spiritual limitations of the heroic lay and the new doctrine of salvation, resolves the conflict by putting the heroic life in perspective against the promise of a future reward. The structural problem confronting him is how to illustrate the futility of this life as a background for the permanence of the next."[21] Andersson traces a series of reversals to conclude, "the larger reversal from bad to good in the monster segment is subject to another reversal from weal to woe in the dragon segment. The dragon brooding over his treasure is an apt emblem of the latent menace that broods over the history of kings and heroes."[22] Nevertheless, the reversals in the poem's structure contribute to other patterns as well. The poem's bipartite, tripartite, and episodic, or digressive, qualities invite readers to think about parallels and contrasts between characters, for example Sigemund/Heremod, Hama/Higelac, and Hroðgar/ Beowulf, and to compare the most important characters to nearly every other character introduced. Thus toward the end of the poem, the account of the dragon's hoard as the material remains of a long-dead civilization, especially the elegiac "Lay of the Last Survivor," anticipates Wiglaf's and the Geatish survivors' anxiety concerning their dismal future prospects. However, the introductory account of Scyld's arrival provides a very different context for understanding the Geats' situation at the end of the poem. Scyld's kingly behavior, the narrator avers, resulted in a remedy not only for his own destitute arrival but also for the Danes' leaderless condition.

Balancing—or at least in tension with—the mysterious and tragic end of the last survivor's civilization, and the anticipation of a similar end for the Geats, is the power of individual heroic behavior to create a greater civilization than had been previously known. James Earl writes, "The fall of the Geats is symbolic of the death of a civilization, just as the founding of Denmark is symbolic of its birth. When the hero dies, civilization as we see it in the poem will die with him."[23] But this interpretation depends on the beliefs that "*Beowulf* takes place in an age between myth and history," that "The Heroic Age mediates temporally between this world and the other," and that the "Heroic Age always reveals the fallen nature of the present age by contrast."[24] According to Earl, the hopeless eschatalogy of its pre-Christian culture led the Anglo-Saxons to emphasize apocalyptic themes of Christianity, with one result being that "*Beowulf* focuses on the collapse of the heroic world, a collapse that results in the world of history as we know it and at the same time displays the essential nature of history as collapsing, falling, eschatalogical."[25]

Not all worldviews, however, understand the essential nature of history to be quite so gloomy. Both Bede and Eusebius articulate in their ecclesiastical histories guarded hope that virtuous action in a world blessed by Christ's incarnation could result in great human accomplishment. Both historians were grappling with the reality that the apocalypse and new Kingdom of Heaven were not as imminent as the first Christians believed. Thus the waiting for salvation could/should be grounded not only on faith but also on works. Eusebius's history, which recounts events from the Apostolic Age to his own, ends with the union of Christianity and the Roman empire under Constantine, a time of great hope for Christians. Similarly, Bede sees both ups and downs in the history of Christianity in England, but he concludes Book V, chapter 23, saying, "This, then, is the present state of all Britain, about two hundred and eighty-five years after the coming of the English to Britain, but seven hundred and thirty-one years since our Lord's Incarnation. May the world rejoice under his eternal rule, and Britain glory in his Faith! *Let the multitude of isles be glad thereof, and give thanks at the remembrance of his holiness!*"[26] What we call the Golden Age of Northumbria and the later tenth-century Gregorian reform in England both attest to cycles characterized by reversals in fortune rather than a steady decline. Well before the Anglo-Saxon period in England, Christians had experienced many events suggesting futility in the face of what appeared to be the end of human civilization. In the year A.D. 70 the Romans destroyed the temple in Jerusalem, in the sixth century the Roman Empire fell to Germanic militant tribes, and, perhaps even more significant, controversies over doctrinal issues threatened the Christian community from within. Nevertheless, the original impulse driven by the Acts of the Apostles to spread the word of God to all the nations had, by the time *Beowulf* was written, resulted in a new Christian civilization in England.

In addition to having a poetic structure emphasizing cycles, changes, and reversals, some of the poem's images contribute to the theme of cycles and change. Two important images the poet uses to depict this theme are the exchange of treasure and sleep after feast. To a very large extent heroic behavior is defined in this poem by the giving of treasure. Thus Heremod is not heroic because he is stingy and hoards his treasure rather than distributing it generously. Hroðgar, Hygelac, and Beowulf are generous with their treasures and thus earn the loyalty of their retainers. The frequent exchange of gifts, often weapons and armor—either at a celebratory feast or unwillingly on the battlefield—contributes both to plot, character development, and to theme. Sometimes the exchange of weapons is later the motive of revenge;

sometimes an exchange is later insufficient to prevent further outbreaks of war; sometimes the exchange of weapons is part of a great warrior's duty to protect his people. But the exchange of gifts emphasizes simultaneously the splendor and greatness of treasure and its uselessness if it is hoarded. Thus the poem suggests the treasure that accompanies Scyld on his burial ship is not wasted. Similarly, the poem depicts the burning of treasure on a pyre with heroes such as Hnæf and Hildeburh's son as sign of heroism and right behavior.

However, the poem presents conflicting attitudes toward the Dragon's treasure at the end of the poem. Beowulf believes that winning the dragon's treasure and leaving it to his people is a compensation for his death. He says to Wiglaf,

> Go now in haste,   that I may see
> the golden gods,   have one full look
> at the brilliant gems,   that by its wealth
> I may more easily   give up my life
> and the dear kingdom   that I have ruled so long.
>   (2747–51)

Later Beowulf thanks the Lord of all for allowing him to see the treasure before he dies:

> I give thanks aloud   to the Lord of all,
> King of glories,   eternal Ruler
> for the bright treasures   I can see here,
> that I might have gained   such gifts as these
> for the sake of my people   before I died.
>   (2794–98)

Significantly, the poem places Beowulf's comments on the dragon's treasure immediately before Beowulf gives Wiglaf his rings and armor (*beah ond byrnan* [2812]). Each of these passages suggests a positive valence for treasure. Wiglaf, however, expresses some ambivalence. He is eager to show the others the splendor of the treasure ([3101–3]) ["Let us hurry now, make a second [journey] / to see the hoard, bright-[gemmed] gold, / the marvel in the cave."]), but he says,

> The hoard has been opened
> at terrible cost.   That fate was too strong
> that drew [the king   of our people] toward it.
>   (3084–86)

For Wiglaf the treasure seems to signify not only the greatness of his lord's accomplishment but also the enormity of the loss.

The narrator presents a different point of view, saying that the treasure, after its burial, is as useless as it was before (þær hit nu gen lifað, / eldum swa unnyt [3167–68]). The word *unnyt* occurs one other time in the poem, when Beowulf tells Hroðgar he has come to Denmark to help because he had heard that Heorot was standing empty and useless to all warriors [411–13] ["that this great building, / brightest hall, stands empty, useless / to all the warriors"]). Many critics see these details as evidence of the failure of heroism, extending the sense of the treasure's uselessness to a sense that all human deeds are useless and material goods offer only illusory value. Linda Georgianna sees in the deferral and delay of Beowulf's final speech a poet "intent on disengaging his audience from the forward movement of the heroic story in order to suggest the limits of heroic action and perhaps of heroic narratives as well."[27] I argue that Beowulf's attitude as he approaches each of his battles with monsters exemplifies a more nuanced stance. Beowulf knows "witig God / on swa hwæþere hond halig Dryhten / mærðo deme, swa him gemet þince" (685–87), but he knows that good deeds are important as well. Thus after being informed of Æschere's death, he reminds Hroðgar,

> Better it is
> for every man   to avenge his friend
> than mourn overmuch.   Each of us must come
> to the end of his life: let him who may
> win fame before death.   That is the best
> memorial for a man   after he is gone.
>   (1384–89)

These pagan values, vengeance and fame, bring Beowulf close to a Christian understanding of the choices available when humans are faced with the mysteries of loss and death. One might even see evidence of belief that knowledge of God is possible without revelation, though expressing such a Pelagian belief might lead to accusations of heresy.

Nevertheless, Charles Donahue has traced in Irish writings what he calls an "Insular Mode" of Christianity that survived the Augustinian stamping out of Pelagianism, following writers like Irenaeus and Origen, instead of Augustine and Orosius, by reading in St. Paul's letters evidence of "natural good," and "natural knowledge of God."[28] Morton Bloomfield interprets *ofer ealde riht* ["the Eternal Ruler"] in line 2330 as evidence that "pre-Christian moral law of whatever origin was considered something of a unity before the time of the *Beowulf* poet. The tendency to assimilate the best part of paganism to the Old Testament is one way converted pagans could accept the New Law and still maintain pride of ancestry."[29] Perhaps even more important, though, is the evidence of Pope Gregory's instructions to the missionaries in England. Bede presents in book I, chapter 30, of his *Ecclesiastical History* the text of Gregory's letter of instruction:

> when by God's help you reach our most reverend brother, Bishop Augustine, we wish you to inform him that we have been giving careful thought to the affairs of the English, and have come to the conclusion that the temples of the idols among that people should on no account be destroyed. The idols are to be destroyed, but the temples themselves are to be aspersed with holy water, altars set up in them, and relics deposited there. For if these temples are well-built, they must be purified from the worship of demons and dedicated to the service of the true God. In this way, we hope that the people, seeing that their temples are not destroyed, may abandon their error and, flocking more readily to their accustomed resorts, may come to know and adore the true God.

After more specific instructions Gregory justifies his instructions saying, "It was in this way that the Lord revealed Himself to the Israelite people in Egypt, permitting the sacrifices formerly offered to the Devil to be offered thenceforward to Himself instead. So He bade them sacrifice beasts to Him, so that, once they became enlightened, they might abandon one element of sacrifice and retain another."[30] Gregory is drawing on the theological idea of correction-and-fulfillment, an important part in the earliest Christian theologians' appropriation of Jewish law and Old Testament scripture.[31] The record of pre-Christian pagan rituals in the Old Testament, now understood figuratively rather than literally, allows later Christian missionaries to use pagan practices as vehicles for the conversion process.

Thus the *Beowulf* poet need not have seen Beowulf's confidence in the power of good deeds as simply antithetical to Christian truth. Beowulf may also illustrate a belief that the step to Christian belief was "natural" for Anglo-Saxons, since so much of their culture could be read with the idea of correction-and-fulfillment. Roberta Frank finds evidence of this attitude in the ninth-century Anglo-Saxon paraphrase of Orosius and King Alfred's translation of Boethius' *Consolation of Philosophy*.[32] Indeed, Frank points out that King Alfred's *Boethius*, unlike the original work, insists that wealth, power, and temporal possessions all can be used for good purposes in a Christian world.[33]

Similarly, the image of sleep after feasting, associated with many of the important reversals of the beginning of the poem, simultaneously underscores the transitory nature of human existence and firmly grounds heroic behavior and mortality in everyday situations.[34] In doing so the poet highlights some of Christianity's attraction for the Germanic pagans. As the speaker in "The Wanderer" understands, mortal life is like a winter storm; Christian eternity offers the only sure haven. So pagans may feel secure in times of peace and sleep, warm in the hall, but that security is bound to fail. Christians acknowledge eternal salvation as incompletely revealed but the only sure comfort. So Æschere, sleeping peacefully, is vulnerable despite Beowulf's heroic deeds. Furthermore, this poet is not content simply to depict heroic action in situations where everyone knows what is expected— on the battlefield or in a siege. He also depicts the vulnerability of humanity when seemingly safe, especially through Æschere's death.

Perhaps most significant to my argument concerning the *Beowulf* poet's insistence on the individual's responsibility for right action is the use of the word *edwenden*, change or reversal, in lines 280, 1774, and 2188, and its close relative, *edhwyrft*, in line 1281. *Edhwyrft* and *edwenden* in one occurrence denote change for the worse; in the other two, *edwenden* denotes change for the better. That is perhaps significant in itself, but a closer examination of the passages is yet more revealing.

In the first passage Beowulf is speaking to the coast guard, identifying his reason for landing on the Danish coast. He says,

> From a generous mind
> I can offer Hrothgar   good plan and counsel,
> how, old and good,   he may conquer his enemy,
> if reversal of fortune   is ever to come to him,
> any exchange   for baleful affliction,
> cooling of care-surges   hot in his heart;
> or else ever afterwards   through years of grief
> he must endure   terrible suffering,
> so long as that hall   rises high in its place.
>   (277–85)

Beowulf's description of Hroðgar's situation reveals a youthful optimism in our hero, for he not only uses *edwenden* to represent something similar in meaning to *bot*, "remedy"; he also acknowledges only two possibilities in Hroðgar's future: stasis, as depicted in the parallel static images—Hroðgar forever suffering and the hall forever standing tall—or change for the better. The possibility of change for the worse is completely absent from the speech. Beowulf's point of view here—and later when he promises Hroðgar and his men safe sleeping in Heorot (1671–76)—contrasts sharply with his later

prophetic account to Higelac of the disastrous results of Freawaru's marriage
to Froda's son ("But seldom anywhere, / after a slaying, will the death-spear
rest, / even for a while, though the bride be good" [2029–31]).

The second instance of the word *edwenden*, in line 1774, also contrasts
sharply with the first. Hroðgar is speaking rather than Beowulf, he uses the
word to denote change for the worse, and he uses it in a context specifically
concerned with convincing Beowulf of the inevitability of change—for the
better or worse depending on circumstances.

> Thus, fifty winters,   I ruled the Ring-Danes
> under these skies   and by my war-strength
> kept them safe   from spear and sword
> throughout middle-earth—   such rule that no one
> under the heavens   was my adversary.
> And look, even so,   in my homestead reversal:
> my nightly invader,   our ancient enemy.
> I bore great heart-care,   suffered continually
> from his persecution.   Thanks be to God,
> the Eternal Lord,   I came through alive,
> and today may look   at this huge bloody head
> with my own eyes,   after long strife!
>   (1769–81)

This passage is part of the speech generally called "Hroðgar's Sermon,"
in which the older, more experienced Hroðgar warns the young Beowulf
of the dangers of pride and complacency. Unlike the Beowulf of the first
part of the poem, Hroðgar knows there is no stasis in this world; he knows
halls and other human artifacts seem perpetual representatives of mankind's
achievements but in fact decline and decay are inevitable sequences to
prosperity and growth.

Hroðgar's speech makes several important points about change. He
brings together his own pattern of success followed by decline followed by
a new prosperity, Heremod's pattern of success followed by decline, and
the inevitable eventual decline of all mankind—mortality. But the use of
edwenden comes ten lines from the end of this eighty-four-line speech, just
before Hroðgar modulates to his heartfelt thanks to God for his survival
of the years of strife and his invitation to Beowulf to share in the feast of
celebration. Hroðgar as much as says he, too, at one time thought that all
change was for the better, but he has learned otherwise through experience.
Thus Hroðgar insists on the inevitability of change, that "the glory of
this might" is temporary, transitory, fleeting, but within the dominantly

optimistic atmosphere of Beowulf's superhuman achievements and the Dane's recovery, after years of suffering. This is similar to the narrator's use of *edhwyrft*—when Grendel's mother came into Heorot, she brought reversal of fortune to the men there.

The third occurrence of *edwenden* comes toward the end of the poem, this time in a narrative comment on Beowulf's youth. Here it emphatically denotes change for the better: Beowulf in his early years was not very promising—an *aeðeling unfrom*—but *Edwenden cwom / tireadigum menn torna gehwylces* (2188–89) ["A change came to him, / shining in victory, worth all those cares"].

The second of these passages is the most important for an understanding of cycles and change in *Beowulf*. Hroðgar's sermon is about the inevitability of change and death, yet it ends on an optimistic note. The theme and structure of the speech can perhaps be seen as a paradigm of the poet's worldview. Man's powers and glory, even in a heroic world, are finite and fleeting, yet despite the Heremods and Grendels of the world, despite man's mortality and potential for evil, true virtue is powerful, and each falling action can be succeeded by a rise. The bad times as well as the good times are finite. Especially important is Hroðgar's insistence that one blessing of mankind is his control over his own behavior. Heremod failed as a king not because of any tragic flaw beyond his control but because he allowed pride to rule his actions. Even more suggestive is Hroðgar's own situation, since he suffered despite his virtuous actions; nevertheless, his suffering did not turn him from his kingly responsibilities.

Significantly both Hroðgar and Beowulf attribute the happy resolution to a combination of heroic behavior and divine grace. Both evoke a Gregorian sense that individual acts of virtue can alter the course of events in a postlapsarian world and an Augustinian sense that one inhabits the City of God or the City of Man by choosing to turn toward or away from God. Though the pagan Hroðgar, like his Christian brothers, cannot perceive a fully revealed salvation, he, like his Old Testament brothers, can imagine something better than the pagan inevitability of destruction. Thus he has confidence that Beowulf, although young and perhaps naive, can learn from Hroðgar's experience, history, and his own experience and therefore can avoid some of the dangers that accompany possession of power in a heroic world. Beowulf's account to Hygelac suggests he has indeed learned the lesson of Hroðgar's sermon. The *Beowulf* poet knows about Christian apocalypse as an alternative to pagan eschatology. The poet may suggest that his virtuous pagan characters, like some of the Anglo-Saxons Augustine encountered in his missionary activities in England, have a natural attraction and openness to Christian truth.

Does this convergence of a pagan and a Christian poetic worldview apply to the second, more elegiac, part of the poem? I believe it does although the differences in tone, pace, and structure between the two parts of the poem are striking. In the first part, the main plot moves forward fairly steadily with the episodic subplots very much in the background, slowing the progress but not really disrupting it. Though success, prosperity, and joy are constantly interchanged with failure, decline, and sorrow, the positive predominates. In the second half of the poem we see a reversal of this structure: The main plot is often subordinated to the complicated, frequently unchronological account of the Swedish-Geatish wars. The chronological narration of the Dragon's rage and destruction and Beowulf's final days takes up much less space in the second half of the poem than do the historical subplot, the passages recounting the background of the treasure, and the other "digressive" material. When the tone of sorrow at man's mortality and the transitoriness of all things human briefly lifts, as when Beowulf asserts "My heart is bold, / I forego boasting against this war-flyer" (2527–28), the effect is, as Joseph Harris notes, "peculiarly unsettling."[35] The pace of the main action slows as it is constantly interrupted by the rapid narration of the major historical events of the last three generations, matter that is full of action, violence, and power.[36]

But is the end of the poem concerned not only with the death of a great hero, but also of a great heroic age? Is the "second part of the poem... dark with the shadow of ineluctable doom" as Professor Brodeur has argued?[37] Does the phrase "dom Godes" (2858) convey only the modern meaning of "doom," with its post-Christian, existentialist sense of futility, or does it retain the pagan sense of judgment, discretion, choice, even glory? Is there evidence that a heroic society might prosper again after Beowulf's death? James Earl suggests that the poet has chosen the Geats as Beowulf's nation because legend and history presented them as a nation of great heroes that had been annihilated.[38] Other critics, however, trace Mercian kings back to the Geats, suggesting Wiglaf migrated to England after the destruction of his people. Some details in the text suggest that Wiglaf has the potential to be to the Geats what Scyld was to the Danes at the beginning of the poem.

First, Wiglaf's behavior during the dragon fight is impeccable. When Beowulf says this is my fight alone, Wiglaf does not argue—he obeys. But when Nægling fails, changing the entire situation utterly, Wiglaf uses his head, assesses the danger that results from the transient nature of all human artifacts, and acts honorably. Despite the obvious significant danger to himself and the seeming hopelessness of the situation, he leaps out to help the greatest man living without a moment's hesitation. In effect, he follows

Gregory's advice and does what he can do. His behavior contrasts sharply with his cohorts' passive helplessness. Moreover, the narrative information that his wooden shield is immediately consumed by flame and the later observation that Wiglaf could only strike the dragon lower than Beowulf did highlights Wiglaf's courage. Ironically it takes this man of lesser stature to reach the dragon's vulnerable spot. Perhaps Wiglaf's success even parallels Beowulf's success in overcoming Grendel by fighting without armor or sword.

Second, Wiglaf behaves thus—bravely, intelligently, humbly, giving all of himself—in his very first battle. This contrasts sharply with Beowulf himself, who rose to glory after an unpromising youth. If Beowulf in his youth was *sleac* yet he became such a remarkable leader, what great potential must Wiglaf have, when we see him behaving so well in his first test?

But a great leader perhaps is not enough. Does the Geats' behavior at the end of the poem suggest any possibility of recovery? The messenger unequivocally portends disaster. But one can imagine a messenger bearing the tale of Hygelac's or of Heardred's death having a similarly gloomy view of the future. When Beowulf had to get home across the sea by himself with those thirty suits of armor, surely the Geats were in as dangerous a situation. After Hreðel died of grief and his son Hæðcyn was killed by Ongenþeow, surely Geatish messengers foretold times of sorrow to ensue. Inevitably the Swedes will attack, for the death of any king results in political instability, but Geatish loss is not inevitable. Nor is the end of the Heroic Age necessitated by the ending of the poem. The Geats' response to Beowulf's death is something like the early Christians' response to Christ's crucifixion. Christ's death only seems heroic after the resurrection or in light of revelatory prophecy. In its mode of correction-and-fulfillment the Christian era invites a reexamination of values, but it also demands of Christians the vision to see, albeit dimly, the possibility of new kinds of heroism. Thus Bede depicts in Coifi's speech to Edwin a recognition beyond Coifi's of the shortcomings of any material or worldly reward, and a new awareness of apocalypse as opposed to eschaton.[39]

In acknowledging they have no right to the treasure Beowulf has rightfully won, the Geats, Wiglaf in particular, evince a mature understanding of right behavior—precisely the kind of behavior that was the subject of Hroðgar's sermon. They also express a distrust of material goods that coincides with Christian belief. They should not take pride in their king's victory, for they, excepting Wiglaf, have behaved abominably. But by acting as though the battle with the Dragon has been an outright loss, by mourning the loss of a king rather than celebrating his victory, they are perhaps ready to begin the reestablishment of a new political stability by infusing heroic ideals with a Christian realism that simultaneously acknowledges postlapsarian instability and the secure promise of divine grace.

At the core of the heroic ideal in *Beowulf* is the belief that great deeds of men do not die with them, that they are immortal. The final lines of the poem demonstrate that Beowulf's great deeds do live on in the memory of his people; they remember that he was "of the kings in this world, / the kindest to his men, the most courteous man, / the best to his people, and most eager for fame" (3180–82). Just as Beowulf has been guided by honor and his love for Hygelac, Wiglaf and his followers may go on to new times of prosperity. Suffering, sorrow, pain, like joy, happiness, and prosperity, will inevitably change. As the *Deor* poet says, "*þæs ofereode, þisses swa mæg!*" Beowulf, in his youth, could imagine a stasis—an unending sorrow—but the maturer vision of the poem epitomized by Hroðgar's sermon insists that all of human life—sorrow and happiness—is transitory. The *Beowulf* poet, like Gregory, seems to have envisioned a physical world contiguous with the spiritual world beyond, a world in which Christian revelation emphasizes the power of virtuous behavior. This confidence in man's ability to alter the world for the better if he chooses right behavior is a large part of what makes *Beowulf* more than a Germanic pagan epic.

NOTES

1. Some important studies of style, structure, and theme in *Beowulf* are Edward B. Irving, *A Reading of Beowulf* (New Haven: Yale University Press, 1968), esp. 31–42; Arthur Gilchrist Brodeur, *The Art of Beowulf* (Berkeley: University of California Press, 1971), esp. 51, 60, 71–87; Theodore M. Andersson, "Tradition and Design in *Beowulf*," *Old English Literature in Context*, ed. John D. Niles (Cambridge: D. S. Brewer, 1980), 90–106; and George Clark, "The Hero and the Theme," *A Beowulf Handbook*, ed. Robert E. Bjork and John D. Niles (Lincoln: University of Nebraska Press, 1997), 271–90. A very different kind of analysis also in *A Beowulf Handbook*, Seth Lerer's "Beowulf and Contemporary Critical Theory" concludes: "[theoretical approaches] may reveal what in the end may be the truly human quality of *Beowulf*: its recognition that the open-endedness and ambiguity of language mark us as creatures of the historical moment and that such a language gives voice to the social worlds in which our literature is made and understood" (339).

2. Robert Barr, S.J., *Main Currents in Early Christian Thought* (Glen Rock, N.J.: Paulist Press, 1965), 110.

3. Carole Straw, *Gregory the Great: Perfection in Imperfection* (Berkeley: University of California Press, 1988).

4. Ibid., 5.

5. Ibid., 4.

6. Ibid., 2–3.

7. Ibid., 10.

8. See Philip B. Rollinson, "The Influence of Christian Doctrine on Old English Poetry," *Anglo-Saxon England* 2 (1973): 276–80, for an overview.

9. Peter Brown, *The Making of Late Antiquity* (Cambridge: Harvard University Press, 1978), 98–99.

10. *Oxford Dictionary of the Christian Church*, 3rd ed., s.v. "Pelagianism."

11. Brown, 101.

12. R. A. Markus, *Speculum: History and Society in the Theology of St. Augustine* (Cambridge: Cambridge University Press, 1970), 14.

13. Markus, 18.

14. W. F. Bolton, *Alcuin and* Beowulf: *An Eighth-Century View* (New Brunswick, N.J.: Rutgers University Press, 1978), 175–77.

15. In *Thinking about Beowulf* (Stanford: Stanford University Press, 1994), James Earl distinguishes between the eschatalogical and the apocalyptic: "The eschaton (Greek 'last thing') is the end of the world"; "An apocalypse, according to its Greek derivation, is an uncovering, a revelation, a revealing of something hidden. The idea of an apocalypse, then, depends upon a prior sense that something is hidden—something we know, insofar as we know it is hidden; but something we do not know, insofar as it is hidden from us" (43; 41).

16. Straw, 10.

17. Ibid.

18. Citations of *Beowulf* are from Fr. Klaeber, *Beowulf and the Fight at Finnsburg* (Boston: D.C. Heath, 1950).

19. The translations are from Howell D. Chickering Jr., *Beowulf: A Dual-Language Edition* (New York: Anchor Books, 1977).

20. In "The Great Feud: Scriptural History and Strife in *Beowulf*," *Beowulf Basic Readings*, ed. Peter S. Baker (New York: Garland, 1995), Marijane Osborn argues, "The poet controls his two perspectives [pagan and Christian] simply by distinguishing between the natural wisdom possible to pagans and the revealed knowledge he shares with us" and cites Augustine as a patristic model the *Beowulf* poet may have drawn on, 121.

21. Andersson, 95.

22. Ibid., 103.

23. Earl, 46.

24. Ibid., 45.

25. Ibid., 46.

26. Bede, *A History of the English Church and People*, trans. Leo Sherley-Price, rev. R. E. Latham (Harmondsworth, Eng.: Penguin, 1975), 332.

27. Linda Georgianna, "King Hreþel's Sorrow and the Limits of Heroic Action in *Beowulf*," *Speculum* 62 (1987): 829–30.

28. Charles Donahue, "*Beowulf* and Christian Tradition: A Reconsideration from a Celtic Stance," *Traditio* 21 (1965): 55–116.

29. Morton W. Bloomfield, "Patristics and Old English Literature: Notes on Some Poems," *Essential Articles for the Study of Old English Poetry*, ed. Jess B. Bessinger, Jr., and Stanley J. Kahrl (Hamden, Conn.: Archon Books, 1968), 66.

30. Bede, 86–87.

31. See Jaroslav Pelikan, *The Emergence of the Catholic Tradition (100–600)*, vol. 1 of *The Christian Tradition: A History of the Development of Doctrine* (Chicago: University of Chicago Press, 1971), 14ff. Pelikan notes that even before the Gospels were written, the idea that the Old Law will be confirmed but superceded by Christ's incarnation, that the Old Testament's purpose was to prepare for and prefigure the New Law of Christ, may have been recorded (16).

32. Roberta Frank, "The *Beowulf* Poet's Sense of History," in *The Wisdom of Poetry: Essays in Early English Literature in Honor of Morton W. Bloomfield*, ed. Larry

Benson and Siegfried Wenzel (Kalamazoo, Mich.: Medieval Institute Publications, 1982), 58–59.

33. Frank, 62.

34. See Howell D. Chickering, Jr., *Beowulf: A Dual–Language Edition* (New York: Anchor Books, 1977), 302–3, for an overview.

35. Joseph Harris, "Beowulf's Last Words," *Speculum* 67 (1992): 26.

36. See Stanley B. Greenfield, "Geatish History: Poetic Art and Epic Quality in *Beowulf*," in *Hero and Exile: The Art of Old English Poetry*, ed. George Hardin Brown (London: Hambledon Press, 1989) for a discussion of the way "historic destiny, in a centrally significant way, universalizes and makes epic this Old English heroic poem," 26.

37. Arthur Gilchrist Brodeur, *The Art of Beowulf* (Berkeley: University of California Press, 1971), 83. Greenfield also argues "the epic hero's fate awakens in us a poignancy, a pathos, akin to but different from the pity or compassion we feel for the suffering hero of drama. It springs from epic's presentation of man's accomplishment against the background of his mortality, from the implications the hero's fall entails for his people, from a sense of futility in the splendid achievement, a resignation and despair in the face of the limits of life," "*Beowulf* and Epic Tragedy," in *Hero and Exile*, 16.

38. Earl, 47.

39. Ibid., 45, argues that the contrast of apocalypse and eschaton contributes to the *Beowulf*'s "dark Christian vision." I suggest, in contrast, that an Anglo-Saxon poem about Geatish history may suggest the poet sees in English history, as Bede did, the possibility of a Christian empire uniting disparate peoples.

Works Cited

Andersson, Theodore M. "Tradition and Design in Beowulf." In *Old English Literature in Context*. Edited by John D. Niles, 90–106. Cambridge: D.S. Brewer, 1980.

Barr, Robert, S.J. *Main Currents in Early Christian Thought*. Glen Rock, N.J.: Paulist Press, 1965.

Bede. *A History of the English Church and People*. Translated by Leo Sherley-Price and revised by R. E. Latham. Harmondsworth, Eng.: Penguin, 1975.

Bloomfield, Morton W. "Patristics and Old English Literature: Notes on Some Poems." In *Essential Articles for the Study of Old English Poetry*. Edited by Jess B. Bessinger, Jr., and Stanley J. Kahrl. Hamden, Conn: Archon Books, 1968.

Bolton, W. F. *Alcuin and Beowulf: An Eighth-Century View*. New Brunswick, N.J.: Rutgers University Press, 1978.

Brodeur, Arthur Gilchrist. *The Art of Beowulf*. Berkeley: University of California Press, 1971.

Brown, Peter. *The Making of Late Antiquity*. Cambridge: Harvard University Press, 1978.

Chickering, Howell D., Jr. *Beowulf: A Dual-Language Edition*. New York: Anchor Books, 1977.

Clark, George. "The Hero and the Theme." In *A Beowulf Handbook*. Edited by Robert E. Bjork and John D. Niles, 271–90. Lincoln: University of Nebraska Press, 1997.

Donahue, Charles. "*Beowulf* and Christian Tradition: A Reconsideration from a Celtic Stance." *Traditio* 21 (1965): 55–116.

Earl, James W. *Thinking about Beowulf*. Stanford, Calif.: Stanford University Press, 1994.

Frank, Roberta. "The *Beowulf* Poet's Sense of History." In *The Wisdom of Poetry: Essays in Early English Literature in Honor of Morton W. Bloomfield*. Edited by Larry Benson and Siegfried Wenzel. Kalamazoo, Mich.: Medieval Institute Publications, 1982.

Georgianna, Linda. "King Hreðel's Sorrow and the Limits of Heroic Action in *Beowulf.*" *Speculum* 62 (1987): 829–830.

Greenfield, Stanley B. "Geatish History: Poetic Art and Epic Quality in Beowulf." In *Hero and Exile: The Art of Old English Poetry*. Edited by George Hardin Brown. London: Hambledon Press, 1989.

Harris, Joseph. "Beowulf's Last Words." *Speculum* 67 (1992): 1–32.

Irving, Edward B. *A Reading of Beowulf*. New Haven: Yale University Press, 1968.

Klaeber, Fr. *Beowulf* and the Fight at Finnsburg. Boston: D.C. Heath, 1950.

Lerer, Seth. "*Beowulf* and Contemporary Critical Theory." In *A Beowulf Handbook*. Edited by Robert E. Bjork and John D. Niles, 325–39. Lincoln: University of Nebraska Press, 1997.

Markus, R.A. *Saeculum: History and Society in the Theology of St. Augustine*. Cambridge: Cambridge University Press, 1970.

Osborn, Marijane. "The Great Feud: Scriptural History and Strife in *Beowulf.*" In *Beowulf: Basic Readings*. Edited by Peter S. Baker. New York: Garland, 1995.

Pelikan, Jaroslav. *The Emergence of the Catholic Tradition (100–600)*. Vol. 1 of *The Christian Tradition: A History of the Development of Doctrine*. Chicago: University of Chicago Press, 1971.

Rollinson, Philip B. "The Influence of Christian Doctrine on Old English Poetry." *Anglo-Saxon England* 2 (1973): 276–80.

Straw, Carole. *Gregory the Great: Perfection in Imperfection*. Berkeley, Calif.: University of California Press, 1988.

GALE R. OWEN-CROCKER

The Fourth Funeral:
Beowulf's Complex Obsequies

THE PRACTICAL DETAILS

Beowulf's is the only funeral of the four to include mention of the labour involved,[1] and it does so twice. The first instance precedes the funeral, when Wiglaf instructs hall-owners to bring in wood for the pyre in the interval while the barrow is ransacked and the dragon's treasure removed: 'then Weohstan's son, the hero brave in battle, commanded it be announced to many men, hall-owners, leaders of people, that they should fetch from afar wood for the pyre' (lines 3110–13). Cremation is very expensive in terms of wood[2] and undoubtedly a funeral on a royal scale would require a lot of timber; but the way in which all Beowulf's subordinate chiefs are expected to supply fuel for his pyre makes the practical collection of wood seem like the delivering of tribute. The second example is that the poet gives the details of how long it took to build Beowulf's barrow, as well as some indication of its construction: 'it was high and broad ... and they built [it] in ten days ... they made a wall round the remains of the burning' (lines 3157–61). These details give the final funeral of the poem an immediacy which is not present in the others; the time scale is quite feasible.[3] The fact that the *Beowulf*-poet chose to include such details here while omitting them from the other funerals makes a contrast between the treatment of characters and events of the remote past and that of Beowulf, in a more tangible past. The impression of verisimilitude may be

---

From *The Four Funerals in* Beowulf: *And the Structure of the Poem*, pp. 85–113. © 2000 by Gale R. Owen-Crocker.

purely literary, a feature of epic tradition, however; there are details both of the bringing of wood for a pyre and the building of a barrow in *The Iliad*.[4]

Beowulf's funeral is preceded by another practical detail—the disposal of the dragon's body. The dragon is pushed over the cliff in a truncated travesty of a burial at sea: 'they also pushed the dragon, the worm, over the cliff; they let the wave take [him], the flood swallow the guardian of treasures' (lines 3131–3). This, with its verbal echo of Scyld's departure (*lèton holm beran*, line 48) and possible reminder of a dragon ship[5] contributes to the cyclic effect of the poem as it ends, in the same way it began, with the funeral of a great king.

The shoving of the dragon into the oblivion of the ocean also reminds us of the proximity of the sea. The first description of the dragon's barrow includes the geographical details that it is situated 'on a plain, near the ocean waves[6] ... by the headland' (2242–3) but this open, natural aspect is largely ignored in the dragon-fight and rifling of the treasure, which take place around and inside the ancient, stone-built structure which is the dragon's lair. The cowards retreat to the enclosure of the woods, further inland, presumably, and the events seem to take place a long way from the *ecgclif* where the rest of Beowulf's armed retainers miserably await the outcome (*eorlweorod ... modgiomor sæt, / bordhæbbende*, lines 2893–5). Now we return from a supernatural world where a stream surges hot from the fire of a dragon to unpleasant practicalities which ordinary men can deal with: fifty feet of dead reptile (line 3042) to be disposed of in the enormity of the sea and a funeral fire to be made.

The funeral ceremonies reflect Beowulf's own request:

> '... Command the veterans to make a bright mound, after the fire, at the sea's cape; it must tower high on Whale's Headland as a memorial for my people, so that afterwards, seafarers, who urge ships from afar over the spray of the floods, will call it "Beowulf's barrow".'
>   (lines 2802–8)

The instruction has been repeated by Wiglaf:

> '... He was still alive then, wise and conscious; the old man spoke many things in sorrow, and commanded to greet you, asked that you make, according to the deeds of a friend, in the place of the fire a barrow, high, great and famous, just as he was the most illustrious warrior, widely throughout the earth, while he was able to enjoy the prosperity of a stronghold.'
>   (lines 3093–100)

Whereas Beowulf's chief concern is his fame, Wiglaf takes the hero's achievements for granted, and is concerned that the magnitude of his illustriousness should be reflected in the proportions of the barrow.

Although we were told that Scyld Scefing gave the commands for his funeral (*swa he selfa bæd, / þenden wordum weold wine Scyldinga*, lines 29–30), we were not told what those instructions were and, as a result, the ship funeral came upon us as a surprise—a magnificent ritual unfolding as each detail was revealed. There is no surprise about Beowulf's funeral; it has always been assumed he would be burned, by the narrator as well as the protagonists, as if this were quite usual (which of course it was not, to the poet's Christian audience) and the building of the barrow has been well prepared for. The element of surprise will come only on the burial of the dragon's treasure with Beowulf's remains.

It is notable that all Beowulf asked for was the barrow for his people to remember him by (*to gemyndum minum leodum*, line 2804). This modesty is in keeping with the picture his household retainers later paint of his character as 'most unpretentious, kindest to [his] people' (lines 3181–2) and contrasts with the public display of magnificence which Scyld evidently ordered for his funeral (*he selfa bæd*, line 29). We may note that Scyld's virtue (*þæt wæs god cyning*, line 11) is measured by his ruthless subjection of neighbouring tribes; Beowulf's by his restraint.

THE FUNERAL

Beowulf's is the most prolonged of the four funeral descriptions in the poem. This is partly achieved by the expansive style, more marked in the barrow rituals than the cremation, though the amplification is largely achieved by repetition and apposition, rather than the inclusion of specific detail. The funeral is also made grander by the doubling of ritual and mourning speeches. Firstly there is the cremation, with its practical details of the building of the pyre, the enumeration of grave-goods and the burning of the body. This is accompanied by two instances of mourning, a general lamentation of Beowulf's retainers (lines 3248–9) and a paraphrase of the mournful chant (*giomorgyd*, line 3150) of a Geatish woman. Secondly there is the interment of the ashes in a barrow, which involves, again, some practical details of construction and a brief account of grave-goods, this time the treasure taken from the dragon's hoard. Again there are two instances of mourning, a description of the lament of twelve sons of princes (with the poet's approving comment on its suitability); and finally, the poet's paraphrase of the lament and epitaph provided by Beowulf's hearth-companions (*heorðgeneatas*, line 3179) which famously, and ambiguously, closes the poem.

As Fred Robinson says, 'Scholars ... are troubled by the fact that
Beowulf's funeral rites are not merely grander than the funerals of other
characters described in the poem, but peculiarly complex in a way that
makes them unique.'[7] The double funeral ritual has troubled critics since
the archaeologist Knut Stjerna argued the inaccuracy and inconsistency of
the burning of weapons followed by the burial of the dragon's treasure.[8]
In fact, a double ceremony is only unique in the context of *Beowulf*. In Ibn
Fadlan's narrative there was a double funeral, though the ingredients were
different from *Beowulf*—first burial then exhumation for burning;[9] and in
every Germanic funeral where ashes were gathered up from the site of the
pyre and placed in a container for interment in a cemetery or enclosure in
a barrow elsewhere, there must have been two rituals. In Beowulf's case the
first ceremony is the funeral proper; the second, which follows ten days later,
after the completion of his monument, is more like a memorial service. The
noisy, spontaneous emotion which accompanied the burning is replaced by
a more dispassionate eulogy expressed in formal circumstances by men of
noble rank. Stjerna's objection that the burning of weapons was inaccurate
is no longer valid,[10] though the practice was certainly unusual in England;[11]
and though unburnt grave-goods are not usually included in cremation
burials, this is not without precedent either (see below). Stjerna thought that
the whole of the dragon's treasure was burnt, and the whole of the dragon's
treasure was buried, in two conflicting accounts. As I will show, the nature
and literary function of the two sets of grave-goods are different.

THE BURNING

The poet devotes the first stage to the preparation of the pyre on which are
hung weapons and armour and in which is placed the corpse.

> Then the people of the Geats equipped a strong pyre for him on
> the earth, hung round with helmets, battle swords, bright mail
> coats, as he was deserving; then the lamenting warriors laid in the
> midst the famous chief, the dear lord.
>   (lines 3137–42)

The pyre is more realistic than that of Finnsburg. Though the height
and visibility of the Frisian pyre are implied, the construction is taken for
granted.[12] Beowulf's pyre is firmly established on the earth and the poet
emphasises the strength of its structure: *unwaclicne* occupies an entire
metrical unit and carries stress on the negator *un*.[13] It is emphatically not
weak, and as such reflects Beowulf's own strength. Unlike Hnæf who 'was
ready on the pyre' (*wæs on bæl gearu*) and his nephew, who 'went up' (*astah*)

as if unassisted by human hands, Beowulf is placed by loving hands 'in the midst', which, assuming this means 'in the midst of the pyre' and not 'in the middle of the grave-goods', is the most practical arrangement for burning a body in the open air.[14]

Beowulf's funeral inevitably invites comparison with Scyld's, for, though the manner of disposing of the body is different, the situation is similar—the loss of a great king who has brought more-than-human qualities to his realm. The poet uses similar terms, but rarely repeats a formula exactly, for example *alegdon ðd ... mæne þeoden ... hlaford leofne* (lines 3141–2) echoes but does not duplicate *aledon þa leofne þeoden ... mærne* (lines 34–6). Similarly, though Beowulf receives the same kind of grave-goods as Scyld—weapons and armour—the exact terms differ. *Hilde-* is again in compound, but a different compound (*hildebordum*, line 3139, as opposed to *hildewæpnum*, line 39). The effect of this thematic echo which is not an exact lexical echo is subtle: cyclic but not repetitive. Swords are not mentioned this time but shields and helmets are included. The poet, always selective, has perhaps chosen here the objects which would make most visual impact when displayed around the pyre, shields ranged like the rows of shields carried along the outside of a Viking ship,[15] or set around the outside of a hall when sea-weary travellers reached land (lines 325–6); mail coats like the trophies of their defeated enemies hung on monuments by the Romans.[16]

The helmets set up reverberations of triumph and destruction. They remind us of Beowulf's achievements—we recall the boar-helmets of the band of brave retainers he took to fight Grendel (lines 313–15), the inlaid helmet presented to the hero by Hrothgar (*wirum bewunden*, line 1031) and the *hwita helm* he wore for his plunge into the mere (line 1448); but they also recall the boar-image on the all-consuming fire at Finnsburg (lines 1111–12) and the slow crumbling through time of the plated helmet in the Last Survivor's Lay (lines 2255–6).

The grave-goods seem particularly appropriate to Beowulf. Helmets and mail coats were evidently high-status grave-goods in Anglo-Saxon cemeteries; and shields, though not particularly rare, are usually found only in the graves of fully adult men.[17] Beowulf's age and experience have been particularly stressed in his final fight.

The funeral description has opened matter-of-factly, with simple alliteration at line 3137, increasing to double with the focus on the massive pyre, *ad on eorðan unwaclicne* (line 3138). As in Scyld's funeral the reference to weapons and armour is marked by alliterative complexity: *helmum behongen, hildebordum, beorhtum byrnum, swa he bena wæs* involves interlinear alliteration from the second element of the compound *hildebordum* to *beorhtum byrnum ... bena*, while the unstressed *he* of *behongen* also alliterates (not essential, metrically) anticipating the *b* sound and interweaving it with the double alliteration on *b*. A return to simple alliteration marks practical detail (lines 3141, 3143), though the retainers' mourning is marked by the ornament of interlacing *l* sounds in the double alliteration on *b*, (*bæleð biofende*, *hlaford leofne*) and the long vowels (*io*, *a*, *eo*) onomatopoeically reflect their grief.

As in Scyld's case, the tributes are multiple, not just the single sword, helmet and mail coat which might symbolically equip a warrior for battle in Valhalla or some similar pagan Other World, but an indication that Beowulf was the owner of vast resources. They are hung round his pyre *swa he bena wær* ('as he was deserving', line 3140) reflecting that status in the same way as Wiglaf's conception of the barrow. As the mail coats are 'bright' they are not, presumably, taken from the dragon's treasure which has been rusting in the ground for hundreds of years, unless the poet's desire to show them positively has led him into an inconsistent description. It seems more likely that this cremation-offering of helmets, shields and mail coats comes from the Geat's own resources, and represents Beowulf's public success as a king in the same way that Scyld's weapons and battle garments symbolised his reputation.

Fire has been the expected outcome since Beowulf's death, narrated over three hundred lines earlier:

> That, for the old man was the last word from the thoughts of his breast, before he tasted the fire, hot surges of hostility; his soul went from his heart to seek the judgement of the righteous.
>   (lines 2817–20)

After the long anticipation the action of the fire is swift and powerful:

> Then the warriors began to kindle the greatest of funeral fires on the hill; woodsmoke ascended, dark over the flame, the roaring-fire mingled with weeping—the raging wind subsided—until it had broken the body, hot at the heart.
>   (lines 3143–48)

The fire itself is magnificent. Set *on heorge*, 'on the hill', the sea-cliff which Beowulf had chosen as a highly visible site for his barrow, the cremation is described in superlative terms, *bælfyra mæst*, in a passage which is rich both visually and aurally. The last action of the retainers is their kindling of the fire (*Ongunnon ... weccan*, lines 3143–4) after which the elements themselves take over, ascending, roaring, storming and finally breaking the 'bone-house', the body that was Beowulf. The action of the fire and the human grief become inseparable. Darkness (here the colour of the smoke) is an obvious metaphor for misery[18] and the sound of the flame and weeping are linked with a grammatical complexity which is lost in translation.[19] The alliteration simultaneously achieves pyrotechnic elaboration. The *w* sound of the double alliteration at line 3144 (*wigend weccan; wudurec astah*) is echoed in the double alliteration on *sw* in the following line (3145; *sweart ofer swioðole, swogende leg*) and reiterated in the next (3146; *wope bewunden—wind blond gelæg*). Here also the *b* of *-blond* is anticipated by the unstressed *be-* of *bewunden* and there is end-linked alliteration on *leg* and *gelæg*. The description of the fire ends with cross alliteration *oð þæt he ða banhus gebrocen hæfdel* (line 3147), the alliteration of the unstressed *he* and an enjambement on *h* which links the lines, the grammatical structures and the thematic sections of the passage: *oð þæt he ða banhus gebrocen hæfdel hat on hreðre. Higum unrote*, lines 1347–8).

The funeral allows the corpse of Beowulf (characterised as *mærne þeoden ... hlaford leofne*, 'famous chief ... dear lord', lines 3141–2) a dignity that the Finnsburg corpses were denied. There is no melting head or spurting wounds or even a more realistic oozing fat and escaping body fluids. The practical problems of dealing with unburnt bone are ignored[20] as Beowulf's corpse rapidly subsides into hot ash. It is a mere *banhus* now (line 3147), a 'bone-house' that was once the repository of the spirit but is so no longer, *gebrocen* ('broken', line 3147) by the fire. In the poet's choice of the word *hreðre* (line 3148) it is as if body and fire become one. It echoes the *hræðre* of line 2819, when it signified Beowulf's breast from which the spirit departed, but it may also refer to the hot core of the fire.[21] There is a finality about the destruction of Beowulf's body which was absent from Scyld's ship funeral. Though the dead king's physical presence is constantly invoked at the burning (as *Him, he, mærme þeoden* and *hlaford leofne*)[22] once the cremation is completed he is gone.

Though the structure of the poem at this point consists of a concentrated description of the cremation followed by reference to the mourning, the burning and the lamentation were evidently seen as taking place simultaneously, since weeping is interwoven with the noise of the fire *swogende leg / wope bewunden* ('roaring fire, with weeping mingled', lines 3145–6) and the final reference to the burning, *Heofon rece swealg* ('Heaven swallowed the smoke', line 3155), follows the account of the woman's song.

> Depressed in soul, they lamented their grief, mourned the liege lord. Likewise the Geatish woman[23] lamented for Beowulf, with bound hair [?], sang a sorrowful song, said often that she greatly feared evil days for herself, many slaughters, fear of the foe, humiliation and captivity. Heaven swallowed the smoke.
> (lines 3148–55)

Beowulf is first mourned by a group of warriors in terms which resemble, but do not directly echo, the grief of Scyld's retainers. The poet mostly prefers to use near–synonyms, *wigend* (line 3144) as opposed to *gesipas* (line 29), though the *hæleð hiofende* (line 3142) recall the *hæleð* under *heofenum* to whom Scyld's destiny remained a mystery (line 52). The distinctive *mod* of the earlier mourners (*murnende mod*, line 50) reappears in an emotive compound, *modceare* (line 3149), but though both groups mourn their king, the relationship is expressed in different terms, *mondryhtnes* ('liege lord', line 3149) as opposed to *wine Scyldinga* ('friend of the Scyldings', line 30). Double alliteration on the lugubrious *m*, reinforced by the back vowels in *mod-* and *mon-* mark, onomatopoeically, the mourning of Beowulf's retainers: *modceare mændon, mondryhtnes cwealm*. The line is complicated by a play on *c/c* which was probably visual rather than phonological. (The former was probably pronounced [tʃ] and the latter [k].) The *m* sound continues into the cross-alliteration of the following line, *swylce **giomorgyd** sio **Geatisc meowle***, linking the mourning retainers with the lamenting woman (lines 3149–50).

Much of the passage concerning the mourning woman is illegible,[24] though enough of the text survives to show the elaborate sound patterns in lines 3149–50 and double alliteration in, at least, line 3155. *Meowle*, 'woman' is clear, and the preceding word has been read under ultraviolet light. The verb *giomorgyd* is also visible, providing a clear echo of Hildeburg's grief at a funeral: *ides ... geomrode giddum* ('the lady ... lamented in dirges', lines 1117–18) though the structure is inverted and the poet chooses the synonym *meowle* here rather than the poetic *ides* which earlier linked Hildeburg to Wealhtheow and, with ironic incongruity, to Grendel's mother (line 1259).

It is useless to speculate on the identity of the woman from the details supplied. Klaeber's perpetuation of the idea that she is old, from the supposed fact that her hair is bound up, has little support, textually or culturally[25] though it continues to be repeated without question.[26] The woman is surely archetypal.[27] She has the prescience which Tacitus claims was attributed to women in the Germanic world[28] and the fate she fears is common to women of conquered races. The Geatish woman's expectation of humiliation and captivity is, however, particularly apt in view of the fact that the likely aggressors are the Swedes; Hygelac and Heardred subjected Ongentheow's queen to exactly these things, and in a world where revenge is of major importance, reprisals are likely.

The woman's song seems to be a long prediction of disaster; though Klaeber's *sæde, bearmdagas* and *ondrede* are reconstructions, *geneabbe* ('often', line 3152) is readable, as are the details that she considers her own fate (*bio byre ...*) and that this will be harsh (*bearde*, line 3153). It may be that a woman mourner was a traditional feature of Germanic funerals[29] and it is worth noting that the singing of the slave-girl witnessed by Ibn Fadlan was prolonged.[30] In the case of *Beowulf*, however, the suggestion that the lamentations were often repeated conveys a sense of time passing, time in which the funeral fire completes its destruction of the king's body. The isolated half-line which concludes this section returns us to the action of the fire: *Heofon rece swealg* ('Heaven received [or 'swallowed'] the smoke', line 3155). Ibn Fadlan testifies to the belief among the pagan Viking Rus people that the wind carries a cremated man to paradise. Conceivably, the poet, who is able to maintain the double perspective of pagan protagonists and Christian audience, wishes to imply that Beowulf's people understood that his soul was carried to Paradise in the smoke; but by using the term *heofon* for the enveloping sky the poet reminds the audience of the Christian belief in Heaven. For the Christian audience, Beowulf is not carried away in the smoke, or at least only his mortal remains are; his soul, we have been told, went to seek the judgement of the righteous at the moment he died (lines 2819–20).

THE BARROW

Then the people of the Weder-Geats made a barrow on the cliff. It was high and broad, widely visible to seafarers, and they built in ten days the memorial of the one bold in battle. They made a wall round the remains of the burning as very wise men might find most splendid.
(lines 3156–62)

The opening of the barrow-building section is structured in a similar way to the burning section with *Geworhton ða* (line 3156) matching *ða gegiredan* (line 3137), and *Wedra leode* (line 3156) the equivalent of *Geata leode* (line 3137). This seems to be followed in the same way by a reference to the position and construction of the structure, the barrow balancing the pyre, *blæw on blide, se wæs heah ond brad* (line 3157) as the equivalent of *ad on eorðan unwaclicne* (line 3138), though both *hlæw* and *hriðe* are editorial emendations.[31] *Heah* and *liðiendum*[32] echo Beowulf's own request for his barrow 'tower high ... so that seafarers after will call it "Beowulf's barrow"' (lines 2805–7) and demonstrate that his wish is fulfilled. The lugubrious sounds are absent now as activity dominates. The rapid unstressed syllables opening the Type B half-lines reflect the action

```
    x      x    /    x    /
    se wæs heah ond brad
```

x   x /   x /
and betimbredon

while the enormity of the task and the edifice itself are echoed in the long,
slower syllables of

/   x   /
heah ond brad

/   x   x /   x
wide gesyne

and

x   /   /   x
on tyn dagum

a Type C half-line with heavy central stress, leading to the climactic, heavily
stressed

/   \ x   /
beadurofes becn

The elaboration of alliteration is largely absent here, though there is
double alliteration at lines 3160 and 3161 (*beadurofes becn, bronda lafe* and
wealle beworhton, swa hyt weorðlicost), and, dependent on emendation, at line
3157 (*hlæw on hliðe, se wæs heah ond brad*). There is probably cross-alliteration
at line 3162 (*foresnotre men findan mihton*) though *fore-* is an intensifier, not
lexical. The effect is much less rich than in the description of the cremation
itself.

The details of the barrow imply that it was an elaborate construction.
Betimbredon (line 3159) perhaps indicates a wooden chamber grave beneath
the barrow, a rare feature found in some of the richest pagan Anglo-Saxon
burials and also known from Viking Age Scandinavia.[33] *Wealle* (line 3161)
can mean 'a wall' in the modern sense of the term, but it is not necessary
to postulate a free-standing rampart.[34] The poet, who has used *wealle* in
describing sea-cliffs (for example lines 572, 1224) and the interiors of the
monsters' lairs (for example, lines 1573, 2323) perhaps meant it as a synonym
of *hlæw* and was merely restating that an impressively towering tumulus was
built to enclose the site of the pyre. The archaeological evidence available
suggests that in pagan Anglo-Saxon England barrows were not normally

built on the cremation site,[35] but this detail may not be purely imaginative as there is precedent for it in Sweden,[36] notably in the case of the Vendel-period hunter's grave at Rickeby, discussed in Chapter 4.

> They placed in the barrow rings and clasps, also all of the orna-
> ments which brave-minded men had taken from the hoard before.
> They let the earth hold the wealth of men; gold in the soil, there
> it still lives now, as useless to men as it was before.
>   (lines 3163–8)

It appears that jewellery is placed, unburnt, in the barrow, though this is inconsistent with the preceding speech of the Messenger, which indicated that all of the dragon's treasure was to be placed on the pyre:

> '... Not shall some single thing melt with the proud one, but there
> is a hoard of treasures, countless gold grimly purchased, and now,
> ultimately, rings bought with his own life; these must the burning
> consume, the fire enfold....'
>   (lines 3010–15)

Possibly critics have misunderstood the poem at this point, and the jewellery has shared Beowulf's pyre, to be included in the barrow as the melted remains of rings and clasps, though the text, 'They placed in the barrow ...' (line 3163), does suggest an additional act of dedication, not simply the burial of what has already been burned. It does not seem to have been usual, either in Anglo-Saxon England or in Scandinavia, to place additional, unburnt, grave-goods with a cremation. In the 'folk-cemeteries' unburnt grave-goods are found with inhumations; but in cremations any remains of metal, usually from clothing fasteners, are normally burnt and melted. However, bone combs and metal tweezers, utilitarian objects, have sometimes been found unburnt in urns, with the ashes. One might speculate that these were very personal possessions, used in the grooming of the corpse for its final appearance, though there is no obvious reason why they were not thrown in the fire. The unique, probably royal, cemetery at Sutton Hoo, however, demonstrates a more extensive use of the custom of adding unburnt possessions to a cremation, which offers closer parallels to the text: under several of the barrows unburnt objects which were probably personal treasures, such as bone gaming pieces, vessels and bone or ivory boxes, as well as more utilitarian shears and combs, had been placed in the burial pit with the cremation in its container.[37] The dragon's treasure was perhaps considered, similarly, to be very personal and precious to Beowulf.

It is noticeable that the objects said to be buried in Beowulf's barrow do not include weapons. This may reflect actual practice in Anglo-Saxon England, where the custom of burying weapons in graves declined as barrow burial became established.[38] At this point the poet selects for mention the items of jewellery from the dragon's hoard, which evidently contained a wide range of objects,[39] some of gold, some decorated with gold,[40] and some, capable of rusting, not gold. *Beg ond siglu* are the most likely of the treasures to have been made of precious metal, enabling the poet to ruminate on the immortality of gold. Characteristically, the poet uses rather general terms, and we can only guess what might be meant by them, if indeed the author had any clear picture at all. Rings (*beg*, *beagas*) are the items of jewellery most frequently mentioned in Old English literature, where they carry emotive force. In *Beowulf* the rings mentioned are chiefly torques for the neck, a category which is not represented in Anglo-Saxon archaeology,[41] though there are many surviving examples from Viking culture. *Sigl* is a rarer word. The most compelling interpretation of it for the modern audience has to be the gold, filigree and garnet objects from seventh-century Anglo-Saxon deposits, including the Sutton Hoo Ship Burial and Taplow, since this is the most splendid Anglo-Saxon metalwork known to us. The rarer surviving jewellery from the later Anglo-Saxon period[42] is mostly less impressive in materials, techniques and design and does not offer obvious parallels, though accidents of survival may convey a false impression of austerity and the poet could have been drawing on royal or religious splendours now lost.[43]

As the poet again begins to describe treasure, the alliterative patterns become elaborate once more. The sibilant at the end of line 3163 is echoed in the repeated *sw* of the correlative *swylce ... swylce* of the following line, which also has transverse alliteration on *h* and vowel sounds: *siglu, / eall swylce hyrsta, swylce on horde ær*. The *h* sound is continued into line 3165, which also alliterates on *n*: *niðhedige men genumen hæfdon*, and recurs once more in the final stress of line 3166, *healdan*. The poet's comment on the treasure ends with double alliteration on vowel sounds (presumably; the line is emended) interweaving with another correlative construction alliterating on *sw*: *eldum swa unnyt swa hit æror wæs*. These correlative constructions are important in juxtaposing time. The first (*swylce hyrsta, swylce on horde ær*) reminds us that Beowulf's treasure was once the dragon's hoard. The second (*eldum swa unnyt swa hit æror wæs*) links the treasure's present uselessness to the centuries of the dragon's possession.

The nostalgic description of buried treasure jerks abruptly into the present at line 3167: the monosyllabic *nu* is startling, a rare *u* sound in a section where the predominant vowels are *e* and *e*-diphthongs, *forleton eorla gestreon eorðan healdan, / gold on greote, Þær hit nu gen lifað* (lines 3166–7).

It combines with the unexpected present tense, unusual stress on the adverb of time, 'still' (*gen*) and the animism of the verb *lifað* to add a philosophical dimension to the narrative. This statement about the gold is at the heart of the barrow-making passage, just as the destruction of Beowulf's body (with its lexical emphasis on 'the heart') is central to the burning section.

The position and ornamentation of the passage about treasure, culminating in the musings about the uselessness of the gold, indicate its importance; but what does the poet mean? Is he aware that pure gold will not rust and crumble like the iron of a helmet (lines 2762–3) but can keep its beauty despite being buried a thousand years or more, as modern archaeologists have discovered? The poet has warned before about the potential for corruption in buried gold: 'treasure easily may, gold in the ground, overpower each of the race of men, hide it who will' (lines 2764–6). Is this image of treasure that is there for the taking a deliberate tantalisation of the audience?

Is the poet saying that treasure is only valuable when it is being used by men, as we have seen in the giving and receiving of gifts throughout the poem? Is this particular treasure 'useless' because it has been hoarded away by the dragon, after surviving the people who once made use of it? If so, the poet would be condemning the action of the Geats in burying the treasure with Beowulf's ashes. The king had rejoiced that he had won it for his people; perhaps their duty was to move forward and use that treasure for their nation's future rather than to look backward and bury it as a tribute to their dead leader. Conversely, the Messenger's speech suggests that the treasure is buried as tribute to Beowulf, but that in any case troubled times lie ahead which will brook no frivolity:

> '... The nobleman shall not carry the treasures as a memento, nor shall the beautiful maiden have a ring-adornment on her neck, but, sad in mind, deprived of gold, more often than once they must tread a foreign land, now the one wise in battle has laid aside laughter, entertainment and the joy of song....'
> (lines 3015–21)

A Christian moral may be implicit, and is particularly likely in view of the number of Christian echoes in the lines that follow: the poet may be saying that all treasure is useless to men. The attractiveness of material possessions, the status symbols of the heroic world of Scyld and Hrothgar, has been undermined as the poem has progressed. The knowledge that an ancestral sword was the catalyst for the outbreak of war between Heathobards and Danes, that boar-helmets failed to save the men at Finnsburg, that

treasure will rust and crumble in the ground, perhaps leaves the audience
more inclined to think along the lines of Christ's words from the Sermon on
the Mount: 'Do not lay up for yourselves treasures on earth ... but lay up for
yourselves treasures in heaven ... For where your treasure is there will your
heart be also' (Matthew 6:19–21).

The narrator had told us, though not until after Beowulf had won it, that
the treasure was protected by (*bewunden*, 'wound round by', line 3052) some
supernatural power, *galdre*. The lexical range of this term as used elsewhere
seems to cover 'incantation', 'charm', 'magic', implying superstition rather
than Christianity, though not overt paganism. Some critics have interpreted
galdre as 'curse', concluding that the treasure is cursed and that Beowulf's
death in fighting against the dragon is the working out of that curse.[44] Yet
the poet tells us that God lifts the spell to allow his chosen one to take the
treasure: 'only God himself, the true King of victories, allowed to him whom
he wished to open the hoard, even to such a man as seemed to him fitting'
(lines 3054–7). This clearly indicates that Wiglaf's plundering of the hoard,
and Beowulf's vicarious role in that, was divinely approved and permitted.

This treasure is ambivalent; it is as a 'heathen hoard', 'heathen gold',
that we first encounter it (lines 2216, 2276) yet here God is taking a hand in
its recovery. If the gold is indeed cursed, the Geats would probably be wise
to bury it again without touching it, but that is not the tone of the text. The
gold, like everything else in a poem set in a pre-Christian society, is literally
heathen, but heathenism is only perceived as wrong if Christian morality is
being promoted. When the gold is hidden in the earth, hoarded by a dragon,
it is 'heathen' and by association, evil. When a good man, aided by God,
liberates it, is it no longer evil? Certainly Beowulf rejoices in his triumph in
winning it. Is he to be condemned for that? Beowulf's winning of the treasure
should perhaps be seen as a peak of achievement which his bereaved people
can never hope to emulate. Their burial of the treasure in his barrow may
then be a gesture carried out in the spirit (though not in the words) of the
biblical King David's prayer of gratitude: 'all things come from thee and of
your own do we give thee ... For we are ... sojourners ... our days on the earth
are like a shadow and there is no abiding.'[45]

The account of the mourning for Beowulf begins more soberly with
two lines of simple alliteration (lines 3169–70).

> Then round the barrow rode men brave in battle, the sons of
> princes, twelve in all. They wished to lament their grief and
> tell of the king, to recite a song and speak about the man. They
> reverenced his nobility and deeds of courage, extolled his might;
> so it is fitting that a man should praise his friend and lord with

words, cherish him in his heart when he must be led forth from
the body.
   (lines 3169–77)

Traditional material seems to be interwoven with Christian associations
here. The ritual of riding round the corpse, while uttering a eulogy, is
paralleled in Virgil's *Æneid*[46] and the fifth-century account of Attila the Hun's
funeral;[47] but the fact that the *Beowulf*-poet specifies twelve noble mourners
is reminiscent of the twelve disciples of Christ.[48] That parallel would not be
recognised by the protagonists themselves, of course, for they were heathens.
Though *winedryhten* is primarily a secular term,[49] and the achievements for
which Beowulf is praised here are worldly ones, the sentiment that 'it is
indeed right that we should give him praise' is liturgical, originating from St
Hippolytus:[50] 'so it is fitting that a man should praise his friend and lord in
words' (lines 3174–5). It is found in the eucharistic dialogue, which comes at
a formal meeting together of Christians,[51] just as Beowulf's mourners here
are depicted formally, anonymous and conjoint. Their eulogy (*wordgyd*) is
apparently metrical, a reference perhaps to the tradition of oral formulaic
composition,[52] in which, as Bede presented it in his seminal description of
the feast attended by Cædmon,[53] each man was expected to contribute in
turn.[54] The fact that the poet uses rhyme here (*wordgyd wrecan, ond ymb wer
sprecan*, line 3172) underlines the formality of their utterance, and a return
to double alliteration—(lines 3171–4, 3176) with interweaving sibilants
in lines 3172–3 (*sprecan ... -scipe*) and *d* sounds in lines 3174–5—indicates
heightened emotion though not of the same intensity as before.

'The sons of princes' who mourn here are clearly distinguished
members of Beowulf's comitatus, riding on horseback rather than walking.
They are described as 'brave in battle' (*hildedeore*) apparently without irony;
the cowardice of Beowulf's last band of retainers and the disgrace of the
Geats is forgotten or suspended.

The passages containing the lament of the sons of princes and
that containing the final reference to mourners are bridged by the word
swa, which can mean 'so', or 'thus' or 'in this way'. *Swa* here might be
retrospective, and the final mourning passage a variation of the lament of
the sons of princes. It seems more likely, though, that the lament and the
epitaph are intended to be complementary elegies from two different groups
of people. The sons of princes are public mourners, members of Beowulf's
comitatus, not necessarily all of them Geats; some could have been foreign
warriors attracted by Beowulf's fame.[55] The final group of mourners are
identified as *heorðgeneatas*, 'hearth-companions', the group of retainers most
intimately associated with him.[56] This marks a return to the *Geata leode* who

had arranged their hero's cremation ('they prepared a pyre for him', lines 3137–8), whose weeping mingled with the sound of the fire.

> The Geatish people, hearth-companions, lamented the fall of their lord in this way: they said that of kings in the world he was the most benign and unpretentious[57,58] of men, kindest to [his] people and most eager for glory.
>   (lines 3178–82)

The poetry is once more highly patterned here. Line 3179, which has double alliteration (*hlafordes hryre, heorðgeneatas*) is subtly linked to the preceding line by repetition of the *l* sound (*leode / hlafordes*) and an echo between *Geat-* and *geneat-* that exploits both alliteration and rhyme. Line 3180 has transverse alliteration, *cwædon þæt he wære wyruldcyninga*, with both the *c* and the *w* of *cwædon* being repeated in the other stresses of the line. The last two lines of the poem repeat the metrical pattern AC:

$$/ \ x \ / \ x \qquad x \ \ / \ \ / \ x$$
manna mildust   ond monðwærust,

$$/ \quad x \ / \ x \qquad x \ \ / \ \ / \ x$$
leodum liðost   ond lofgeornost

the juxtaposed stresses of the C half-lines creating a forceful effect which combines with the cumulative superlatives *mildust … monðwærust … liðost … lofgeornost* to create a conclusion that is strong, not weak.

The hearth-companions' praise is not of famous victories, but, perhaps surprisingly in view of Beowulf's reputation as one who crushed his enemies to death, of a lord who was merciful and kind. This ostensibly simple epitaph is packed with associations. The poet is again couching a eulogy for Beowulf in both heroic and Judaeo/Christian terms.[59] Elsewhere in Old English *milde* is descriptive of the quality of treatment requested from God,[60] and an expression of the Christian virtue of both seculars and ecclesiatics.[61] Originally, perhaps, signifying generosity, or benign rule,[62] Old English *milde* was also used to translate Latin *mitis* and *mansuetus* ('gentle').[63] The quality of gentleness (*mansuetudo*) was proverbially associated with the biblical Moses by the Church Fathers (just as patience was associated with Job and obedience with Abraham),[64] following the scriptural reference to Moses as *vir mitissimus super omnes homines* ('the gentlest man over all men', Numbers 12:3). In the Old English poem *Exodus*, the last description of Moses, as *manna mildost*, evokes this tradition.[65] Gernot Wieland's suggestion that the description of Beowulf as *manna mildust* is a deliberate reference to Moses is plausible.[66] In terms of the structure of the poem, a Moses parallel so close to the end of the poem neatly balances the link between Moses and Scyld which I have suggested near the opening of the poem (lines 7 and 46; see pp. 18–19, above), which reflects exactly the method of composition by association of ideas that is suggested in the second part of this book. An opening which evokes the arrival of Moses together with the arrival of Scyld, and a conclusion which evokes the last appearance of Moses (at least in the Old English poetic version of his story) embedded within the last reference to Beowulf is a manifestation of the bringing together of beginnings and endings which, as Tolkien noted, characterises this poem.

Manna mildust is here alliteratively linked with *monðwærust*, a significant conjunction since it occurs often enough in Old English poetry and prose to be labelled 'formulaic'.[67] Mary Richards notes that it 'always appears in a religious context',[68] relating to Christ, an archangel, a saint, a bishop and the virtuous. She concludes that 'to be *mildust ond mon[ðw]ærust* is to be an excellent Christian indeed and an excellent candidate for sainthood'.[69]

The final word of the poem is *lofgeornost*. We must not forget that near the beginning of the poem, immediately before recounting Scyld's funeral, and with reference to our hero's namesake, the Danish Beowulf (or Beow), the poet has asserted: 'in every nation a man must thrive by deeds of *lof*' (lines 24–5).[70] The fact that, immediately after the Geatish Beowulf's funeral, his successful pursuit of *lof* should be acknowledged is a final instance of the poem's cyclic, elliptical construction (see Chapters 7–10). The narrator's earlier statement can be seen as prophetic, and the echo of it a satisfying fulfilment, pronounced with resounding rhetoric. *Lofgeornost*, the poet's final word, is, however, ambiguous. It has been interpreted as 'most eager for fame'[71] and cited as evidence that Beowulf is ultimately culpable, having succumbed to the sin of Pride.[72] However, although the compound *lofgeornost* is documented in Old English homiletic texts in a pejorative sense[73] as Roberta Frank points out, the Old Norse cognate *lofgjarn* and other compounds of *-gjarn* are used uncritically as terms of praise in skaldic poetry, which may be contemporary with *Beowulf* if the latter is a late Anglo-Saxon composition.[74] Furthermore, its first element, *lof*, occurs almost exclusively in a favourable sense, ranging from praise of men to praise of God, including the psalms. The poet of *The Seafarer* puns on two meanings, playing off the heroic virtue of posthumous fame (*lof lifgendra*, line 73) against the heavenly glory achieved by a life of Christian virtue ('and his glory afterwards shall endure with the angels, always for ever, the bliss of eternal life, joy with the heavenly host' [lines 78–80]).[75] The second element of the compound, *-georn-*, when documented elsewhere, means 'desirous', 'eager'. The citations convey a praiseworthy, positive attitude, not greed. *Lofgeornost*, then, is a term of approbation, but it may have meant something different in the reported speech of the Geat protagonists from its significance for the Christian poet and his audience. The ethical tone established with *manna mildust ond monðwærust, / leodum liðost* makes it clear that in his dealings with his subjects Beowulf was a good man by Christian standards. In his behaviour to others who are not his people, Beowulf has been agreeable and generous, exhibiting the Christian virtue of 'turning the other cheek';[76] and, appropriately for a man of such goodness, his soul has already 'gone to seek the judgement of the righteous' (lines 2819–20).[77] That the hearth-companions, as pagans, would not appreciate the finer points of Christian belief is only in keeping with the double perspective the poet established on the subject of death at the opening of Scyld's funeral. The only *lof* the Geats can understand is renown, and that of course Beowulf achieves; and it cannot have been lost on the architect of this most carefully constructed poem, that in bestowing on his pagan, fictional hero the Christian gift of a written account, he was fulfilling for him that most heroic of ambitions—posthumous fame.

NOTES

1. 'Above-average labour investment in grave construction' is now a recognised indicator of social status; Heinrich Härke, 'Early Anglo-Saxon social structure', in Hines (ed.), *The Anglo-Saxons from the Migration Period to the Eighth Century* (1997), p. 145.

2. The demand for traditional cremation has contributed to deforestation in India. Modern (indoor) crematoria use gas or electricity.

3. Carver estimated that Sutton Hoo Mound 2 could have been built by ten men working a ten-hour day for seven days (assuming they had the equivalent of wheelbarrows); Carver, *Sutton Hoo: burial ground of kings?* (1998), p. 166.

4. See Chapter 1, notes 7 and 8.

5. See Chapter 2, p. 24.

6. Kiernan *wæteryðu*.

7. Fred C. Robinson, 'The tomb of Beowulf', in Fred C. Robinson (ed.), *The Tomb of Beowulf and Other Essays on Old English* (Oxford, Blackwell, 1993), pp. 3–19, at p. 4.

8. Stjerna considered the complex account to be the product of two distinct versions, in the earlier of which Beowulf's body and the dragon's treasure were burned, and in the later a grave was prepared and the treasure buried; Knut Stjerna, 'Beowulf's funeral obsequies', in Stjerna, *Essays* (1912), pp. 197–239, esp. pp. 200–1.

9. Garmonsway and Simpson, *Analogues* (1968), p. 341.

10. For example, at the Viking Age cemetery of Lindholm Høje, Denmark, burnt possessions were found with ashes and charcoal in burials which were sometimes marked by stone settings. 'Prized possessions might first have been smashed or mutilated so as to be useless, like the "killed" sword from Wallstena'; Graham-Campbell and Kidd, *The Vikings* (1980), p. 95.

11. 'between nil and 1.2% of cremations in any one cemetery'; Härke, 'Changing symbols', in Carver, *Age of Sutton Hoo* (1992), p. 150.

12. It was 'easily seen', line 1110, and the dead warrior 'ascended' it, line 1118. If

we accept Klaeber's emendation of *að* to *ad* there would be a simple reference to the pyre being 'prepared' (*geæfned*) at line 1107.

13.   /   x   /   x   / /   \   x

ad on eorðan unwaclicne.

Sievers Types A and D.

14. See Chapter 3, p. 54.

15. The Gokstad (Norway) funeral ship had thirty-two overlapping shields, painted alternately yellow and black, tied to each side. (Roesdahl, *The Vikings* (1991), p. 86). Such arrangements are depicted in art; see for example, Graham-Campbell and Kidd, *The Vikings* (1980), plate 8 (a picture-stone from Gotland, Sweden).

16. Karl Schumacher, *Germanendarstellungen*, Katalogue des Römisch-Germanischen Zentralmuseums zu Mainz, I (Mainz, Römisch-Germanisches Zentralmuseum, 1935), plate 21, no. 96; plate 35, no. 151.

17. Härke, 'Changing symbols', in Carver, *Age of Sutton Hoo* (1992), p. 156. It may be significant that the seax, the weapon with which Beowulf killed the dragon, is, when deposited as grave furniture, found only with adult men, predominantly with those in the upper age range.

18. The poet spoke of Beowulf's dark thoughts (*þeostrum geþoncum*) at line 2332.

19. Verbs take on adjectival function: *swogende*, which describes *leg*, is a present participle and *bewunden* a past participle, not, as might seem from translation, a past tense. The fire, which is roaring, is 'wound round with weeping'. *Leg* is an emendation. The manuscript has *let*, which, if we kept it, would be a verb. I follow Klaeber's punctuation for *windblond gelæg*, though it is not very satisfactory and the sequence of the action is not clear. *Windblond* is a *hapax legomenon* and is not written as a compound in the manuscript (the two syllables come on different lines). *Blond* could equally be the preterite of a strong verb (such as **blindan*). *Gelæg* is a confusingly near homonym for *leg*, 'fire' or 'flame', though, as in this passage the word *leg* is an emendation, this observation may not be relevant.

20. Cf. Barely, *Orosius* (1980), p. 17.

21. The subject of the clause is *he*, which refers back to *leg*, 'the fire'. 'Hot at heart' is a poetic formula: the hot baths in *The Ruin* are *hat on hreþre* (lines 40–1; Dobbie, *Exeter Book*, ASPR, III (1936), 228) and *hate on reðre* describes dragons dwelling at Hell's door in *Christ and Satan* (line 98; Dobbie, *Minor Poems*, ASPR, VI (1942), 138).

22. The naming of the hero in the paraphrase of the woman's song is editorial reconstruction.

23. Klaeber's reconstruction of *geameowle* has been superseded. *Geatisc* was read from ultraviolet photographs of 1938, by John C. Pope, *The Rhythm of Beowulf: an interpretation of the normal and hypermetric verse-forms in Old English poetry* (New Haven and London, Yale University Press, 1960), pp. 232–3, and has been generally accepted.

24. Lines 3121–58 occupy fol. 198 of the manuscript. Kiernan argues that this folio forms part of a sheet which had been removed from its original position and used as a cover for the manuscript, and that it was in this place, after the incomplete poem *Judith*, at the time of the Ashburnham House fire. The burning of this vulnerable page, and subsequent crumbling of the vellum, account for the damage which is greater than on other folios; Kiernan, *Beowulf and the Beowulf Manuscript* (1981), pp. 152–4.

25. '**bunden-heord** ... *with hair* BOUND *up* (ref. to an old woman; in contrast with the flowing hair of young women)', Klaeber, *Beowulf* (1950), p. 311. The *b* of *bundenheord* is reconstruction. *Heord* is well documented as a noun meaning 'herd' but not adjectivally as '-haired'. Even if the reconstruction and definition were accepted, there is no evidence

of early Anglo-Saxon women's hair and headdress styles. Women in late Anglo-Saxon manuscripts are always shown with heads covered, whether they represent maidens (the constellation Virgo; the Virgin Mary) or other women, with the exception of personified Vices. The only support for the woman being old seems to be a Latin gloss *an[us]* above *meowle* (Zupitza, *Beowulf* (1959), p. 144, n. 1.) Interpretations of the character are discussed in detail in Tauno F. Mustanoja, 'The unnamed woman's song of mourning over Beowulf and the tradition of ritual lamentation', *Neuphilologische Mitteilungen*, 68 (1968), 1–27, esp. pp. 1–13.

26. I find it in the most recent edition of the text, Mitchell and Robinson, *Beowulf* (1998), p. 160, note to line 3151.

27. In *The Iliad*, XXIV, Hector's mourning is led by Andromache his widow, Hecuba his mother and Helen, his sister-in-law, the cause of the Trojan War. Andromache anticipates captivity for herself, slavery and violent death for her child; Murray, *Iliad*, II (1925), 616–20.

28. *Germania*, 8; Peterson and Hutton, *Tacitus* (1914), p. 274.

29. Discussed in Owen, *Rites and Religions* (1981), p. 87.

30. In this case the girl had a vested interest in prolonging it; she was to be murdered at the end of the ceremony!

31. MS hl : : on liðe. Zupitza, *Beowulf* (1882), p. 144, line 5.

32. *wæ* of *wægliðendum* is reconstructed.

33. See Chapter 4, n. 10.

34. Thus Robinson: 'Having erected a splendid *heorh* or tumulus ... they surround it with a splendid wall'; 'The tomb of Beowulf' (1993), p. 5.

35. 'Pyres have not certainly been recorded in association with Anglo-Saxon cremation cemeteries and may be assumed to be elsewhere'; Tania Dickinson and George Speake, 'The seventh-century cremation burial at Asthall Barrow, Oxfordshire: a reassessment', in Carver, *The Age of Sutton Hoo* (1992), pp. 95–130, at p. 118. The problematic barrow cremation at Asthall is a possible exception (Dickinson and Speake, pp. 116–19). The normal practice where some or all of the ashes were collected (some may not have been) was that they were placed in containers, and interred elsewhere, often in communal cemeteries. Ceramic urns were used in most cases, though in the late pagan period higher status cremations in barrows sometimes merited unusual containers (metal in Sutton Hoo Mounds 4, 5, 6 and 7 also Brightwell Heath 3, Suffolk and possibly Asthall, Oxfordshire; wood in Sutton Hoo Mound 3) (Dickinson and Speake, Table 1A, p. 128). The authors also list twelve late sixth- to early seventh-century cremations in copper-alloy vessels which were not under barrows, of which the only evidence of high status is the use of the metal vessel (Table 1B, p. 129), and reject six sites previously claimed to be cremations under barrows (Table 1C, p. 130).

36. 'Die eigentliche Kremation scheint in der Regel direkt am Grabplatz vorgenommen worden zu sein.' ['The cremation proper seems, as a rule, to have been carried out directly on the burial place']; Sten and Vretemark, 'Osteologische Analysen' (1992), p. 89.

37. This was certainly the case in Mounds 3–7, though looting had reduced the gravegoods; Carver, *Sutton Hoo: burial ground of kings?* (1998), pp. 107–10.

38. 'as an élite symbol, weapon burial was complemented, and partly superseded, by an alternative (barrow burial)'; Härke, 'Changing symbols', in Carver, *Age of Sutton Hoo* (1992), p. 164.

39. The hoard reflects both military life and the 'joys of the hall'. It includes rings, decorated gold (line 2245), sword, cup, helmet, mail coat and harp (mentioned in 'The

Lay of the Last Survivor', lines 2252–63). On raiding the dragon's lair, Wiglaf notices gold (line 2758), including a golden standard (lines 2767–71), but its brightness is counterbalanced by vessels and helmets (lines 2760–4, 2775), composite objects made with base metal which, as the Last Survivor anticipated, have rusted and disintegrated. Vessels, though not mentioned here, have been particularly prominent. It is a vessel which is stolen from the dragon (lines 2282, 2300, 2306) and as the reptile lies dead it is surrounded by cups and dishes, as well as by precious swords, eaten through with rust (lines 3047–9). It is significant that 'large numbers of vessels are a hall-mark of the highest-status burials among the germanic peoples from the Roman Iron Age onwards and in England characterize the early seventh-century phase of rich, adult male, primary barrows'; Dickinson and Speake, 'Asthall Barrow' in Carver, *Age of Sutton Hoo* (1992), p. 110.

40. There is gold associated with the helmet mentioned in 'The Lay of the Last Survivor', where (though the first part of the relevant word is editorial reconstruction), it clearly refers to an ornament that is anticipated as falling off, not a structural part of the object: *Sceal se hearda helm (hyr)stedgolde, / fætum befeallen. -gode*, like *fætum*, is in the dative case and does not agree with *helm*.

41. The main category of rings to survive from both the pagan and the Christian Anglo-Saxon period is the finger-ring. That larger rings did indeed exist, and were not merely literary convention, is confirmed by non-literary text and art. A woman named Wynflæd bequeathed a wooden cup that was ornamented with gold to her son so that he could use the gold to enlarge his ring (*his beah*; Dorothy Whitelock, *Anglo-Saxon Wills* (Cambridge, University Press, 1930), p. 12, lines 18–20). King Edgar appears to wear a simple gold ring on his right upper arm in the drawing of him in BL MS Cotton Vespasian A. viii, fol. 2v.

42. The decline of burial with grave-goods in the seventh century means that there is less metalwork surviving from the Christian Anglo-Saxon period than before. There may in fact have been less jewellery circulating in society with the growth of a money economy in the Middle Saxon period. I owe this comment to Stephen Glosecki.

43. Documentary evidence suggests that seculars gave great quantities of gold to the Church; Dodwell, *Anglo-Saxon Art*, Chapter VII, 'Jewellery, gold and silver', pp. 188–215.

44. The curse is discussed as a structural device in Chapter 10.

45. I Chronicles 29:14–15. I am grateful to Rev. Martin Collins for this reference.

46. XI, lines 189–90; Fairclough, *Virgil* (1950), I, 246.

47. Opland, *Oral Poetry* (1980), pp. 52–3.

48. M. B. McNamee, '*Beowulf*—an allegory of salvation?', *Journal of English and Germanic Philology*, 59 (1960), 190–207, at p. 204.

49. St Andrew addresses God in this way in *Andreas*, line 919; Krapp, *The Vercelli Book*, ASPR, 11 (1932), 28.

50. 'It is meet and right' is from *The Apostolic Tradition* (IV, 3) of Hippolytus (c. 215) (*The So-Called Egyptian Church Order*, ed. Connolly, *Texts and Studies*, VIII, 4 cited in Henry Bettenson (ed.), *Documents of the Christian Church* (London, Oxford University Press, 1943, reprinted 1959), p. 106). I am grateful to Rev. Martin Collins for this information.

Klaeber (p. 230) noted that this 'sounds like an echo of the divine service' and pointed out the resemblance to the opening of the Old English poem *Genesis [A]* lines 1–3 and 15–18 (Krapp, *Junius Manuscript*, ASPR, 1 (1931), 3). Line 1, *Us is riht micel* is particularly relevant. Robinson, noting the comparison, adds that the *Genesis* opening 'is based upon the Common Preface to the Mass' ('The tomb of Beowulf' (1993), p. 15).

51. The 'meet and right' part of the dialogue derives from the assent of members of the Jewish *chaburah* to the president of the *berakah*, 'essentially a corporate occasion'; Gregory Dix, *The Shape of the Liturgy* (Westminster, Dacre Press, 1943, 2nd edn 1945), pp. 126–7.

52. This has already been taken for granted in the poem, for example lines 867 ff.

53. Bede, *Historia Ecclesiastica*, IV, xxxiv (xxii) (hereafter *HE*); B. Colgrave and R. A. B. Mynors (eds), *Bede's Ecclesiastical History of the English People* (Oxford, Clarendon, 1969), pp. 414–16.

54. Opland considers, but rejects, choral performance (*Oral Poetry* (1980), p. 206). For poetry on horseback, here, at Attila's funeral and the Sigemund Lay (*Beowulf*, lines 864–917), see Opland, pp. 52–3, 202–5.

55. Wulfgar was a foreigner at Hrothgar's court (*þæt wæs Wendla leod*, line 348) and Beowulf's retainer Wiglaf was a Swede (*leod Scylfinga*, line 2603).

56. In *The Battle of Maldon*, Byrhtnoth, after organising his army, dismounts to fight 'among the people where it was dearest to him, where he knew his hearth-troop to be very loyal' (lines 23–4); Dobbie, *Minor Poems*, ASPR, VI (1942), 7.

57. Reconstructed from the Thorkelin transcripts, which read *mondrærust*.

58. I take my translation from Bede's Latin *mansuetissimus ac simplicissimus* (*HE*, IV, xxvii; Colgrave and Mynors, *Bede's Ecclesiastical History* (1969), p. 430), which is rendered by *milde* ... 7 *monþwære* in the Old English version (*HE*, IV, xxvii, where it refers to Abbot Eata; J. Schipper (ed.), *Konig Alfreds Übersetzung van Bedas Kirchengeschichte*, C. M. W. Grein, R. P. Wülcker and H. Hecht (eds), *Bibliothek der angelsächsischen Prosa*, 13 vols (1872–1933), IV, 2 vols (Leipzig, Georg H. Wigand, 1898), II, 511, line 4094). Beowulf has not been so modest that he has hidden his light under a bushel: he has made heroic boasts at appropriate times; but if we compare him to Scyld who was famous for subjecting his neighbours, Hrothgar who built a hall more splendid than the sons of men had ever heard of and Hygelac who arrogantly attacked Frisia, he appears to have led a quiet life.

59. The reading of many twenty-first-century readers will inevitably be coloured by the children's hymn 'Gentle Jesus meek and mild' but we should not be confused by the coincidence of language into thinking that Old English *milde* indicates submissiveness or that Beowulf allegorises Christ here. The hymn is modern (composed by Charles Wesley). Though the Old English formula *milde* 7 *monþwære* is applied to Christ in Blickling Homily VI (R. Morris (ed.), *The Blickling Homilies of the Tenth Century* (London, 1874–80), p. 71) its use is not restricted to Christ.

60. For example, in the West Saxon Gospels *God beo þu milde me* (Luke 18:13; Liuzza, *Gospels*, (1994), 140). Here *milde* renders Latin *propitius* ('favourable'). In the Old High German Wessobrunn Prayer, which is considered to reflect the influence of Anglo-Saxon missionaries, the cognate phrase *manno miltisto* applies to God; Wieland, '*Manna mildost*', (1988), pp. 87–8.

61. It is, for example, included in the metrical eulogy for Edward the Confessor in the *Anglo-Saxon Chronicle* for 1065 (G. P. Cubbin (ed.), *The Anglo-Saxon Chronicle: a collaborative edition*, III, MS D (Cambridge, D. S. Brewer, 1996), p. 79) and is applied to Abbot Eata in the Old English Bede (see n. 58, above).

62. 'Old English *milde*, in common with its Germanic cognates, could have technical force as a term for the generosity of the lord or king towards his subordinates' (Charles D. Wright, 'Moses, *manna mildost* (*Exodus* 550a)', *Notes and Queries*, 229 (n.s. 31) (1984), 440–3, at p. 440). Wealhtheow twice uses the word, once in reference to the appropriate manner of Hrothgar to the Geats who have rescued him (lines 1171–2) and once in her description of the Danish courtiers' behaviour to one another (lines 1228–9). Josephine

Bloomfield argues that in this heroic context 'generosity' is meant by the word, in a discussion of the watering-down of Old English epithets in Klaeber's translation; 'Diminished by kindness: Frederick Klaeber's rewriting of Wealhtheow', *Journal of English and Germanic Philology*, 93 (1994), 183–203, at pp. 190–2, esp. n. 26.

63. Wright, 'Moses' (1984), p. 441.

64. *Ibid.*, 441–3. Wright notes the use of this commonplace in Irish saints' lives and an Anglo-Saxon coronation *ordo*.

65. Krapp, *Junius Manuscript*, ASPR, I (1931), *Exodus*, line 549. The reference to Moses as *manna mildost* in the poem is incongruous in context: Moses has just witnessed the drowning of the Egyptian army and is about to predict the destruction of other enemies. It is understandable only as a proverbial epithet, taken from the different context (his restraint in comparison with the indignation of his brother and sister) in the Old Testament.

66. Wieland, *'Manna mildost'* (1988), 89–91. Though I accept similarities between Beowulf's achievements and those of Moses (particularly as related in the Old English poetic *Exodus*) notably with regard to the mere and the Red Sea, I do not share Wieland's thesis that Beowulf should be seen as the equivalent of an Old Testament figure like Noah and Moses.

67. Mary P. Richards, 'A reexamination of *Beowulf ll*. 3180–3182', *English Language Notes*, 10 (1973), 163–7.

68. Ibid., p. 165.

69. Ibid., p. 166.

70. *lofdæd* is a *hapax legomenon*. Klaeber glosses it 'praiseworthy (glorious) DEED'.

71. Thus Kevin Crossley-Holland (trans.), *Beowulf, The Poetry of Legend: Classics of the Medieval World* (1968, new edn 1987, Woodbridge, Boydell), p. 139.

72. See, for example, Margaret E. Goldsmith, *The Mode and Meaning of 'Beowulf'* (London, Athlone Press, 1970), pp. 224–8, 239; Andy Orchard, *Pride and Prodigies: studies in the monsters of the Beowulf-manuscript* (Cambridge, D. S. Brewer, 1995), pp. 169–71. George Clark attributed to Tolkien the reinterpretation of Beowulf as flawed and shows how Tolkien's view changed between 1936 ('*Beowulf* the monsters and the critics', *Proceedings of the British Academy*, 22 (1936), 245–95) and 1953 ('The homecoming of Beorhtnoth Beorhthelm's son', *Essays and Studies*, 6 (1953), 1–18). 'After the [Second World] war, Tolkien saw defeat as a moral refutation'; George Clark, 'The hero and the theme', in Bjork and Niles, *Handbook* (1997), pp. 271–90, at p. 280.

73. Wulfstan, for example, speaks of being *lofgeorn for idelan weorþscype* ('eager for empty honour') in a list of sixteen examples of un-Christian behaviour which include being *gitsiende* ('covetous'), *idelgeorn* ('lazy') and *ofermod* ('proud'). (D. Bethurum, *The Homilies of Wulfstan* (Oxford, Clarendon, 1957), pp. 206–7, lines 1–2.) See Joseph Bosworth and T. Northcote Toller, *An Anglo-Saxon Dictionary*, I (Oxford, University Press, 1898, reprinted 1976) and T. Northcote Toller, *Supplement*, II (Oxford, University Press, 1921) with Enlarged Addenda and Corrigenda by Alistair Campbell (Oxford, Clarendon Press, 1972, reprinted 1973), **lof-georn**. We might note, though, that in Ælfric's condemnation of *iactantia*, 'boastfulness', cited by Orchard (*Pride and Prodigies* (1995), p. 171), to be *lofgeorn* is condemned when it is accompanied by hypocrisy and the giving of gifts only for the glory it brings; Walter William Skeat (ed.), *Ælfric's Lives of Saints*, EETS o.s. 76, 82, 94, 114 (London, N. Thübner, 1881–1900, reprinted as 2 vols, 1996), I, 356–8, lines 300–5.

74. Frank, 'Skaldic verse and the date of *Beowulf*', in Chase, *Dating* (1981), p. 135.

75. Dobbie, *Exeter Book*, ASPR, III (1936), 145.

76. We might cite his courteous (*wine min*) handling of Unferth's insult (lines 530–2). This, like his agreeable encounter with the coastguard (lines 286–319, 1890–1903), has less harmonious parallels in Norse poetry (see Frank, 'Skaldic verse and the date of *Beowulf*', in Chase, *Dating* (1981), pp. 132–3). Although willing and eager to take revenge for wrong on behalf of Hrothgar and for the deaths of his own kings, Hygelac and Heardred, Beowulf has been a non-aggressive and honourable ruler '[I] did not seek out treacherous quarrels, nor did I swear a quantity of perjurous oaths' (lines 2738–9).

77. Robinson (in 'The tomb of Beowulf' (1993), pp. 6–19) argues that the liturgical echoes in the account of the sons of princes' chant and the words of praise in the hearth-companions' eulogy point to the euhemerisation of Beowulf, a deification of a human king which would have been deplored by the Anglo-Saxons. While I accept that the Christian Germanic people were familiar with euhemeristic explanations of pagan deities (accurate or inaccurate), the name 'Beowulf' does not occur in the genealogical lists which include Woden and Scyld. Robinson's reading of the eulogies contributes to a 'dark' interpretation of the passage, and ultimately of the whole poem, which I do not share. For me, the religious language in the passage is not heretical, but an indicator of Beowulf's goodness.

JUDY KING

Launching the Hero:
The Case of Scyld and Beowulf

Listen! We have heard of the glory in days gone by of the kings who
ruled the Spear-Danes, how those princes performed deeds of valour![1]

*B*eowulf opens on to the world of the Germanic past as the poet introduces
his main narrative with the genealogy and some of the history of the Danish
kings. This acts as a prelude to his account of the creation of Heorot and
the terrible moment when Grendel is aroused. It leads inevitably, too, to
the entrance of the hero who, although not yet present in the events of the
narrative, is clearly in the poet's mind.[2] Beowulf the Dane, renamed by the
poet, foreshadows Beowulf the Geat,[3] as the poet sets up in the opening
portrait of Scyld the first panel of a diptych to be completed with the portrait
of the hero. Thus Scyld's arrival and departure, the nature of his kingship and
the destination of his soul are described in the "Prologue" to the exclusion
of all other information concerning him, and the same aspects of Beowulf's
own life will be illuminated as a result.

The "Prologue" has been widely seen as a passage of straight narration
which provides us with the standard of behaviour common to the main
characters (monsters aside), and this is so regardless of whether the poem
is interpreted as demonstrating an identity or a convergence of viewpoint
between pagan characters and Christian author. That the "Prologue" does
not in fact set the ethical tone may be substantiated from the poem itself, as

From *Neophilologus* 87, 3 (July 2003), pp. 453–471. © 2003 by Kluwer Academic Publishers.

233

well as from other poems within the Old English poetic corpus and Latin works well known to the Anglo-Saxons. A close look at even the first eleven lines suggests a complex attitude to the material on the part of the poet.[4]

The opening lines of the poem indicate that the poet is setting his own tale in a bygone age and using traditional methods, but not necessarily that it is a tale in common currency. Like many other poems in Old English, *Beowulf* announces itself with "Hwæt" [Listen!] and uses the "ic gefrægn/we gefrunon" [I/we have heard] formula to create a context within which the poet's own narration is to be situated and understood. As Parks in particular has shown,[5] this formula appears to derive from an oral tradition where the narrator had only his own memory, and that of his audience, to rely upon; the resultant concept of the narrator would then have carried over into poetry which is clearly literate, such as the poems of Cynewulf. I would add that the use of similar phrases in homilies—for example, in the *Blickling Homilies*, where we read, "Listen! We have heard that the evangelist said that the Saviour was led into the wilderness ..."[6]—demonstrates the same movement from orality to literacy, and a similar appeal to authority.

If however the opening of *Beowulf* is traditional, it says nothing about the type of poem which we are about to read. Just as it does not presuppose an oral poem, it does not necessarily indicate a secular one, given that overtly Christian Old English poems open in identical fashion. *Exodus*[7] begins,

> Listen! Far and near all over the world we have heard of the laws
> of Moses ...
>   (*Exodus*, 1–2)

while two of the hagiographical poems open similarly, *Andreas* with a reference to tales of all twelve apostles—

> Listen! We have heard of twelve under the stars in days of old
>   (*Andreas*, 1–2a)

—and *Juliana* with a reference to accounts of the persecutions under Maximian:

> Listen! We have heard heroes consider, men bold in deeds judge,
> what happened in the days of Maximian, the impious king who
> throughout the world instituted a persecution—killed Christian
> people, razed churches....
>   (*Juliana* [*The Passion of Saint Juliana*], ed. Muir, 1–5)

Other poems such as *Daniel* and *The Phoenix* use the "ic gefrægn" formula without "hwæt".

In contrast, the Christian epic poets who write in Latin adopt an entirely different approach. Modelling themselves closely on Latin and Greek epic, they feel obliged to replace the Muse with Christ:[8] Prudentius, for example, opens the *Psychomachia* with an invocation to Christ—"Christe, graves hominum semper miserate labores" [O Christ, you who have always taken pity on the heavy toils of humankind][9]—and a request that Christ himself describe the forces which aid the soul in the fight against evil:

> dissere, rex noster, quo milite pellere culpas
> mens armata queat nostri de pectoris antro.
>   (*Psychomachia*, 5–6)

> [Explain, O king of ours, with what army the soul is equipped in
> order to be able to drive sins from the cavern of the breast.]

Anglo-Saxon writers follow this example. Alcuin's *Versus de patribus regibus et sanctis Euboricensis ecclesiae*[10] opens with the invocation, "Christe deus" [O God Christ] (*Versus de patribus*, 1) as the strength and wisdom of the Father, and to the saints or "cives ... Olympi" [citizens of Olympus] (8), the "gens diva Tonantis" [divine race of the Thunderer] (9). Later in his poem, Alcuin overtly rejects the classical gods of poetry and song when he states that, had Bede not written a poem on St Cuthbert, he would do so himself,

> non Pana rogitans Phoebi nec numen inane,
> sed tua cum toto suffragia corde precarer,
> ut mihi rorifluam donares, Christe, loquelam....
>   (*Versus de patribus*, 747–49)

> [not invoking Pan or the empty power of Phoebus, but I should
> entreat your aid with all my heart, that you might bestow on me,
> O Christ, language flowing like dew....]

Aldhelm, in the preface to his *Enigmata*, similarly rejects the "Castalidas nimphas" [Castalian nymphs][11] in favour of divine inspiration. Bede also feels the need to modify the conventional classical invocation. In his abecedarian hymn on St Etheldreda, his Muse is the Trinity, and he presents his subject as a negation of that of Virgil or Homer:

Alma Deus Trinitas, quae saecula cuncta gubernas,
    adnue iam coeptis, alma Deus Trinitas.
Bella Maro resonet: nos pacis dona canamus,
    munera nos Christi; bella Maro resonet.
Carmina casta mihi, fedae non raptus Helenae;
    luxus erit lubricis, carmina casta mihi.
Dona superna loquar, miserae non proelia Troiae;
    terra quibus gaudet, dona superna loquar.[12]

[Gracious Divine Trinity, which governs all the ages, prosper now my undertakings, Gracious Divine Trinity.
Let Virgil resound with wars: as for us, we shall sing of the gifts of peace, the bounties of Christ; let Virgil resound with wars.
My songs will be pure, not the abduction of shameful Helen, lust will be for the lewd, my songs will be pure.
I will tell of celestial gifts, not the battles of wretched Troy; gifts in which the earth rejoices, I will tell of celestial gifts.]

However, Anglo-Saxon poets writing in Old English, with a different poetic tradition behind them, appear able to keep the formulaic opening without offence to the Creator. One might speculate that the oral poems which preceded the literate in their culture did not call upon the gods, and that therefore no transmutation was needed. Whether or not this was the case, it is clear that the opening of *Beowulf* would not necessarily indicate to its original audience that it is a secular rather than a religious poem.[13]

The opening lines, similarly, do not imply that the poem is of the same kind as the poems concerning Danish kings of the past to which the poet here refers; that is, it is necessary to differentiate between the status of the texts within which the "new" poem is being situated and the poem itself. It is reasonable to suppose that the tales of Scyld and other Danish kings have taken the form of oral lays rather than written texts. There are examples within *Beowulf* itself of minstrels singing what are clearly short encomiastic poems about heroes and kings; we have, too, Alcuin's oft-quoted question to the monks of Lindisfarne, "Quid Hinieldus cum Christo?" [What does Ingeld have to do with Christ?], as well as the catalogue of material for songs in *Widsith*, a poem which, although slight, contains important clues for understanding what the *Beowulf* poet is doing in his own work.[14]

The traditional opening of *Beowulf* sets the tale which the poet is about to tell in the context of those tales which "we"—the poet and his audience—already know, that is, tales or lays of the Danes of the past which are currently popular.[15] Such a lay appears to be summarised and characterised in the short sketch of Scyld which immediately follows the opening, with these lines constituting less a portrait of Scyld than the poet's summary of what is known of him from poetry or song.[16] However, the tale which the poet is about to tell is not necessarily included in the group of tales to which he refers in the opening lines;[17] whilst we may agree with Niles that the narrator, far from being individualised, "speaks from his deep familiarity with the stories of Germanic antiquity, a familiarity that he has gained from oral tradition", it is an unfounded assumption that "Of these he has chosen one for retelling".[18] Tolkien similarly believes that we are dealing with an old tale which probably already combined the Scyldings, monsters, and a foreign champion;[19] that the poet is re-shaping rather than inventing his material has always been the general view of the poem's genesis.[20]

There is, however, evidence that the poet is creating a largely fictional work, for its hero, otherwise unknown, appears to be inserted into a known historical background. Further, as Tripp claims, "the *poet's story* is what is new. What is old and known is the material he alludes to in telling it".[21] Here we may note that the "we ... gefrunon" of the opening lines is the only example of the plural version of the formula in the poem, the many other occurrences being in the singular form ("ic gefrægn", "ic hyrde", or "mine gefræge"). Although these terms seem to be used indiscriminately in other Old English poetry, it must be likely that with his sole use of the inclusive version of the formula the poet is characterising common material (his summary of the poems about Scyld) and distinguishing this material from that of his own creation. I would, then, suggest that the use of "ic gefrægn" after the sketch of Scyld—in relation to the foundling story which the poet attaches to Scyld, the marriage of Yrse to Onela,[22] and the building of Heorot, as well as throughout the "Beowulf" material which makes up the body of his poem—may indicate that he is composing fiction, albeit on a historical base.

The poet's attitude to the current poetic output, visible in the opening lines, continues throughout the poem. Tales such as those of Finn and Ingeld (the latter particularly interesting given Alcuin's problem with it in a monastic context) are referred to in the poem; indeed, they are retold, albeit perhaps with an emphasis different from that of the original version. The so-called digressions are as much a comment on the poetry of the age as on its past history, as *Beowulf* answers Alcuin's objection not by disdaining such material but by reinterpreting it. One could apply to *Beowulf* Parks' view of *Sir Gawain and the Green Knight* as "an indicator of a larger cultural turning away from the celebration of warfare as a principal theme of narrative literature".[23] As Hill argues in relation to *Beowulf* itself, the poem "does not simply celebrate one of the ancient heroes, but ... its subject is ultimately the tradition of Germanic heroic literature as a whole".[24]

The nature of the summary of Scyld's reign with which the poem begins substantiates such a view:

> Often Scyld Scefing took away mead-benches from bands of foes, from many tribes, he terrified warriors, from the time when he was first found destitute; he experienced consolation for that, he flourished under the skies, prospered with honours, until each of the neighbouring tribes over the whale-road had to obey him, pay him tribute; that was a good king!
>
>   (4–11)

This passage summarises in brutal terms the apparent content of lays about Scyld—the violent, imperialistic deeds for which he would be celebrated as the founder of the dynasty. It may also be seen as the portrait of a particular type of kingship, ending as it does with "þæt wæs god cyning". Two views of this passage predominate. Firstly, some critics believe that Scyld is set up as an ideal of kingship according to the poet's standards,[25] with Florey going so far as to ask whether Scyld may embody all of the qualities associated with God.[26] This view is bound up also with the general belief that the poem is complimentary to the Danes.[27] However, it is clear that in the Grendel affair the Danes are incapable of resistance (as Beowulf points out to Hunferth, a failure of courage or will is involved), and it is up to an outsider to bring them help.

The alternative view holds Scyld to be an example of the heroic kingship which will be gradually embodied in the life of Beowulf himself and which it is the poet's aim to show as misguided and ultimately disastrous in both the political and spiritual spheres. Of these critics, Bernard Huppé is perhaps the most prominent. Reading the poem within an Augustinian framework, he sees Scyld's role as providing "a thematic context by which the hero may be judged", with both kings condemned by the poet as inhabitants of the Earthly City.[28] Dahlberg agrees, seeing Scyld as an example of pagan kingship, who "rules by force and terror", and to whom Beowulf is linked by the formula "þæt wæs god cyning" as well as by the final word of the poem, "lofgeornost" [most eager for glory], with its alleged reference to glory of the secular kind.[29]

Underlying each of these positions is the assumption that Scyld and Beowulf share the same ethos, and yet there is ample evidence that the poet is depicting in the portrait of Scyld a set of values which it is the task of the rest of the poem to challenge and to redefine. Such a change of direction would not be unprecedented in Old English poetry.[30] As we have seen above, in *Juliana* a villain (Maximian, persecutor of Christian heroes) rather than, as is more common, the heroes themselves, is referred to as the subject of tales known to poet and audience.

Scyld is not a villain of the order of Maximian, but his values do differ from those of the hero of the poem. Perhaps a closer parallel exists in the opening of the ninth-century *Waltharius*, which describes the Huns in similar terms to Scyld, whilst the portrait of Attila will prove to be in many ways a sympathetic one:

> Hic populus fortis virtute vigebat et armis,
> non circumpositas solum domitans regiones,
> litoris oceani sed pertransiverat oras,
> foedera supplicibus donans sternensque rebelles.[31]

> [This brave people grew strong by valour and arms; not only did they dominate the neighbouring regions but they had also passed through the areas of the shore of Ocean, making alliances with suppliants and overthrowing the rebellious.]

Within the poem, the chief indication that the portrait of Scyld is not entirely complimentary lies in its contrast with the portrait of Beowulf, particularly in regard to his lack of aggression towards human enemies. The hero's different way of ruling is especially evident in his "confession". As Beowulf lies dying, he focuses on his restraint, especially in relation to staying within his own borders, keeping only what is rightfully his, refraining both from feuding and from swearing oaths which he did not intend to keep:

> I awaited my destiny in my own land, held what was mine prop-
> erly, did not seek out treacherous quarrels, nor did I swear many
> oaths wrongfully.
>   (2736b–2739a)

These aspects of the review of his kingship appear largely as negatives, as they do in the poet's own assessment of the hero (not at all did he slay his hearth-companions when drunk; his was not a savage heart (2179b–80)). These negatives both imply that Beowulf's conduct has constituted an exception to the prevailing code and invite comparison with rulers who conformed to it. Such a ruler is Scyld, who went outside his own borders, provoking conflict in order to increase his power. Scyld is a negative exemplum, although to a lesser degree than Heremod or Modthryth, and it is his portrait which initiates the study of kingship integral to the poem.[32] *Beowulf* is nearly over by the time we read the two assessments of the hero quoted above, and they are the culmination of all that we have seen of him in the intervening lines.

According to the poet, however, Scyld was a "god cyning". We might be tempted to term this irony: certainly there is irony in *Beowulf*[33] and even a precedent for the ironic use of a very similar phrase in Old English poetry, when the poet of *Daniel* exclaims "that was a good piece of work" (24b) in relation to the Hebrews' relapse into paganism. However, irony is not exactly the correct term here. "þæt wæs god cyning!" marks the end of the summary of Scyld's kingship, as the poet passes to a second narration concerning Scyld where he speaks more personally, using "ic gefrægn" rather than "we gefrunon". He now concentrates firstly on the securing of the Scylding dynasty by means of an heir, and then on Scyld's funeral, incorporating details of his arrival in Denmark and his relationship with the people whom he rules. It is clear from this material that Scyld is not totally condemned by the poet.

Scyld's arrival is implied to be part of God's plan for the Danes, just as Beowulf's own coming will prove to be, even though it is Scyld's son Beowulf who is said to be sent by God "as a consolation to the people" (14a).[34] In his reference to the coming of Scyld, the poet applies to him the foundling story which other sources, including Æthelweard's Latin Chronicle, apply to Sceaf,[35] who, in *Beowulf*, is probably the father of Scyld (he is "Scyld Scefing" (4a)). The association of the tale with Scyld may indicate the poet's desire to create a "saviour" story in connection with the eponymous founder of the Scyldings. The miraculous nature of Scyld's arrival, as well as his lowly beginnings, will be paralleled in the events of Beowulf's own life,[36] and recalls the career of the biblical David, who came from the sheepfold to the throne of Israel.

That God's purpose may be accomplished through pagans is implied in the poet's assertion, "The Ruler had power over all of humankind, as he still does now" (1057b–58);[37] it is demonstrated also in Alcuin's *Versus de patribus* where the "Saxon" conquest of England (and the Saxons, like Scyld, have come over the sea to a new kingdom) is seen as part of God's plan for replacing the sinful Britons with a people destined to produce powerful Christian kings:

> Hoc pietate Dei visum, quod gens scelerata
> ob sua de terris patrum peccata periret
> intraretque suas populus felicior urbes,
> qui servaturus Domini praecepta fuisset.

Quod fuit affatim factum, donante Tonante
iam nova dum crebris viguerunt sceptra triumphis
et reges ex se iam coepit habere potentes
gens ventura Dei.
     (*Versus de patribus*, 71–78)

[This was decided by the goodness of God, that the wicked
race should vanish from the lands of their fathers on account of
their sins, and that there should enter their cities a more for-
tunate nation, one which would keep the Lord's precepts. This
was satisfactorily accomplished when soon, by the grace of the
Thunderer, with frequent triumphs a new power grew strong and
the race destined to be God's began to have powerful kings from
among its own people.]

For Augustine the spread of the Roman Empire was part of the Divine
Plan. He may condemn empire-building, asking rhetorically, "Inferre autem
bella finitimis, et inde in cætera procedere, ac populos sibi non molestos sola
regni cupiditate conterere et subdere, quid aliud quam grande latrocinium
nominandum est?" [To make war on one's neighbours, and then to go on to
destroy and subdue peoples without being provoked and from the mere desire
for rule, what should this be called other than large-scale brigandage?],[38] but
he explains in *De civitate Dei*, V.16 ("De mercede sanctorum civium civitatis
æternæ, quibus utilia sunt Romanorum exempla virtutum" [Concerning the
reward of the holy citizens of the eternal city, to whom the examples of the
virtues of the Romans are useful]) that the Roman Empire was allowed to
extend and prosper by God

ut cives æternæ illius civitatis, quamdiu hic peregrinantur (11
Cor. V, 6), diligenter et sobrie illa intueantur exempla, et videant
quanta dilectio debeatur supernæ patriæ propter vitam æternam,
si tantum a suis civibus terrena dilecta est propter hominum
gloriam.
     (*De civitate Dei*, V.16; *PL* XLI.116–17)

[in order that the citizens of that eternal city, as long as they are
pilgrims here (II Corinthians 5.6), may diligently and soberly pay
attention to those examples, and see how great is the love owed
to the celestial homeland on account of eternal life, if the earthly
homeland has been so greatly loved by its citizens on account of
glory among humankind.]

In *Beowulf*, Danish history is similarly seen as part of God's plan. Scyld and the fate of the Danes are set from very early on within a religious dimension, with the events seen as involving not only men but the Deity as well—the human drama has cosmic significance.

The account of Scyld's funeral demonstrates how beloved he was of the Danes: the poet refers to him as "leof landfruma" [the beloved ruler of the land] (31a) and "leofne þeoden" [the beloved prince] (34b), and stresses the worth of the treasures which accompany him out to sea (see 38–40a). These two aspects of Scyld's kingship—loved at home and feared outside his own land because of his expansionist policies—are paralleled in Alcuin's portrait of Edwin of Northumbria before his conversion:

> Qui mox accipiens sceptri regalis honorem
> quaesivit propriae genti bona, largus in omnes,
> nec per sceptra ferox, sed de pietate benignus,
> factus amor populi, patriae pater, et decus aulae,
> assiduis superans hostilia castra triumphis,
> imperioque suo gentes superaddidit omnes,
> finibus atque plagis qua tenditur insula longa.
>   (*Versus de patribus*, 115–21)

> [Soon accepting the honour of the royal sceptre, he sought what was good for his own people; he was generous to all, nor did he wield his power fiercely, but was kind through his sense of duty, and became beloved of his people, the father of his homeland, and the delight of the royal court, overcoming enemies' strongholds in continual triumphs, and he added to his kingdom all the nations held within the boundaries and territories of this vast island.]

In the affection which he inspires in the Danes, Scyld contrasts especially with Heremod who, after an auspicious beginning, became a curse on his people and ended by falling "on feonda geweald" [into the power of enemies] (903a),[39] perhaps suffering the fate which Byrhtnoth wishes to avoid when he prays to God for his own soul:

> I beseech you that ravagers from hell may not be allowed to harm it.
>   (*The Battle of Maldon*, 179b–80)

Portraits of Heremod-like characters abound in Gregory's *Pastoral Care*, in illustration of the truth that prosperity may lead to pride and ultimately to downfall. Thus, in the West Saxon version, Saul, after becoming king, "is turned to pride, and continues in vainglory",[40] and David's treatment of Uriah would suffice to damn him despite his previous good works unless "tribulation and hardship had helped him againa" (*WSPC*, 36). It is clear that Heremod, rather than Scyld, is an example of the worst that the heroic ethos can produce. "þæt wæs god cyning!" is not ironic when applied to Scyld; he *is* a good king, but only by the standards of his own society.[41]

The distinction between the ways of life of Scyld, Heremod and Beowulf is to be found in Augustine's *De civitate Dei* where they are put into a Christian context, especially in connection with Augustine's views on the high-minded Romans of the past. In fact, portraits of characters resembling Heremod, Scyld, and Beowulf occur in close proximity. The depiction of the noble Roman (see *De civitate Dei*, V.15; *PL* XLI.160) is later modified by the comment that true virtue cannot exist

> sine vera pietate, id est veri Dei vero cultu ...; nec earn veram esse, quando gloriæ servit humanæ. Eos tamen qui cives non sint civitatis æternæ, quæ in sacris Litteris nostris dicitur civitas Dei.... utiliores esse terrenæ civitati, quando habent virtutem vel ipsam, quam si nec ipsam.
> (*De civitate Dei*, V.19; *PL* XL1.166)

> [without true piety, that is, the true worship of the true God ...; nor can that be true virtue when it serves human glory. And yet those who are not citizens of the Eternal City, which in our holy Scriptures is called the City of God..., are more useful to the earthly city when they possess even that kind of virtue than if they do not.]

This portrait, which may remind us of Scyld, is enclosed between two other types. On one side we have those Romans who wanted only domination, such as Nero, who "hujus vitii summitatem et quasi arcem ... primus obtinuit" [first attained the height of this vice, and, as it were, its citadel] (*De civitate Dei*, V.19; *PL* XLI.166), the kind of ruler depicted within *Beowulf* in the character of Heremod. On the other, we have those who "vera pietate præditi bene vivunt" [endowed with true piety live well] (*De civitate Dei*, V.19; *PL* XLI.166) and who, if skilled in the art of government, make the best rulers; such men, says Augustine, realise that it is to God that they owe their virtues. This description could serve as a portrait of Beowulf who, in his struggles with the monsters which menace humankind, will entrust himself to God and use "the strength of his power, the ample gift, which God had given to him" (1270b–71).

Details of Scyld's funeral further the religious context into which his life is set. The rites may seem completely pagan in conception,[42] but a very close parallel has been discovered by Cameron in the Latin Life of Saint Gildas.[43] St Gildas, author of the *De excidio Britanniae*, gives instructions for his own burial, asking his followers to lay his body in a ship and push the ship out to sea, leaving it to drift where God wills. There are verbal parallels close enough to suggest direct influence, or the influence of a common source: "then they carried him off to the current of the sea, his own companions, as he himself had bidden" (*Beowulf*, 28–29) corresponds closely with the Life's "Discipuli veto illius tollentes corpus eius fecerunt, sicut praeceperat eis" [Indeed his disciples carrying his body did as he had ordered them]; Scyld drifts "on Frean wære" [into the keeping of the Lord] (27b) and Gildas asks to go "quo Deus voluerit" [wherever God might wish].

Gildas' own last rites may not seem very "Christian", but they bring to mind the "peregrinatio pro amore Dei", albeit taken to its ultimate conclusion. The possible use of this material by the *Beowulf* poet in his account of Scyld's funeral could indicate that he is drawing upon a literary source to reconstruct a practice of which he has heard (the burial at Sutton Hoo perhaps),[44] but he sends Scyld off with this comment:

> People cannot say for certain, hall-dwellers, heroes under the heavens, who received that cargo.
> (50b–52)

The poet's emphasis on the perpetual ignorance of Scyld's fate makes little sense on the literal level, and would seem to indicate that his voyage into the unknown has metaphorical significance.[45] The image of a journey was common in Christian writings, as it is today, to describe the soul's departure from the body and progression to meet its Maker. It is used elsewhere in *Beowulf*, for example when "fæder ellor hwearf" [his father had passed elsewhere] (55b) explains Beowulf the Dane's accession, and in the "Christian Excursus":[46]

> Ill will it be with him who because of his grievous malice must shove his soul into the fire's embrace, he must not expect consolation or change in any way at all. All will be well with him who is allowed after his death-day to seek out the Lord and ask for peace in the Father's embrace!
> (183b–88)

The "Excursus" may provide a parallel, but it furnishes also a contrast with the lines relating to Scyld, as it describes the known destination of the journey of the good and evil soul. As regards the fate of those such as Scyld, who have exemplified the standards of their society, "God ana wat" [God alone knows].[47] Scyld's soul continues on, but his ultimate destiny is obscure.

The "Prologue", then, launches us into the main action of the poem, a poem which will differ from those works in celebration of Germanic heroes which the audience is wont to hear, as the depiction of Scyld provides the context into which the hero comes and by comparison with which he is ultimately to be judged. If Huppé is correct in saying that the relief which Scyld brings to the Danes is founded upon war,[48] it is not true that Beowulf at the end "has become involved in his world and in the ethos of the feud".[49] Beowulf, for Huppé, would promote only "by antithesis" the concept of the Christian hero.[50] Certainly, antithesis is involved, but on the level of the opposition between heroic and Christian ethics the antithesis is between Scyld and Beowulf.

The poet has deftly moved the plane of events from an apparently secular world to a framework within which those events have religious significance. The "Prologue" tells us that no-one can know the fate of a pagan who lives according to the old heroic ethos. However, the poem as a whole is designed to demonstrate the fate of a pagan who follows quite different principles, and in this case the poet does not declare his ignorance. When, after bequeathing his kingdom and armour to Wiglaf, Beowulf dies, his soul leaves his breast "secean soðfæstra dom" (2820), that is, to seek out the glory of the just.[51]

NOTES

1. *Beowulf*, 1–3. All quotations from *Beowulf* are taken from Klaeber's edition (*Beowulf and The Fight at Finnsburg*, ed. Fr. Klaeber, 3rd ed., with First and Second Supplements (Boston, Massachusetts: D.C. Heath, 1950); I omit, however, Klaeber's indications of syllable length, the use of Thorkelin transcripts and conjectural readings, as well as his capitalisation of part of the opening line, where he follows the manuscript. Line numbers of further quotations will be given alongside quotation in the text. Translations from Old English and Latin throughout this article are my own; in the latter case, however, translations cited in these notes have been consulted in checking my own work. I have on the whole translated as literally as possible in order not to obscure any similarities of phraseology.

2. As Irving says, "Even though Beowulf has not even been mentioned in the first 193 lines, we have really been talking indirectly of no one else" (Edward B. Irving, Jr, *Introduction to Beowulf* (Englewood Cliffs, New Jersey: Prentice-Hall, 1969), 38–39).

3. The manuscript's "Beowulf" (in 18a and 53b) is often assumed to be a scribal error, or even an error on the part of the poet, for the "Beow" or "Beaw" of the genealogies

(see Klaeber's edition, xxvi, for early proponents of this view; it is still widespread to-day, for example in George Jack's introduction to his edition of the poem, *Beowulf: A Student Edition* (Oxford: Clarendon Press, 1994), 11). The view closest to my own on this subject is that of Paul Dean, for whom the early mention of Scyld's son Beowulf leads to confusion when the hero states "Beowulf is min nama" (343b), a confusion which points up the parallels between the two characters (see *"Beowulf* and the Passing of Time", *English Studies* 75 (1994): 193–209 and 293–302, at 197). James W. Earl believes that "Beowulf", an untraditional name, "is given its own traditionality right within the poem" by its use for Scyld's son (see *Thinking About Beowulf* (Stanford, California: Stanford University Press, 1994), 23).

4. I intend to use the term "poet" for the narrating voice as well as for the poem's author, on the grounds that in much Old English poetry poet and narrating voice are indistinguishable in any meaningful sense; where there is irony one can identify it as such and ascribe it to the poet as fittingly as to the narrating voice in a poem like *Beowulf*. As Ursula Schaefer remarks in connection with the use of "we" in particular: "The deictic value of the first-person plural pronoun is that it includes the speaker and those to whom he or she speaks. Hence this pronominal reference may indeed be interpreted as the mani-festation of the unity of the knower(s) and the known" ("Hearing From Books: The Rise of Fictionality in Old English Poetry", in *Vox Intexta: Orality and Textuality in the Middle Ages*, ed. A. N. Doane and Carol Braun Pasternack (Madison, Wisconsin: University of Wisconsin Press, 1991), 117–36, at 123). It is reasonable to assume that in the poet's time this bond existed in the real world as it does within the world of the poem. In those poems where the first-person narrator is also an actor in the drama (*The Dream of the Rood*, for example, or the "elegies"), it is more useful to draw a distinction between poet and narrator, although even in these poems the poet is creating for himself a position of authority (as the recipient of a heavenly vision, or, in *The Seafarer*, as a sailor accustomed to extreme hardship) from which he may provide Christian teaching to his audience. Stanley B. Greenfield, in "The Authenticating Voice in *Beowulf*", *Anglo-Saxon England* 5 (1976): 51–62, makes the point that the narrator is an "authenticating voice" rather than a persona; however, his conception of the stance of the narrating voice does not allow for fine distinctions such as the particular tone of "þæt wæs god cyning!" as applied to Scyld which I propose below.

5. See Ward Parks, "The Traditional Narrator and the 'I Heard' Formulas in Old English Poetry", *Anglo-Saxon England* 16 (1987), 45–66; his later article, "The Traditional Narrator in *Beowulf* and Homer", in *De Gustibus: Essays for Alain Renoir*, ed. John Miles Foley (New York: Garland Publishing, 1992), 456–79, draws heavily on the 1987 essay.

6. *The Blickling Homilies*, ed. Richard Morris, Early English Text Society, Original Series 58, 63, and 73 (Oxford: Oxford University Press for The Early English Text Society, 1874–80; rpt. as one vol. 1967), 29. "Hwæt" is used by characters within the poems either to begin a speech (as when, in *Beowulf*, the hero replies to Hunferth (see 530a)) or to emphasise a point (as when Hrothgar praises Beowulf by reference to his mother (see *Beowulf* 942b)).

7. *Exodus* is here cited, as will be all Old English poems other than those in the Exeter Book, from *The Anglo-Saxon Poetic Records: A Collective Edition*, ed. Elliott van Kirk Dobbie and George Philip Krapp, 6 vols. (New York: Columbia University Press, 1931–1942), by Krapp and Dobbie's title and line numbers only. Poems contained in the Exeter Book will follow the edition of Bernard J. Muir (*The Exeter Anthology of Old English Poetry: An Edition of Exeter Dean and Chapter MS 3501*, 2 vols. (Exeter: University of Exeter Press, 1994)), and will be cited, in the main text where necessary, by the conventional name

of the poem, followed by Muir's alternative title if relevant, a reference to Muir as editor, and line numbers.

8. On the replacement of the Muses in early Christian poetry, such as the works of Juvencus and Sedulius, see Ernst Robert Curtius, *European Literature and the Latin Middle Ages* (1948), trans. Willard R. Trask, Bollingen Series, 36 (New York: Pantheon Books for the Bollingen Foundation, 1953), 235–36.

9. *Psychomachia*, in Prudentius, [*Opera*], ed. and trans. H. J. Thomson, 2 vols, Loeb Classical Library (London: Heinemann, 1949–53), line 1; this work will be cited henceforth alongside quotation by line only.

10. See Alcuin, *The Bishops, Kings, and Saints of York*, ed. [and trans.] Peter Godman, Oxford Medieval Texts (Oxford: Clarendon Press, 1982). This text will be cited alongside reference as *Versus de patribus*, an abbreviation of its Latin title, followed by line number only.

11. "Praefatio" to the *Enigmata Aldhelmi*, in *Aldhelmi opera omnia*, ed. Rudolf Ehwald, Monumenta Germaniae Historica, Auctores Antiquissimi, 15 (Berlin: Weidmann, 1919; rpt. 1961), 97–149, at line 10, p. 98.

12. *Bede's Ecclesiastical History of the English People*, ed. Bertram Colgrave and R. A. B. Mynors, Oxford Medieval Texts (Oxford: Clarendon Press, 1969), IV.20; pp. 396–98.

13. As John Miles Foley says, "To put it most simply, the oral traditional idiom persisted because—even in a written incarnation—it offered the only avenue to the immanent poetic tradition, the invisible but ever-present aesthetic context for all of the poems" ("Texts That Speak to Readers Who Hear: Old English Poetry and the Languages of Oral Tradition", in *Speaking Two Languages: Traditional Disciplines and Contemporary Theory in Medieval Studies*, ed. Allen J. Frantzen, SUNY Series in Medieval Studies (New York: State University of New York Press, 1991), 141–56, at 155).

14. Both Heorot and Hrothgar are mentioned in *Widsith*, together with two other personages from the poem:

> Hrothwulf and Hrothgar held peace together, uncle and nephew, for the longest time, after they had driven out the race of the Vikings and humbled the vanguard of Ingeld, hewn down at Heorot the host of the Heathobards.
>   (*Widsith*, ed. Muir, 45–49)

These lines provide some surprises for those who consider the main narrative of *Beowulf* to be an inherited story with historical foundation. In a passage concerning Hrothgar and Heorot, one would expect to hear of their saviour, Beowulf. Further, the destruction of Heorot by fire, assumed by many readers of the poem to have occurred during the defeat of the Heathobards, is not mentioned, nor indeed is the presumed treachery of Hrothulf in relation to Hrothgar's sons. In *Widsith*, uncle and nephew appear to have ruled peacefully together, just as the *Beowulf* poet first shows them to us, or as do Hygelac and Beowulf after Beowulf's return from Denmark. In fact, the peaceful co-rule of Hrothulf and Hrothgar seems to the *Widsith* poet more noteworthy than the slaughter of the Heathobards.

15. As Dean sees, the poem begins with "an appeal to our common *past* experience, specifically our memory of certain kinds of story" (see Paul Dean, "*Beowulf* and the Passing of Time", 196; the italics are Dean's).

16. Knowledge of such songs may be relevant to the vexed question of the poem's dating; however, there was from the earliest period of Anglo-Saxon settlement a clear connection between Scandinavia and pre-Viking East Anglia. R. T. Farrell summarises archaeologists' views on a Swedish connection in *Beowulf, Swedes and Geats* (London: Viking Society

for Northern Research, 1972), at 43–45; John Hines details the Scandinavian character of East Anglian finds in *The Scandinavian Character of Anglian England in the Pre-Viking Period*, BAR British Series, 124 (Oxford: BAR, 1984), especially at 227–300, and "The Scandinavian Character of Anglian England: An Update", in *The Age of Sutton Hoo: The Seventh Century in North-Western Europe*, ed. M. O. H. Carver (Woodbridge, Suffolk: The Boydell Press, 1992), 315–29.

17. For Ward Parks, however, it "would not be unreasonable to characterise the entirety of *Beowulf* ... as a retelling of one or several of the stories alluded to by the poet in the original 'we heard' of the poem" ("The Traditional Narrator and the 'I Heard' Formulas in Old English Poetry", 59). Fred C. Robinson similarly claims that *Beowulf* "is itself a retelling" (see *Beowulf and the Appositive Style* (Knoxville, Tennessee: University of Tennessee Press, 1985), 27).

18. See John D. Niles, *Beowulf: The Poem and Its Tradition* (Cambridge, Massachusetts: Harvard University Press, 1983), 199. Robert P. Creed ("The Singer Looks at His Sources", in *Studies in Old English Literature in Honour of Arthur G. Brodeur* (Eugene, Oregon: University of Oregon Books, 1963), 44–52), develops his idea that the oral songs within *Beowulf*, such as that concerned with Sigemund, mirror the way in which the poet has heard his own material; in "The Remaking of *Beowulf*", in *Oral Tradition in Literature: Interpretation in Context*, ed. John Miles Foley (Columbia, Missouri: University of Missouri Press, 1986), 136–46, he reiterates his belief that the poet is retelling an old tale, conjecturing that he remakes "the tale of the beneficent heathen god into the tale of the beneficent hero" (see "The Remaking of *Beowulf*", 146).

19. See J. R. R. Tolkien, "*Beowulf*: The Monsters and the Critics" (1936), in *The Monsters and the Critics, and Other Essays* (London: George Allen & Unwin, 1983; rpt. 1997), 29.

20. This point concerning the received view is made by Helen Damico in *Beowulf's Wealhtheow and the Valkyrie Tradition* (Madison, Wisconsin: University of Wisconsin Press, 1984), 15.

21. Raymond P. Tripp, Jr, "The Archetype Enters History and Goes to Sleep: What Beowulf Does in Heorot", *In Geardagum* 2 (1977): 74–92, at 76; the italics are Tripp's.

22. I follow here the usual reconstruction of line 62; Alfred Bammesberger has however suggested that this passage is an incorporated gloss (see "Hidden Glosses in Manuscripts of Old English Poetry", *Anglo-Saxon England* 13 (1984): 43–49, at 49).

23. Ward Parks, *Verbal Dueling in Heroic Narrative: The Homeric and Old English Traditions* (Princeton, New Jersey: Princeton University Press, 1990), 159–60.

24. See Thomas D. Hill, "The Confession of Beowulf and the Structure of *Volsunga Saga*", in *The Vikings*, ed. Robert T. Farrell (London: Phillimore, 1982), 165–79, at 177; Hill, however, bases his argument on the portraits of Sigemund and Heremod and their verbal links with Grendel rather than, as I do here, on the portrait of Scyld and the opening lines of the poem.

25. For Edward B. Irving, Jr, for example, "we are presented at the outset with a paradigm of praiseworthy conduct in Scyld, the *god cyning*" (*A Reading of Beowulf* (New Haven, Connecticut: Yale University Press, 1968), 44); according to Bruce Moore, Scyld has "the poet's absolute approval", and "Beowulf's triumphs bring with them the hope that there may be a complete return to the Scyld ethos" (see "The Thryth-Offa Digression in *Beowulf*", *Neophilologus* 64 (1980): 127–33, at 132); for Moore, Hrothgar represents a falling away from the ideal, as when "þæt wæs god cyning" is used of Hrothgar "the tone is somewhat uneasy" (see "The Thryth-Offa Digression in *Beowulf*", 133, fn. 15). Keith P. Taylor perpetuates this view, claiming that Scyld is "considered noble and a *god cyning*,

at least by the *Beowulf* poet, primarily because of his brave deeds and specifically because of his ability to exact tribute from those around him" (see "*Beowulf* 1259a: The Inherent Nobility of Grendel's Mother", *English Language Notes* 31.3 (1994): 13–25, at 20); as I hope to argue elsewhere, I view Hrothgar's kingship as an improvement on Scyld's, whose ethos is one which the hero works to replace with a more "Christian" way of life. For Leo Carruthers, too, Scyld is "the ideal against which other kings will be judged", with the application of "þæt wæs god cyning" to Scyld (11b), Hrothgar (863b) and Beowulf (2390b) associating all of them in a "universal statement of approval" (see "Kingship and Heroism in *Beowulf*", in *Heroes and Heroines in Medieval English Literature: A Festschrift Presented to André Crépin on the Occasion of His Sixty-Fifth Birthday*, ed. Leo Carruthers (Cambridge: D. S. Brewer, 1994), 19–29, at 20).

26. See Kenneth Florey, "Grendel, Evil, 'Allegory', and Dramatic Development in *Beowulf*", *Essays in Arts and Sciences* 17 (1988): 83–95, at 85); he sees also in the rule of Scyld a "pastorally simple world" ("Grendel, Evil, 'Allegory', and Dramatic Development in *Beowulf*", 86).

27. The dating problem is linked for most critics with possible periods when a poem complimentary to the Danes could have been written, with critical energy expended in showing that relations with Scandinavia remained healthy despite Viking attacks; see for example, Norman F. Blake, "The Dating of Old English Poetry", in *An English Miscellany Presented to W. S. Mackie*, ed. Brian S. Lee (Cape Town: Oxford University Press, 1977), 4–27, at 25, and Nicholas Jacobs, for whom "from 927 onward the Danes constituted a widely accepted element in English society, and an English poem complimentary to them is conceivable at least down to the resumption of raids in 980" (see "Anglo-Danish Relations, Poetic Archaism and the Date of *Beowulf*: A Reconsideration of the Evidence", *Poetica* (Tokyo) 8 (1978): 23–43, at 40). Fidel Fajardo-Acosta, however, believes that the Christian Anglo-Saxon poet was interested in condemning the way of life of the barbarian Danish tribes who were semi-pagan and also proverbial enemies of the English at the time of the poem's composition (see "Intemperance, Fratricide, and the Elusiveness of Grendel", *English Studies* 73 (1992): 205–10, at 207).

28. See Bernard F. Huppé, *The Hero in the Earthly City: A Reading of Beowulf*, Medieval & Renaissance Texts & Studies, 33 (Binghamton, New York: Medieval & Renaissance Texts & Studies, State University of New York at Binghamton, 1984), 21.

29. See Charles Dahlberg, *The Literature of Unlikeness* (Hanover, New England: University Press of New England, 1988), 43 (includes quotation) and 50–52.

30. On the "opening theme" of Old English poems see Michael D. Cherniss, "The Oral-Traditional Opening Theme in the Poems of Cynewulf", in *De Gustibus: Essays for Alain Renoir*, ed. John Miles Foley (New York: Garland Publishing, 1992), 40–65, at 43–45. In a brilliant essay, Cherniss isolates the opening theme and discusses its elements in relation to the poems of Cynewulf.

31. *Waltharius*, in *Waltharius and Ruodlieb*, ed. Dennis M. Kratz, The Garland Library of Medieval Literature, Series A, 13 (New York: Garland Publishing, 1984), 3–70, at 4, lines 6–9. Line 9 is an obvious paraphrase of Virgil's "parcere subiectis, et debellare superbos" [to spare the conquered, and to crush the proud by war] (Virgil, *The Aeneid of Virgil*, ed. T. E. Page, 2 vols (London: Macmillan, 1894; rpt. 1951), VI.853), part of the delineation of Rome's mission as expressed by the shade of Anchises.

32. Kemp Malone suggests a political reason for the difference in their style of kingship: Scyld rules an empire, whilst Hygelac, and later Beowulf, rule a single nation (see "Symbolism in 'Beowulf': Some Suggestions", *English Studies Today* 2nd series (1961): 81–91). However, it seems clear that Beowulf does not harbour imperial longings.

33. See especially Richard N. Ringler, "'Him seo wen geleah': The Design for Irony in Grendel's Last Visit to Heorot", *Speculum* 41 (1966): 49–67; Robert W. Harming, "Sharing, Dividing, Depriving—The Verbal Ironies of Grendel's Last Visit to Heorot", *Texas Studies in Literature and Language* 15 (1973): 203–13; Elizabeth Liggins, "Irony and Understatement in *Beowulf*", *Parergon* 29 (April 1981): 3–7; Robert Costomiris, "The Potential for Humour in the Ironic Elements of *Beowulf*", *Old English Newsletter* 26.3 (1993): A-38/39. Recognition in the Middle Ages of irony in epic is discussed by Dennis M. Kratz in *Mocking Epic: Waltharius, Alexandreis and the Problem of Christian Heroism*, Studia Humanitatis (Madrid: Porrua, 1980), 3–4.

34. This phrase, or a variant, is often used of Christ and the Holy Ghost, as in, for example, the expanded version of the Creed in the Old English version of the Benedictine Office, which states that Christ "to frofre gewearð foldbuendum" [became a consolation to earthdwellers] (see *The Benedictine Office: An Old English Text*, ed. James M. Ure, Edinburgh University Publications: Language and Literature, 1 (Edinburgh: Edinburgh University Press, 1957), 88, line 8. Crépin considers that the phrase is diverted in *Beowulf* from its more usual religious application to the "heirs and heroes" of the poem (see André Crépin, "Wealhtheow's Offering of the Cup to Beowulf: A Study in Literary Structure", in *Saints, Scholars and Heroes: Studies in Medieval Culture in Honour of Charles W. Jones*, ed. Margot H. King and Wesley M. Stevens, 2 vols (Collegeville, Minnesota: Hill Monastic Manuscript Library, Saint John's Abbey and University, 1979), 1.45–58, at 51). However, these two uses are consistent, as in *Beowulf* the "heirs and heroes" of the poem are seen as agents for divine aid.

35. See *The Anglo-Saxon Chronicle: A Revised Translation*, ed. and trans. Dorothy Whitelock (London: Eyre and Spottiswoode, 1961), 44, fn. 12 and fn. 14. For a study of the variants in the genealogical relationship of Sceaf and Scyld, and the stories attached to them, see Audrey L. Meaney, "Scyld Scefing and the Dating of *Beowulf*—Again", *Bulletin of the John Rylands University Library* 71 (1989), 7–40. According to R. D. Fulk (see "An Eddic Analogue to the Scyld Scefing Story", *Review of English Studies*, n.s. 40 (1989): 313–22), Karelian and Eddic analogues suggest that the Scyld foundling story was originally told of Beow.

36. Adrien Bonjour draws attention to these parallels between Scyld and Beowulf, which, however, he believes to be "more or less accidental" (see *The Digressions in Beowulf*, Medium Ævum Monographs, 5 (Oxford: Basil Blackwell, 1950), 5).

37. That "Metod" refers to God here (as, I believe, in all of its occurrences in the poem) is clear both from the statement itself and from the immediately preceding lines, where the poet declares that it was "witig God" [wise God] and "ðæs mannes mod" [the man's spirit] that forestalled "wyrd" [the course of events] (see 1056–57).

38. *Ad Marcellinum de civitate Dei contra paganos, in Patrologiae cursus completus*, Series Latina, ed. J.-P. Migne (Paris, 1844–64), XLI.13–804, at V.16, *PL* XLI.160; this series will be cited henceforth as *PL*, and this particular work cited alongside quotation by its accepted title, *De civitate Dei*.

39. The references to Heremod in the poem raise many questions. Does his fall through pride and subsequent exile re-enact the fate of Satan, or perhaps of Man, in the "Creation to Apocalypse" pattern discernible in *Beowulf* as a whole? It appears to be Heremod's fall which leaves the Danes without a leader, and it is this vacuum which Scyld is sent to fill. One wonders, too, whether "Heremod" may mean "hostile mind", and whether his end might be intended to recall the apocryphal fate of the rather similarly named Herod.

40. *King Alfred's West-Saxon Version of Gregory's Pastoral Care*, ed. Henry Sweet, 2 vols, Early English text Society, Original Series, 45 and 50 (London: N. Trübner & Co. for the

Early English Text Society, 1871–72), 34. This work will henceforth be cited alongside quotation as *WSPC*, by page only, as there is continuous pagination in the two volumes.

41. Marjorie Daunt believes that "in *Beowulf*, god is charged with pre-Christian heroic values" (see "Some Modes of Anglo-Saxon Meaning", in *In Memory of J. R. Firth*, ed. C. E. Bazell, J. C. Catford, M. A. K. Halliday and R. H. Robins, Longmans' Linguistic Library (London: Longmans, 1966), 66–78, at 68); however, as I hope that my argument here will suggest, the meaning of "god" will be redefined during the course of *Beowulf*. Florey, on the other hand, takes an over-liberal view, claiming with no supporting evidence that "the poet assures us that by all standards" Scyld was a good king (see "Grendel, Evil, 'Allegory', and Dramatic Development in *Beowulf*", 85).

42. L. Whitbread summarises the literary record of Scandinavian ship burials in "*Beowulf* and Archaeology: Two Further Footnotes", *Neuphilologische Mitteilungen* 69 (1968): 63–72; as he points out, the nature of Scyld's rites makes them incapable of exact parallels from archaeology, but the funerals of King Haki, Sigvard "Ring" and Baldr are very similar, although these all involve cremation on a launched vessel (see "*Beowulf* and Archaeology", 64–65). Interestingly, Haki is laid in the ship "when he is dead or nigh to death" ("*Beowulf* and Archaeology", 64); in light of this I wonder whether my unease concerning the condition of Scyld (he is "felahror" [very active] (27a), and he no longer "wordum weold" [wielded (with) words] (30), a phrase possibly concerned with the power of speech) is justified. If he is still living, the metaphorical level which I suggest below concerning the voyage of his soul would be even more powerful.

43. See A. F. Cameron, "Saint Gildas and Scyld Scefing", *Neuphilologische Mitteilungen* 70 (1969): 240–46; I reproduce here some of his parallels and cite the text through him. Meaney considers a direct connection between the two texts "very probable" (see "Scyld Scefing and the Dating of *Beowulf*—Again", 35). The Life is usually dated between the ninth and eleventh centuries, but it seems to incorporate earlier material (see "Saint Gildas and Scyld Scefing", 242–43).

44. The Sutton Hoo ship, at first though to be a cenotaph, is now considered likely to have contained a burial (see Angela Care Evans, *The Sutton Hoo Ship Burial*, rev. ed. (London: British Museum Press for The Trustees of the British Museum, 1994), 39–40).

45. We might compare Cynewulf's ignorance of his own prospective fate: "Min sceal of lice / sawul on siðfæt, nat ic sylfa hwider" [My soul must leave the body on a journey, I myself do not know whither] (*Juliana* [*The Passion of Saint Juliana*], ed. Muir, 699a–700). It is noticeable that the *Beowulf* lines are often misunderstood as referring to past ignorance: E. G. Stanley, for example, who appears to see the journey as metaphorical, nevertheless takes "Men ne cunnon" [People do not know] as expressing the pagans' ignorance concerning the fate of the soul, life after death in general (see "The Narrative Art of *Beowulf*", in *Medieval Narrative: A Symposium*, ed. Hans Bekker-Nielsen, Peter Foote, Andreas Haarder and Preben Meulengracht Sørensen (Odense: Odense University Press, 1979), 58–81, at 72).

46. This term is applied to lines 175–88, or restricted to the poet's comments in 178b (or 180b)–188. Many critics, including Tolkien, have regarded it, at least in part, as an interpolation (see the introduction to *Beowulf with the Finnesburg Fragment*, ed. C. L. Wrenn, rev. W. F. Bolton (London: Harrap, 1973), 63).

47. Thus I must disagree with Bonjour, who feels that, in contrast with Beowulf's funeral, mourning is put into the background in favour of the brilliant and splendid funeral scene, the royal banner flying at the mast, with the journey out to sea "almost an apotheosis", symbolic of a glorious future for the Scyldings (see *The Digressions in Beowulf*, 9–10, quotation at 9).

48. See *The Hero in the Earthly City*, 21.

49. See *The Hero in the Earthly City*, 35. G. V. Smithers is another critic who regards Beowulf as I would Scyld, as "an exemplary hero according to the Germanic warrior code" (see "Destiny and the Heroic Warrior in *Beowulf*", in *Philological Essays: Studies in Old and Middle English Language and Literature in Honour of Herbert Dean Meritt*, ed. James L. Rosier (The Hague: Mouton, 1970), 65–81, at 80).

50. See *The Hero in the Earthly City*, 40.

51. For a full discussion of the meaning of the phrase "soðfæstra dom", including the reasons for my belief that it must indicate the salvation of Beowulf's soul, see Judith A. King, "'The Spirit Giveth Life': A Reading of *Beowulf* in a Literary Context", unpublished PhD thesis, Flinders University, Adelaide, Australia, 1998.

Chronology

ca. 500	Traditional date for the migration of the continental Germanic tribes (Angles, Saxons, Jutes, etc.) to England; Ambrosius Aurelianus and the Britons defeat the Saxons at Mount Baden.
ca. 540	Gildas publishes his *De Excidio et Conquestu Britanniae*.
ca. 560-616	King Aethelbert (the first English ruler to accept Christianity) reigns in Kent.
ca. 597	Gregory the Great sends Saint Augustine as the Church's emissary to Christianize Britain.
ca. 625-700	Sutton Hoo ship burial, which may be the grave of Raedwald, King of East Anglia.
ca. 657-680	The poet Caedmon's tenure at the monastery of Streoneshealh. According to Bede, he is the first English Christian poet. The writing down of his verse by the scholars of Whitby is the first recorded writing of Old English poetry.
669–690	Tenure of Theodore, Archbishop of Canterbury.
ca. 686	Last pagan dynasty (on the Isle of Wight) comes to an end.
ca. 700–750	Composition of "The Dream of the Rood."
ca. 731	Bede's *Historia Ecclesiastica* completed.

ca. 735–804   Reign of Alcuin of York.

ca. 757–796   Reign of King Offa of Mercia.

793   Viking raiders attack the monastery at Lindisfarne; Alcuin writes his letter to King Ethelred.

865–877   Viking army conquers Northumbria, East Anglia, and most of Mercia.

871–899   King Alfred's reign in Wessex; the probable period for the translation of Bede's *Historia Ecclesiastica* into Old English.

878   Danes defeat Wessex forces at Chippenham; Alfred withdraws to the Somerset marshes.

880   Alfred returns.

886   Alfred captures London.

ca. 892   Compilation of the first *Anglo-Saxon Chronicle*.

893–896   Alfred staves off another Viking army.

937   *The Battle of Brunanburh* is entered in the *Anglo-Saxon Chronicle*.

959–975   Reign of Edgar, King of all England; era of great ecclesiastical reform.

ca. 975   Compilation of the Exeter Book.

978   Murder of Edward the Martyr.

979–1016   Reign of Aethelred Unraed; era of Archbishop Wulfstan and Abbot Aelfric of Eynsham.

991   Vikings defeat Ealdorman Byrhtnoth's warriors at the Battle of Maldon on the Blackwater in Esssex.

ca. 1000   Probable date of the extant manuscript of *Beowulf* (composition may be contemporary with the manuscript).

1014   Wulfstan composes the *Sermo Lupi ad Anglos*.

1016–1035   Reign of Cnut the Viking.

1042–1066   Reign of Edward the Confessor.

1066   In January, Harold, earl of Wessex, assumes the throne; killed October 14 at the Battle of Hastings. King William of Normandy (William the Conqueror) assumes the British throne.

1086   William orders the composition of the *Domesday Book*.

CHRONOLOGY OF EVENTS AND CHARACTERS IN THE POEM

495   Beowulf born to Ecgtheow and a daughter of the Geatish king, Hrethel.

502	Beowulf sent, at seven, to Hrethel's court for his upbringing.
503	Hrethel dies of sorrow because his second son, Hæthcyn, killed his first-born son, Herebeald. Hæthcyn, succeeds to the Geatish throne. Hrothgar, the Danish king, builds a great hall, Heorot, and Grendel begins his nightly raids on it.
503	The sons of the Swedish king, Ongentheow, raid the Geats.
510	Hæthcyn and his brother Hygelac raid the Swedes. King Ongentheow and Hæthcyn die in battle. The victorious Hygelac succeeds to the Geatish throne.
510-514	Beowulf's youthful adventures: the seafaring contest with Breca and battles with sea-monsters and giants.
515	Beowulf kills Grendel and Grendel's mother, thus relieving Hrothgar and the Danes of an affliction that had gone on for twelve years.
524	Hygelac is killed while raiding in the Netherlands. According to the poem, Hygelac is avenged by Beowulf, who becomes the Geatish regent during the minority of Heardred, Hygelac's son.
525	Hrothgar dies; his nephew Hrothwulf (rather than a son of Hrothgar) succeeds to the Danish throne.
532	Oththere, the Swedish king, dies; his brother Onela succeeds him. Ohthere's sons, Onela's nephews, seek refuge with the Geats. Onela attacks the Geats and kills his nephew Eanmund and the Geatish king, Heardred. Beowulf becomes king of the Geats.
535	Beowulf assists Ohthere's surviving son, Eadgils, to invade Sweden; Onela killed, Eadgils succeeds him.
ca. 800–900	The poem, somewhat resembling its present form, is first committed to writing, probably after a long circulation in oral tradition.

Contributors

HAROLD BLOOM is Sterling Professor of the Humanities at Yale University. He is the author of 30 books, including *Shelley's Mythmaking* (1959), *The Visionary Company* (1961), *Blake's Apocalypse* (1963), *Yeats* (1970), *A Map of Misreading* (1975), *Kabbalah and Criticism* (1975), *Agon: Toward a Theory of Revisionism* (1982), *The American Religion* (1992), *The Western Canon* (1994), and *Omens of Millennium: The Gnosis of Angels, Dreams, and Resurrection* (1996). *The Anxiety of Influence* (1973) sets forth Professor Bloom's provocative theory of the literary relationships between the great writers and their predecessors. His most recent books include *Shakespeare: The Invention of the Human* (1998), a 1998 National Book Award finalist, *How to Read and Why* (2000), *Genius: A Mosaic of One Hundred Exemplary Creative Minds* (2002), *Hamlet: Poem Unlimited* (2003), *Where Shall Wisdom Be Found?* (2004), and *Jesus and Yahweh: The Names Divine* (2005). In 1999, Professor Bloom received the prestigious American Academy of Arts and Letters Gold Medal for Criticism. He has also received the International Prize of Catalonia, the Alfonso Reyes Prize of Mexico, and the Hans Christian Andersen Bicentennial Prize of Denmark.

ARTHUR GILCHRIST BRODEUR was Professor Emeritus at the University of California, Berkeley. He is the author of *The Climax of the Finn Episode* (1943), *The Riddle of the Runes* (1932), and translator of *The Prose Edda* by Snorri Sturluson (1916).

RICHARD J. SCHRADER has been Professor of English at Princeton University and currently at Boston College. He is the author of *God's Handiwork: Images of Women in Early Germanic Literature* (1983), *Old English Poetry and the Genealogy of Events* (1993), and editor of *H.L. Mencken: A Documentary Volume* (2000).

JOHN D. NILES has been a Professor of English at the University of Wisconsin-Madison. He is the author of *"Beowulf": The Poem and Its Tradition* (1983), *Homo Narrans: The Poetics and Anthropology of Oral Literature* (1999), and an editor of *Anglo-Saxonism and the Construction of Social Identity* (1997).

SETH LERER has been the Avalon Foundation Professor in Humanities and Professor of English and Comparative Literature at Stanford University where he served as Chair of the Department of Comparative Literature from 1997 to 2000. He is the author of *Literacy and Power in Anglo-Saxon Literature* (1991), *Chaucer and His Readers: Imagining the Author in Late-medieval England* (1993), and *Courtly Letters in the Age of Henry VIII: Literary Culture and the Arts of Deceit* (1997).

ANDY ORCHARD has been a Professor of English and Medieval Studies and Director of the Centre for Medieval Studies at the University of Toronto. He is the author of *The Poetic Art of Aldhelm* (1994), *Dictionary of Norse Myth and Legend* (1997), and *A Critical Companion to Beowulf* (2003).

EDWARD B. IRVING Jr. has been a Professor at the University of Pennsylvania. He is the author of *A Reading of "Beowulf"* (1968), *Rereading "Beowulf"* (1989), and a contributing editor of *Old English Studies in Honour of John C. Pope* (1974).

SCOTT DeGREGORIO has been an Assistant Professor of English Language and Literature at the University of Michigan, Dearborn. He is the author of an article on Bede for *The Literary Encyclopedia* (2002) and is the author of "The Venerable Bed on Prayer and Contemplation" (1999) and "Þegenlic or Flæsclic: The Old English Prose Legends of St. Andrew" (2003).

PHYLLIS R. BROWN has been an Associate Professor and Chair of English at Santa Clara University. She is an editor of *Modes of Interpretation in Old English Literature: Essays in Honour of Stanley B. Greenfield* (1986),

Women Writing Latin: From Roman Antiquity to Early Modern Europe (2002), and *Hrotsvit of Gandersheim: Contexts, Identities, Affinities, and Performances* (2004).

GALE R. OWEN-CROCKER has been Senior Lecturer in English Language at the University of Manchester, UK. He is the author of *Dress in Anglo-Saxon England* (1986)—revised and enlarged (2004) and editor of *King Harold II and the Bayeux Tapestry* (2005) and "Medieval Clothing and Textiles" (2005).

JUDY KING is a member of the research staff at Flinders University in Australia. She is the author of "Chamber Theatre by Any Other Name" (1972).

Bibliography

Allen, David G. "The Coercive Ideal of *Beowulf.*" In *Literary and Historical Perspectives of the Middle Ages*. Edited by Patricia W. Cummins, et al. Morgantown: West VirginiaUniversity Press (1982): 120–132.

Andersson, Theodore. *Early Epic Scenery: Homer, Virgil and the Medieval Legacy*. Ithaca, New York: Cornell University Press, 1976.

Baker, Peter S. "Beowulf the Orator." *Journal of English Linguistics* 21.1 (1988): 3–23.

Battaglia, Frank. "The Germanic Earth Goddess in *Beowulf.*" *The Mankind Quarterly* vol. 31, no. 4 (1991): 415–446.

Bauschatz, Paul C. *The Well and the Tree: World and Time in Early Germanic Culture*. Amherst: University of Massachusetts Press, 1982.

Bennett, Helen. "The Female Mourner at Beowulf's Funeral: Filling in the Blanks / Hearing the Spaces." *Exemplaria* vol. 1, no. 4 (1992): 35–50.

Benson, Larry D. "The Literary Character of Anglo-Saxon Formulaic Poetry." In *PMLA* 81 (1966): 334–341.

Bessinger, Jess B., and Robert P. Creed, eds. *Franciplegius; Medieval and Linguistic Studies In Honor of Francis Peabody Magoun, Jr*. New York: New York University Press, 1965.

Bloom, Harold, ed. *"Beowulf": Modern Critical Interpretations*. New York: Chelsea, 1987.

Bloomfield, ed. *The Interpretation of Narrative*. Cambridge: Harvard University Press, 1970.

Bolton, W.F. *Alcuin and Beowulf.* New Brunswick, N.J.: Rutgers University Press, 1978.

Bonjour, Adrien. *The Digressions in Beowulf.* Medium Ævum Monographs, 5. Oxford: Blackwell, 1950.

Brennan, Malcom M. "Hrothgar's Government." *Journal of English and Germanic Philology* 84 (1985): 3–15.

Brown, Phyllis Rugg, et al., eds. *Modes of Interpretation in Old English Literature: Essays in Honour of Stanley B. Greenfield.* Toronto: University of Toronto Press, 1986.

Burlin, Robert B. and Edward B. Irving, eds. *Old English Studies in Honor of John C. Pope.* Toronto: University of Toronto Press, 1974.

Busse, W. G., and R. Holtei. "*Beowulf* and the Tenth Century." *Bulletin of the John Rylands University Library of Manchester* 63 (1981): 285–329.

Butts, Richard. "The Analogical Mere: Landscape and Terror in *Beowulf.*" *English Studies* 68 (1987): 113–121.

Calder, Daniel G., ed. *Old English Poetry: Essays on Style.* Berkeley: University of California Press, 1979.

Camargo, Martin. "The Finn Episode and the Tragedy of Revenge in *Beowulf.*" *Studies in Philology* vol. 78, no. 5 (1981): 120–134.

Chambers, R.W. *Beowulf: An Introduction to the Study of the Poem with a Discussion of the Stories of Offa and Finn.* 3rd edition. Cambridge: Cambridge University Press, 1959.

Chase, Colin. "Beowulf, Bede, and St. Oswine: The Hero's Pride in Old English Hagiography." In *The Anglo-Saxons: Synthesis and Achievement.* Edited by J. Douglas Woods and David A. E. Pelteret. Waterloo: Wilfrid Laurier University Press (1985): 37–48.

Chase, Colin, ed. *The Dating of Beowulf.* Toronto: University of Toronto Press, 1981.

Chickering, Howell D. "Lyric Time in *Beowulf.*" *Journal of English and Germanic Philology* vol. 91, no. 4 (1992): 489–509.

Clark, George. *Beowulf.* Boston: Twayne Publishers, 1990.

Davis, Craig R. *Beowulf and the Demise of Germanic Legend in England.* New York: Garland, 1996.

Deskis, Susan E. *Beowulf and the Medieval Proverb Tradition.* Tempe, Ariz.: Medieval & Renaissance Texts & Studies, 1996.

Damico, Helen. "Þrymskviða and Beowulf's Second Fight: The Dressing of the Hero in Parody." *Scandinavian Studies* vol. 58, no. 4 (1986): 407–428.

Damico, Helen and John Leyerle, eds. *Heroic Poetry in the Anglo-Saxon Period: Studies in Honor of Jess B. Bessinger, Jr.* Kalamazoo, Mich.: Medieval Institute Publications, 1993.

Donahue, Charles. *"Beowulf* and Christian Tradition: A Reconsideration from a Celtic Stance."*Traditio* 21 (1965): 55–116.

Earl, James W. *Thinking about Beowulf.* Stanford, CA: Stanford University Press, 1994.

———. *"Beowulf* and the Origins of Civilization." *Speaking Two Languages: Traditional Disciplines and Contemporary Theory in Medieval Studies.* Edited by Allen J. Frantzen. Albany: State University of New York Press (1991): 65–89.

Earl, James W. "Transformation of Chaos: Immanence and Transcendence in *Beowulf* and Other Old English Poetry." *Ultimate Reality and Meaning* vol. 10, no. 3 (1987): 164–185.

Feldman, Thalia Phillies. "A Comparative Study of Feond, Deofl, Syn, and Hel in Beowulf." *Neuphilologische Mitteilungen* 88 (1987): 159–174.

Fenny, Sarah J. "The Funeral Pyre Theme in *Beowulf.*" *De Gustibus: Essays for Alain Renoir.* Edited by John Miles Foley, J. Chris Womack, and Whitney A. Womack. New York: Garland (1992): 185–200.

Foley, Joanne De Lavan. "Feasts and Anti-Feasts in *Beowulf* and the *Odyssey.*" *Oral Traditional Literature: A Festschrift for Albert Bates Lord.* Edited by John Miles Foley. Columbus, OH: Slavica (1981): 235–261.

Foley, John Miles. *Traditional Oral Epics: The Odyssey, Beowulf, and the Serbo-Croatian Return Song.* Berkeley: University of California Press, 1990.

Frank, Roberta. "'Mere' and 'Sund': Two Sea-Changes in *Beowulf.*" In *Modes of Interpretation in Old English Literature.* Ed. Phyllis Rugg Brown, Georgia Ronan Crampton, Fred C. Robinson, and Kim R. Stafford. Toronto: University of Toronto Press (1986): 153–172.

———. "Old Norse Memorial Eulogies and the Ending of *Beowulf.*" In *The Early Middle Ages.* Edited by William H. Snyder. Binghamton: The State University of New York at Binghamton (1982): 1–19.

Frantzen, Allen J. "Writing the Unreadable *Beowulf*: 'Writan' and 'forwritan,' the Pen and the Sword." *Exemplaria* vol. 3, no. 2 (1991): 327–357.

Fry, Donald K. *The Beowulf Poet: A Collection of Critical Essays.* Englewood Cliffs, N.J.: Prentice-Hall, 1968.

Fulk, R.D., ed. *Interpretations of Beowulf: A Critical Anthology.* Indianapolis: IndianaUniversity Press, 1991.

Godden, Malcolm and Michael Lapidge, eds. *The Cambridge Companion to Old English Literature.* Cambridge and New York: Cambridge University Press, 1991.

Goldsmith, Margaret E. *Mode and Meaning of "Beowulf."* London: Athlone Press, 1970.

Greenfield, Stanley B. *A Critical History of Old English Literature.* New York: New York University Press, 1965.

Greenfield, Stanley B. & Fred C. Robinson, eds. *A Bibliography of Publications on Old English Literature, from the Beginnings through 1972.* Toronto: University of Toronto Press, 1980.

Greenfield, Stanley B. & Daniel G. Calder, eds., *A New Critical History of Old English Literature.* New York: New York University Press, 1986.

Haber, Tom Burns. *A Comparative Study of Beowulf and the Aeneid.* New York: Phaeton, 1968.

Hanning, Robert. "*Beowulf* and Anglo-Saxon Poetry." In *European Writers: The Middle Ages and the Renaissance, I: Prudentius to Medieval Drama; II: Petrarch to Renaissance Short Fiction.* Edited by William T. H. Jackson. New York: Scribner's (1983): 51–87.

Hansen, Elaine Tuttle. "Hrothgar's 'Sermon' in *Beowulf* as Parental Wisdom." *Anglo-Saxon England* 10 (1982): 53–67.

Harris, Joseph. "Beowulf's Last Words." *Speculum* 67 (1992): 1–32.

Hart, Thomas Elwood. "Calculated Casualties in Beowulf: Geometrical Scaffolding and Verbal Symbol." *Studia Neophilologica* 53 (1981): 3–35.

Hill, John M. *The Cultural World in Beowulf.* Toronto: University of Toronto Press, 1995.

———. "Beowulf and the Danish Succession: Gift Giving as an Occasion for Complex Gesture." *Medievalia et Humanistica* 11 (1982): 177–197.

Howe, Nicholas. *Migration and Mythmaking in Anglo-Saxon England.* New Haven: Yale University Press, 1989.

Huisman, Rosemary. "The Three Tellings of Beowulf's Fight with Grendel's Mother." *Leeds Studies in English* 20 (1989): 217–248.

Huppé, Bernard F. *The Hero in the Earthly City.* Binghamton: State University of New York at Binghamton, 1971.

Irving, Edward B. Jr. *Rereading Beowulf.* Philadelphia: University of Pennsylvania Press, 1989.

Kendall, Calvin B. *Voyage to the Other World: The Legacy of Sutton Hoo.* Minneapolis: University of Minnesota Press, 1992.

Kiernan, Kevin. *Beowulf and the Beowulf Manuscript.* New Brunswick, N.J.: Rutgers University Press, 1981.

Lapidge, Michael. "*Beowulf,* Aldhelm, the *Liber Monstrorum* and Wessex." *Studi Medievali* 3rd ser. 23 (1982): 151–192.

Lawrence, William W. *Beowulf and Epic Tradition.* New York and London: Hafner PublishingCompany, 1961.

Leake, Jane Acomb. *The Geats of Beowulf: A Study in the Geographical Mythology of the Middle Ages.* Madison: University of Wisconsin Press, 1967.

Magoun, Francis P. Jr. "The Oral-Formulaic Character of Anglo-Saxon Narrative Poetry." *Speculum* 28 (1953): 446–467.

Newton, Sam. *The Origins of Beowulf and the Pre-Viking Kingdom of East Anglia.* Cambridge: Brewer, 1992.

Nicholson, Lewis E., ed. *An Anthology of Beowulf Criticism.* South Bend, Ind.: University of Notre Dame Press, 1963.

Niles, John D. *Beowulf: The Poem and Its Tradition.* Cambridge, Mass.: Harvard University Press, 1983.

————, ed. *Old English Literature in Context.* Bury St. Edmonds, England: Brewer-Rowan & Littlefield, 1980.

Ogilvy, Jack David Angus. *Reading Beowulf: An Introduction to the Poem, Its Background, and Its Style.* Norman: University of Oklahoma Press, 1983.

Parker, Mary A. *Beowulf and Christianity.* New York: Peter Lang, 1987.

Parks, Ward. "Ring Structure and Embedding in Homer and Beowulf." *Neuphilologische Mitteilungen* 89 (1988): 237–251.

Purdy, Strother B. "Beowulf and Hrothgar's Dream." *Chaucer Review* vol. 21, no. 2 (1986): 257–273.

Robinson, Fred C. *Beowulf and the Appositive Style.* Knoxville, Tennessee: University of Tennessee Press, 1985.

Sisam, Kenneth. *The Structure of Beowulf.* Oxford: Oxford University Press, 1965.

Stanley, Eric. *In the Foreground: Beowulf.* Cambridge and Rochester, N.Y.: D.S. Brewer, 1994.

Swanton, M. J. *Crisis and Development in Germanic Society 700–800: Beowulf and the Burden of Kingship.* Goppingen: Kummerle, 1982.

Tolkien, J.R.R. "*Beowulf*: The Monsters and the Critics." *Proceedings of the British Academy* 22 (1936): 245–295. Issued separately 1936, paginated 1–53.

Whallon, William. *Formula, Character, and Context: Studies in Homeric, Old English, and Old Testament Poetry.* Washington, D.C.: The Center for Hellenic Studies, 1969.

Whitelock, Dorothy. *The Audience of Beowulf.* Oxford: Clarendon Press, 1951.

Williams, David. *Cain and Beowulf: A Study in Secular Allegory.* Toronto: University of Toronto Press, 1982.

Acknowledgments

"The Structure and Unity of *Beowulf*" by Arthur Gilchrist Brodeur. From *The Art of Beowulf* by Arthur Gilchrist Brodeur. Berkeley and Los Angeles: University of California Press (1959): 71–87. © 1959 by The Regents of the University of California. Reprinted by permission.

"Succession and Glory in *Beowulf*" by Richard J. Schrader. From the *Journal of English and Germanic Philology* vol. 90, no. 4 (October 1991): 491–504. © 1991 by the Board of Trustees of the University of Illinois. Reprinted by permission.

"Locating *Beowulf* in Literary History" by John D. Niles. From *Exemplaria* Vol. V, no. 1 (Spring 1993): 79–109. © 1993 by the Center for Medieval and Early Renaissance Studies. Reprinted by permission.

"Grendel's Glove" by Seth Lerer. From *ELH* 61 (1994): 721–751. © 1994 by The Johns Hopkins University Press. Reprinted by permission.

"Psychology and Physicality: The Monsters of *Beowulf*" by Andy Orchard. From *Pride and Prodigies: Studies in the Monsters of the* Beowulf-*Manuscript*. Woodbridge, Suffolk, and Rochester, N.Y.: D.S. Brewer (1995): 28–57. © 1995 by Andy Orchard. Reprinted by permission.

"Christian and Pagan Elements" by Edward B. Irving Jr. From *A Beowulf Handbook*. Edited by Robert E. Bjork and John D. Niles. Lincoln: The

University of Nebraska Press (1998): 177–192. © 1998 by the University of Nebraska Press. Reprinted by permission.

"Myth and History" by John D. Niles. From *A Beowulf Handbook*. Edited by Robert E. Bjork and John D. Niles. Lincoln: The University of Nebraska Press (1998): 216–232. © 1998 by the University of Nebraska Press. Reprinted by permission.

"Theorizing Irony in *Beowulf*: The Case of Hrothgar" by Scott DeGregorio. From *Exemplaria* Vol. XI, no. 2 (Fall 1999): 309–343. © 1999 by Pegasus Press. Reprinted by permission.

"Cycles and Change in *Beowulf*" by Phyllis R. Brown. From *Manuscript, Narrative, Lexicon: Essays on Cultural Transmission in Honor of Whitney F. Bolton*. Edited by Robert Boenig and Kathleen Davis. Lewisburg: Bucknell University Press (2000): 171–292. © 2000 by Associated University Presses, Inc. Reprinted by permission.

"The Fourth Funeral: Beowulf's Complex Obsequies" by Gale R. Owen-Crocker. From *The Four Funerals in Beowulf: And the Structure of the Poem*. Manchester and New York: Manchester University Press (2000): 85–113. © 2000 by Gale R. Owen-Crocker. Reprinted by permission.

"Launching the Hero: The Case of Scyld and Beowulf" by Judy King. From *Neophilologus* vol. 87, no. 3 (July 2003): 453–471. © 2003 by Kluwer Academic Publishers. Reprinted by permission.

Every effort has been made to contact the owners of copyrighted material and secure copyright permission. Articles appearing in this volume generally appear much as they did in their original publication—in some cases foreign language text has been removed from the original article. Those interested in locating the original source will find bibliographic information in the bibliography and acknowledgments sections of this volume.

Index

Characters in literary works are indexed by first name (if any), followed by the name of the work in parentheses